WORDS
WITHOUT
BORDERS

Happy birthday
to The amazing
Lynn!
Much love, Ann,
Louisa,
Alex

WORDS

WITHOUT

BORDERS

The World Through the Eyes of Writers

AN ANTHOLOGY

Edited by SAMANTHA SCHNEE,
ALANE SALIERNO MASON, *and* DEDI FELMAN

Anchor Books

A Division of Random House, Inc.

New York

AN ANCHOR BOOKS ORIGINAL, MARCH 2007

*Copyright © 2007 by Samantha Schnee, Alane Salierno Mason,
and Dedi Felman
Introduction copyright © 2007 by Andre Dubus III*

Grateful acknowledgment is made to Penguin Books India for permission to reprint
"Ulat-Puran" by Rajshekhar Basu from *Selected Stories* by Parashuram, copyright © 2006
by Rajshekhar Basu, English translation copyright © 2006 by Sukanta Chaudhuri.
Reprinted by permission of Penguin Books India.

Library of Congress Cataloging-in-Publication Data
Words without borders : the world through the eyes of writers / edited by
Samantha Schnee, Alane Salierno Mason, and Dedi Felman—1st Anchor Books ed.
p   cm.
ISBN: 978-1-4000-7975-9
I. Schnee, Samantha.   II. Mason, Alane Salierno, 1964–   III. Felman, Dedi.
PN6019.W67   2007
808.83—dc22
2006022501

Book design by Jo Anne Metsch

www.anchorbooks.com

Printed in the United States of America
10 9 8 7 6 5 4

CONTENTS

ANDRE DUBUS III

In November 1979, I was living in Austin, Texas, when Iranian students in Tehran overran the American embassy, and the hostage crisis began. In those early moments of what would become a 444-day standoff, young white men from Houston and Dallas cruised the streets in their late-model cars, stopping to beat up any man or boy who looked even remotely Iranian. Among the battered were Sudanese, Italians, El Salvadorans, Egyptians, Ethiopians, and quite a few Mexicans. They were called "sand nigger" and "camel jockey" and told to *go home*. Go Home.

Twenty-two years later, on a clear blue morning in September, we were attacked by a handful of men from a fundamentalist cult of a militant arm of an ancient religion, and we answered those attacks with attacks of our own, one of which was the beating of an elderly Sikh on a bus in Boston. Three men took him for Middle Eastern because he wore a turban, which somehow meant Muslim, which then meant terrorist, and they pummeled him.

We are, of course, a country of immigrants. We come from the very cultures we no longer seem to know. A recent *National Geographic* study tested 18-to-24-year-old Americans, 83 percent of whom could not find Afghanistan on a map. Seventy percent could not find Israel or Iran. Only 37 percent could locate Iraq. When asked the religion of India's majority population, nearly half answered Muslim when it is Hindu. A full 80 percent of Americans do not have passports, and there is this alarming statistic from *Words Without Borders*: "50 percent of all the books in translation now published worldwide are translated *from* English, but only 6 percent are translated *into* English." Our own president has publicly referred to Slovakia as "Slovenia," has called Kosovars "Kosovarians," Greeks

"Grecians," and East Timorese "East Timorians." When he was running for office in 1999, he was quizzed by a reporter and could not name the president of Chechnya, the general who had taken power in Pakistan, or the prime minister of India.

There are theories as to how we've become so ignorant of other cultures around the world: geography and foreign languages are no longer taught in schools; U.S. media companies have cut back on world news coverage; we are isolated between two oceans and have friendly neighbors to the north and south and can afford the luxury of being provincial. The real reasons for our collective ignorance are probably more complex, but whatever the roots, the consequences are dire: we have never been less isolationist in the variety of goods and services we consume from around the world, and never have we been more ignorant of the people who produce them. This is, if nothing else, fertile territory for misunderstanding, unresolved conflict, and yes, war.

The translation and publication of this volume, therefore, have never been more timely or necessary. Yet there are rewards here that go beyond politics and even age-old questions of war and peace; to go more deeply into the experience of the other—no matter how "foreign"—is to go more deeply into our own experience as well. Leo Tolstoy wrote: "Art is transferring feeling from one heart to another." In this essential collection of stories from around the world, genuine feeling and more are transferred from Africa, Asia, Latin America, Europe, and the Middle East. The emotional landscape of many of these is hardship of some kind: drought, war, poverty, living under totalitarian rule. In each, however, is the affirming cry of human expression.

In Argentine writer Juan José Saer's "Baked Mud," young men living through a drought spend their afternoons in the shade of a store's patio, drinking wine and buying more for "Sebastián 'deaf man' Salas, so he'd tell us about droughts he had seen that were worse than this one, just to know that such calamities occurred every once in a while and that it did not mean that this bitch of a life was coming to an end." But this story is less about fearing the natural world and more about the nature of love between a father and son, the real fear that it can dry up as quickly as a river and never return.

Marcela Solá, in *Kind's Silence,* introduces us to a woman whose family home has been marked by Peronists to be burned down. Tacked beside the door is a sign: "There is a traitor here, may those on our side know it and when the moment comes, act." Meanwhile, Kind has entered into an unlikely but completely believable friendship with a refugee Nazi general. They both share a love for Mozart, and Kind believes in the power of the imagination.

> The world cannot be seen. A glance does not necessarily mean the truth. The world came to me through imagination, a certain internal touch, large fingers that reach from inside, that brush across the surface of things, people, and colors, feeling their inner workings, without ever looking at them, those things and people that are so desired, so distant, so inaccessible.

The general, on the other hand, believes in power.

> Like Goethe, I've always preferred injustice over disorder. But I probably let you live because survivors are witnesses to what power can do. It's a mistake to think they will be cause for embarrassment. Secretly, all those who have or have had power belong to the same brotherhood and respect its every manifestation, even if they don't realize it. In this country, Kind, there isn't a single person who doesn't want it, who doesn't fear it, who doesn't find pleasure in exercising it. There are some, like myself, who know what humans are really made of. That's all there is, power, and someone has to take charge.

Solá's prose here is spare and naturalistic, and while she examines the subjugation of one group of people by another, she has plumbed so deep as to cast light on the illusive and shadowy nature of the soul itself. This is what art and literature can do, open us to the mysteries among and within us.

Certainly this is clear in Giorgio Manganelli's "Experiment with India"; here we begin to experience an Italian's perception of Madurai, India, and the universal dreamworld it evokes:

> Like the fleshy and velar world of dreams, this is a place not of true and false but of a fantastic power, something violent, scornful, laughable, sinister the way an animal of the underbrush might be, with its ingenious coat and sly limbs; a religion that has the mortality and the soft complicity of guts; that, like a corridor of dreams sealed in a loving soul, alternates and connects nightmares, revelations, enigmas, meaningless words, solemn discourses hardly begun and immediately incomprehensible, prophecies, the mysterious joys of flight and falling, of the loss of self, in death or in ecstasy.

There is ecstasy in simply reading this passage—abundantly impressionistic in its insights—one we are fortunate to read at all because it has been painstakingly translated for this collection, one of whose central strengths is its breadth and scope: here lies the organically aesthetic pleasure of contrasts; to go from the lushness of Manganelli to the spare, bleak verse of Bosnian poet Senadin Musabegović:

> In 1993, I measured one meter, ninety-one centimeters. I was standing next to a window two meters high, watching a corpse that had been hit by a sniper and was now spread across four flagstones on the sidewalk. Its fingers touched the asphalt, the sun reflected off its golden bracelet three times. I could not count the droplets of steam that were gathering on the windowpane:
> The seconds followed in a row:
> one,
> two,
> three,
> four . . .
> In a fraction of a second I felt on my head the ruler with which my father's hand measured the border between me and the world.

The world. There is so much of it here. In Norwegian writer Johan Harstad's "Vietnam. Thursday." a depressed psychoanalyst treats a Vietnamese woman who was badly burned as a girl in the napalm bombing of her family's village. An adult now living in Norway, the woman is obsessed, literally, with a 1957 magazine photograph of adoring, joyful fans at an Elvis Presley concert.

> She says, "Look carefully at the picture. Look as hard as you can, because you will never see it again. Pictures like that don't get taken anymore. Perhaps that's what makes it so sad. The fact we missed it. The fact I can never sit there in the front row, wide-eyed, and think that right now, at this very moment, I am happy. And there you have it, Vietnam, the feeling it gives—that nothing can ever be like that—that I shall always sleep on my side at night, because my skin is still too sore to lie on—that I will never once experience what it is to be so open, so innocent, so ecstatic, as they are in that picture; that's what hurts. That I am so close to the picture, that I stand in the front row every time I hear him, every time I play one of his records, but I can never be there, because it didn't happen the way it should—because at some moment in time, Vietnam happened."

In Johan Harstad's capable hands, Vietnam has become an adjective for despair, for a wounded and lingering state of mind.

One of the strongest stories here is by Egyptian writer Gamal al-Ghitani, who Nobel laureate Naguib Mahfouz calls in his introduction "the most important Arab novelist today." Arab. The word for so many Americans has become burdened with associations of oil and terrorism and war. But here, in "A Drowsy Haze," al-Ghitani simply paints a masterful portrait of a man in Cairo who senses his own death is upon him and spends his last day preparing for it as best he can. This is not a dark or foreboding tale but one suffused with the light of acceptance and gratitude grounded in universal mystery. It is not a long story, but by its closing moment in the Imam al-Husayn Mosque, we, too, have become the dying protagonist pausing before the Quranic verse on the wall: "'Say: No reward do I ask you save love of kindred. . . .'

"Why did he want to weep every time he read that?"

Love of kindred. Failing at it. Loving well but enduring the loss of love anyway. Loving again: family, lovers, the world. In Palestinian writer Adania Shibli's "Faint Hints of Tranquillity," a young translator has seen too much killing, of children especially. She has become world-weary far too soon and wishes for only this: "The petals, then, have fallen from the almond trees before I had a chance to touch them. . . . All I wish from this life before it ends is to join the spring and enjoy its bloom even though I don't know how or where or by what right."

One of the subtle strengths of this story is the revelation that the protagonist no longer knows what her rights are. The trauma of her daily experience has skewed her perspective.

This collection of stories, translated from the original languages of its authors, does just the opposite; instead of narrowing our vision, it expands it; instead of propping up insidious ethnic stereotypes, it shatters them. These voices from China and Argentina, Bosnia and Norway and Iran, from Egypt and Romania and Nigeria, from Haiti and Lebanon and Indonesia, and still more, these are the voices we have forgotten in languages we no longer speak or never did. Whether we know it or not, these are the notes in the world symphony in which we all play a part. The writers and translators have done their work here. It is up to us now to listen to the expression of our fellow human beings with whom we share this planet. This is our duty, yes, but it is also a deeply moving pleasure, one that will also allow us, ultimately, to become more gracefully and truly ourselves.

WORDS

WITHOUT

BORDERS

MA JIAN

A sign painted on the wall of the hospital cafeteria reads: PRACTICE REVOLUTIONARY HUMANISM. *But the hospital won't care for those who can't pay for care; it leaves them begging at its gates. The crowds gawk, but don't intervene. Parents of those in need of help are helpless. What's left?*

Ma Jian is impossible to classify. He writes politically, but he isn't a political writer. He employs surrealism without being a surrealist. Is he a comic nihilist? A tragic comedian? Ferocious? Generous? All and none, he explodes any title you might try to apply to him.

Except, perhaps, for "revolutionary humanist."

This story about a hospital is a hospital. A good, humane hospital, a revolutionary hospital that doesn't look like anything that came before it. But its characters aren't its patients. Its readers are.

Where are you running to? Characters in this story are running to different places—some to their pasts, some to their futures. Some are running to ideas of themselves, some to ideas that don't include people.

Readers are always running toward the same place when they open a book. We're trying to get to a greater understanding of ourselves. Books have no burden to entertain. Television and film and music are entertaining enough. Books don't need to be political or surreal or comic or tragic. They need to help us understand ourselves. Everything else a book does is incidental to that.

Writers are all running, too. They're running to meet their readers.

—JONATHAN SAFRAN FOER

WHERE ARE YOU RUNNING TO?

"Where are you running to?" shouts Zhao Chunyu, chairwoman of the local neighborhood committee, as she stands in the entrance to the staff accommodation block.

She's wearing cotton trousers and a tracksuit top that's faded to the color of old bricks. Her freshly washed hair, which was cut by her husband, Old Liu, is fluffing out in all directions, making her round face look even larger and her narrow eyes even smaller. At the moment, however, these small eyes are popping with rage; her arms are tightly folded across her chest, and a smell of raw celery is escaping from her mouth. A few minutes ago, she was chopping up vegetables for dinner. Old Liu walked in and, without washing his hands, broke off a stick of celery to have with his beer. Chunyu popped a piece into her mouth as well, and as they munched away, their son, Kai, leaped from his stool and rushed out of the door. Chunyu moved the bowl of celery onto the piano, out of Old Liu's reach, then followed her son downstairs.

"Where are you running to?" she shouts again.

"I don't want to play 'Pleading Child.' I hate slow pieces!"

"Well you can play 'Perfectly Contented' instead!"

"No, I won't play anything by Schumann! I refuse!"

"All right then. Tonight you can practice Chopin's Revolutionary Etude for a couple of hours. It's very fast, and it has that passage you like so much where the left hand plays in octaves."

"No, I won't play it! I won't!" Kai is shouting so loudly everyone in the block can hear. One wouldn't expect a ten-year-old child to be capable of producing such a noise.

"Come back here!" As Chunyu jumps down the two concrete steps below the entrance, Kai grabs on to a small willow tree that's just been planted, swings around in a half circle, then shoots off like a bullet down a small alleyway.

Chunyu hesitates for a while. Above her, she can hear her neighbor Old Jia saying to Old Zun, who lives on the third floor, "If Kai doesn't get into music school this time, he's had it. Next year he'll be too old."

"He's always playing the same pieces," Old Zun replies. "I know them by heart." Then he shouts down to Chunyu, "Your piano's sounding terrible these days! You should pay someone to come and tune it."

Chunyu ignores the men's remarks. She and her husband spent every last yuan they owned to buy that piano. Chunyu hasn't always been so poor—she was born into a wealthy family. When the Communists liberated China in 1949, she cut herself off from her parents and took active steps to join the party. As a result, she was able to secure a place at Beijing's Central Academy of Music. Unfortunately, just before she was due to graduate, an officer discovered an old photograph she'd been hiding that showed her playing the piano to a group of her parents' bourgeois friends. She was consequently labeled a rightist, and as Old Liu, who was her boyfriend at the time, refused to denounce her, they were both sent to a labor camp in the remote northwest where they remained for twenty-four years.

Chunyu scrapes back her hair and runs down the alleyway in pursuit of her son, shouting, "Come back, you little beast!"

In the light of the setting sun, she sees Kai swooping down the alley like a cockerel in flight. She steps up her speed. Since she isn't wearing socks, her feet grip well to her rubber-soled shoes. She feels as though she has the wind under her feet.

When she was eighteen, after a year of running more than ten kilometers a day from her Beijing lodgings to the Academy of Music and back, she became champion of the academy's annual long-distance race. Although she's now fifty-three years old, her legs are still strong. Last month she managed to chase after and catch a thief who'd stolen a tape recorder while wandering around her block pretending to deliver leaflets on a new brand of lipstick.

"Come back. If you don't stop, I'll kill you!"

Her son is wearing his school uniform: a white cotton suit with blue piping along the seams. His red necktie is as bright as a cockscomb. He pumps his arms as he runs. Chunyu is convinced that as long as she maintains her speed, she'll be able to catch him in less than twenty seconds. But she soon realizes that she can't match his pace, just as a duck can never match the pace of a chicken. She suspects that she's put on weight again. She's been concerned about her weight for the last ten years, ever since she and Old Liu were rehabilitated in 1981, and released from the labor camp. As soon as she returned home, and arranged for a family portrait to be taken in a photographer's studio to celebrate the event, her body started to balloon. As an adolescent, Chunyu was one of the prettiest girls in the town. Whenever she walked down the street, men would stop and gawk. But when she returned from the camp, her face looked so old that no one recognized her.

The little rascal who's running in front of her now was just three months old when the family portrait was taken. Chunyu was just forty-three, and still had a lot of life left to devote to the party and to herself. Within a few months, Old Liu's party membership was reinstated, and he was assigned a post in the political office of a coal processing plant. Chunyu was appointed cultural officer of the Municipal Music Association, a post she held for nine years, until last year when she was promoted to chairwoman of the local neighborhood committee.

Back in 1981, her daughter, Xin, who was twelve years old, was preparing to take the entrance exam to the local music school. Chunyu had the key to the Music Association's piano room. During the day, she used the piano for teaching purposes, and let Xin practice on it in the evening. Chunyu bought all the sheet music that her daughter needed, and charged it to the Music Association. The family was now well provided for, and had a goal to work toward. Everything seemed to be going well. In 1983, Chunyu and Old Liu received eight thousand yuan in compensation for the years they spent in the labor camp. After Liu paid the 260-yuan party membership fee, they had just enough left over to order a small upright piano, which was delivered to them a year later. As life became easier following the implementation of the Open Door Policy, Chunyu's spirits improved, and so did her appetite. But, unlike Old Liu, she liked to keep active. Every day, she'd get up at dawn and hold dance classes outside the Open Door Club. She wanted to retrieve all the lost years of her youth, and was determined to keep her weight down to under seventy-five kilos. But she needn't have worried, because since Xin became ill six years ago, and then died two years later, Chunyu hasn't put on a gram of weight.

Her legs are now aching from the sudden sprint she made a few minutes ago. She's worried that her left kneecap has become dislodged. She watches her son swerve to the right and scurry down Construction Alley. That's where his school is.

"I bet he's going to jump over the school wall," she thinks to herself. "The little terror. He knows that I'm afraid of heights. I get vertigo just walking downstairs." When Chunyu was six years old, she once jumped off the balcony of her parents' apartment to avoid having to play the piano to her mother's friends. By then she could already play Beethoven's "Für Elise" and Mendelssohn's "Spring Song" by heart. She injured herself so badly in the fall that she had to stay at home for three months. When she returned to school she was unable to catch up with the other children, so her parents decided to send her to a private music school instead, where she could concentrate on the piano.

"What's the hurry?" cries a friend of Old Liu's as Chunyu dashes past.

"Kai's trying to run away!" Chunyu shouts back, without turning around. It occurs to her that when her son was younger she didn't pay enough attention to him. She focused all of her energy on Xin. She was convinced that as long as Xin followed the practice plan that she'd devised, she would easily get a place at Beijing's Central Academy of Music. Xin looked just like Chunyu did as a young girl, but was even more talented. In the labor camp, when Xin saw a piano for the first time, in the film of the model play *The Red Lantern,* she immediately announced that she wanted to be a pianist when she grew up. Chunyu drew the notes of a keyboard along the edge of their brick bed, and within a few days, Xin was able to tap out the notes for the song "Nothing is redder than the sun, and no one is dearer to us than Chairman Mao Zedong." Xin's musical talent gave Chunyu a sense of purpose. She was determined that her daughter would become a great pianist, and succeed where she herself had failed.

But Chunyu could never have guessed that just four years after the family was released from the labor camp, her daughter would develop bone cancer. Xin was admitted to the hospital, and for the first two years, Chunyu's work unit paid for all the medical costs. But when Xin reached the age of eighteen, the payments came to an end. Without medical treatment, Xin's condition deteriorated drastically. The chief surgeon, Dr. Han, told Chunyu that Xin needed an emergency operation, and before this could take place, the hospital would require a payment of 40,000 yuan.

This sum was the equivalent of five years of Chunyu's and Old Liu's combined incomes. After a long discussion, the couple decided that Old Liu should take early retirement. From this he would gain a onetime pension award of 20,000 yuan. They calculated that they could then get 9,000 yuan from selling their piano and fridge, and borrow another 2,000 from close friends, which would give them a total of 31,000 yuan—just 9,000 yuan short of the sum the hospital demanded.

Through a backdoor connection, the couple asked an acquaintance to give the hospital director two bottles of French wine and two gift-wrapped jars of Nescafé and Coffee-mate. After accepting this bribe, the director agreed that Xin's operation could go ahead immediately, and gave the couple two weeks to pay the remaining 9,000 yuan. Xin underwent surgery the next day. After the operation, Dr. Han informed the couple that although the tumor had been successfully excised from Xin's pelvic bone, the cancer had spread to her stomach, and that she would now need a course of chemotherapy. For this additional treatment, the hospital required a further 10,000 yuan.

In an effort to start raising the money, Old Liu bought a wooden handcart and wheeled it around town looking for work. Many buildings were being demolished at the time, so there was plenty of work to be found. Old Liu could make forty or fifty yuan a day carting rubble from building sites to rubbish heaps. Two weeks later, Old Liu handed the hospital the few hundred yuan that he'd made, and promised to pay the rest of the money as soon as he could. The director of the hospital told him that this money would cover only one more dose of anti-inflammatory drugs, and that once this was administered, his daughter would have to leave the hospital. Chunyu was devastated.

In the afternoon, she and Old Liu lifted Xin onto their wooden handcart and prepared to wheel her home. But after they emerged from the hospital gates, Old Liu squatted down and refused to move. He knew that if they took their daughter home, there would be no hope left for her. Ten minutes later, in a fit of rage, he marched over to the burial clothes store across the road, picked up an angle iron that was lying on the ground, and smashed the mural that decorated the shop's outside wall. He'd heard someone say that the beautiful girl in the mural, who was pictured waiting to ascend to heaven, looked very much like Xin. In fact, the long-haired artist, a member of the so-called "Wild Beast" school, apparently, who'd painted the mural had had a crush on Xin in the past. Old Liu had once spotted his daughter following the artist into the hamburger bar that had just opened in the center of town. Before Xin had made it through the door, Old Liu had rushed over and grabbed her by the collar, then dragged her back home. A couple of years later, the artist was arrested for "hooligan behavior" and sentenced to twelve years in prison. After he'd destroyed the mural, Old Liu stormed into the burial clothes shop, picked up a paintbrush and a large sheet of paper, and wrote:

Dear friends, please help me!

   My name is Liu Xin. I live at 13 Beisi Road. I am eighteen years old. In late 1984 I developed bone cancer. I have spent the last two years in hospital. Although a tumor has been removed from my pelvic bone, the cancer has spread to my stomach. I now need six months of chemotherapy, which will cost 10,000 yuan.

   I am paralyzed from the waist down, and suffer from incontinence. If I don't receive help, I doubt that I'll have many days left in this beautiful world. So I am coming out onto the streets today to ask my dear friends to take pity on me and offer some financial support. I will be eternally grateful for any help that you can give.

When he finished writing this appeal, Old Liu returned to the hospital gates and placed it over his daughter's body. Xin looked as frail as a flower crushed by heavy rain. She had a high fever and could barely open her red and swollen eyes, but was nevertheless able to whisper to her parents that she wanted to go home. Chunyu thought to herself, "If we take her home, she'll be as good as dead. At least if we stay here outside the hospital we still have a glimmer of hope." She wiped the tears that fell from Xin's eyes, then pulled the cotton sheet more tightly over Xin's body, so that her bare flesh was hidden from view.

On this hot summer afternoon, there were flies everywhere, especially near the hospital. Around the fruit stalls outside the hospital gates, the ground was littered with rotten watermelon skins, orange peel, and empty ice-cream cartons. Several people from outside town who, like Chunyu and her family, couldn't afford to pay for medical treatment, also loitered at the gates. The middle-aged woman lying down behind the rubbish bins had been waiting there for three months. Her legs were covered with boils. In her hand, she clutched a piece of cardboard on which she'd written the details of her illness. The coins that passersby gave her were only enough to buy food and drink—they certainly wouldn't have paid for any medical care.

Many pedestrians stopped by the gates to read the appeal that Old Liu had written. Someone told the couple that in the outskirts of town, not far from the private crematorium, a traveling doctor had set up business. Apparently he could cure many illnesses, and his fees weren't high. But there were always crowds of people waiting to see him, and one had to queue for several days. Others told them that this traveling doctor was a charlatan and that he prescribed the same medicine for every illness. They said that the police had planned to arrest him, but had been forced to change their minds after the local newspaper reported that a colleague of the wife of the local party secretary had been cured of uterine cancer by his treatment.

In the evening rush hour, the crowd gathering around Xin grew even larger. Old Liu was afraid that someone might recognize him, so he crouched in a dark corner behind the handcart. Chunyu told him to return home and fetch the tape recording of Xin playing the piano. After he'd left, Chunyu wiped the sweat from her daughter's brow and folded back the cotton sheet so that people could see her face. With great effort, Xin attempted to pull the sheet over her head again. A look of determination shone from the eyes of this girl who'd grown up in a labor camp. Whenever someone stopped to take a look at her daughter, Chunyu would tell them what a talented musician she was. "Look at her hands!" she'd cry. "They're so long and delicate. If she recovers from this illness, she's bound to get a place at Beijing's Central Academy of Music. She'll bring glory to our town!"

People started reaching into their pockets and handing money to Chunyu. Some were too embarrassed to hand it to her directly, and chose to place it on the handcart instead. After Dr. Han finished work, he walked out through the front gates. When he saw Xin lying on the handcart, he went over to her and said, "Be careful, it's very hot out here. Your scars haven't healed yet. You don't want them to become infected, do you?" Then he turned to Chunyu and said, "I know it's a doctor's duty to care for their patients, but my hands are tied: I have to follow the hospital regulations. I wish I could help, but there's nothing I can do. Still, you can't stay out here like this. It will create a lot of problems for us."

Chunyu's mind turned to the Chairman Mao slogan that was painted on the wall of the hospital's cafeteria. It read: CURE THE SICK AND HEAL THE WOUNDED; PRACTICE REVOLUTIONARY HUMANISM. Then she looked at Dr. Han and said, "Old Liu and I both work for the government; Xin comes from revolutionary stock. Surely there's something that can be done. Of course we don't want to cause any problems for the hospital, but if we take her home, she'll be as good as dead."

Drops of sweat glistened on Dr. Han's pale and drawn face. He whisked away the flies that were settling on his nose, then brought out from his leather bag a ten-yuan note, placed it in Xin's hand,

and said, "This is just a token. If I were you, I'd go home and try to find some other way of raising the money." When the crowd saw Dr. Han make this gift, they clapped their hands. Within seconds, the doctor became surrounded by other sick people asking for money too. He made his excuses and walked away as fast as he could.

When Old Liu returned with the recording of Xin's piano playing, the atmosphere improved. Many people got off their bicycles to listen to the music. The traffic came to a standstill. People on the edge of the crowd tried to muscle their way in to see what the sick girl looked like. Chunyu held up in the air the appeal that Old Liu had written, so that everyone at the back could read it. Then, at the top of her voice, she started commentating on the pieces that Xin was playing:

"Comrades, Ladies and Gentlemen, my daughter is much more talented than me. This is the piece she was planning to play last year in the Central Academy of Music's entrance exam. It's Beethoven's 'Appassionata' Sonata. The piece was held in high regard by the revolutionary leader Comrade Lenin. He used to listen to it every day.

"This is the first movement. Listen to the chords ripple across the keyboard like the fluttering shadow of a ghost. The theme is quizzical, unsettling. It's constantly asking questions about the meaning of life. Here's the theme again, although you'll notice that this time it's changed a little. Listen to my daughter play the syncopated rhythms. Her fingering has power and confidence . . . Revolutionary comrades, my daughter's bone cancer has spread to her pelvic cavity. But if we can raise enough money to give her six months of chemotherapy, she'll make a full recovery, and continue to contribute to the revolutionary cause. She's been able to endure hardship since an early age. When she was born, she weighed just one and a half kilograms. We were living in a labor camp at the time, and I hadn't eaten any meat for a whole year. When she was ten, she still weighed only fifteen kilos. Then, a few years ago, the gentle breezes of the Open Door Policy came and blew our troubles away. We thank the party for the new life it has given us. Both my husband and I have been rehabilitated. The party even awarded me compensation. We wanted to help our daughter make something of herself, to repay the kindness that the party had shown us. How were we to know that before she'd got anywhere, she'd be struck down with . . ." Chunyu's voice petered out and her eyes welled with tears.

"Listen," she continued. "This is the third movement. The tape's a bit scratchy here, I'm afraid. Do you hear that repeated note in the background? The right hand is playing flowing arpeggios while the left hand is hammering rapid, staccato chords. It conjures images of wild horses galloping across the plains. You can feel the tide of history surging forward, the irresistible momentum of life. The Central Academy of Music's examiners would have paid special attention to this part.

"Listen to my daughter play those diminished-seventh arpeggios. You can tell that, despite her gentle exterior, she has a will of steel. That's her great quality. Her determination and optimism allow her to convey the most valiant struggles undertaken by mankind.

"Listen: this is the march of time, the future no one can avoid!" Chunyu was so carried away by her words, her head was pouring with sweat.

After a while, the crowd began to stir. Someone had called a policeman over. Fortunately, Chunyu knew him. The policeman cast his gaze over the crowd, causing it to disperse immediately, then criticized Chunyu for creating such a commotion and ordered her to go home.

Old Liu jumped up from his dark corner, apologized profusely, and grabbed hold of the cart's handles. The policeman glanced at the appeal draped over Xin's body and said, "That paper is the size of a poster. You know that it's forbidden for members of the public to write anything on a sheet of paper that size. You're a party member, Old Liu, you should be aware of the law." The policeman snatched hold of the paper and ripped it in half. Chunyu and Old Liu apologized again and started wheeling their daughter home. They had managed to collect more than sixty yuan that afternoon. This was more than Old Liu made wheeling rubble around all day. But they calculated that even if they continued at this rate, it would still take them more than a year to raise the money that their daughter needed.

But they didn't lose heart. From then on, every morning Old Liu would place his daughter on the handcart and wheel her around town begging for money. He chose a letter-size piece of cardboard, wrote out a new appeal on it, and tied it to the side of the cart. Whenever he saw a policeman approach, he'd flip the cardboard around to hide the words from view.

After he'd begged his way through every street of the old town, he ventured into the newly built district by the sea. He parked the cart outside luxury hotels and nightclubs, and played his daughter's tape. Sometimes a smartly dressed businessman would throw him a five- or ten-yuan note.

At first the people there tolerated their presence, but by the fourth day, the situation changed. When Old Liu wheeled his daughter to the gates of an expensive hotel, a security guard rushed over and told him to get lost. He retreated to the entrance of a hair salon, but was shooed away by the manageress, who accused his daughter of being a fake. In the sweltering heat of the afternoon, the stench issuing from his daughter's body attracted swarms of flies, and most people were afraid to approach, apart from two drunkards from another town, who walked up to Xin, ran their hands over her face, and said, "Will you do it with us? We'll pay you a hundred yuan, but you'll have to give us the full works."

Old Liu dared not lash out at them. Xin was so upset that she closed her eyes and never opened them again. In an attempt to raise her spirits, Old Liu bought her a carton of orange juice, but as he was afraid that people would accuse her of being a fake if they saw her drink from it, he wheeled her to a deserted street before he put the straw to her mouth. She had been unable to move for several days, now; she'd lost most of her hair and her skin was rotting away in places. She knew that she was about to die. She'd learned the truth about her condition the day she was kicked out of the hospital, and she understood that it was to try and save her life that her parents had sold almost everything they owned.

The next day, undeterred, Old Liu took his daughter back to the new district. As he approached the gates of a three-star hotel, the head of the Municipal Cultural Department came walking out with a cadre from the Provincial Propaganda Department. When the department head spotted Old Liu, he raised his eyebrows and said, "However bad things get, you shouldn't let yourself sink so low. It's a good thing you're a party member, otherwise you'd get into a lot of trouble for bringing such shame to our town. If this got into the papers, it would become a political matter. You know very well that the local government brings foreigners to this street to show them the success of the Open Door Policy. A foreign visitor could turn up at any time, and imagine what they'd think if they saw you!"

Old Liu broke into a heavy sweat; he looked as though he'd fallen into a river. Without a word, he bowed his head and wheeled his daughter away. At this point, Xin broke a three-day silence and said, "Let's go back now. I want you to take me to the hamburger bar." Old Liu had collected only eight yuan that morning, which was only enough to buy one hamburger. But he was eager to fulfill his daughter's wish. He wheeled her to the hamburger bar in the center of town, and parked the cart outside the glass door. There was air-conditioning inside, and bright lights. He couldn't hear what the people inside were saying, but they all had an air of bourgeois prosperity. He was afraid. He'd never stepped inside such a clean place before. On the front window, a color poster showed visions of crisp chicken, and bread rolls filled with beef and shreds of lettuce. He didn't know how one was supposed to eat these things. In the papers, he'd read of various new terms such as "set menu" and "happy meals." But he'd never been inside such a restaurant before; he had no idea what food to order or how much it would cost.

Old Liu thought back to what the head of the Municipal Cultural Department had said to him, and felt his anger well up again.

Then he glanced down at his dying daughter, and with sudden resolve, flung the glass door open and charged inside.

A few minutes later, he came out again, clasping a small styrofoam box that he placed beside his daughter. So that she'd be able to eat the hamburger in peace, he wheeled her over to the entrance of an empty building. Xin lifted the hamburger to her nose and inhaled its smell. She took a bite, but couldn't swallow. Old Liu propped her head up, but she was still unable to swallow the food. Xin whispered apologetically, "I just wanted to know what it smelled like."

Chunyu still remembers the day Old Liu came back with the uneaten hamburger, which he then cut in half and shared with her. Because from that night on, her daughter fell into a deep sleep from which she never woke.

Now as Chunyu runs toward the intersection in the center of town, she feels her heart pound against her chest and her legs begin to flag. Suddenly, to her amazement, she sees her son sprinting toward her. She tries to grab him as he passes, but he's running so fast that he slips straight through her fingers.

"Where are you running to?" Chunyu shouts. As she swirls around, her foot gives way and she falls to the ground. After her son hears her go down, he stops and turns round.

"Help me up!" Chunyu cries.

"I'll never play the piano again."

"Your sister has gone. You're our only hope now." As she says this, Chunyu thinks about how her daughter died without ever having tasted a hamburger. "If you come home with me and do a couple of hours' practice, I'll take you to the hamburger bar on Sunday," she adds.

"You've promised to take me there eight times already," the son replies, squatting down.

"When your sister and I were your age, we could play all of the Bach partitas by heart."

"I want to study computers."

"No you don't, you just want to play computer games."

"My teacher said I should go into the army. I was the quickest in our class at jumping over walls and climbing up ropes."

"I bet you also won the long-distance races," Chunyu sneers, rubbing her sore ankles.

"No, I came third."

"Come home with me and do your practice!"

"No!" Seeing his mother rising to her feet, Kai jumps up and runs away again.

Chunyu chases after him. She thinks to herself, "I was a champion long-distance runner as a student, and for the last few years I've been exercising every morning. It shouldn't be too hard for me to catch the boy." Gradually she increases her speed, narrowing the gap separating her from her son.

"Chairwoman Zhao, can you stop for a moment?" cries a woman who lives in the red block opposite hers. "Granny Wu's wandering through the streets again. Can't you go and sort the problem out?"

"There's nothing I can do about it. Anyway, the exercise will do her good."

"That's not a very responsible attitude," the woman shouts as she watches Chunyu run off into the distance.

A few minutes later, Chunyu passes the entrance to the Writers' Association. She has no idea where her son has gone. When she reaches the bright window of an electrical goods store, she stops and looks around, but her son is nowhere to be seen. She glances through the window at the imported television, oven, and tape recorder, which are illuminated by pink fluorescent light. She looks at the foreign lettering on the stickers, and the high prices marked on the labels.

This area is not controlled by her neighborhood committee. It's part of the zone earmarked for the "Three-Year Great Urban Renewal Project." Several old buildings are already half-demolished. If her son has hidden himself inside one of them, she'll never be able to find him. Chunyu decides to give up her pursuit of Kai, and head for Granny Wu's home instead. Granny

Wu shares her one room with her daughter and granddaughter. The daughter, who got divorced five years ago, has recently acquired a new boyfriend. When the young couple want to have sex, they wait until the child is asleep and then ask Granny Wu to go out for a walk. Sometimes the old woman ends up having to wander the streets all night.

Although Chunyu has been chairwoman of the neighborhood committee for only a year, she has achieved a great deal. At first she ran disco dancing classes for the elderly. When the party called for government workers to promote Chinese culture, she started teaching traditional silk ribbon dancing instead. Some months ago, a girl called Aihe ran away from home because her father didn't like her working as a nightclub hostess. The father would spend all day by the telephone, waiting for his daughter to call. Chunyu paid him a visit and persuaded him to come and play the drums for her ribbon dance group. Thanks to his great contribution, the dance group was singled out for praise by the local party committee. Chunyu has also managed to persuade the twenty-four fertile women in her neighborhood to either have a cervical cap fitted or to undergo sterilization. Recently, the higher authorities granted her neighborhood a quota of three births, giving her authority to award three women a license to conceive. Although many women offered her gifts in the hope of gaining a license, she refused all bribery. She chose three women, based entirely on seniority and length of marriage, and wrote their names on the board outside her office for all to see. There are two newlywed couples in the neighborhood, and Chunyu makes a point of visiting them every week to top up their supplies of condoms. As a result of all this hard work, the higher authorities have named Chunyu a Model Family Planning Officer.

On her way to Granny Wu's home, she passes the Open Door Club. This is where she holds her ribbon dance class every morning. Inside, a ping-pong competition is taking place. A large crowd has gathered to watch. She searches the hall for a sign of her son.

"Time is Money, Efficiency is Life," she mumbles to herself. "When I catch him, I'll make sure he makes up for these two hours of practice time that he's wasted!" Her anger rises. "Kai!" she cries out suddenly. "It's time to go home!"

Her son never skips school, and doesn't usually complain about his piano practice. The last time he refused to play the piano, Chunyu talked him into it by promising to buy him a desk. Unfortunately, after the desk arrived, Chunyu took to serving their evening meals at it (as there's no other table in the room), and using it as a resting place for her bottles of soy sauce, sesame oil, and vinegar. Old Liu, who's turned to drink since the death of his daughter, also likes to prop his elbow on the desk when he sits down for a beer. As there's no room left for Kai at the desk, he's forced to do his homework on the lid of the piano.

Chunyu thinks back to the privileged childhood she enjoyed before Liberation. Although her father was executed after the Communists took over, she successfully cut herself off from her disgraced family and gained a place at the academy. If she hadn't been labeled a rightist a few weeks before she was due to graduate, she could have become a famous concert pianist and have traveled the world. She could also have equipped her home with the domestic appliances that most average households can now afford.

Chunyu looks up and realizes that she has made her way to Red Scarf Park. In a couple of minutes she'll be home. She feels a wave of hunger and thinks of the pig's trotter that she left simmering on her stove. "I hope Old Liu's remembered to add the vegetables," she mumbles under her breath.

Suddenly, behind her, she hears her son's footsteps. She recognizes the distinctive noise of his soccer cleats: each step sounds as though his foot is biting into the earth. She turns around and sees her son walking toward her.

"What did you do with the money I gave you to buy salt this morning?" she asks.

"I bought some salt with it."

"Salt costs two and a half jiao a jar. What about the two and a half left over?"

"I bought it at the supermarket. It's more expensive there."

"Well then, you'll have to come home with me and do three hours of practice, not two." As she says these words, Chunyu pounces on her son and grabs him by his collar. But since the zip of his jacket is undone, Kai is able to wriggle out and make a quick escape.

"Where are you running to?" Chunyu shouts, as she chases after him. Having rested for half an hour, she can now run as fast as a hound. Waving her son's white jacket in her hand, she chases him all the way to the broad avenues of the new district.

"Where are you running to?" Only she can hear the sound of her voice in these wide, commercial streets. She runs past a line of restaurants; the neon signs dazzle her eyes. She feels drab and dumpy when she spots the waitresses in their red lipstick and silk cheongsams. She skirts around a line of parked limousines. All the men who step out of them are wearing imported leather shoes. On these streets, even the porters look at her with disdain. Chunyu thinks to herself, "If I'd been born thirty years later, perhaps I'd be wearing high-heeled shoes now, playing the piano in the lobby of a luxury hotel." She remembers playing five Bach preludes at a party her parents threw for sixty guests. It was the photograph of this performance that later caused Chunyu to be condemned as a rightist, and that changed the course of her life.

As Chunyu passes a brightly lit hair salon, she wonders whether Old Liu is drunk by now. Unable to control herself, she shouts, "He really is a disgrace!" Chunyu reflects that she's lived for almost half a century, but still has nothing to show for herself. A sudden impatience grips her. She wants to catch up with the life she lost all those years ago. She wants to catch up with the new generation, catch up with her son, catch up with her ideals and aspirations. A van painted with the slogan UP WITH PRODUCTION, DOWN WITH POPULATION! whizzes past her, nearly knocking her down. As Chunyu dodges back onto the pavement, her target becomes submerged in the crowd and she finds it hard to keep her eyes focused on it. But fortunately, her target starts glancing back now and then, to check that she's still following him. Chunyu conceals herself behind a tall man and continues to pursue her son. After a while the man looks round and says, "You're a bit past it to play that game now, aren't you? Next time you go for a piss, just take a look at yourself in the mirror!" Chunyu realizes that the man has taken her for a prostitute. She feels so humiliated, she wishes she could bury herself beneath the ground. In a panic she yells, "It's time to go home, son!" then jumps back onto the road again and continues to run. She can hear people mutter, "Who does she think she is, trying to pick up men at her age? And then pretending to be looking for her son! Has she no shame?"

For a moment, Chunyu blacks out. She's trembling all over; her legs feel so heavy she can barely lift them from the ground. She dares not look around; she must focus on the target ahead. When her vision returns, she fixes her eyes on her son as he flickers in and out of view. She can't turn back now.

Her son runs through a busy shopping center, then races up onto the new spaghetti junction by the sea. As Chunyu follows him up, the pavement peters out and she's forced to join the cars on the road. The elevated roundabout circles a large statue of Chairman Mao. All she can see is a stream of cars whirling around the statue, then shooting down one of the four exits. In the middle of the roundabout, she glimpses her son standing at the foot of Chairman Mao. Chunyu wants to run straight over to him, but there are so many cars, she dares not cross the road. Instead, she follows the stream of traffic, trying after each circuit to edge herself a little nearer to the center. Soon there are cars in front of her, behind her, to her left and right. She can't stop. She's running so fast, she can hardly see a thing; her target is becoming more and more blurred. But she's not afraid of the cars any longer: she wants to race them. She's certain that if she manages to overtake the cars, she will be able to reach her son.

At last she lets her son's jacket fall from her hand. After another circuit of the roundabout, her clothes become drenched with sweat. She unzips her tracksuit top and flings it off. She's running in her vest now, and feels a lot cooler. A sense of freedom that she's never experienced before courses through her body. At last she feels that she has caught up with herself. The smell of the sea breeze transports her back to her childhood. She can hear herself play Beethoven's "Appassionata" Sonata. The faster she runs, the clearer the notes become. She wants to catch up with her past. As she races onward, she kicks off one shoe, then the other, and suddenly she feels that she's flying, flying to a place not far from where she's always wanted to be.

Just at this moment, she hears her son chasing up behind her, yelling at the top of his voice, "Mother, where are you running to? Where are you running to?"

Translated from the Chinese by Flora Drew

ABOUT THE AUTHOR

Ma Jian is the author of *Red Dust,* which won the Thomas Cook Travel Award, *The Noodle Maker,* and *Stick Out Your Tongue.* He was born in Qingdao in 1953 and moved to Hong Kong in 1986, shortly before his works were banned in China. After the handover of Hong Kong from the British to the Chinese in 1997, he moved to London, where he now lives.

CAN XUE

Unlike other Chinese writers, Can Xue claims that her literary roots are in the West, having nothing to do with Chinese literature. On the surface, her work seems influenced by writers like Kafka, Borges, and Calvino, but according to her, she has also learned the art of fiction from many classical Western writers, such as Shakespeare and Dante. In recent years she has written extensively about classical Western literature, of which she has always been an avid reader. "Meteorite Mountain" is one of her most recent stories, representative of the quality of her fiction. I found it quite moving, especially toward the end of the story, when the search for the little sister has become an enlightening experience, and when the narrator comes to view her sister as someone who lives a life of passion and fulfillment. She says her sister "could strike springwater out of the rocks with the force of her passion; there was nothing she could not do." For me, that's a glorious moment in the story.

Can Xue doesn't trust reason and always follows her instinct in writing fiction. In her own words: "From the very beginning I've felt that the irrational way of writing is the best way of making fiction." By the same token, she is interested only in the inner worlds of her characters, and tries to get rid of the superficial interferences of the external world in her work. Since 1988, when she began to write full-time, she has gradually gained a sizable readership in China and drawn a good deal of critical attention, yet she has been regarded as an eccentric. She believes that in two or three decades her works will have more readers.

To be honest, I don't share most of her literary views, since I do believe in reason and have my misgivings about some of the modern Western authors she admires. But I trust that some readers will find Can Xue's fiction unique and liberating. I admire the firmness of her conviction and belief, as one has to be an idealist to write artistically.

—HA JIN

METEORITE MOUNTAIN

My little sister left, after all. Nothing I said could make her stay. She left for Meteorite Mountain, more than a hundred miles away. A few months ago, she had come across a young shepherd from the mountain. It was love at first sight, and now she has thrown caution to the winds and dropped everything to join him. In my daydreams, the mountain was carpeted with mossy grass. I did not bother to ask myself whether grass could grow on a meteorite, or if that mountain was a meteorite at all.

In the stillness of the night, I would sit outdoors on a stone seat next to my boyfriend, teacher Yuanpu, and we would speculate on what was going on in my sister's life. We sighed as we thought of her, but we were also secretly jealous, as nothing so romantic had ever happened in our lives.

Little sister had always relied on me. She never knew her own mind. I always made decisions for her. We two sisters were survivors of a great disaster, and had settled here in this out-of-the-way rural spot through the good offices of a distant relative. But life here was no pastoral idyll; the fierce struggle for survival had tempered me into a woman of steel. Not so little sister. Doe-eyed and innocent, she was oblivious to the realities of life around her and always tried to escape into her own dreamworld. Sometimes I lost patience with her, especially during the backbreaking, busy farming season. But then I was also proud that I had little sister tucked under my wing.

Little sister's lover was a lanky young fellow who owned five hundred head of black mountain goats. I was told that there were several shepherds in the Meteorite Mountain area, but that he owned the biggest herd. The two had met at a snack place in the township. My sister finished her noodles and stood up to go, but had left her basket of vegetables under the table. She was going to sell them in the market. The shepherd called her attention to the basket, and they exchanged a few words. What followed was just beyond comprehension—little sister dropped everything then and there and followed him home and did not return till three days later. She had slipped away from under my nose for three whole days! It turned out that this young fellow was afflicted with a strange disease; when it attacked, he would faint from the pain and had to remain where he was until the spell was over. According to my sister, the pain had attacked him twice during the three days that she was there. She could not bring herself to leave. Not for his sake, mind you, but for the sake of the goats. "When he is down with the pain, he is not my lover," sister said absentmindedly. I was dead set against sister spending the rest of her life with this sickly young man, but it seemed that teacher Yuanpu saw it differently. He was intrigued by the life of the shepherds, and bombarded little sister with questions about the charms of this meteorite Arcadia. Thus, without being aware of it, I myself was also drawn to the place.

"Truly this Huimin is a young man out of the ordinary," Mr. Yuanpu pronounced as he set off to teach his classes at the village elementary school. He meant the young shepherd.

To judge by appearances, Huimin the shepherd did not look like a sick man. His eyes were clear and his movements agile. And he had clever fingers, too. The first time he visited, he brought me two straw hats, followed later by straw sandals and bamboo baskets, all exquisitely woven, exuding the fragrance of nature and teasingly suggestive of his place of abode. Huimin always came by boat on his visits and left the same day, never staying overnight at our place. I wanted to see what his home was like. When I said so to little sister, she shook her head vigorously:

"No, no. Don't go. That kind of place. . . . You will be disappointed."

"What do you mean?!" I asked angrily.

"Come on, don't get mad at me. What I mean is, the place is not worth seeing."

"Not worth seeing! Then why do you marry yourself into that place?"

"That's me. What am I worth? It's just me."

Little sister always dodged my questions with this kind of quibbling, and I ended up losing interest in her affairs. I told teacher Yuanpu about sister's whims, and he laughed.

"Let's be happy for them."

Teacher Yuanpu's words are not to be trusted. He teaches at the village elementary school, but was more interested in taking the children swimming in the river. One-third of the school year was spent in "swimming" lessons. His irresponsible style of teaching led many parents to take their children out of school. At one time he had to make daily visits to the parents' homes to get his students back. We have been engaged for the last two years. On first acquaintance, I could not stand him, since unlike him I was a literal-minded person who took things seriously. But later I was attracted to him for his sunny temperament, realizing that he had a knack for effortlessly solving the knotty problems of life. He's the elusive type, and when we were together, every word he uttered would leave me puzzled. Take right now for instance, I just didn't understand why he should feel happy for little sister, and why he laughed.

"Why poke your head into that dirt-poor corner?" he said to me gently, "It must be a troubled place. Why don't we let distance preserve for us the mystery of your sister's new home?"

"It's not dirt poor. He has five hundred goats."   .

"Who knows. Seeing is believing."

My discussion with teacher Yuanpu ended in frustration for us both. On top of which, little sister mocked me for not leaving well enough alone. But several months later, she literally got up and walked away. Now I was alone in this old house, which seemed to echo its own emptiness. I did not ask teacher Yuanpu to move in. I felt that his moving in would be the end of our relationship; I wanted things to remain as they were.

Before she left, little sister told me that she was really leaving for the goats, that if the goats were lost, she and Huimin would lose their means of living and would starve. "The goats are like magicians," she ended up saying. As she was talking a blue streak, teacher Yuanpu's eyes wandered off into the distance and he muttered absentmindedly, "Very well, very well."

Now we were sitting under the bay tree, breathing in its luscious fragrance. Under the light of the moon, teacher Yuanpu's pale, oval-shaped face wore a look of perplexity.

"I'd rather say there's something wrong with little sister. The solitary mountain will help her mature, and she will soon be whole again. I have been to Meteorite Mountain many times before," he said, and added, "Goats could hardly find footing on those naked rocks."

"That's not at all what Huimin and sister have been saying about the place."

"Well, there may have been changes during the past few years, but no matter what you say, a bare, rocky mountain cannot turn into green pasture."

"Then why are you happy for sister?"

"My happiness for her is pouring from the bottom of my heart."

"I don't care what you say, I'm taking a boat trip down there."

"Oh, don't ruin your own dream."

I finally made the boat trip to Meteorite Mountain, accompanied by teacher Yuanpu. Although it was downstream all the way, it took us four days and four nights, with two stops in between.

The first time we went ashore was to buy matches. I opened one box and found it empty. When I started to say *hey, we have a problem,* the fat storekeeper furrowed her brow and started screaming, and right away two swarthy-looking giants darted in from nowhere. Teacher Yuanpu dragged me out in a flash, and we ran for our lives.

That night in my dreams, I fought the battle over and over again, charging into that contraband store and being driven out. I used my fists, drumming on the creaking bed boards so violently that teacher Yuanpu couldn't sleep. By the time I woke up, our boat had covered a long stretch downstream. On both shores, strange-shaped rocks greeted my eyes as I sat on the deck, not a speck of green in sight. I began to believe teacher Yuanpu's account of the place. But what I couldn't understand was, why did it take four days and four nights when our boat was going downstream? I put the question to the boatman. At first he didn't understand my question. When I repeated it, he looked at the two of us piteously, without giving a direct answer.

"Just look at you two, thin as reeds, you have no business going to that kind of place."

Teacher Yuanpu and I slept fitfully the following two days, unaware of anything around us. On the morning of the third day, however, hair-raising sounds of wild animals assailed us from the mountains on both sides of the river. The sounds rose and fell like waves, as if heralding an imminent attack. In answer to our questions, the boatman explained that the mountains were populated with tigers and these were the sounds of their roaring. Neither of us had seen a tiger in our lives and we paled in fright. But the boatman said that so long as we did not moor, we would be safe. However, with the coming of dusk, he moored the boat anyway. When we protested, he pretended not to hear us, collected his things, and went ashore, headed for a wineshop. By now, the tigers' roars seemed closer than ever. Teacher Yuanpu and I huddled against each other in the cabin, quivering with fear. Suddenly we felt a heavy object land on the boat with a thud, and we were sure that our final hour had come. But after waiting a long time, nothing happened. Being bolder than teacher Yuanpu, I pushed open a crack in the opening of the cabin and peeped out, holding my breath. There was indeed a bulky object at the prow. After a while, we heard the boatman approach, humming some drunken tune or other, and we were sure that he would end up in the tiger's jaws. But no bloody incident took place; the boat moved slowly forward while the tigers in the mountains continued to roar.

"How do we know they're tigers? There may be other wild animals," said teacher Yuanpu, his teeth chattering in fear. He had completely lost his composure.

We finally reached our destination and left the wild animals' roaring behind us. Teacher Yuanpu said that the place had totally changed since his visits many years ago. At my insistence, he searched his memory and succeeded in finding a crooked mountain path. We were indeed on a rocky mountain; there was not a blade of grass, not to mention foliage. The climb was not steep, though. Dark, crimson-colored rocks stretched away before us, forming a twisting path with no end in sight.

"Meteorite Mountain is right ahead, behind this mountain." Teacher Yuanpu pointed with his finger.

I was soon to see my sister, but I did not feel happy. I was crest-fallen to realize that my sister had lied to me. Whatever was it that made her move to this wretched place?

"We are here," teacher Yuanpu announced as he flopped down next to the path.

I looked around, bewildered. He had to be joking—there was nothing around us except rocks and more rocks. There was no sign of life.

"Come on," he remonstrated, "don't be so stubborn. Can't you take a closer look at the rocks?"

Acting on this advice, I looked harder and saw at a distance a green skirt drying on a rock. That was my sister's skirt. But I still saw no signs of domestic habitation. I thought to myself, even if there were no sheep, there would still be people living in houses. Teacher Yuanpu saw what I was thinking. With a smile flitting between his eyes, he said casually, "Let's go over and take a look." Obviously alerted by the sounds of our feet slapping over the rocky surface, little sister turned up right in front of us, as if coming out of the ground under our feet. Huimin followed in her wake. They were both skin and bones with faces as black as coal, but apparently in high spirits.

"Big sister will never get used to life here. I've been saying it all along. But see, she's turned up anyway! And we are totally unpre-pared . . . ," little sister chattered away.

She clasped my arm and led me down toward the foot of the mountain.

I gave a sigh of relief. So they didn't live on this wretched mountain after all.

"Your skirt," I reminded her.

"You mean it might be stolen? Never. Think, who will come up this mountain? This is our mountain, mine and Huimin's."

Our walk downward ended at an open space. Blades of grass sprouted from crevices between the rocks underfoot, and there was even an occasional shrub, but there was not a bird in the sky. The spot was like a village hewn out of rock. We saw people assembled in the open space, busy moving away a huge pile of rocks. My eyes swept over the scene, but I still couldn't locate any sign of human habitation.

"We're home," I heard Huimin, walking behind us, tell teacher Yuanpu.

"Where?" I asked in a loud voice.

Little sister squeezed my hand, reminding me not to be so impatient. And then I saw it, a dark hole gaping from the stony surface. In single file, the four of us walked down the steps leading into the hole. At the end of about ten steps, the gap widened into a large space. Huimin lit an oil lamp.

"Sit down anywhere," he said as he placed the lamp in an aperture carved in the stone wall.

The inside of the cave, with the stone floor smoothly chiseled, was the size of an ordinary room. I turned and saw sister and teacher Yuanpu already comfortably settled on the floor, so I also sat down. There was no furniture, no clothes, no cooking utensils of any kind. How could this be a home?

"We eat and drink on the mountain. You have no idea the kind of life we have," little sister announced gleefully.

"Supposing it rains, won't the cave be flooded?"

"Rain? From my grandfather downward, no one has ever seen a drop of rain," Huimin muttered in a low voice.

His words reminded me of the fragrant straw weavings that he had given me. I asked where the black mountain goats were. Huimin stared at me as if caught off guard, then immediately seemed to have remembered something. Ignoring my question, he suggested we go to see the piece of land that they "relied on for a living." He stood up, blew out the lamp, and we four exited the cave.

Once out in the open, I took a closer look at the surface beneath my feet and discovered a row of openings extended as far as the eye could see. Obviously this village carved out of rocks was quite populous.

The piece of land on which sister and Huimin "relied on for a living" was at quite some distance. We walked until the path finally ended in a stretch of earth, and we heard the low humming of many voices.

It was a long and narrow strip of earth between two mountains. The red-colored soil was carved up neatly into rectangles, clearly marked.

"That patch is ours," Huimin pointed to the third rectangle from where we stood.

The patch was covered with sweet potato vines. Looking around, we saw that all the other patches were likewise planted with sweet potatoes.

"The soil here is rich," little sister said proudly, "It doesn't take much work to get a good harvest of sweet potatoes."

There were several villagers sitting on the edge of the potato plots. The humming of voices came from them. Now they gazed at us idly from afar.

Each plot came to about a third of a hectare; by the condition of the vines one could tell at a glance that the sweet potatoes were growing abundantly. How could sweet potatoes grow between rocks with no water? Strange!

"They depend on underground water," Huimin said, anticipating my question. Pointing to the vines he added, "The underground water is invisible."

"Then how do you know there is water under this spot?" I asked.

"You can tell by looking at the sweet potato vines," Huimin replied as he bent to scoop up a fistful of the dry red soil. "The surface soil is always dry," he told us. "If you dig a little, it is still dry. But underground water is definitely there. No one has actually found underground water, but we know it is there from the vines of the sweet potato. The sweet potatoes grown from this soil are crisp and sweet. The truth of the matter is . . . just like when we were up the mountain. . . ." He winked and didn't go on.

"And what about up the mountain?" I turned to little sister and asked her disdainfully, "What's the mystery about the rocky mountain?"

"A grand mystery indeed!" little sister replied tauntingly.

I felt that she was pulling my leg. I turned to teacher Yuanpu and he, too, was winking at me. I was enraged.

Seeing my thunderous looks, little sister hastened to say, "Don't be angry. We are talking about water. Just think, it never rains here, and there are no wells in the village, how do you think we survive? The answer to the mystery is up the mountain. Tap the rocks, and water will flow."

"I never heard of such a thing!"

"Indeed it is true. I'm not saying that springwater will bubble up whenever we want. No. One must endure, and when one reaches the extreme of endurance, things will happen. At first I couldn't stand it here. Now I can't bear to leave."

We had an evening meal back at their home. Huimin and little sister brought sweet potatoes from a smaller cave nearby. We peeled the sweet potatoes with knives and ate them raw. Little sister said it was the only way to eat sweet potatoes, because of the lack of water. I had never tasted such good sweet potatoes in my whole life. But there was not much moisture in them, and I became thirsty soon after the meal. It suddenly occurred to me that I had not had any water the whole day long. However, none of the others showed any signs of thirst. Moreover, teacher Yuanpu seemed to have changed in a subtle way now that he was on Meteorite Mountain. He seemed to have forgotten that he was supposed to be my boyfriend. In this place, which was totally alien to me, he on the contrary seemed to have metamorphosed into an "insider" like my little sister. Faced with this situation, I tried to control my thirst and put on a nonchalant front, sitting down with my back against the stone wall of their cave.

"Isn't the moon lovely?" little sister said in a husky, seductive voice. "Let's go up the mountain to capture the love that was lost."

Saying which, little sister rushed out in great glee. The two men seemed unmoved, but followed her out nevertheless. Suddenly recalling what she had said about there being water up the mountain, I became excited at the prospect and joined them.

The climb was not steep, but the mountain was completely bald, with nothing to hang on to as we made our way up. I quickly tired and was more thirsty than ever. Coupled with the fact that I had not bathed in the last couple of days, I felt that I couldn't bear it any longer. But the other three seemed totally at ease. Weren't they thirsty? I couldn't help exclaiming, "I'm dying of thirst!"

Little sister dodged behind a huge rock and emerged with a drinking glass. She said, "I saved half a glass of water yesterday."

I snatched it from her hand and gulped down two mouthfuls before I realized what I was doing. Embarrassed, I handed the glass to teacher Yuanpu, who declined. I stared at him in disbelief, while little sister took the glass away from my hands. She didn't drink any, but put the water back behind the rock.

Although my whole body felt filthy, the air was fresh and wholesome. There was not a sliver of cloud in the sky, only the moon shining down serenely. Up there on the mountain with not a shred of foliage, I felt exposed and threatened. But the immediate threat was thirst. The two mouthfuls of water I had gulped down had only made me thirstier. As I followed the others farther up the mountain, my thoughts remained on that glass of water left behind, my heart in a turmoil of regret. Why hadn't I finished the water in the glass? Why pretend politeness with those hypocrites?

As I turned around to retrieve that glass of water, little sister shouted at me, "You will lose your way!"

I had no choice but to turn back and stagger after them. After a while, I felt my legs giving way. No matter how I tried, I just couldn't keep up with the three figures ahead of me. How vigorous they seemed as they kept climbing. The fatigue and fear of the last few days, now compounded by this parching thirst, was more than I could bear, and losing control, I slid and fell down.

The instant I was down, the sound of gurgling water hit my ears. I thought it was a delusion, and closed my eyes, trying to block it out. But the sound was insistent and grew louder. Water splashed over my feet and soaked my pants. I jumped up, but quickly bent down to catch the water with my mouth. After drinking my fill, I decided to take a bath. There was no one around anyway. I undressed completely and started to wash myself. By now the water was cascading from above and bounced up like a fountain as it hit the rocks below. I was completely mystified. As I finished washing and dressed myself, the water stopped. The wind rose and all signs of water disappeared from the rocks as if it had never been. Just then I saw teacher Yuanpu descend toward me, his head down.

"Where's my sister?" I asked. At the same time I couldn't help noticing what a beautiful moonlit night it was.

"She is with Huimin. The ecstasy of love. In the cave over there," he pointed vaguely to somewhere behind him. As he reached me, I saw water dripping down his face from his wet hair.

"Where did the water come from?"

He did not answer, but pulled me down hastily to sit next to him as he put his head dejectedly between his knees. At that moment, he was again my boyfriend. I stroked his wet hair and asked softly what had happened. He mumbled, "Shockingly violent. This damned mountain. I had never imagined. . . ."

Looking down the mountain, I could see flashes of firelight moving about. It was the villagers of the rocky village returning home. I tried to imagine little sister and Huimin locked together in a night of love. I mused over her decision to settle down in this dirt-poor place. Teacher Yuanpu must have been contemplating the same questions, but he understood them more than I did, and thus the shock to him was a bigger blow. I had never seen him so downhearted. He had been away for barely a half hour; I wondered what kind of terrible scene he had witnessed in that short interval to bring about this change.

I turned my thoughts to going down the mountain. Although it was not steep, there was no discernible path downward. Following little sister and Huimin uphill had not been a problem, but going down seemed dangerous.

"Don't even think of it," teacher Yuanpu said, with his head still down. I asked what he meant, and he said, "There are rattlesnakes everywhere. You haven't seen them yet. We mustn't move; if we do, they will come out. The only thing we can do is to wait till daybreak."

He stretched out his right hand. Under the moonlight, I saw the mark of a snakebite on his palm, and blood on the wound. Strange that it had not swollen and that his hand could move as usual. Teacher Yuanpu gazed at the bite wound and said, between clenched teeth, "The poison is in my heart, do you understand such things? I feel terrible." Suddenly words began to pour out of him feverishly: "You come here giddily. Once arrived, however, there's no going back. You saw the villagers down there. You saw them sitting in the sweet potato fields. Did you think they were growing sweet potatoes? Absolutely not. That's not what they are working on. The soil here is rich; you plant the cuttings and don't ever bother about them again. Their real work is moving rocks. They move rocks the year round. I saw the stone mausoleums that they built. Years ago . . ."

I felt that teacher Yuanpu was getting too worked up, and tried to change the subject.

"Little sister and Huimin don't work with rocks. They are having fun up the mountain."

"No!" he thundered. Even in the dusk, I could see his face glowering, a dark purple. "They have been moving rocks up there on the mountain. Rocks are their love. Listen, can you hear it?"

Yes, I could hear it. The sound of explosions seemed to come from the very core of the earth, muffled, somewhat unreal.

"It is their homemade explosives," teacher Yuanpu said coldly.

Suddenly I was scared to be next to him. I moved away and asked timidly, "What about you—will you end up dying here?"

He did not answer. In that instant, I saw how detached and distant he had become. I had no clue as to what he was thinking. How could he ever have been my boyfriend? What did he really feel for me? He sat there on a rock, having sustained a mortal blow, but I had no clue as to what that blow was. And now he was weeping. He wept as he said, "Life is so short. I have not lived my fill."

In the morning, when little sister found me, I was in a tight embrace with teacher Yuanpu lying on the rocks. We had become one person in our dreams. Little sister was disheveled and looked tired, but her face shone with determination as never before. Huimin, his face coal black, stood beside her holding an iron bar and a hammer in his hands.

"We two have been working through the night in the bowels of the mountain. See, my feet are hurt."

Little sister limped before me, making a circle as Huimin held her up gently. This little couple's love was so palpably moving.

That same day we descended the mountain, and did not return to little sister's home despite her urging.

Our return trip took only two days and two nights, although it was upstream all the way.

Now teacher Yuanpu has moved in with me. In the stillness of the night we always sit beneath the bay tree, facing Meteorite Mountain, musing on life over there. Teacher Yuanpu told me very firmly there was nothing on earth that attracted him as much as Meteorite Mountain. But he did not want to go again. That visit with me was the last, he decided. As he said it, he did not seem sad, and I was glad for him.

By now, the images of Huimin and little sister are blurred in our memories. We are still concerned about them but we will not sail downstream to visit anymore. I even think it's fortunate little sister is married off to that place, leaving me with this unending longing for her. Perhaps nature intended her to work in the bowels of the earth. As for teacher Yuanpu, I feel that he is two beings. He lives in the village, but another part of him is elsewhere living another life, where he is someone like Huimin. It was actually my union with teacher Yuanpu that made me gradually discover the true inner core of little sister. Little sister found what she had been looking for all her life in the violence of the rocky mountain. She could strike springwater out of the rocks with the force of her passion; there was nothing she could not do. The past seemed like a dream. How strange that my gentle little sister had her heart and soul stolen away by that lanky young man. In truth it must have been fated. Probably Huimin had been waiting, waiting for little sister to grow up, for everything to turn out as it did.

Translated from the Chinese by Zhu Hong

ABOUT THE AUTHOR

Can Xue is the pen name of Deng Xiaohua. She was born in Changsha, Hunan, and still lives there. She first began writing in 1983, and her stories have appeared in various literary magazines in mainland China as well as in Hong Kong and Taiwan. She is the author of *Dialogues in Paradise, Old Floating Cloud: Two Novellas,* and *The Embroidered Shoes.*

JO KYUNG RAN

Born in 1969, Jo Kyung Ran received her undergraduate degree in creative writing from the Seoul Institute of the Arts, and while still a student there, published her first book, a story collection called The French Optician, *which won her the Donga-Ilbo Prize. That year, her first novel,* Time for Baking Bread, *was also released, and it won the first Literary Community New Writer's Award. Seemingly overnight, she was a literary sensation and, as these things go in South Korea, she was quite famous.*

As these things go in every country, however, her rise to stardom was a bit more complicated than appearances might suggest. For one thing, she was a shut-in for half of her twenties. She had failed her university entrance exams and couldn't find a job, and she became obese and friendless. Ashamed, and without a single clue as to what she would do with her life, she did not leave her room for five years. All she did, nearly every minute of the day, was read books, and as she read, she had a shamanistic transformation of sorts. The books began to "speak" to her, telling her that she should become a poet. Finally, at the age of twenty-six, she started university, gravitated quickly to writing fiction, and published her first book when she was twenty-eight.

Of late, women writers have been flourishing in Korea—a rather startling development in a country that still clings to rigid Confucian patriarchal traditions, a country in which nearly all of the scholars and critics, who wield enormous power, are men. Also until recently, much of Korean literature has centered on the historical or sociopolitical, subjects sanctioned by the academy and government as appropriate "culture content": folktales, feudal epics, earnest representations of peasant life, honorable depictions of laborers in the industrial age, anguished stories of Japanese colonial rule and the subsequent civil war that divided the country into North and South (referred to there as the "tragedy of the murder of brothers"). Quite frankly, a lot of this work—especially in the shoddy translations endorsed by the government—came across as rather bleak and dry.

Better, more innovative books were being written, but they remained under wraps.

But the political situation in South Korea has loosened, and a new wave of writers, of which Jo Kyung Ran is certainly a prominent part, is ushering forth something different, something fresh and urgent. Jo's prose is both haunting and whimsical as she delves into a deeply interior life, one rent with dreamy, impressionistic dislocation. Her style is thoroughly contemporary, yet, at the same time, she seems to subscribe to the traditional motif of writer as shaman. Indeed, she has professed to feeling she is simply channeling a supernatural voice: "I'm just . . . a bridge between here and there, the world that is seen and the world that is unseen." Whatever the case, it is a voice that is chillingly unique, and undeniably her own.

—DON LEE

LOOKING FOR THE ELEPHANT

The Polaroid camera I have is a Spectra. It uses film about 1.5 times larger than an ordinary Polaroid, and it's more expensive. He bought it for my birthday a few years ago. I remember how happy I was when I unwrapped the present and saw it was the camera I had wanted so much. He took the first picture. I'm looking down a little, my head slightly bowed. The lipstick smudge on my wineglass is still plainly visible. I must have asked him, Should I take one of you? He shook his head. With one pack of film you can take ten pictures—there were nine left. He didn't want me to, but I wish I had taken one of him to keep that day. Because we suddenly broke up shortly after that. And now I can't love him, and I can't hate him anymore. The camera—I brought it back home and got a shot of my family gathered around the table.

I usually sleep lying straight, flat on my back. When my stomach bothers me, I roll over onto my left side and fall asleep facing the wall. But no matter what position I sleep in, one of my arms stretches out—like it's a habit—and ends up dangling down from the bed. Suddenly, I feel the sensation of someone gently holding my hand. I wake with a start. The room is dark. The warmth lingers on my palm. I try flexing the fingers of the hand that dangles from the bed. I feel like somebody sneaked in—he's lying on the floor or sitting at the foot of the bed, not even a tremor of movement. But I don't even consider leaping out of bed or quickly snapping on the light. For some reason I don't think it would be right. It wasn't easy at first. The presence terrified me— so much that I had to sleep with the light on for a long time. But now I'm quite accustomed to the presence. Slowly, I force out my breath. I mean, I'm hoping it will figure out that I'm awake. After a little while I switch on the light. There's nobody there. Not a trace of anybody having been there. But now I know. *He's* been here. At first I wondered if it might be one of the spirits of this house. Or is it my dead grandmother, or my aunt, or my uncle?

My father is from Yeosu. I've been there only once since I became an adult. I don't like it, because that's where my father was born. Too many bad things happen there. My father's half brothers and half sisters drink way too much—they're always fighting and crying. One of my uncles goes out onto the savage ocean for months at a time to catch the fish he sells at market. My father left his hometown when he was nine, after his mother died. She died on her birthday. For once, my grandfather, my seafaring uncles, and my aunts all gathered together in one place. My grandmother must have waited a long time for that day. She cooked a puffer fish soup and committed suicide by eating it all by herself. And not just any day—it had to be her birthday. I saw my grandmother in the one picture that's left of her. Like my mother's mother, who died young from breast cancer, she was dressed all in white, frowning. Both my grandmothers had thick black eyebrows. I decided I liked my father's mother—because I think her death was dramatic. After she died, my father left home and came up to

live in Seoul, and when he got married, he registered this place as
his permanent address. But I know he loves Yeosu. I know that he
privately dreams of going back there someday. I also know that
whenever something about Yeosu comes up on TV shows like
My Hometown at 6, he looks at me. Ha! Not a chance! I jerk my
head and look the other way. Aunt Yonsook is the youngest of my
father's siblings. She's especially fond of my father's children, that
is to say, her nieces: my sisters and me. Every season, she would
send us fish by courier—dried sole, croaker, and skate—and she
called us all the time. She wanted to move up to Seoul, but after
I was grown, she never came even once. Every holiday or memo-
rial service she'd say, I should go, I should really go and see you
all, and she would cry. She was the one who cried the most of all
my father's siblings. That's why I was afraid of her. When she got
married, she was prettied up in a long dress with her black hair
hanging all the way down to her waist. I heard that her sailor husband (I only saw his face once) used to beat her. She had two kids
with him before she got a divorce. I also heard that she was sending the money she made from her shop and her side job at the
seashore to pay for the children's education. They said she was
tough. My mother liked Aunt Yonsook a lot. That young thing,
she would say. Come to think of it, there wasn't much difference
in our ages even though I was her niece. Then Aunt Yonsook had
a fight with her lover and jumped out of his fifth-floor apartment.
A suicide. My father's siblings berated her lover and accused him
of murdering her. On the day of the autopsy, my father's younger
brother, Uncle Dosong, went to the morgue instead of him. My
father was drunk—he couldn't stop the dry heaves. Up to now,
my father has given up smoking exactly three times. The first time
was the day he came back after cremating my aunt. The autopsy
wasn't able to determine whether her death was a suicide or a
homicide. They said that the man who had been her lover took
care of the funeral. I guess that meant he paid the expenses.
I heard all this from up here in Seoul. Go down to Yeosu? I shud-
dered. The funeral turned into utter chaos. The five surviving siblings were all drunk, and they yelled and cried, clutching one

another by the collar. That was the night I first felt the strange presence in my room. After holding my breath and lying there for a long time, I floated up from my body. I looked at the foot of the bed and down at the floor. I called my dead aunt's name in the dark room, Aunt Yonsook? I felt a coldness brush past my face. Those nights went on for a very long time. I didn't say anything about it to my mother or my sisters. My family was afraid to talk about the dead. I just got used to it by myself. And after a while I didn't feel the presence at all, not until the night after my uncle died. Uncle Dosong, who saw Aunt Yonsook's autopsy with his own two eyes, was diagnosed with liver cancer at Severance Hospital two years after she died. He came and stayed in our house while he was an outpatient. My father's siblings are all tall and well built—but Uncle Dosong became emaciated, his face grew dark. In that condition, he turned down my parents' offer of their bedroom and slept in a fetal position on the living room sofa. When I had to go to the bathroom in the middle of the night, I couldn't go downstairs. I was afraid my uncle might be lying there dead. It felt like my bladder would burst. My uncle went back down to Yeosu with his face black as a goat's. He died two months later. Even then, I didn't go to Yeosu. My father quit smoking again. I started waking up often around dawn. I couldn't shake off the feeling that somebody was sitting at the foot of my bed or curled up on the floor where there was hardly space for a person to lie down. My palms were always clammy with sweat. I tried calling, Uncle Dosong? Nobody answered—not Aunt Yonsook, or Uncle Dosong, or my grandmother who killed herself a long time ago. Finally, I fell asleep with my Polaroid camera still in my hand.

Every Polaroid picture has a serial number printed on it. The first picture he took—the one of me on my birthday, sitting in a local café with my head bowed—has the number 0318 4149 printed on the back. If I had gotten a shot of his face after that, it would have the number 0318 4150. But number 0318 4150 is the picture of my family. They had just returned home after their evenings out and were all gathered around the table with a small cake on it. All right, everyone, look this way! I had just broken up with him when I clicked the shutter. I took up to the tenth picture in the pack, number 0318 4158, a portrait of my friend on her birthday—and when my youngest sister's boyfriend came over, I got a shot of the two of them posed in the living room. I shot a magnolia just beginning to bloom, and I shot my old sneakers. While I used up 4152, 4155, and up to 4157—having already shot number 0318 4151—winter passed, spring came, and summer went. I never got another chance to get a picture of his face. I was down to the last shot, number 0318 4158. I slept holding my Polaroid. I woke up. I held my breath and—*click*— I pressed the shutter as if I were on an ambush. The film popped out like I had snatched it from the camera. I quickly turned on the light, pressed the film hard against my hot, sweaty palm to make it develop faster. Slowly, faint forms started to emerge. The joy of Polaroids is the short time you wait while they develop, being able to see your pictures right away, right there. It's like the anxious waiting at the door, and each time it opens, you think it might be the person you've been watching for. But I couldn't feel that kind of excitement that night. Excitement! I was scared, like someone was clutching the nape of my neck with both hands. I look quietly at the picture, at the colors and the shape so vivid in those 9 x 7.3 centimeters. It isn't my dead grandmother, or Aunt Yonsook, or Uncle Dosong, and it isn't some spirit of the house. There it is—a great big elephant.

I started living in this house eleven years ago. It's multifamily housing now, but eleven years ago it was a small single-story home with a narrow yard. My father bought that house. He tore it down and built one based on his own sketches. While the new house was under construction, our family of five all lived in a single room nearby. When they had to raise their voices to argue about something, my mother and father would go to a local inn.

My father built one more room on top of the roof. That's the rooftop room where I've lived until now, where I am writing this. This was supposed to be my youngest sister's room. I used to write downstairs, squatting on the floor. I wanted to have a huge desk. When my youngest sister went away for a while, I called some of my other sister's male friends and they helped me empty my room downstairs and move up here. That night I wrote my youngest sister a letter. Her reply: Well done, sis. The rooftop room had no space to put a desk, so I bought a shiny little table. Now the lacquer is peeling from the edges in spots and the legs wobble, but it's still usable. Even if I get a bigger room, I don't feel like changing my desk anymore. But I still do dream of a big desk with lots of drawers and compartments. People have to learn to be satisfied with less than enough, my mother always said. In my rooftop room I would read, write, and make phone calls in the middle of the night. Years passed in the blink of an eye. When I couldn't write, or every time I had a bad fight with someone in the family, I felt like leaving this house. When I went downstairs at night to use the bathroom, I would accidentally step on the legs or stomachs of my family members sleeping in the dark on the floor of the living room. We'd startle each other in the dark and scream, Who's there! Who are you? I banged the wall of my room with both fists. It didn't crumble. The house my father built was more solid than I thought.

Sunday afternoon I went to the Seoul Grand Park in Gwachon. It was a few days after I saw the elephant. A very windy day, and it was jam-packed with people. In the zoo, a chrysanthemum festival was opening. People were taking pictures in front of the multi-colored chrysanthemums in full bloom, and in the flamingo cage next door, the flock of long-legged flamingos were flapping their wings. I went straight to the front of the elephant pen. An African elephant, with its long trunk swaying, slowly walked around inside the broad S-shaped enclosure. I couldn't help feeling disappointed. The distance between the elephant and me was farther than I had expected. It was too far—it wasn't worth taking a picture. I got closer to the elephant. When it went left I ran that way; when it turned its body around, I quickly ran back to the right. The elephant is really popular. Every gap in the long, curving fence was jammed with children and adults. I guessed the elephant in that pen was an old bull. Old males live alone. In the early morning and evening they forage for plants, and they rest in the shade of trees during the day. They sleep standing up—though there are times when they sleep lying on their side. The elephant that came to my room lay on that cramped floor and slept with its massive body curled up tight around its trunk. As if I might try to steal it or something. I couldn't tell whether it had big tusks, so there was no way to know whether it was a male or a female. The elephant had been walking back and forth on the same path through its pen; once in a while it seemed lost in thought and paused with its thick legs bent, gazing out at us. Then, as if to say that it was nothing after all, it went clomping back again, retracing its steps. Each time the elephant flapped its ears, it sent a cold breeze through the front of my clothes. I took the Polaroid camera out of my shoulder bag. I put in a new pack of film. If there had been a Polaroid better than the Spectra, he probably would have bought it for me. But it wasn't easy to find film for it. I ordered it specially from the owner at the photo shop. When I went to pick up the film, the owner told me that the Spectra wasn't widely distributed, so it would always be hard to get film for it. He said if I took it back to the place of purchase, they would exchange it for a regular Polaroid. Like a refund. I ordered three packs of film at once. It was his last present to me. Suddenly, the elephant stopped walking and—with a *thump*—put its front feet up on the inner rail on our side of the pen. There was another pen two or three meters away, and the gap in between was dug out like a ditch. It looked as if the elephant could jump right across. I was tense. I couldn't be sure if the elephant would come flying up at me like a bird. I pressed the shutter just as it raised its long trunk. The print popped out. The elephant took its front feet down and turned its body around. Clever beast. It's unlikely it heard the sound of the shutter, but I'll say it did, anyway. The zookeeper opened the steel gate and came out. He gave the elephant a bun, and the elephant took it in its trunk and ate it. It was 4:40 PM. The elephant followed the keeper in through the steel gate and disappeared. As soon as it was gone, all the people left the front of the pen at the same time. I went over to the next pen, to the Asian elephant. But the Asian elephant was already gone. I read: The Asian elephant has weak eyesight. Because its neck is short, it cannot look behind itself. Cannot look behind itself. Now I was sure. The elephant that came to me that night was not Asian but African. The elephant—it has weak eyes, but its hearing and sense of smell are excellent. It can run up to fifty kilometers per hour. The surface of its body is covered with thick bristles. The front teeth in its upper jaw grow into long tusks. The elephant—largest land animal on the face of the earth.

I felt that something was unsatisfactory. But I didn't want to know too specifically. I kept going out, eager to get out of the house, though there was nowhere to go. One day he showed up with a bunch of different self-improvement pamphlets. He took me by the hand and we went around looking at rooms. By coincidence, all four places we saw were rooftop rooms. I ripped the pamphlets to shreds right in his face. We ate some hot soup and rice for dinner. We crossed the street via the pedestrian overpass and went into a newly built twenty-story officetel[1] building. The custodian gave us the key. There was a big desk, a wardrobe, a bed, a shiny sink. I pulled him by the hand. I pointed outside the window where cars were whizzing by. This place isn't going to work out. Maybe not. Yeah, it'll be too noisy. That's what I was thinking, too. We returned the key and came out of the officetel. We went to eat some fried chicken. It was less than half an hour after we'd had dinner.

Even now my heart pounds when I hear my mother's footsteps coming up the stairs to my rooftop room. My mother came up to my room. She said we would have to leave our house. There was

---

[1] An office and hotel with single-unit rentals.

so much my parents had been keeping from us. She said our house was going to be foreclosed and put up for auction. My father's older brother had borrowed money from him twice and then disappeared. I couldn't blame my father. Everyone was just trying to get by. For the first time, I understood the expression, "One day we found ourselves out on the street." My father quit smoking. Stayed in his room all day. Ate his meals by himself. His face became black and gaunt like my dead uncle Dosong's. My mother's ears dripped blood. I only wished my little sisters could stay in school. I suppose it was no different from my parents keeping those dire things hidden from us three daughters. I stabbed a kitchen knife between the red bricks of the house. The house was very solid. We began the fight to keep it. I ran around—all over the place—to take care of things. It was important and someone had to do it. I'm sorry I can't do anything to help, he said. I'm not as afraid of losing the house as I am of losing you, I blurted out to him, terrified. He cried. Don't cry, I consoled him. I didn't cry. My pent-up tears burst forth only when the elephant came to see me again. I buried my face in its big belly, and covering my mouth with my hand, I sobbed and sobbed.

Once in a while he calls me. How are you? His voice is sad and tender. I laugh dismissively. How are you doing? He's asking after me, but he's also asking about the house. Then he asks another thing. Did the elephant come again? There are times when he seems to be more interested in the elephant than in me. The day I went to the zoo, I took three pictures: the elephant with its front feet on the rail, the elephant suddenly raising its trunk into the sky, wriggling its buttocks as it walks, the elephant trudging toward the setting sun with its head bowed low. My lonely elephant.

Sometimes I ask myself how I came to live in this house all this time. Surely, there must have been a chance for me to end up living somewhere other than here. Among those chance events was my turning twenty, and the incident that my family still remembers—my kidnapping. It's strange, but I can't seem to remember my twenties. Maybe it's because I never told anyone about those days. Last fall, I went to give a guest lecture at S—— University. As I was about to enter the lecture hall, someone blocked my way. She said my name. I stared right through her, then said with a sigh, Ah, it's Yonjong. She said she had seen a poster for the event on a campus bulletin board. I really wanted to know if it was you. I was visibly uncomfortable. I took her business card and hurriedly said good-bye. She must have been studying computer graphics all that time. Looking at her card, I saw that she was now a senior researcher at the Electronic Visual Media Research Center at the university. I remember that even after I went into the lecture hall, I couldn't speak for a while and just sat there. Yonjong was one of the people who knew me back then. I said I would get in touch, but I didn't. A year went by. Finally, a little while ago, I sent her an e-mail: Yonjong, I wonder how everyone from back in those days remembers me. And where are they all now? Do you still remember what I looked like back then? I had just had dinner with the head editor of a Web site, and we were walking along a street in Shinsadong looking for a place to get some tea, when someone called me from behind. Hey, Fatty Jo! I didn't stop walking. I didn't even look back. Why was it so hard to find a teahouse? I walked faster, faster. My companion cautiously took my elbow. I think someone is calling you over there. When I heard the Hey! I instantly recalled whose voice it was. That's odd. I was about twenty-two when I met those people—it had already been more than ten years ago. I can still hear that insistent voice calling me. I turn my head to look with an indifferent eye. Hey, Fatty Jo! Ah, how do you do? Hey, is it really you? It's been a long time. I greet Director Jong and Assistant Manager Pak politely. Wow! Look at her! They laugh. I used to go to work with my hair in my first perm ever, tied in back like a country girl. I shampooed every morning and I wore stockings. Every time I dried my wet hair with the dryer, I thought to myself, Where shall I go today? I often didn't show up for work.

Once, I was absent for three straight days the same week. At lunchtime I went out by myself to a big bookstore in the building across the street where there used to be a fast-food place in the basement. I would eat a hamburger and read a book. A whole book. When I was tired of reading, I would call someone on the pay phone. I would also peek into the galleries near work. When I went back to work, my coworkers would look at me disapprovingly. It was four hours past lunchtime. I didn't eat out with my coworkers and I didn't socialize with them after work. Sometimes I would stay by myself at the office and read a book or spend a long time looking at the 4-D graphics that my coworkers had been working on. With the computer, my coworkers created stars, they made camels walk across the desert, they built apartments. They also created Flash animations. It's not shown anymore, but there used to be a commercial for a cold medicine called Blupen made by a certain pharmaceutical company. It was an animated commercial that showed a bottle of Blupen rushing like a train toward a child with a fever. I had helped create the frames for that. There was nothing they couldn't make. I stayed behind after work. When I was alone, I grabbed the mouse and clicked buttons at random. In the morning, I heard my coworkers cursing, Who did this? Who erased everything? I was always expressionless. When I went downstairs to the bathroom, someone grabbed me from behind and pulled my backside against his groin. Don't you know how to smile? He was an interior designer who was often in and out of our office. After work, Assistant Manager Pak said he would drop me off near my house. I got into his car. He told me to put my seat belt on. I pulled out a length of seat belt, too long. I hesitated, then I put it around my neck. Hey, don't you know how to put on a seat belt? Is there a problem? I said. I looked at him with a sullen face. His flabbergasted expression is still clear in my mind. Even now, whenever I get a ride in someone's car, I privately fret that I might put the seat belt on wrong like I did that time. So you write. Director Jong and Assistant Manager Pak knew about my present situation. Yes. Let's get together with Yonjong and Assistant Manager Kim Jong sometime. Yes. They must have been truly pleased to run into me. Director Jong and Assistant Manager Pak kept chuckling. They asked me to write down my contact info. I wrote some phone number. I don't even know whose it was. I hated myself for being fat, I hated myself for cutting work, I hated myself for not being able to understand the computer graphics manuals I was forced to read. I worked at that company for seven months. Then I turned in my resignation. It was Director Jong who said I should reconsider. What else are you going to do? he asked. Sometimes, when I go to Shinsadong or Gangnam I look at the World Book Center. I can still see myself standing inside that bookstore at the age of twenty-two, lost in some book. I used to live in this city back then. I never got a reply from Yonjong.

If I hadn't been able to get back home after the incident, this is not where I would be living now. And my family would not be the family I have now. I was kidnapped when I was four by a middle-aged woman who couldn't have children. She took me to a beauty parlor to alter my appearance. She must have asked them to give me a perm. She stepped out for a while. That was my chance. I bawled my eyes out. Even at four years old, I was able to remember Bongshin Church. The owner of the beauty parlor held my hand and took me there, and that's how I got back home. The house I lived in then was demolished, but Bongshin Church is still there.

I've started to eat before my father, before he even lifts his spoon. When my sisters get out of work late, they call me first though I'm still asleep. My father is smoking again. In the morning my mother shines my shoes. In the room on the roof, the piles of books are steadily growing. There's too much stuff in your room, my father says, worried. I didn't care. I got myself a TV set, a printer. There wasn't room to walk. I moved some of my books down to the living room. I bought some new bookshelves. I got rid of the living room sofa. There was another sofa by the refrigerator, and I put bookshelves there, too. Each time I put up a new bookshelf, I felt as if I were uprooting a grove of trees, but the feeling never lasted more than half a day. The things from the living room, and the wardrobe that the three of us sisters shared, got moved into the main bedroom. My father put up a column in the downstairs living room to support my room on the roof. But even then he paced back and forth every day, anxious that the ceiling would collapse from the weight, and meanwhile I wondered if my parents could stretch their legs and sleep in a room so crammed with their daughters' stuff.

On the same night he said, I'm sorry I can't do anything to help, he wrote me a long letter. It was about himself, full of helplessness and regret. At the end of the letter he added this: Things deeply felt cannot help but last. He wrote: People cannot always live and love in the same way; nothing remains as it was. He wrote: We must change in order to remain the same. And he also wrote this: That is how love must grow. A letter. A very sad word, *letter.* After we split up, I never took that letter out to read it again. And there's another letter I could never read again. Once in a while I think about it. And I think, So why did we split up? In the end, because of saving the house, I lost him. I look at the picture of my family—the one I took on my birthday when I got home after breaking up with him. They don't know the table is the elephant's head, that the sofa is the elephant's back, and they're smiling, digging their sharp elbows into it. Look, I'm telling you this is an elephant! If I said that, they would all just laugh and say, She's writing another story. The elephant is pretending to be asleep and his eyes are closed, but I know he's not sleeping. I never forget to keep a butter-coconut biscuit or a banana, just in case. Because I don't know when the elephant might come again.

My father went down to Yeosu, showing off his three daughters like medals. It was 1996, so I was twenty-six—it was the year I started college. That night there was a drinking party. Someone got drunk and burst into tears. I mingled with my relatives, and I drank a good amount myself. The next day, the entire extended family went together on a picnic. We rented a Bongo minibus and sped off a long way down the coast. We went on a boat ride there. Odong Island was visible in the distance. It was a hot midsummer day. No one can remember the name of that island now. Me neither—no matter how hard I think about it, I can't remember where the island was that we went to that day. But then, Yeosu is a place with so many nameless islands you couldn't possibly count them all. But it occurs to me now that maybe the island wasn't even in Yeosu. Aunt Yonsook organized and brought all the food. My uncles, cousins, and aunts stood in front of the grill and cooked the meat and blood clams. They ran into the ocean to swim and play with a ball. The cousins who took after their fathers were all slim and long-legged. They laughed merrily in the hot sun. The sound startled me. I dropped the parasol I was carrying, and for the first time in my life, I saw my father swimming. He was quick, confident, agile as a seal. The first time I saw him swim. I must have entirely forgotten that this was where my father was born. Uncle Dosong, just back from a stretch at sea, had a large bottle of *soju* dangling from his mouth. Uncle, please don't drink too much—I told him what he didn't want to hear, like I was talking to my father. I think it was around then that Uncle Dosong's liver problems started. Leave him alone, said my father. Aunt Yonsook had brought the food, but she hardly had time to eat anything. She was too busy clearing away the meat grill, cooking the clams and seafood she'd kept frozen solid for months in the freezer, boiling chickens. My other aunts washed the dishes under the command of her loud voice. They were sharing a large bottle of *soju* too. They quickly went through a whole pot of Dolsan mustard leaf kimchi. My mother, drunk from three glasses of *soju,* spread out a mat and lay down. The sun was really hot. The ocean looked infinitely deep. My uncles and cousins waved to me from out in the water. I shook my head. Not one of us three sisters knew how to swim. They threw me in the ocean the day I was born, said Aunt Yonsook. I took off my socks and threw them aside. It took courage to go into the water. Holding my sisters' hands, I walked into the ocean one step at a time. Then my third uncle, Doyoon, suddenly pushed me hard on the back and I fell in with all my clothes on. I could hear my aunts, uncles, and cousins all laughing even from deep down. I was not afraid. I couldn't be sure, but maybe my arms and legs would move instinctively and I could swim like Aunt Yonsook. I was my father's daughter, after all, and he was a salty old dog who could look at an anchovy's shit and tell you what it had eaten. I walked out of the water all flustered. Around me, my father, my three uncles, three aunts, and six cousins were all having a leisurely swim. Now, two are gone. Those who are left call my mother regularly. I hear that one of my uncles got water on the knee awhile ago, and another hurt his back and can't go out to sea anymore. It scares me that people keep dying. I hate the monsoon, I hate blizzards, and I hate wars. There are times when I'd like to see the faces of the dead once more, but that will only be possible in the distant future. The sun went down. The *soju* was finished, and the watermelon, the octopus, the grilled bulgogi, the lettuce—all finished. Aunt Yonsook's husband took charge and cleared everything up. He did the driving, too. He didn't look like the type who would beat a person like a dog, but the subtle slant of his eyes bothered me. We all went back to the house of one of my uncles. It was a long way. My father, my uncles, and my aunts stayed up drinking until dawn. And somebody argued and started crying, but then, right away, they were all cackling with laughter again. My father's second mother is over eighty—maybe when she dies I'll go down to Yeosu again. Black hairs are starting to poke up again on my grandmother's head. When my father is drunk, he brings up that summer outing. And he talks about his younger days in Saudi Arabia, Iran, and Kuwait. He used to write us twice a week. My mother wrote him a letter every day, and because of her badgering, we three sisters dutifully wrote him once a week. Letters that read: Daddy, we're all well and we're doing all right in school, we'll study hard—and nothing more to say after that. My father's letters, which crossed the blowing sands of the desert, were the same: Listen to your mother and concentrate on your studies. Daddy is doing fine. Only the dates were different. The letters we exchanged like this for ten years are in a big earthenware storage jar on the rooftop. It's like burying winter kimchi—a layer of plastic spread inside the pot with the letters sealed up inside. My father did that. To this day, I have never once opened that pot. But I've already started to worry about what I should do with those letters after my father passes away. Every day we're paying off the house, and every day we're losing the house, but fortunately there hasn't been any real change so far. In the morning, my father brings in the paper from the front steps, my mother shines the shoes, and we three sisters leave for work. When I'm out of earshot, my father sadly complains that no one seems to notice the old cacti are blooming, and my mother gives us that look. She doesn't come up to my room. When I get a phone call, she puts the receiver outside my door and goes back downstairs. How much longer can my mother climb up and down those stairs with the pain in her joints? I go downstairs a lot even when I'm reading a book or writing. I wish one of us would hurry up and get married and leave this house. If a room were free, we could move the stuff from the main bedroom there and we could put the sofa back in the living room. But I'm afraid I may be the last of the sisters, remaining in this house until the very end. My father still worries that the room on the roof will collapse—his heart pounds—and I worry that his daughters' possessions and books have invaded his bedroom. I'm not the happiest person in the world, but I'm not the most miserable, either. When I'm upset or my pride is injured, I sit at the table for an hour or two trimming anchovies. If we don't have any, then I'll shell peanuts. I frequently dress up and go to an Italian restaurant to eat pasta and drink wine. My mother still tells me that people have to learn to be satisfied with less than enough. Now I know what that means. Though I must admit it has taken a long time. I'm still living in this house. This is where my happiest and unhappiest moments are. My room on the roof is warm. It's winter now. I can hear the spoons being laid out on the table downstairs. Let's eat! my mother shouts up to my room. All right! I answer right away. And I *thump thump thump* down the stairs.

Sometimes I wait for his call. He's the only one who understands my elephant story. He listens. I can pick up the phone and ramble on for an hour about my elephant. I don't take pictures anymore, but something still appears. Now and then the house moves—it squirms—and I think to myself, Ah, the elephant has come.

Translated from the Korean by Heinz Insu Fenkl

ABOUT THE AUTHOR

Jo Kyung Ran earned her undergraduate degree in creative writing from Seoul Institute of the Arts and debuted in 1996 with *The French Optician*. That same year her novel *Time for Baking Bread* won the first Literary Community New Writer's Award. Her published works include *Changing Season, Beautiful Knife, Your Side, My Purple Sofa, Binoculars, Glass Zoo,* and *Family Prayer.*

SENO GUMIRA AJIDARMA

Unlike writers in the more developed countries of the world, third-world writers don't have the luxury of devoting themselves completely to the development of their personal writing style or technique. They have an extra task, what I would call "nation building." Perhaps a writer shouldn't have to have this task, but in the third world, participating in nation building is, I feel, an honor, not a burden. Of all the younger Indonesian writers whose works I am acquainted with, Seno Gumira Ajidarma seems to me to be keenly aware of this responsibility. He writes not just because of the need to express himself—which is every writer's need—but to comment on social inequities and, through his work, institute or attempt to effect changes for the better in the world around him. Indonesian history has been marked by long periods of repression and it is up to the nation's younger people and, more specifically, its writers, to keep that situation from recurring. The future of Indonesia—whether we can become the free and self-sustaining nation that we proclaimed ourselves to be almost sixty years ago—cannot be predicted at present, but the realization of that goal will depend on the strength of the country's younger generation. People like Seno Gumira Ajidarma give me hope that the younger generation will achieve for this country its founding goals.

—PRAMOEDYA ANANTA TOER
Translated from the Indonesian by John H. McGlynn

CHILDREN OF THE SKY

These children are not of woman born; they are born from the womb of poverty. At birth they immediately become three and a half, eight, or twelve years of age. When the night is completely dark, without even a sliver of moon in the sky, they appear on main streets, slithering out of sewage drains with their bodies covered with mud. Slithering forward, they crawl, then, finally, stand, immediately extending their hands at intersections. From the sewage drains, a huge number of young children emerge. First their arms appear from the drainage holes to push aside the metal coverings, then they creep out, their bodies covered with mud that drips from them onto the asphalt. Pleasant little children, kids with eyes as bright as comets but whose eyelids droop sadly. When the mud on their bodies dries and turns into a grime that will stick to them for years, they extend their hands toward the windows of cars without hope of obtaining anything at all.

As they stretch out their hands, they make their faces look sad. Sometimes they clap their hands and move their mouths as if they are singing when in fact they're only moving their mouths without making any sound because the drivers in the cars aren't going to hear them anyway, and even if they could would never consider their voices to be beautiful or to have even a semblance of beauty when compared to a voice that is generally considered beautiful, even though children's eyes are still beautiful, in fact as beautiful as when they were born, whereupon they instantly turn into beggars who employ underhanded and deceitful tactics to elicit sympathy, even though their eyes have the purity of eyes of children everywhere around the world, with an abiding allure, because children everywhere are always pure regardless of whether or not when they become adults they turn out to be the nastiest and basest and most uncivilized and most rotten and most insolent persons there could be.

The people in the cars that fill the streets never know where these children come from. All they know is that they're suddenly there with their mud-covered bodies, sticking out their hands and begging with a look in their eyes, which appears to be at once pitiful and fabricated because when the light turns from red to green and the cars speed away in a flash, as if wanting to leave reality behind, those children go back to joking around and jumping rope just like they were in some kind of dreamland or a playground for the children of royalty, even though the space in which they play is no more and no less than a patch of rough cement, not in the least bit smooth, where the light changes from green to red again. The people in the cars feel no sense of pity when looking at those children. The people in cars spout clever phrases that confirm how ill advised it is to teach children to beg as they turn up the volume of their CD players belting out Puccini's "Quando me'n vo soletta" as those children striking tambourines and homemade clackers made from bottle caps nailed to a piece of wood look at the windows of the cars darkened by film with a 60-percent blackout ratio to see passengers in the backseat not looking at them at all but intently reading *The Economist*.

During the day the mud on their bodies dries and flakes off but leaves a residue of grime on their skin like a darkening mold that might not ever be expunged, just as their own destiny on the streets, which fate has forged, cannot be changed even if they bathe one hundred times a day in the slowly moving river whose dark waters are further darkened by pitch-black oil from some unknown source, carrying with its slowly moving course clutters of plastic refuse or an unidentified human corpse that is ignored by all until it has bloated with rot like a cat's carcass with its distended belly bobbing on the water, no one knowing who the person might have been or whether he or she had died alone in some unidentified place and had been given no burial nor awarded a ceremony of any kind, even though it's probably better to die and be freed from the solitude of streets so packed with people that none of the passengers in the passing cars are able to understand even a trifling of the suffering apparent outside, because in doing all they can to eschew such knowledge and free themselves from any kind of curiosity, they prefer not to take notice of the bleakness of poverty that stands right before their eyes with saddened faces, their hands extended toward them with other faces that are similarly obscure, mouthing unknown songs while clapping their hands.

Outside the cars' windows darkened by film with a 60-percent blackout ratio and an air-conditioned interior that makes the outside temperature even hotter, children with sun-bleached hair and dirty clothes full of holes meander from one car window to another with such lack of expectation it appears that they are not hungry at all and are only acting out the bitter role that they must forever continue to play because the world has always had such roles and it would be a miracle if the world had no beggars or poverty or suffering or bitterness or anything else that makes happiness something so extraordinary.

But why do those children look happy? Their eyes have the brightness of comets, and the look on their faces is one of purity and innocence, until the time comes when they reach a point where boys of twelve years of age begin to pay for the services of the cheapest prostitutes beneath the bridge and girls at the age of twelve become prostitutes. From one day to the next and from one year to another life provides lessons to girls on how to use their bodies until their bodies cannot be used and become discarded garbage in the form of a vagrant's corpse beneath an overpass, which proves to be useful as a cadaver to be carved up by medical students in their anatomy classes. Their skulls are preserved, their hearts are stored in apothecary jars, and one day these students become fabulously wealthy from the knowledge they gained from the nerve structure and the muscles and the glands and all the other innards they removed from the corpse of that unknown woman who was most likely a low-paid prostitute whose life had begun in a sewage drain.

In the dark, bleak, and acrid-smelling drains, masses of children await their turn to emerge. They will always be there and cannot be expunged or made to disappear as they continue to multiply until they come to be found popping out of each and every sewage drain in the city. As soon as they emerge from the drain they immediately put on a mournful face and extend their hands to signal that they need money to eat but only for just that day, as if they don't know that they were born to feel hunger and that they were born to be beggars to serve as proof that poverty exists. They extend their hands toward one window after another while trying to peer inside where people are reading *The Asian Wall Street Journal* beneath minispotlights while moaning and sighing that trade has become so difficult and that international currency rates are causing their debts to bloat. In the calculations of their accountants, they are far poorer than the beggars outside their car windows who, despite their baseness and filth and disgusting appearance, have no debts whatsoever. Not a single cent. They take a deep breath. Life is so difficult, they think. As entertainment they turn their car into an opera house. Listen to Montserrat Caballe resound, "Spira sul mare e sulla terra."

I am thinking about all of this while looking at the clouds—an ocean's expanse of white cotton like a heaven for the most beautiful of children. Outside the window of the plane, the sun seems different, its light softer with violet, golden, and reddish colors that plate the soft and inviting pillows of clouds. The stewardess offers me a choice of beverages and I choose a white wine with a name that is difficult to pronounce but one that will complement the fish I eat with a napkin at my neck and a knife in my left hand and a fork in my right, the way civilized people eat, as I watch the fleeting clouds with the color and texture of yogurt extending to infinity and what is truly a dreamlike scene. The headphones on my ears take me to La Scala in Milan, where I hear Placido Domingo singing, "L'alba vindice appar." When I turn again to the window his voice seems to emanate from the sky, as if he himself is there, with his audience stretching their legs on the clouds.

A sojourn through the clouds makes one feel the world is so vast. You can skip from one layer of clouds to the next. You can imagine yourself to be a flying horse or even Lembu Andini, the vehicle for Batara Guru, chief of the gods, going in and out the breaks in the clouds that glow with irresistible changing colors, from one moment to the next, from one mood to another, from one world to another world. The sky is never the same as the earth. Each cloud layer portends a different meaning and story. Exploring the sky is navigating a world of never-ending stories, ever so expansive and ever so promising of something behind the clouds that is completely and quintessentially interesting. But I am also watching you stroke the cat, like a goddess scampering from here to there, from one dream to another, appearing for a moment and then disappearing again. "Elucevan le stelle." Do you still listen to Puccini? I am still in the airplane with my seat belt on as I eat a civilized meal. The violet clouds are tinged with red. I take a sip of wine, then belch, and the aroma of the salmon I ate just previously infuses the air.

The stewardess takes my tray. I can no longer see you outside the window. Where have you gone? Will you still be there to greet me after I am back on land? I have grown too accustomed to partings—everything always ends like this. "Tutto e finito." It's always sad to realize that each discovery within oneself denotes a kind of parting. The clouds separate. Rays of sunlight flow like a river. The plane becomes a ship. The clouds are a floating layer of soapsuds. And then from behind the sealike expanse of clouds those children appear.

Children whose bodies are covered with mud float up from the sewage drains and through the clouds to extend their hands toward the windows of the plane. I am stunned. I take off my headphones. Is this just my imagination? No, it's not, because the other passengers are in a commotion. At each window of the plane, on both sides, one, two, three children appear with their hands extended and with a sorrowful look on their faces and a false-seeming look in their eyes while other children are slapping their clappers as their mouths move in time with a song that is unidentifiably but obviously not an aria while other children whose only capital is clapping their hands stare with eyes that show little expectation of obtaining anything, so used are they to hand waves of refusal.

Passengers seated in the middle rows are taking off their seat belts and wedging their way to the windows on both sides of the plane, some of them whipping out cameras and minicams to record the scene outside. The flight attendants, normally so firm with their orders for calm, join the hysteria and shamelessly shove passengers aside to look outside the windows. A miracle. Children of the world's sewage drains whose only appropriate home is darkness and whose only appropriate life is poverty are rising upward through the clouds, the thick fleeting clouds, to continue their beggarly activity. The children spread across the sky, flitting here and there with tambourines and clappers or with only the clapping of their hands to beg at each airplane that passes through the earth's atmosphere. They rise up from sewage drains that seem to contain an unlimited supply of mud-covered children, floating directly into the sky toward passing planes in order to extend their hands to the windows. On earth the children extend their hands with a look in their eyes that says they know they will be refused. "We are begging not because we need money," their eyes say, "but because we were born as beggars." Thus the children rising from the sewage drains directly to the airplanes do so without expecting that the plane windows will open and they will receive one hundred or two hundred rupiah in coins, especially since no known plane has windows that can open and close for the distribution of alms.

In the twilight sky, beauty stretches out like a heavenly river. The sky's canopy is made bright by another sun. The plane's passengers are stunned to hear the call of the faithful, that God is great, softly entering the body of the plane from outside. At the windows, the mud-covered children with such pure eyes stare at us as we in the plane stare back at the children's eyes. What kind of poverty might it be that can never be eased and what kind of wealth might it be that cannot be used to change this poverty?

In the heavenly call of the faithful that drowns out any earthly operatic song, the children float, continuing their journey upward. I try to look up but all I can see are the ambient flashes of a brilliant light.

Translated from the Indonesian by John H. McGlynn

ABOUT THE AUTHOR

Seno Gumira Ajidarma was born in Boston in 1958 while his father was a student there. He began working as a journalist at the age of nineteen, and in 1980, he graduated with a degree in cinematography from the Jakarta Institute of the Arts. Since that time he has produced a number of screenplays but has achieved much greater success as a short story writer and novelist. To date he has published twenty-eight books and has been awarded numerous national and international literary awards, most recently in 2004 for his novel *Country of Twilight* (*Negeri Senja*). A previous novel, *Jazz, Perfume & the Incident,* is one of a select number of contemporary Indonesian novels that have been translated and published in English.

PARASHURAM

Parashuram was the pen name of Rajshekhar Basu (1880–1960), probably the greatest twentieth-century humorist in Bengali. The pen name is not, apparently, an homage to the Parashuram of mythology, the Brahmin sage who made it his mission to decimate the Kshatriya, or aristocratic, caste with his ax; although Basu directed his satire toward his contemporaries, his humor was regenerative rather than destructive. For his pen name, Basu simply borrowed the surname of someone at hand, the family goldsmith, Tarachand Parashuram, revealing that, from the beginning, his interest lay in the hidden potential for idiosyncrasy in local and ordinary actors, and also in comically conflating, as the modernists did, the banal with the mythic.

He came from a distinguished family, took a master's degree in chemistry from Calcutta University in 1903, joined Bengal Chemical and Pharmaceutical Works Ltd., founded in 1901, as a chemist, and rose, before long, to the high-ranking position of "manager." His brother, Girindrashekhar Bose, was the first Freudian psychoanalyst of the non-Western world. Basu's means of engaging with a rather odd contemporary reality of bhadralok *(Bengali middle-class) propriety and comic subterfuge was not to consign his subjects to a psychoanalyst's couch, as his brother might have, but to treat them with an indulgent but penetrating satire, often leading them to confess to oddities they might have been too embarrassed to admit to a doctor. He is extremely difficult to translate; among the main reasons for this is his verbal play, exhibited especially in the way he records the diverse ways in which Bengali is spoken, and loquaciously or prevaricatingly transmuted, by the various communities and types settled in Calcutta.*

Though it may be tempting to read the story below as an early version of the "Empire writes back" theme, an impetus that postcolonial Indian writing in English is so often identified with, I think it would be a mistake to do so, and to miss its subversive richness. Not long ago, an Indian writer (in the English language) was moaning about how he was fed up reading about young Indians who worked at call centers after learning Scottish and American accents. *"I'd like to hear of people in California striving to pick up the Patna accent,"* he said crossly. *Parashuram's story is both an extraordinarily shrewd analysis and marvelously opportunistic response to this desperate, fulminating desire for parity, to the psychology of the colonial subject's desire for revenge, its anger seen from both outside and within, and transformed into laughter. Laughter and the detached perspectives and freedoms of the imagination give us an equality that the granting of our wishes cannot, the story appears to suggest; our longings, if they came true, would be the stuff of comic dystopia.*

—AMIT CHAUDHURI

THE SCRIPTURE READ BACKWARD

Scene: The Richmond Bengalo-Anglian Pathshala.[1] *Mr. Cram, pundit in charge. Tom, Dick, Harry, and other boys.*

Cram. Hurry up now, it's four o'clock. Dick, read out the last bit of the history lesson.

Dick. [Reads from his textbook in Bengali] "Europe's days of woe are over. All hatred, violence, and conflict between its races are at end. Under the soothing influence of the dordanda rule of the mighty Indian Government" . . . What does *dordanda* mean, Pandit Mashai?

Cram. Don't you know? *The big rod. Under the soothing influence of the big rod.*

Dick. . . . "the big rod with its cool sheltering shade, all Europe is now basking thankfully in a blessed state. From Ireland to Russia, from Lapland to Sicily, peace reigns everywhere. France no longer tries to slit Germany's throat, the races of England can

---

[1]Pathshala: an elementary school of the traditional Indian type.

no longer squabble with each other, Austria and Italy have ceased to fight over possession of the Meti Pond."[2] Where's the Meti Pond, Pandit Mashai?

Cram. Why don't you look at that map in front of you? It's that sea near Italy. It used to be called the Mediterranean. The Indians couldn't pronounce the name, so they started calling it the Meti Pond—just as they call Ulster Belestera, Switzerland Chhachhurabad, Bordeaux Booze-shop, Manchester Nimta. Get on with your reading.

Dick. "The condition of the Europeans is gradually improving. Their greed has been curbed, their barbaric love of luxury dispelled; they look less toward this world and more toward the next. The children of India have crossed the seven seas and thirteen rivers to selflessly spread peace, order, and civilization through these wild and remote lands, unvisited even by the Pandavas of yore."[3] Is all this really true, Pandit Mashai?

Cram. It must be, if it's put down in print and taught by order of the government.

Dick. But my dad says it's all *bosh.*

Cram. He can say what he likes. He's a lawyer, he doesn't live on government pay.

Dick. "All you well-disposed children of England, never forget that the Indian Government has brought endless benefits to your nation. Prepare yourselves from this point of your lives to be peaceful, obedient, and patriotic subjects of the Empire when you grow up."

Tom. Brr—rr—rr—

[2]Meti Pond: satirizes the way Englishmen used distorted Anglicized forms of Indian names that they could not pronounce.

[3]Pandavas: in the *Mahabharata,* the five sons of King Pandu. Having lost to their cousins the Kauravas in a wager at dice, they had to go into exile, during which they traveled to many distant countries. "Unvisited even by the Pandavas" implies a very remote land indeed.

Cram. What's that? Feeling cold? Whatever made you wear a dhoti and kurta again? You'll die of pneumonia trying to ape the Bengalis.

Tom. Dad's orders, Pandit Mashai. I've got to go straight from school to a party at Khan Sahib Gobson Toady's house—he's got some new title or other from the government. There'll be a lot of Indian gentlemen, so Dad said I mustn't wear native clothes.

Cram. But why dress like a Bengali? You could've worn north Indian leggings and a high-collared coat.

Tom. You see, sir, Dad says the Bengalis are the most cultured race of all, so . . . brr . . .

Cram. Home with you, quick, at least get yourself a shawl. O my God, have you tripped over yourself now?

Harry. Just look at the way Tom's trailing his dhoti—like a skipping rope!

From the Church publication, **The Kingdom Come:**

Destruction is at hand. The Indian Government has robbed us of our wealth and our livelihoods. We peace-loving churchmen have never protested, for we do not lust after the loaves and fishes of this world, and scripture exhorts us to render to Caesar what is Caesar's due. But what do we hear now? Our very religion is under attack! A law is being passed to ban horse racing! Will our holy shrines like Ascot and Epsom be reduced to cremation grounds? Bishop Stonybroke has reportedly advised the government that the scriptures make no mention of horse racing, hence a ban on racing is not contrary to Christian doctrine. Alas that we should hear such words from a man of religion! Can the bishop be ignorant that horse racing is the time-hallowed dharma of the English nation, and that such traditional practices rank even above the Bible? There might be yet worse to come: we hear of imminent legislation to ban the consumption of alcohol. Does the Indian Government want to rob us of our ancient scripture-approved drink to boost the sale of Indian tea?

From **The Statesman**, *with which is amalgamated*
The Englishman's Friend:[4]

We warmly congratulate Khan Sahib Gobson Toady. He richly
deserves the high honor awarded him, and we are truly delighted.
It is the first time such a high rank has fallen to a native's lot. At
the same time, we would caution the government not to cheapen
such titles through excessive and indiscriminate award: that would
cause chagrin to Indian Rai Sahibs and Khan Bahadurs, thereby
impeding Europe's progress. Let Europeans be content with
native titles like knight, baron, marquis, or duke. However, as
Mr. Toady has indeed become a Khan Sahib, we would urge him
to assiduously guard the signal honor of his station. We hope he
will not let the shadow of the seditious Liberty League fall on him.

*The women's quarters of Gobson Toady's house. Mrs. Toady, her two
daughters, Fluffy and Flappy, and their governess, Jyotsna Didi.*

Jyotsna. Flappy, I simply don't know what to do with you, my
   dear. Is that any way to do your hair? Shame on you, both your
   ears sticking out like that! You're not a child anymore, but you
   just won't learn. See how nicely your sister's done her hair.

Flappy. Let her. I can't hear anything if my hair keeps flopping
   over my ears. I'll get myself a shingle, like Miss Lanky Gosling
   down the road.

Jyotsna. What next? Shingle your hair, then shave your head and
   pluck off your eyebrows—you'll look irresistible, just like an
   adjutant stork. What you need is a mother-in-law to lick you
   into shape.

Flappy. Little Pussy Friskers
         Shaved off her whiskers;

---

[4] *The Statesman, The Englishman's Friend*: *The Statesman* was a pro-English newspaper of the time. It is still published, of course with an outlook more appropriate to the times. The second title suggests *The Englishman,* the predecessor of
The Statesman and, predictably, still more pro-English and establishmentarian.

And sharpening her paw
Scratched her mum-in-law.

Jyotsna. You shameless girl! Mrs. Toady, I just can't control your younger daughter.

Mrs. Toady. Shame on you, Flappy, you seem to be getting more and more defiant every day. Don't you appreciate all that Jyotsna-di's doing for your education?

Flappy. I don't want to be educated. Let her educate Fluffy.

Jyotsna. There you go again. Why "Fluffy"? Can't you say "Didi"? O my goodness, you're sucking your pencil! What a disgusting habit! All right, you'd better go into the next room and practice that Urdu ghazal.

Mrs. Toady. Jyotsna-di, can I take a betel leaf from your box? Thank you.

Jyotsna. Look, Mrs. Toady, you really shouldn't keep saying *thank you, please,* and *sorry* all the time. It's a very rude habit. This is the kind of thing that's holding back your race. We think it's hypocrisy to profess gratitude or contrition for such trivial matters. Here you are, chew a bit of this tobacco leaf.

Mrs. Toady. No, thanks—oh, sorry! My head starts to reel if I chew tobacco leaves. I'll have a cigarette instead.

Jyotsna. It's thoroughly indecorous for women to smoke cigarettes. You really must make the effort to start on tobacco leaves.

Mrs. Toady. But they're both tobacco after all.

Jyotsna. So what? One's smoke, the other's fiber. Smoke is for men, fiber is for women. Fluffy, have you finished that Bengali novel?

Fluffy. It's very hard to understand, I can't make it out at all.

Jyotsna. There's no need for you to understand it; all you need do is learn select passages by heart. You have to show people you're acquainted with good Bengali literature. But your accent really is dreadful. To mix in polite company, the first thing you need is a proper Bengali accent, and then a few Urdu songs. Just count "one, two, three" in Bengali.

Fluffy. Ek, dui, tin, shar . . .

Jyotsna. Not *shar, char.*

Fluffy. Char, painch . . .

Jyotsna. Not *painch, panch.*

Fluffy. Painsh . . .

Jyotsna. PANCH!

Fluffy. Phanch . . .

Jyotsna. This really is the last word. Mrs. Toady, don't give Fluffy any more chocolates, let her have fried gram instead, otherwise her tongue won't ever loosen. I tell you what, Fluffy, keep repeating this Bengali tongue twister . . .

Gobson Toady. [offstage] Dearie . . .

Mrs. Toady. Coo-ee! Where are you?

Gobson. In the bathroom. Fetch me a few more mangoes, will you?

Jyotsna. Mangoes in the bathroom?

Mrs. Toady. It's the only way. Gobby says, "If I'm to eat mangoes I should eat them the Indian way." But he's not as adept at it as you are, so he keeps spilling juice onto his clothes, the carpet, the tablecloth—everywhere! So I've told him to practice eating mangoes in the bathroom. He's sitting there, holding the fruit in both hands, with juice dribbling down his chin. *Horrid!*

Jyotsna. That's a good solution. But look, Mrs. Toady, it's against all rules of polite behavior to call your husband "Gobby." Call him what you like when you're alone—Gobby, Hubby, anything—but not in front of other people. If you need to refer to him, say "uni" in a respectful way. And if you don't want to be so deferential, just say "he."[5]

Mrs. Toady. Oh, is that how it is? All right. Excuse me for a minute, will you? I'll take "him" some more mangoes.

From the Commercial Columns of The Statesman:

PURE JOY-LADDUS. Don't ruin your health by eating English biscuits larded with fat. Try our Joy-laddus. They strengthen your

---

[5] *uni,* he: Traditionally, the Indian wife does not refer to her husband by name, but as "he." Bengali has two levels of third-person pronouns: the respectful *uni* and the more informal *sey* or *o.* Either can be used, depending on how formal or respectful the wife wishes to be.

teeth. Nothing but ground rice and molasses. Not touched by machine: made by Bengali women with their own hands. Five shillings a packet. Available everywhere. Manufacturers: Rasamay Das, Lizard Market, Kolkata.

AMBERGRIS POWDER. Memsahibs need not feel frustrated anymore. This miraculous powder will remove the unfortunate natural pallor of their skins and give them the complexion of Bengali women. If you want to enhance the dark effect, mix in a little verdigris. As used by Ramachandra Ji. Price, five shillings a phial. Marketed by Sheikh Azhar, Leadenhall Street, India House, London.

From The London Fog:

There will be an Imperial Sacrificial Assembly[6] of Kings in London in the coming month of Ashwin. The Grand Satrap himself will preside over the ceremonies as representative of the Indian Government. Priests, ascetics, mullahs, and *maulanas* will flock here from India. The feeding and fanfare will continue for two months. The cost, as ever, will be borne by the impoverished Europeans.

Even after ceaselessly sucking the whole of Europe dry, they are not satisfied. Mother India is lolling out her tongue, slavering as she says, "O my stepchildren, rejoice—let me lick your bones once more."

At the same point of time, the Pan-European Liberty League[7] will hold its conference at the Hague. O Britons, wherever you may be, from Land's End to John O'Groat's, join this great international gathering. If you have the remotest smidgen of honor, do not go anywhere near the Sacrificial Assembly. Only ponder for a moment

[6]Imperial Sacrificial Assembly: The *rajasuya yajna,* where the emperor presides over a great sacrificial ceremony, while subordinate and tributary rulers perform subservient roles in the worship. The parallel here is with the Delhi Durbar held by George V in 1911.

[7]A clear parallel to the Indian National Congress.

the straits to which your *Merrie England,* that once flowed with milk and honey, has been reduced. You have no food, no cloth, no beef, no butter, no cheese—even your beer is about to run dry. You can bake bread only if wheat is brought in from across the seas. The wool from your sheep is no sooner sheared than it is carried off to the Punjab, to be brought back as ready-made blankets to wrap your bodies. The cotton fabrics of India have destroyed your renowned linen industry. Fie, fie, whose garments do you wear? They conceal your nakedness but not your shame; they keep out the cold, yet you shiver as you wear them. Your finest breeds of cattle have been exiled to India, where Hindus and Muslims fatten in concord on their milk, curds, and ghee. You are forgetting the taste of beer and whiskey, while Indian hemp and opium slowly take possession of your brain. The great temple of India's wealth and luxury is being raised upon your ruins. You are shivering in the December cold for want of coal, yet millions of tons of coal are being burned at your expense on Cheviot Hill to create an artificial volcano. Why? So that Indian officials might work through the winter at the secretariat there. They cannot stand the English cold.

O Europeans, divided among yourselves, prone to internecine strife, will you not even now lay aside your petty sectarian interests? Will there yet be no end to the conflict of English and Celtic, French and German, capitalist and worker, male and female?

Hyde Park. Speaker: Sir Tricksy Turncoat

Turncoat. My countrymen, thank you for giving me the opportunity to say a few words. I do not know how to address you, for my heart is full. O chosen people of God, dwellers in the greatest land on earth, O you descendants of Britons, Saxons, Danes, and Normans, you English nation . . .

McDoodle. Don't say English, say British. What about the Scots?

Turncoat. Of course, of course. O you British nation, just think once of your past history. O heroes of Hastings, Crecy, and Agincourt, whose triumphal flag once flew over England, Scotland, Ireland, France . . .

McDoodle. That's a lie. Your triumphal flag never flew over Scotland.

Turncoat. All right, all right. I'll leave Scotland out of it. . . . whose triumphal flag once flew over Ireland, France . . .

O'Hooligan. Oireland! Say that again!

Turncoat. O, very well, your triumphal flag didn't fly anywhere. O you British nation, commingled of the English, the Scots, and the Irish . . .

O'Hooligan. Begorrah! We're not British, we're Celts.

Turncoat. Quite, quite. So then, all my British and Celtic brothers, why are you assembled here today?

O'Hooligan. Sure, Oi don't know!

Turncoat. Do I have to tell you why? O you wretched people, don't you know of the ceremony that is about to be held upon the supine breast of your fatherland? It is the Imperial Sacrificial Assembly. The Indian Government will pour out the array of its wealth and power, and all the nobles of Europe will make their obeisance to the Grand Satrap and say, "Victory to Indian Rule!" This *outlandish* business, this *sacrilege* . . .

[Lord Blarney rushes in.]

Blarney. *[aside]* What are you about, Sir Tricksy? You're courting disaster. I've been pleading with the Grand Satrap to make you Steward of the Chiltern Hundreds. Such a cushy job—an absolute sinecure. The Satrap has Toady in mind, but I pressed him so hard that he said he'd think about you. We might have news any minute—and here you are spreading sedition!

Turncoat. Really, really? Never mind, I'll mend matters.

The crowd. Go on, Tricksy, go on!

Turncoat. Oh yes, where was I? O my fellow countrymen, what is your duty in these afflicted times? Will you bring yourself to join this grand farce?

The crowd. Never, never.

Bill Snooks. Say, guv'nor, will they stand treat? How many barrels of the stuff are they going to bring?

Turncoat. Not a drop. They'll only dole out sugar-puffs. So, my friends, where is your place in such an assembly?

Blarney. What's this you're saying, Turncoat?

Turncoat. Don't worry, just keep listening. My friends, will you go to this great ceremony?

The crowd. We'd sooner go to the devil.

Turncoat. No, no, that won't look nice. We have to go—there's no help, for the Indian Government has invited us.

Blarney. Hear, hear.

The crowd. Miaow, miaow.

Turncoat. Please don't take me amiss. Remember, we can't get along without the support and sympathy of the Indian Government—our future depends on their mercy. [*A rotten egg*] Whew, just missed my eye. . . . My friends, I am not afraid to do my duty. I shall frankly utter what I believe to be the truth.

Blarney. Splendid, that's the stuff. There's someone bringing a telegram. Bravo Sir Tricksy, I'm sure the Satrap has appointed you. I'll see what it says—don't stop your speech.

Turncoat. My brothers, what I'm saying is for your own good. I have no selfish interest in the matter. (What does it say, Blarney?) My dear friends, I am willing to suffer any persecution for the good of my country. Your catcalls are my chant of victory. I accept your gift of rotten eggs with bowed head. If you have any other weapon in your quiver . . . [*A cabbage*]—Really, I can't take this anymore! Come on, Blarney, what does it say?

Blarney. Poor Tricksy. That blighter Toady's got the job after all. Never mind, don't be put out. I'll try again for you as soon as I get a chance. The Satrap is an ass. He doesn't realize that Toady's in his pocket anyway. While here are you, a demagogue of such stature—and he lets go the chance to win you over. Tch, tch.

Turncoat. Damn Toady and damn the Satrap! O my countrymen . . .

The crowd. Shut up! Kick him—lynch the traitor!

Turncoat. No, no, let me speak first. You simply must go to the Sacrificial Assembly. But why? To eat their sugar-puffs? To greet them with salaams? To cry victory to the Indian Government? *Never.* You'll go to wreck the sacrifice, to turn everything topsy-turvy—the Indian Government mustn't ever think again that it can keep you happy with shows and sugar-puffs.

The crowd. Long live Tricksy! Turncoat forever!

From "The She-Man," the organ of the female race:

At three o'clock sharp tomorrow afternoon, the All-Britain Women's Army will bring out its rally. The vast procession will start from Regent's Park, pass through Portland Place, Regent Street, Piccadilly Circus, and Trafalgar Square, and end at Parliament House.

The race of males has lorded it over women for thousands of years, but their tricks won't serve their turn anymore. We shall wrest our dues from them by force. The suffrage we have won is a deceit. These cardsharping males have won over the votes by their wiles and practically gained a monopoly over the National Council. This state of things cannot continue. Sixty percent of Britain's population is female. We want a proportionate number of women members. We also want 60 percent of all government jobs. In what way are we inferior to men? We wear divided skirts, cut our hair, smoke cigars, and quaff cocktails. If necessary, we shall apply ayurvedic oils to our face to grow whiskers. We shall keep no truck with men—there's no such crafty and selfish race on earth. They think the world has been made for men. Even their God is of the masculine gender. We shall not bow down to any he-god. We shall get along fine with Isis, Diana, Kali, or Shurpanakha.[8]

O woman, you are no longer a simpleminded *niminy-piminy* housewife. Sharpen your teeth and claws, join this great army in your most fearsome aspect to attack the Houses of Parliament. Drive out all these useless men and seize your rights from the government.

From "The Mere Man," the organ of the male race:

Is the government fast asleep and snoring through its well-oiled nose? The diabolical events that took place in London yesterday

---

[8]Shurpanakha: a female *rakshasa* or demon in the *Ramayana*.

lead us to believe that the land has sunk into anarchy. Berserk women wrought havoc in broad daylight, smashing up shops, scratching and biting at inoffensive males—but where was the Oriya police on whom the government lavishes so much love? They looked on grinning, their mouths stuffed with betel, and urged the female hooligans to greater mischief with laughter and applause. Respected national leaders like Khan Sahib Gobson Toady and Sir Tricksy Turncoat visited the scene with intent to pacify the rioters, but the Oriya sergeants turned them back with the insulting words, "Hey you Sahibs, you'll taste our sticks if you go that way."

The government must be rejoicing at heart, for the more we see such internecine strife, the more it can say that we are unworthy of self-rule.

From The Statesman:

If there be any men of sense among the English, they will have realized by now that their hopes of obtaining self-rule are distant indeed. The Liberty League, the Anglo-Celtic Union, the Heterosexual Pact—all these are brave-sounding names. But when people's blood in this cold country grows hot with violence and hatred, these platitudes are of no worth. When riots break out, the only hope lies with the rod of rule of the Indian Government, and its formidable Oriya police.

We keep hearing that self-rule is the birthright of the British. But O Britons, what does your history testify? You have never known what it is to be free. You have spent your days in bondage, first to the Romans, then one by one to the Anglos, Saxons, Danes, Normans, and such other races of marauders. Those who have come to your land as conquerors have stayed on to be conquered in turn by others. Today there is no way of telling who conquered whom—not one of these races has been able to preserve its identity. Your nationality is not firmly defined; your land is not your own, nor your religion. There has never been unity among you. There is no end to your social and economic divisions.

If such is the state of little Britain, it is best not to speak of all Europe. The nations of Europe have ever been kept asunder by divisions of race, language, and religion. The might of Indian rule alone has cooled the continent's fires. First acquire a little civilization; it will then be time to think of freedom. You are sunk in drink and gambling; even to this day, you dance like savages; you are afraid to take a bath; you do not rinse out your mouth after a meal. For some time to come, it is best for you to live quietly and obediently, in subservience to India in all matters. There will be time enough later to ponder the question of your rights.

Schloss Vomstadt. Prince Vom,[9] the Chinese traveler Lang Pang, and the prince's attendant Kobaldt.

Prince. Well, Herr Pang, you have visited many countries. How do you like our state?

Lang Pang. Not bad at all. You have fields, and water, and bread, and grass, and pigs, and sheep. But the people in the country all seem rather drowsy. Why is that so?

Prince. That's the beauty of it. Think of all the troubles and discontent across Europe: you won't find any of that here. The Indian Government tells us, "In the states we rule directly, we can let our subjects have a little free play if we like, then draw in the reins again. But you're like children—don't you try any funny stuff of that sort: it'll be the end of you. If there's any trouble in your state, we'll throw you out on your ear." So I've just arranged for everyone in the state to have a happy time— they're all stoned. Kobaldt, my man, pass me one of those little

---

[9]*Vom:* punning on *bhom,* a Bengali word meaning "intoxicated" or "stoned." *V* and *bh* are not distinguished in Bengali. Prince Vom represents the Indian rulers or "native princes" of British times, who retained titular rule over their territories but were, as a rule, under stern British control. His state also suggests the state of China at the time, rendered drugged and powerless by the dissemination of opium as a colonial tool. This makes the visit of the Chinese traveler another instance of "the scripture read backward."

pellets—it's three o'clock, and I'm starting to yawn. Oh, Herr
Pang, what a wonderful thing your ancestors discovered!

Lang Pang. But it doesn't grow in our country anymore. Whatever you get comes from India—it's grown just for you.

[Enter the prince's minister, Baron von Bibler.]

Bibler. Your Highness, Sir Tricksy Turncoat has come from England
to see you.

Prince. Here's a nuisance. They won't let me lie down and have a
moment's peace. All right, show him in. Kobaldt, my man, turn
me over onto my left side.

Lang Pang. I suppose I'd better be going.

Prince. No, no, keep sitting. I meet people in the Indian way.
I can't be bothered to grant *audience* to one person at a time,
I have 'em in batches of five or seven. It's less strain, and makes
for better conversation.

[Enter Sir Tricksy Turncoat.]

Prince. How do you do, Sir Tricksy? Do take that chair. So then,
what's the news?

Turncoat. Prince, you've simply got to go to the Hague, to preside
over the session of the Pan-European Liberty League.

Prince. Mein Gott! What's the man saying? Kobaldt, you'd better
give me another of those pellets.

Turncoat. Very well, if you won't go as president, just come along
anyway. We can't do without you.

Prince. Go to the Hague? Are you mad?

Turncoat. Why, what's your problem? Viscount Puff, the Countess
Greymalkin, the Grand Duke Panjandrum—they're all going.

Prince. You can't compare me to them. They're mere British subjects—they can go to hell if they like. I'm the independent lord
of a feudal state, I can't just take off for somewhere like that. If
I ask the Grand Satrap for permission, he'll tell me, "To the
forest with you this instant, you rogue."

Turncoat. At least promise you won't go to the Sacrificial Assembly either.

Prince. Gott im Himmel! You must be mad. I've been preparing
these last six months to go there—I've arranged to spend ten

million or so—and you think I'm going to call it all off at your whim? Oh, that reminds me—Baron, have you checked all the battle-drums? Are there seventeen?

Bibler. Yes, Your Highness. I put them out in the sun, they're nice and tight.

Prince. All seventeen?

Bibler. All seventeen.

Lang Pang. What will you do with battle-drums?

Prince. We'll play on them. When I set out for the Assembly, seventeen battle-drums will begin to beat. Prince Drunkendorff has only thirteen; I have seventeen.

Lang Pang. Why stop at seventeen? You can play seven hundred battle-drums, kettledrums, bagpipes, flutes, horns, or whatever you like, if it takes your fancy.

Prince. Heh, heh, it's not as simple as that. I have to play just the number that the government has allotted me. If there's a single one extra, they'll cut it out. Kobaldt, my man, just tickle me a little under my nose here.

Turncoat. Do you mean to say you can't honor any of my requests?

Prince. I really am sorry. But I assure you, your efforts have my deepest support. Baron Bibler, would you mind withdrawing to the next room for a minute? Well then, Sir Tricksy, it's like this. You can hardly expect me to risk my life and inheritance by teaming up with you people to save the country. But if I live, and you manage to get what you want, why then: should you need a really tough emperor or kaiser or *dictator* for Europe, you can come to me by all means. It's our hereditary trade, it comes naturally to me. So then, Sir Tricksy, would you like to try one of these pellets? It'll soothe your brain. Not used to it? Oh very well then, have a glass of schnapps.

From **The London Fog:**

The Imperial Sacrificial Assembly has ended amid a two-month-long general strike. The people of Europe have preserved their self-respect by boycotting the proceedings—except, of course, for a handful of sycophants. We were not present at the ceremonies, so can report no further details.

From **The Statesman:**

The Imperial Sacrificial Assembly has concluded with great success. Defying the so-called national leaders, the common people of Europe have taken part in this great festival to their unending satisfaction.

The name of Sir Tricksy Turncoat is prominent among those who have afforded the government all assistance in conducting the Assembly. It is reported that Sir Tricksy will soon be appointed chairman of the commission set up by the government to improve the breed of British sheep, and he will proceed to Kamrup[10] in that capacity.

Translated from the Bengali by Sukanta Chaudhuri

ABOUT THE AUTHOR

Parashuram (Rajshekhar Basu) (1880–1960), writer, scientist, and lexicographer, was born in West Bengal. His twenty-one books, published under the pseudonym Parashuram, include the satires *Shri Shri Siddheshvari Limited* (1922), *Gaddalika* (1924), *Kajjali* (1927), *Hanumaner Svapna* (1937), and *Galpakalpa* (1950), the short stories included in *Krsnakali* (1953) and *Anandibai* (1957), and the essays anthologized in *Laghuguru* (1939), *Bharater Khanij* (1943), *Kutirshilpa* (1943), and *Bichinta* (1955). He also published a number of translations, including *Meghdut* (1943), *Valmiki Ramayana* (1946), *Mahabharata* (1949), and *Hitopadesher Galpa* (1950). His Bengali dictionary, *Chalantika* (1937), is still widely used.

---

[10]Kamrup: a part of the present state of Assam in northeast India. Men were reputed to turn into sheep on going there—supposedly a tribute to the beauty of the women.

GOLI TARAGHI

The scene that begins Goli Taraghi's story "The Unfinished Game" is not an unfamiliar one—the overbooked airline, the crowd of disgruntled passengers each determined to get a seat. But what changes everything here is that this is Iran Air, en route to Tehran. And every surge of the passengers' energy, every slight alteration in their prospects, each instance of casual disregard of the most fundamental rules of airline safety—all of this has less to do with the conventions of modern air travel than with thousands of years of Persian and Islamic culture and, in particular, with a half century of stormy and violent political drama. Preparing to board a flight, our narrator thinks, or imagines, that she sees a woman whom she knew as a girl, and who had for her the power of a living icon or symbol. Gradually, we learn that her idol was, even as a girl, someone who (like the recent governments of their shared homeland) cared about ends more than means, more about victory than compassion. And this knowledge, at once revealed and secret, resonates throughout the story even as the speaker must undergo the sudden immersion in the dictatorial and everyday caprice that governs life in her country. Everything in Goli Taraghi's story is connected to everything else, each element establishes a layer that gives the story added weight and heft, until it adds up to something denser and more communicative than what a less gifted writer could possibly have compressed into so few pages.

—FRANCINE PROSE

THE UNFINISHED GAME

Orly Airport. Iran Air flight number 866.

The Paris–Tehran flight is full. It's no use begging, pleading, threatening, or putting on VIP airs. There is no room for anyone.

Not anyone. Not for the haughty rich, not for the humble poor, not for the elderly, not for the sick, not for those at death's door, and not for foreigners. Not even the French. Nevertheless, for some unknown reason—some kind of hereditary optimism or faith in divine benevolence—the travelers without seats stand firm and refuse to move. The impossible does not exist and no door is absolutely shut. One man who has faith in this miraculous "door" recites under his breath:

If God in his wisdom closes one door, in his mercy He opens another.

The other travelers are also waiting for this "other door." Not only do they not retreat but, with full knowledge and feigned innocence, as if preoccupied with conversation or examining their luggage, they surge forward en masse. If the airline were Air France or Lufthansa, they would have left, because these companies have no miraculous door. Foreign companies have a mechanical door that opens and closes on the basis of scientific principles, and divine mercy has nothing to do with it. The week before, as was well known, it had been even more crowded than today and the number of seats more limited. At the last moment, again the usual miracle manifested (Did the airplane grow? Did the number of seats increase? No one knows). Whatever happened, everyone got on board. Today they are just as certain that in the end that door will open and somehow things will work out. How? No one knows, because the reason is beyond any scientific or mathematical reckoning. However, these seats don't suddenly fall out of the sky and they are not a gratuitous gift. They are also not destined for just anyone. They belong to worthy and deserving individuals, those who are clever and know special tricks. The best way is to find an influential acquaintance behind the scenes or come up with a sad and effective story. The first and last rule is to get ahead of the next person at hand, with a smile or with fists, it doesn't make any difference—the goal is to move forward, with perseverance and obstinately, with nimble steps (tiny kicks), with elbows, with a show of teeth (whether smiling or biting), with force.

An agitated young woman, with shocking red lips and excess baggage (two suitcases, three handbags, two plastic bags stuffed with odds and ends), kicks my foot and thrusts herself forward. She's in a frenzy of a rush, oblivious to the grousing and grumbling on all sides.

"The end of the line is back there; this is the head of the line . . ."

"Have some respect for the rest of us . . ."

"Madam, please move to the back . . ."

Madam's ears are deaf to their complaints. She says that her mother is sick and could die at any moment. She must get on the flight. She alone. She's willing to sit in the aisle of the plane. She's willing to stand. She's ready to hang from the wing or crawl under the suitcases in the hold. She'll do anything they say so long as she gets on that plane. She alone.

Although "she alone" arrived late, with a shamed look and a pained smile, she pushes ahead of everyone, spreading her palpable and deniably unrepentant presence like a thin cloak over seats, tickets, and airline employees. There is another one, a student, who also thrusts himself forward. The student is trembling in distress—true or feigned—and says that his father has Alzheimer's. He's been lost for some time. He went to the movies and never came out. They searched for him everywhere. The cinema had only one exit. The entire audience had come out, except for his father. He urgently needs to get to Tehran to find his father. He says, "Please, get me on the plane by whatever means. Just me."

"She alone" and "just me" stand face-to-face, focused and poised to attack, ignoring the other passengers.

"My dear sir, you should have come earlier. Before your daddy got lost."

"You should have thought about your dear mother before she was on her deathbed."

The others have become curious; they talk among themselves. How could someone go into a cinema and get lost? One asks, "Did they look under the seats?"

"Yes. Backstage, under the stairs . . . They searched everywhere."

"They probably kidnapped your father," says a pessimist wearing smoky glasses. His voice hints that he has information concerning some occult truth.

The young man becomes uneasy. He closes up. He doesn't like this line of thought. He says, "My father is eighty-six years old. Why would they kidnap him?"

The pessimist shakes his head with regret. He says, "For a thousand and one reasons." He fixes his gaze, laden with significance, on the young man.

Once again, it is explained to the respected travelers in a loud voice that there are no seats available. The flight is full. Do you understand? Full—pronounced with final emphasis: Fulllllllll. Cease and desist. Remove yourselves; leave!

No one moves back a step.

"Ladies, gentlemen, there are no seats." The ladies and gentlemen are deaf. This does not pertain to them. They don't move. One sleepy woman (she's come a long way, probably from America) pushes her cart. She yawns, excuses herself, and moves herself to the head of the line. Her handbag is wide open. When she bends over, her keys and coins fall out.

My glance stumbles on her face, follows her lips, the line of her neck, and with an odd curiosity goes in search of her eyes. I want her to take off her sunglasses.

I know this woman. Her face is familiar. I have seen her somewhere. I stare at her more carefully and I don't understand why this encounter makes me uncomfortable and anxious. A pebble has struck the skin of my memories, the flick of a finger on still water. The half-recognized woman is sure of herself. She's not worried. Her ticket is in her hand and her seat is reserved. She is not haggling.

Who is she?

A blurred image appears before my eyes. A shadowy face, colorless, featureless, forms in snippets behind my eyelids. A name rolls on the tip of my tongue, something flits about in my mind and is lost again.

They have brought a young man in a wheelchair. A fragile *setar* rests on his knees. He has long hair and a beard; dark eyes, ashamed eyes. His face is lowered and he looks at no one. A path opens for him.

The half-familiar woman is nervous and exhausted. She searches through her handbag and pockets. People are pointing at her. She looks flummoxed, confused. She has left her passport somewhere. Her scattered gestures are those of a person disturbed, tired, and distressed. She seizes on her passport and laughs. An embarrassed laugh, but simple and without pretense; such a young laugh for a woman her age. Fifty?

Her mouth, with that peculiar laugh, extracts a blurry image from the farthest folds of memory, and my heart drops. A feeling that is laughable at my age.

Azadeh Derakhshan? Maybe.

I sneak a look at her, hastily, furtively, from lowered eyes, over my shoulder . . . sideways . . . face on. A giddy feeling runs through my body, a sort of sweet fear from out of the past. The past meaning fifteen or sixteen years old, Anushiravan Dadgar High School, sports competitions, André's sandwich shop, the neighborhood boys, Lalezar Avenue and Cinema Iran. The past meaning Azadeh Derakhshan, invincible, the champion in all sports and the champion of my dreams. Mornings, I wake up excited at the prospect of seeing her. I am giddy and happy. I finish my chores hastily, pick up my bag, and get myself to the Shemiran bus. Most days, Azadeh Derakhshan is on that bus. She sits at the back of the bus, reading a book. She is two classes above me. She nods a token greeting and goes back to staring at her book. She is the most important student in school and does not easily offer anyone attention.

The successful passengers have checked in their luggage and, like a victorious army, file past the others. I leave "just me" and "she alone" to one side (I ignore the complaints) and position myself at the head of the line.

"Sir . . ."

Sir is busy and doesn't answer. I need to invent a story, a heart-rending, harrowing tale, worthy of a good seat.

I can't. My brain doesn't work. I'm angry and I want that door to open one way or another and get me home. I've earned it.

I make my voice meek and gentle: "Please sir . . ."

Pretty pleases don't get me anywhere. I have to wait. My name is at the bottom of the waiting list.

A woman is looking for a kindhearted passenger with a sure seat to deliver a package of medicine for her mother.

"If this medicine doesn't reach my mother within twenty-four hours, she'll die," she says.

No one volunteers. The old woman is probably condemned to death.

Azadeh Derakhshan (I'm still not sure that's who she really is) accepts the package. She notes down the name and address of the recipient. Whoever this woman is, she is precise and civilized. She can be trusted. The whole while, my insistent gaze is compelled to follow her. This curious gaze crawls along the line of time, flits from one place to another, and is dazzled by the imagined figure of Azadeh Derakhshan.

It's her. A hundred percent sure.

Her eyes, their expression, bits and pieces of her body and face, are just like hers. But for all this, it's not her. Never. Azadeh Derakhshan was gorgeous—young and slim and full of life. But many were gorgeous. Thirty-some years later, most of those gorgeous faces have changed. Or they've died. And now, suppose this woman is Azadeh Derakhshan. So what? Why is it important? It is what it is. I want to say, "To hell with her" and free myself, but I can't. So what if it is her? This encounter, though uncertain and confused, skewers me like a painful wisdom tooth and exhausts me.

The airline's general manager arrives. The decisions are up to him. Assault. Attack. Push. Argue. A polite altercation starts up between two men—a hodgepodge of Persian mixed up with French, some English thrown into the mess. Other passengers are drawn in. It's not clear what the argument is about, or who is in the right.

Someone says, "Gentlemen, you should be ashamed, acting like this in front of foreigners. It's not for nothing that they call us backward."

A voice answers him, "To hell with them. Two thousand years ago we were sleeping on silk sheets and eating off gold dishes. They didn't even exist then."

A woman laughs. She answers, "And now we don't exist and they're sleeping on velvet."

The same voice answers the woman, this time with poetry:

Arabs in the desert eat bugs; in Isfahan even dogs drink ice water.

A ruckus begins. Those who advocate human rights are complaining. It has almost come to a fight.

My mind is on getting a seat when I catch sight of a familiar face among the airline employees. This is what they call the "door of mercy." An ancestral, third-world, aggressively vocal "just me" character surfaces from under my thin layer of civilized modernity. I leap forward and grab the collar of the familiar employee. I greet him like an old buddy, beg and plead, with appropriate modesty and stubborn persistence, until finally, with his head spinning, this acquaintance who can't quite place my face and has no memory of my name (Perhaps this woman has mistaken me for someone else?) makes a hollow promise out of customary courtesy. I grab on to this promise with both hands like a tick, and with his help I crawl and cram myself into the plane. Others also in this same fashion, each one through another "door of mercy," get into the plane, tired and drenched with sweat but victorious, collapsing on the first seat at hand. There are no seat numbers. Or if there are, no one pays them any attention. I don't know where my real seat is, and it's not important. The point is to sit. On my left, by the window, sits a man of the faith reciting prayers under his breath. His eyes are closed, his head nods slowly, and a long string of prayer beads is wound around his fingers. With a swing of his hand he unwinds it, winds it again, unwinds it, winds it again. This continues. Repeats. I look away. The yellow beads circle in my mind and twist around my thoughts. They unwind. Wind. Unwind. Wind. Unwind. I'm getting dizzy. I decide to change my seat.

Azadeh Derakhshan is looking for her proper seat. She reads the numbers carefully and looks at her ticket.

Her seat is at the back of the plane, in the smoking section.
I can hear her complaining. She is not a smoker. The engines begin
to sound. A good prayer, a prayer of mercy and compassion, is
broadcast over the loudspeaker. An old woman exhales a verse of
scripture three times and someone, several rows away, softly
recites a blessing. A number of people are still standing and looking for an empty space to stow their extra bags and hand luggage.
Every corner is filled. Stuff falls out of every compartment above
the seats that they open.

I ask the stewardess, "Can I change my seat?"

She shakes her head and points to the seat belt sign. An old
woman staggers around looking for a prayer room. She's one step
from going head over heels.

The Iran Air plane, with its all-in-the-family crowd and commotion, is its own world. It's like the Tajrish Bridge in the days when
people—men and women, adults and children, old and young—
gathered in clusters in front of the Villa ice-cream shop or at
the lower corner of Sa'adabad Avenue, eating ice cream and
roasted corn, and debating. It's full of to-and-fro and talk and
commotion—arguments, jokes, debates, poetry—full of loose
pages of newspapers and empty cigarette packs and crumpled
napkins tossed underfoot—along with stewardesses rushing
through the motions of locating the emergency exits and how
to use the life jackets in case of a crash, and the pilot reporting on
the altitude above sea level and air temperatures. Nobody heeds
the instructions to sit in their seats and fasten their seat belts, or
pays attention to the red warning lights. Most of them are people
of faith and they trust in fate or destiny. Whatever must happen
will happen. The safety instructions won't change anything.

The first row of the plane, next to the exit, is a headache of a
place. An empty space, six feet square, it's a place for men to con-
gregate and discuss politics, a place for children to play hide-and-
seek, a place for old women coming and going to the restrooms in
a continuous trickle from takeoff until landing.

The airplane jolts up and down and shakes. The passengers are calm; no one thinks of the possibility of a crash or the likelihood of death. Their talk is of the price of meat and poultry, the exchange rate, and the cost of land, and how to get through customs and where (under a coat, at the bottom of a handbag, under one's shirt and belt) to hide fashion magazines and tapes of Western music and videocassettes.

There is an argument behind my head about blankets. As soon as we boarded the pillows and blankets were gone. A man complains, "What is this? For two hundred passengers you don't even have thirty blankets?" The stewardess explains that the honored passengers, over time, have taken the blankets and pillows with them—in other words, stolen them—and she shrugs her shoulders in philosophical regret. The woman behind me has thrown two blankets over herself and says she is sick. She has her head under a blanket and (for real or faking it) she coughs. The passenger beside her is also not feeling so well. She pulls on a corner of one of the claimed blankets. She's sick too, and she sneezes.

The first invalid answers from under the blanket—cough, cough, cough—and twists the blanket tightly around herself. Mrs. Sneeze is no match for her. Kids are running around, pushing and shoving each other. I say, "You baboon! If you kick my leg one more time, I'll skin you alive."

The child stares at me in confused amazement and runs away. Behind the wall of the restrooms he turns and pokes his head out. He makes a face.

Shitty kid.

I wish I could sleep. I'm tired and my feet are swollen in my shoes. I close my eyes. A sudden sadness presses on my heart and an annoying sensation pokes at me from inside. Azadeh Derakhshan wriggles behind my eyelids, swings on my thoughts, leaps from one memory to another, journeys from one year to the next, and, in various shapes, appears and disappears. A while ago, after years and years, I dreamed about her. Azadeh Derakhshan was riding a bicycle and I was running after her. Near the sea, we arrived at the beach together. Azadeh Derakhshan was a champion

swimmer. She dove into the sea and disappeared under the waves.
She left her bicycle for me. I climbed on to it. I pedaled slowly,
gained speed, and fell off at a curve in the road. I woke up in a fit
of tears. Why? I myself didn't understand it.

Azadeh Derakhshan is a champion at track and field, a champion in all sports. No one can compete with her. She is the most
important student at school and the most perfect human being in
the world in my eyes. I want to be her and, in her footsteps, get
ahead of everyone. I want to win that perfect 20 and hang my
scorecard on the walls of the world. Everyone wants to be like
her. Her figure. Her height. Her position. With that short chest-
nut hair and the checkered handkerchief around her neck, knot-
ted at an angle, with that healthy suntanned skin and those high
cheekbones. I know that there are miles between me and Azadeh
Derakhshan. First of all, I'm two years younger than her and two
feet shorter, and my usual score in sports is zero. On the street—
Shahreza Avenue as far as the Pahlavi intersection—I follow
behind her at twenty yards' distance. Each place that she stops,
I stop. Whatever she looks at, I look at. I step on the same cracks
in the pavement, into the same potholes, hold my head high,
throw my shoulders back, one hand free, one hand in my pocket,
just like her.

The stewardess announces that the honored passengers will soon
be served a delicious hot meal. At the mention of food, everyone
rushes to their seats.

The passenger on my left jumps up from his seat. He's not well.
The prayer beads fall from his hand. He takes a large handkerchief
out of his pocket and holds it in front of his mouth.

Dinner.

The stewardess is tired and impatient but she smiles. She has a
simple, kind face. She asks, "Rice with chicken or kebab?"

The passenger next to me lowers his face into his handkerchief
and throws up. I say, "Rice with chicken" and realize that I'm
nauseated and that eating is not possible under the circumstances.

That same vicious kid is running around the restrooms again, pushing and shoving everyone. When he gets close to me, I grab his ear and twist. He screams.

"Where are this kid's parents?"

No one knows.

"Who are they?"

No one answers. The kid has no mother or father.

"Is he yours?"

"No."

"Yours?"

"No."

One of the airline staff takes him by the hand and walks him down the rows. He shows him to all the passengers. No one claims him. Mom and Dad don't exist, or if they do, they don't show their faces.

Someone says, "For sure this child got on the wrong plane."

"Where is his ticket?"

"Where is your ticket, child?"

The kid is a mute. He doesn't answer. His mouth hangs open. He gives me a dirty look and I can see the glint of a dangerous plan rippling in the depths of his eyes.

When dinner is finished they turn off the lights to show a film. I think of Azadeh Derakhshan. Could this sad wreck of a woman sitting a few rows away be the champion of my childhood? Is it possible?

The film is dim and scratched. It tears, cutting off suddenly. The passengers complain. It starts up again. This time there is no sound. Again the sound of complaints all round gets louder. Some are laughing. They turn on the lights. The passengers clap.

The passenger beside me has fallen asleep and a strange sound is coming from his throat. I look around. I have to change my seat. I pick up my bag and set off. On the left, beside the aisle, there is an empty seat. I don't know if it is really empty or its owner is around somewhere. I ask the stewardess. The stewardess has lost patience with the passengers and is annoyed. She says, "Madam, find a seat and sit down."

There is an empty seat two rows farther back, and it is next to the half-familiar woman, the one who might or might not be Azadeh Derakhshan. She is sitting by the window, napping. She has taken her sunglasses off.

To sit or not to sit? I hesitate. There is no other empty seat. My own empty seat was immediately occupied. Everyone is moving around and continuously changing seats. I sit down, and after fastening my seat belt, I throw a quick glance sideways from the corner of my eye. Long eyelashes, a smooth forehead with two thin lines, clear eyes with tiny crow's feet.

The smokers have gathered at the back of the plane. The woman beside me pulls a corner of her scarf over her mouth and coughs. It's a bad seat. She calls the stewardess. She complains.

Her voice has a familiar pitch, with undertones of a bell that stirs up memories, a ringing that reaches me from far away, the morning bell in high school, the recess bell and the shouts of students, the whistle at the start of a game.

Her seat is narrow and uncomfortable and her arm presses lightly against my shoulder. This simple contact, this slight, temporary connection, like an invisible thread, lines up the scattered beads and joins the disconnected pieces.

Azadeh Derakhshan (I decide that is indeed her name, and I make myself comfortable) throws me a sleepy, empty look from the corner of her eye and turns away. She closes her book—it's in English—and stares out the window again.

Strangely sad eyes. Tired, restless hands, work-worn, with prominent blue veins. She is half asleep. Her book slides off her knees. She rests her head on the window frame and sighs, a long sigh from the bottom of the heart, mixed with an unfinished yawn that she swallows along with some mumbled words. She lifts her silk scarf—that same gleaming short hair, with a few strands of gray at her temples—and puts it back on again. She ties the knot tight. For a moment, her face from that time, fresh and young and clear, emerges from the depths of her broken expression, and then, like a sad glance, it retracts and is hidden behind a thin veil.

I don't have the courage to speak. I'm shy. I rehearse in my head, "Excuse me, are you by any chance Azadeh Derakhshan?"

No. It sounds formal and foolish. I should ask, plain and simple, "Azadeh Derakhshan?" As simple as that. Like friends.

What if she doesn't answer? What if she says I'm mistaken?

The mystery woman takes a postcard from her handbag. She starts writing. She's left-handed. Azadeh Derakhshan also held her ping-pong paddle in her left hand and used to dunk the basketball with her left hand. Then it's her. Beyond any shadow of a doubt. But there is so much missing. It's cracked and dusty, faded, like a precious painting left for years in a musty storeroom. For all this, untouched planes of her simple beauty and proud profile still remain.

The sickly youth with his head bowed modestly is seated one row forward. His *setar* is on his knees. A skinny twig of a man, with a bald head and tiny hands and feet, asks to see the *setar*. The modest youth makes no objection. Mr. Twig takes the *setar* out of its case. He is a musician. He tries a few notes. The passengers who are standing gather in a circle around him. They ask him to play a piece. He plays. The others hum along and sing a few lines together.

Azadeh Derakhshan watches, elated and amazed. Under her breath she says, "This is what they call homeland," and she sighs. It's obvious that she has been far from this and homesick. She takes her eyes off the singer and turns to sleep, facing me. Her eyes are closed but she is awake. She's not blinking. What is she thinking about? She doesn't realize that I, the passenger beside her, a person like any other, know her past and have memorized her entire youth like a text.

The schoolyard at Anushiravan Dadgar High School. Mrs. Banoo, the Zoroastrian principal, is after students with a long switch.

Wearing short socks is forbidden, and Azadeh Derakhshan has on short white socks and tennis shoes. Mrs. Banoo strikes at her bare legs with the switch. Next she comes after me. The tip of her switch catches my long braid and she swings me in a circle around the yard like a bundle hanging from a stick.

Azadeh Derakhshan knows English (better than we do, at least, and better than Book One of the Essential English series) and she reads foreign magazines. Or maybe she doesn't read them. But she brings them with her and at the recess bell she sits on the steps in the schoolyard and turns the pages of her magazine. The entire yard is filled with her presence and no one but her is visible. Even the teachers lose their weight and power, and the other students around her are reduced to colorless shadows. She is different from all of them, and especially from me. I am shy and clumsy and however much I try in any one sport—ping-pong, running, long jump, basketball—I can't even make it as a secondhand chump of a champion. In the afternoon when classes are over, we have permission to stay and practice sports. I've chosen the weight toss, of all sports—me, skinny and wobbly, just on my feet again after pneumonia. If the wind blows my way, I'll fall over. I want to win the competition. I want to take the gold medal and show it to Azadeh Derakhshan. I want to be seen and announce my presence. In spite of all the practice and effort, the iron weight lands—plop—in front of my feet. I'm not strong enough to toss it farther than half a meter. I give up this sport. I go after the long jump. I come in last. I take up swimming. I'm short of breath and my heart pounds. I catch pneumonia again and I'm in bed for a month.

Azadeh Derakhshan, knowing nothing of my sad struggle, head and shoulders above everyone, strides along to her own tune, and she's a hundred miles ahead of the other students. She smokes and talks politics. She reads left-wing books and has ideas of her own. They say she will become a great writer. Some of her poems have been published in the literary section of the newspaper *Tehran Mosavar* and the teachers look at her with respect. Nobody can compete with her.

We live in the same neighborhood. Shemiran. We get on the bus and I sneak glances at her. I look so often that she realizes and smiles. Her white teeth gleam. Her look passes over me heedlessly and goes somewhere farther, to a place beyond Anushiravan Dadgar High School and the Shemiran bus. She gets off at the stop before mine. But her conquering look and confident smile stay with me, until the next morning and all the days after.

Where is she coming from? How did she get so fat? Fat and sad. Her fatigue is not that of a traveler in need of sleep. It's the product of years, difficult years. These lines on her forehead, the wrinkles under her eyes, these veins popping on her hands are not transient. They are the work of time and hidden pain, the work of the anger that swells in the depths of her eyes and the wretched anxiety that circles through her hands.

She looks at me quickly and then pulls away. She makes a little more room for me. I am waiting for a look of recognition and a friendly greeting, waiting for some expression of emotion, some mixture of surprise and happiness. I'm still waiting. Azadeh Derakhshan, half-conscious and distant, is submerged in her own thoughts. Me, so-and-so, Anushiravan Dadgar High School, ping-pong matches, the Shemiran bus, strict Mrs. Banoo with her long switch and kind heart, the teachers, exams, cheating, youth, those days . . . No. She doesn't remember any of it. Her look, level and indifferent, passes over my face and she doesn't recognize me. I say to myself, "So, I've changed as much as she has, maybe even more." I see myself in her alien, defeated eyes and a heavy weight settles on my rib cage. I want to lift the mask of time from my face and show her my face of those days. I had not realized that time had also passed through me.

It was arranged that we would play a fencing match in front of Queen Soraya. It was her birthday and several high schools were competing. Our class had the most interesting program of all.

We wore mesh masks on our faces. We had rented white leather gloves and special fencing jackets. There were four of us. We practiced afternoons in the schoolyard, and the P.E. teacher from Firuz Bahram Boys' School had taught us some basic moves of attack and defense.

Queen Soraya, in dark glasses and a striped shirt, sat in a special booth with the important people from the court. The stadium was in an uproar. The cheers and screams and shouts of high school girls were deafening. Queen Soraya was not enjoying the hubbub; she didn't smile. My mind was on Azadeh Derakhshan and I saw no one but her. It was our turn. We entered the playing field and our classmates clapped and cheered for us. We were standing together on one side in a row. Heads high. Shoulders back. Confident. Knights of the Round Table! We gave a special salute with our swords. Three times. Left—right—straight ahead. We set off. At first slowly, then faster and faster we began running. The grass was soft under our feet. We are to stop when we reach a spot in front of the booth, and bow. We had practiced a hundred times and memorized every movement. The gold medal was ours, an absolute certainty. Proud and happy, we held our swords in front of our faces. The mesh masks were dirty, like a thick curtain pulled over our eyes. We were running toward the queen's booth when it happened, who knows how. In one instant, all four of us fell over. Headfirst onto our stomachs, laid out like a picture flat on the grass. At our feet, a thin wire was stretched a few inches above the ground. By accident or on purpose, we never knew. The mesh masks pressed thin, wavy lines into our faces. Our mouths were squished, our noses squashed.

For the first time, Queen Soraya laughed and her companions were happy. They gave us each a bronze medal—in commemoration of having made the queen of Iran laugh. Azadeh Derakhshan won the track and field events. She received the gold medal from Queen Soraya's own hand and preserved the honor of the school.

I take a shortcut through the folds of memory. I arrive at the day when Azadeh Derakhshan is competing in ping-pong against a girl from Nurbakhsh High School. I am anxious. My heart is pounding. Azadeh Derakhshan is inside of me, in my thoughts, my fears, in my skinny young legs that want to run with her step-by-step and pass everyone. What if she loses? This girl's loss is my loss. The Nurbakhsh students and ours, old rivals, are lined up around the gym. My heart is pounding. Azadeh Derakhshan has the ball. The game begins. One–two. Three all, neck and neck. It's an even match, and then at one stage Azadeh Derakhshan falls behind. The competition comes pounding down on her in a torrent. She loses the first round. She wins the second round. Sweat is flowing off her. Her face has turned red and she's breathing hard. Her nostrils are quivering. The students' shouts and cheers, the hoorahs, the clapping hands and stomping feet are spinning in my head. The ping-pong ball flies back and forth between my eyes, and my neck swings left and right, from this side to that, like the pendulum of a crazy clock. Azadeh Derakhshan forges ahead, falls behind. Twenty–sixteen (Azadeh is behind). Twenty–seventeen. Twenty–eighteen. Twenty–nineteen. Twenty all. They're tied. The fateful ball is in Azadeh's hands. Tied again. And again. And again. Twenty all. Azadeh Derakhshan has taken the shape of a wolf. She has chewed her lip and the corner of her mouth is bloody. She must win. She must. She must. At any cost. She will swallow her opponent whole. She'll tear her to pieces. She has no mercy. Then something unexpected happens. Azadeh Derakhshan's opponent curls up. She can't breathe. She doesn't have the strength to resist. She staggers, blue in the face. She's dying. Azadeh Derakhshan doesn't realize. Or if she does, it's not important to her. To hell with her. She thinks of one thing only: she must win. She must. At any cost. The prize stand and the gold medal are hers. Hers alone. Her opponent is wheeling around. The ping-pong paddle drops from her hand and she passes out.

I continue the match in my dreams every night, every night until morning, tossing and turning, breathing hard, eighteen all, nineteen all, twenty all, tied, till the end of the year, all through the summer and years to come. The unfinished game remains inside me and from time to time grabs me by the throat in the shape of some pointless rage or irrational argument.

The airplane has begun to shake unpleasantly. A thick cloud of cigarette smoke blankets the rear section of the plane. That same lost brat runs up and down the aisle, then disappears for a little while.

One way or another, I want to start up a conversation with Azadeh Derakhshan. I am awkward and uncomfortable. I curl up, shy, like a girl who has just reached puberty. I've regressed to that same mute anxiety of youth, that same meaningless bashful smile, just like in the old days.

Azadeh Derakhshan has put on her glasses. She doesn't like the airline meal. She turns the pages of her book.

I take the leap. I ask, "Are you . . . ?" and softly, stuttering with schoolgirl shyness, I pronounce her name.

Azadeh Derakhshan looks at me. She takes off her glasses, lenses thick as magnifying glass. She blinks. I introduce myself. I am waiting. I feel my face turning red. My name rings a puny bell—*ding*—not connected to anyone special. She pulls her eyebrows into an expression of surprise. She gives her neck a nervous twist, and her eyes, uncertain and embarrassed, circle my face and body. She is looking for someone else (younger?). Then, as if waking from a deep dream, she takes a long breath: an expression of fleeting recognition lights up her face and a transparent glimmer, a sort of wholesome, young happiness, flashes in her eyes for an instant. She repeats my name, and this time the name rings louder and longer than the last time—*ding ding ding ding.*

Anushiravan Dadgar High School: the morning anthem, names, half-forgotten names engraved in the mind, students, teachers, events, craziness, memories, pressed into the mold of words that pour in an involuntary rush from her mouth and from mine. You would never think that thirty-six years or more had passed since we last met, that for years and years we had been distant and without news of each other, and that at this very moment we are strangers. For this instant, Azadeh Derakhshan and I are in the past. The sharp, bright reality of Pahlavi Avenue and Mrs. Banoo and the antiquated classrooms of Anushiravan

Dadgar High School and André's sandwich shop are for us more
real than this airplane, this man standing two steps away with a
cigarette in hand, and this dinner tray. I know that in a few hours,
the moment we go our separate ways, the past will fade like a
movie that has closed down, and if by chance we happen to run
into each other again, we won't have anything to say. This encounter, with all its wistful warmth and glow, can happen only
once. It won't be repeated. Its delight lies in just this.

I start somewhere and Azadeh Derakhshan jumps in, runs
ahead of me, and then chases another story. We laugh. We are
friendly and comfortable together. We are young. Neither of us
mentions the ping-pong match. So much the better.

The lights go off inside the airplane. It's time to sleep. We fall
silent. Silent and sad. We have both returned to the present: to ten
after twelve at an altitude of several thousand meters with Tehran
spread beneath our feet; to thoughts of getting through customs;
to worries.

Azadeh Derakhshan is coming from America. It's her first trip
after fifteen years. She says she has two grown sons, one in Canada,
one in Texas. She's a nurse and has worked in a hospital this whole
time, struggling against odds, closed doors. Her mother died in her
absence. She's going back to repossess her house (from a bunch of
strangers) and her husband (from another woman) and get her sons
to return home. What a program she has ahead of her, what a
struggle, what opponents!

I know her husband. It's a small world. The whole city knew that
Dr. So-and-so found a new wife young enough to be his daughter. At some boring party, some nosy woman—one of those
women who has news of every event in the world—whispered in
my ear, "That man in the double-breasted jacket with the gold
buttons and the white shoes, acting like a kid—he's the doctor
who took a second wife. And that's his young wife. His first wife

is in America. Do you remember Azadeh Derakhshan? She was the ping-pong champion, two classes above us."

Azadeh Derakhshan, with what's left of her wasted beauty, is seated beside me and is not talking about her husband. She talks about her sons, and her mother's former cook who has seized the house that's rightfully hers and has no intention of moving. She doesn't talk about the young girl who has taken possession of her husband. And she doesn't talk about herself, about why her hair has all these gray strands, why there are dark rings under her eyes, why she is fat, and why she is so sad. She talks about her sons: about the older one, who is engaged to a Vietnamese girl and has changed his name and identity (Akbar became Ike), and the younger one, who speaks Persian with an American accent and who is angry at his father, and how this anger has made him hot-headed and irrational. She talks about America, about the great loneliness of the busiest city in the world, about her work as a nurse and her struggles—for the sake of her sons.

The wheels of the plane descend and the sound of the pilot's voice echoes in space: "Honored passengers, please do not leave your seats until the aircraft comes to a complete stop—seriously!" The words fall on deaf ears. More than half of the passengers are standing. They are in a hurry. Each one wants to get ahead of the others.

Azadeh Derakhshan is nervous, excited, and worried. She's afraid, with a thousand different fears. Her tired eyes are jittery. She has waited for this moment for fifteen years. She asks, "Things have changed, no? Have they changed a lot? The people? The street names?"

The passengers have closed ranks, back to back. They push one another. They stagger. The airplane is likewise in motion. Azadeh Derakhshan looks out the window, flustered. She's anxious. She's terrified of showing her passport and the possibility of being interrogated, of confronting the gang at the house, and more than anything, of coming face-to-face with her husband and that young girl. She has a hard battle ahead of her.

We say good-bye. Like two strangers. We exchange phone numbers. We make some lame promise and we part ways. I know that we have different paths and will probably never see each other again. For all this, in the short space of this ephemeral stroll in the past, a vague event has taken shape inside of me, and something at the bottom of my heart, in my spirit, has shifted. Time is now more palpable, and I see that it has punished my proud champion with terrible hardship.

Hurry. Shove. Push. The passengers get ahead of one another. Those who travel regularly know the tricks. They know when to run, when to stand, where to cut in and how, with all their bags and baggage, to get past the others at any cost. Getting onto the bus that has come to pick up the passengers has its own special technique. Whoever gets on last stands by the door and consequently gets off first, a hundred steps ahead of the others. Charging ahead, running, panting, he arrives at the police booth and passport control. Having passed these first two obstacles, he runs up the stairs two steps at a time—panting—victorious—and grabs his luggage. This "just me," insofar as a powerful force runs in his veins and all his intelligence and wits have been concentrated on reaching the goal, is first in line at customs. He's in a hurry. He closes his suitcase. Happy and successful, he gets into the first taxi and goes straight to his house. He goes to sleep early and wakes up at the crack of dawn. He gets to work sooner than the rest of his colleagues, rises in the ranks, and gets promoted. He is a winner. He takes first prize in the race of life and death. He retires sooner than So-and-so and So-and-so and So-and-so. His night turns to morning more quickly, his weeks to months, his months to years, and his years to the end of the century. He leaps from that last step of life and stands first in line at the gates of heaven, long before the others he left behind, shuffling in line at customs.

Customs. Azadeh Derakhshan is at the head of the line. Her eyes light on me from the distance but offer no sign of acknowledgment. She looks around, dazed and bewildered. Her headscarf is crooked and her expression miserable. Every bearded man who passes by terrifies her. I'm traveling light and not worried about customs. Personal effects, a few small gifts, some medicines, and a handful of food items are the contents of my baggage. Most likely, according to customs regulations and any logical reckoning, I should be able to get through easily without a headache. I don't plan to argue or haggle. I'm sure of myself. I carry myself like someone with an easy mind and nothing to fear from anyone. And because I have no excess baggage or forbidden items, because I've committed neither crime nor sin (so I think), I'm calm and indifferent. I don't know that standing like this (one hand in my coat pocket and, to all appearances, unconcerned) is a big mistake; I don't realize that having an easy mind and a cool, indifferent look (mixed with unintentional pride) is to my disadvantage.

I've opened my suitcase and, with a look and a movement of my head, I show my impatience. I'm tired. I yawn. The customs officer approaches with an air of polite reserve. He looks calm.

"Madam, we're tired too," he says.

The passenger next to me lays it on thick. "Yes, of course," he says. "You put us to shame. The future of this country belongs to hardworking people like you. Good luck to you."

The officer keeps his head down. He continues with his business. He's used to this type of bogus flattery. He's up to his neck in it. I tell myself I'm lucky that I got a decent customs officer. But for some unknown reason, maybe because of that same self-assurance, I sense that the customs officer doesn't like me and he's not letting me go. He's dragging it out. He's looking for excuses. I try to be polite and humble. I smile. My smile and my humility are obviously false, they're shouting it, and they ruin my chances even further. The very proper officer studies a package of medicines. He sets one box aside.

He says, "This drug is prohibited." He says it softly and calmly, barely audibly. As if his words were addressed to someone else.

No. I mustn't get angry. I mustn't complain and make a fuss. He's probably right. Some drugs have to be verified. But, well, what goes by rules and regulations in this country? Look, that woman walked through easily with three suitcases.

The officer is in a hurry. He repeats, "This drug has to be verified."

"Who has to verify it?"

"It has to go into storage. The person responsible is not here tonight."

"What?" I say, "Go and come back tomorrow? Do you think people have nothing better to do? As if it were that easy."

He answers, "It has nothing to do with me. That's the rule."

"Where is it written?"

He says, "Honorable sister, if you're going to be stubborn I'll confiscate your suitcase." The argument is getting serious. One of us will have to overcome the other. The passenger behind me has a huge suitcase, the size of a large chest. It's the fourth time this year that he's gone abroad and come back. For all that, he keeps his head down and tries to slip, even sneak, through customs easily. He's even brought a television with him, in addition to a hundred pairs of children's socks and a hundred pairs of women's stockings crammed into dozens of plastic bags. He's coming from Germany. He trades in this stuff. He ought to pay customs duties. But he begs and whines. I'm at your service . . . forever indebted to you . . . He rolls over and plays dead. His stories are fabricated and his oaths are lies. The customs officer understands his language. He's familiar with his tricks. The procedure is clear for this type. He haggles with him, wrestles over the price. A little discount on this side, a little whining and begging on that side, and in the end they reach an agreement. They know each other's worlds. The officer's behavior toward me is different. He feels that I think the world owes me (maybe I do) and, however much he pours, my glass will be half-empty.

I am not going to let it go. I'm not going to give way. I try again, "Please, sir, these are vitamins." I read the label out loud, and, "We're allowed to bring in vitamins."

The officer doesn't respond.

I hold the box up to his eyes. I ask, "Do you know how to read?" Bad question. I regret it.

The officer gives me an odd look, a look tinged with anger. I've insulted him. He talks to the person behind me.

A tired traveler, waiting for his turn, says, "Madam, don't you understand simple logic? Come back tomorrow."

I say, "It's written here: disodium chloride, amino acid, potassium . . ."

The passenger pleads, "Madam, do you think speaking in a foreign language will help? Give up."

A porter tries to get my attention.

He whispers in my ear, with a Turkish accent, "Give me a five and I'll get your luggage cleared." I don't pay attention to him. I'm not going to pay a bribe. Not to anyone. The law is on my side. Or maybe it's not. In any case, I intend to fight and win. Why? I don't know. I can't help it. Maybe it's a kind of sickness, some sort of ancient, hereditary habit.

Azadeh Derakhshan has picked up her luggage and is wandering around, looking at people. Everything is new to her. Her headscarf is too long. It's obvious she's come from abroad and might as well be a foreigner.

I raise my voice. An empty bluff.

The officer says, "Madam, don't shout. This drug is prohibited," and he says it with anger.

"No. It's not prohibited."

"Don't argue, sister. I have a job to do."

"I have a job too."

"Please step aside. Passengers are waiting."

The ping-pong ball is bouncing in my stomach. Twenty all. We're tied. I must win. I must. Azadeh Derakhshan is wriggling behind my eyelids. It's she who's giving the orders. An old sound rings in my ears. Students are cheering. All eyes are fixed on me.

A woman says, "Come on, just let it go. It's morning."

I say, "Mind your own business."

She flies hot out of the furnace, her voice rising to a screech. An elderly man, fatherly, sides with me. The woman turns on him. She says one thing, I say another, the old man chimes in, and the officer does too. The Turkish porter repeats, "Give me a five and I'll get your luggage cleared."

I shout, "What are you saying? Go away! Leave me alone. I wouldn't even give you two."

The customs officer says, "Go ask the supervisor for permission."

Now he's talking. At least I'll be dealing with someone else.

"Where is the supervisor?" I ask.

The officer waves a hand: somewhere behind him. I set off. The Turkish porter follows me. The supervisor's office is nearby, the door half-open. I knock. The porter says, "Go on in. Why are you knocking?"

No one answers. A man comes out and hurries off. I knock again: *tak tak tak.*

The porter says, "Don't bother knocking. Go on in. Can't you see there's nobody in there?"

He's right. There's no one in the room. A person holding a letter enters the room. I ask him . . . He shakes his head. He's in a hurry.

A woman is standing near the door. She says, "Go ask at the information desk."

"Where is the information desk?"

The woman says, "There's a free phone at the end of the hallway. Go call from there."

"Who should I ask for?"

"Internal services."

The porter says, "Let's go call. I know how to use the phone."

"Call who?"

"Call internal services."

"Where is 'internal services'? What's it got to do with them?"

"How should I know?"

"Are you stupid?"

The porter gets angry. The veins on his neck are popping out. He says, "Why do you insult me? What an attitude! You're wasting my time. You don't listen to anyone."

The phone at the end of the hallway is free. A man cuts ahead of me. His hand reaches the receiver at exactly the same time as mine. He says, "Excuse me. It's my turn."

He is stronger. He pushes me aside with his shoulder. He dials.

The porter says, "Come on. Just give me four *toman*. I'll get your luggage cleared."

I snap at him. He gets fired up. He turns red. The veins in his neck pop out again. He says, "What a temper! Why are you picking a fight? What's it got to do with me? Do you think I'm the mayor? If you think you're so right, go argue with him. You're not my boss."

I go back to the customs line. The officer has his head down. Back to the same stew: "It's prohibited. You can't bring it in."

"It's not prohibited. I can bring it in."

"You can't."

"I can."

Eighteen all. Twenty all.

Tied.

"Go file a complaint."

"I will."

"Leave me alone."

"I won't."

I say. He says. He shouts. I shout. I'm breathing hard.

The Turkish porter says, "Is there gold in this box? Leave it in storage. Come get it tomorrow. This officer has work to do. He's said what he has to say. Do you want to insult him in front of all these people? Go home and sleep. Get some rest. You'll get old like this. You'll have a heart attack."

My eyes catch Azadeh Derakhshan in the distance. She is sad and lost. She's been running for a lifetime and has come back empty-handed. Exhaustion runs through my body, along with an unknown anxiety—the sense of a great vacuum and a sudden nausea.

＂ ． ． ．

Azadeh Derakhshan's picture is in the school newspaper. I've hung it on my bedroom wall. Tomorrow we have a ping-pong match. My opponent is a skinny and untalented girl. I'm going to win. For sure. I'm certain. I can't sleep. What if I lose?

The porter senses my sudden grief, and sighs. He shakes his head philosophically. He says, "We fight at home, too. Bloody fights. The landlord said we have to move out at the end of the month. I asked him: Where should we go? My wife orders me around. She told me to go file a complaint. The landlord came after us with a bunch of small-time thugs. He was yelling and screaming. I hit him with a hammer, on the car. My sons jumped into the fray. I don't know how it happened but in the middle of all this, my wife's head was cut open. She's very feisty. You say something as clear as the nose on your face and she'll slap you."

The customs officer is tired. He swallows a yawn. He looks despondent. His mind is elsewhere. He's lost patience. It's late. Most of the passengers have left. Somebody calls him. He goes. Another officer takes his place.

The porter says, "Put the box of medicine in your purse. Don't say anything. Let's get out of here."

The second officer has no idea what's been going on. He has no issues with me. I throw the box of medicine on the table and close my handbag. The first officer's sadness was contagious; I've caught it. Victory and defeat are hollow. Arguing over nothing. I'm weary, and this weariness belongs to old times, to those inner competitions, losses, unfinished matches.

The Turkish porter, grumbling and sleepy, puts my suitcases on his cart. He can't figure me out. It's almost dawn. The customs officials are napping. A flight from Damascus has landed and hundreds of women in black veils are coming up the stairs. Again, the same pleading and begging, the same tricks, the same cheating over a few pairs of socks, a few pennies.

The porter says, "So you made all this scene for what? You make yourself have a fit. If you'd given me four *toman,* everything would have worked out. And I would have had some benefit too."

Maybe.

He asks, "Why didn't you take the box of medicine? Was an argument all that you wanted? My wife loves arguing too. The moment you walk in the door, she draws blood."

He takes his money. He's not satisfied; he wants more. He haggles.

"Taxi?"

"Yes."

I get in the cab. I give the address. I ask, "How much?" I want to settle the price so there won't be an argument at the end. The driver says, "It's on me." Then he waves to someone in the distance and disappears.

I'm too tired to complain. I lean back in the seat and take a nap. I can smell the day coming, the smell of a delicious breakfast and a good sleep in a ready bed, soft and cozy. The smell of a calm and quiet hour of the morning.

Azadeh Derakhshan, lost and wavering, paces in front of the airport entrance. She looks at her watch. She is hot under the collar, arguing with somebody invisible. I don't want to look at her. I turn my face away, and I feel her hidden presence—the medals, the competitions, her endless winning streak—slithering calmly and silently out of my soul. A delicious fatigue, a sort of lazy, sweet surrender, fills its empty space.

A man opens the front door of the taxi. He gets in. He says, "We're going the same way. My stop is ahead of yours. With your permission?"

I say nothing. The cab driver arrives. He gets behind the wheel and steps on the gas. He's in a good mood, in fine form. "This man gets off at the corner," he says. "Then I'll get you where you're going. Then I go home to sleep. You'll arrive safe and sound. A little later, a little sooner, we'll get there in the end."

Vali'asr Avenue is clean, washed with rain, with the same old sycamores full of new sparrows, the same familiar mountains full of strangers hiking. The Shemiran bus has just pulled up at the

Abshar stop. The other passenger says something to the driver. The driver agrees. He brakes quickly and stops in front of a bakery. The man gets out. He buys a few flaps of fresh bread and returns. He offers a big piece of bread to the driver and then to me. He insists. The smell of fresh bread fills the car. I'm hungry. It's a gift from God.

The morning sun, warm and generous, slips over the man's hands and the backseat and the edge of my skirt. It hoists itself up and settles quietly on the driver's shoulder.

We arrive. The driver is busy talking. He refuses my money politely: "Please, I beg you, be my guest." I insist. His name is Ali One-Hand, and he really has only one hand. He has a kind face— a humble face—and gray hair. He sets the suitcase at the gate, with that same one hand. He gives me his phone number, says, "Anytime you need to go somewhere, call me. I'm at your service."

He waits till I go inside and it's certain that I've arrived safe and sound.

The gate opens slowly and a good feeling, like a cozy child's quilt, settles on my tired body. Behind this gate (one more of those doors of mercy) a safe and familiar world waits for me. Kind hands lift my suitcase. The neighbor's dog is in the side street. He comes to welcome me and rubs my shoes with his muzzle. Mr. Ali One-Hand closes the car door. He nods and slowly drives away. A feeling of peace comes over me, and the Iran Air flight, with its chaotic world and its native generosity, its clever losers, its ritual arguments and its exhaustion, its hidden kindnesses and its empty animosities, disappears from my memory, along with Azadeh Derakhshan and that old, unfinished game.

Translated from the Persian by Zara Houshmand

ABOUT THE AUTHOR

Goli Taraghi was born in Tehran. She began her writing career with a collection of short stories entitled *I Am Che*

Guevara Too in 1969. Her first novel, *Winter Sleep,* was published in 1973 and has been translated into English and French. Her most recent books are *Scattered Memories, In Another Place,* and *Two Worlds.* Two of her recent collections of stories, *The House of Shemiran* and *The Three Maids,* have been published in France. Taraghi lives in Tehran and Paris.

JABBAR YUSSIN HUSSIN

Jabbar Yussin Hussin has the privilege of belonging to the oldest literary community in the world. One long-ago afternoon, in the land that would six thousand years later call itself Iraq, one of his ancestors made some rudimentary marks on a clay tablet to document some transaction or other. With that act, more commercial than poetic, this remote forefather of Jabbar's invented writing: in other words, he made possible the epic of Gilgamesh, *the stories of* One Thousand and One Nights, *the works of Aeschylus and Sophocles, the lives of Hamlet and Don Quixote, and the moving stories of Jabbar's own collection,* The Reader of Baghdad.

Jabbar was born in Baghdad in 1954. A few years as a journalist culminated in a death threat; the next, obligatory step was exile. The philosopher Edgar Morin, referring to Jabbar's work, wrote that, "anyone who has suffered exile lives, in his own way, an anthropological experience: exile from the cosmos." It's now nearly thirty years that Jabbar has lived in exile in France, in a small cottage near La Rochelle, where nostalgia for what he had lost impelled him to write. Today Jabbar reads voraciously, writes stories, sketches, newspaper articles, and memoirs, in beautiful Arabic that he strives not to forget. The community of Arab writers is vast, but Jabbar is interested above all in his countrymen, who were unable to read and think freely during decades of tyranny.

Recent events, all too well known, in which the tyrant was conquered and the country humiliated, enabled Jabbar to return to his homeland in 2003. There, amid bombings and diplomacy, he tried to find the places and people that he'd had to leave behind so suddenly years before. He found some, but what he saw more often than not were ruins and ghosts: the National Library of Baghdad pillaged, many of his relatives and friends dead. A curious encounter marked this trip. One morning, on the banks of the Tigris, Jabbar saw a young man sitting on a bench. They greeted each other and after a moment the young man said, "My grandfather told me that wolves ran wild in these parts, and savaged whomever dared set foot here before dawn." Jabbar started. This total stranger of a young man had quoted to him a passage from his story "In the Tracks of Wolves" from the collection The Reader of Baghdad.

The stories in The Reader of Baghdad *move between the fantastic and the documentary, between dream and memory. In one, present reality uncannily mirrors thirteenth-century Arab history in the tale of another invasion and sacking, when Mongol invaders built bridges of books from the National Library of Baghdad and the Tigris ran black with ink. In the story selected here, Baghdad becomes a certain city in the southern hemisphere and the protagonist is not Jabbar but rather Jorge Luis Borges, librarian.*

At the end of a few weeks in Iraq, Jabbar returned to France, the country that now, by force of habit, has become his home. But his long absence had reached its terminus, and the exile, which had turned him into a writer, had finally ended.

—ALBERTO MANGUEL
Translated from the Spanish by Samantha Schnee

———◦———

Translator's Note: *This story is a response to Borges's "Averroes' Search," in which Borges writes about that old master's attempts at understanding the meaning of the words* comedy *and* tragedy. *In that story, Averroes (Ibn-Rushd, 1126–1198—regarded by many as the foremost Islamic philosopher) was working from a translation of a translation. I found it appropriate that my first task in translating this story was to locate the opening quote from Borges. Once I did, I discovered that it must have been falsely translated into Arabic, perhaps because the Borges version is somewhat "blasphemous." In the Borges, the Quran is a place where tragedy and comedy exist, and I assume Borges's Arabic translators changed it. In the original, the last line is not: "In the Quran and the mu'allaqat of the mosque, there is room for neither tragedy's magic nor for comedy," but rather, "There are many admirable tragedies and comedies in the Quran and the mu'allaqat of the mosque." In this way, the translation of the following story—its anecdote about the stuttering scribes, its genesis in another story, which itself is based on history—continues the tradition that Borges began, and, in a way, embodies Aristotle's own take on comedy and tragedy.*

—R. J.

THE DAY IN BUENOS AIRES

With firm, painstaking calligraphy, Averroes added these lines to the manuscript "Destruction of the Destruction": *"Aristotle gives the name 'tragedy' to panegyrics and the name 'comedy' to satires and anathemas. In the Quran and the mu'allaqat of the mosque, there is room for neither tragedy's magic nor for comedy."*
—JORGE LUIS BORGES,
"Averroes's Search," in *The Aleph*

Before his siesta, Averroes—or better yet, "Grandson" as both his father and grandfather, who were judges in Córdoba, called him—recalled a class in medicine he'd attended with his teacher, the Valecian, Abi-Marawan. He tried to remember the year in which he'd last met his teacher, but could not, and instead, the image of a woman crossing an alleyway in a Marrakesh quarter came to mind; it had been morning and Averroes was on his way to meet his majesty Sultan Yusef who would ask him to explain Aristotle. The woman was walking in a leisurely manner with her veil off, and Averroes could barely contain himself. He stopped and leaned back to let her pass, and the image of her face remained imbedded in his memory to this very day. What kind of radiant face did he see? He never told us—nor did Abd al-Wahed al-Marrakeshi, who wrote a lot of stories about Averroes—about the image of that face. But now, this afternoon, he is flung under a white velvety cover, remembering that woman's face and a passage of his teacher ibn-Tufayl's regarding this very matter, that he'd once read in which ibn-Tufayl talks about his "gazelle."

He let his heart wander in the Marrakesh woman's bright face under that distant day's sun. Slowly, the face came nearer, until it was between his eyes and the velvety cover that resembled a Marrakesh caftan. His eyelids became heavy, and the sound of the seagulls' circling reached his ears; he could hear their wings cutting the shore's wind. Soon he saw unfamiliar multicolored birds of the ocean fly above a forest in which a green river ran. Then he fell asleep.

When he awoke, the Marrakesh woman's face was far away. He'd forgotten it in the inundation of sleepiness. He heard men's voices coming from the direction of the Diwaniya[1], and remembered his scheduled meeting with the trader abu-al-Qasim al-Ash'ari who'd just returned from China. He hadn't pondered the rift between al-Ash'ari and Farah, a Quranic scholar, when he'd invited both to his nightly sitting. And now he was hearing something akin to an argument coming from the Diwaniya, the sounds of which were permeated by the low, hushed voice of his redheaded chambermaid who was singing in the courtyard. He didn't call for her as he usually did, but rose quickly and put on his blue robe after washing his face with the water that was in the pot by his bed. He refreshed himself with scent from a bottle and felt the overwhelming flavor of late afternoon lingering on his grayed beard. He recalled the details of his siesta's dream and smiled. He walked to the Diwaniya after glimpsing the red-haired chambermaid reenter to light the lamp of the women's Diwaniya.

He greeted his two guests, and al-Ash'ari kissed both his cheeks. The trader had a shaved beard, his eyes were lined with red kohl, and his face was picking up the lantern's light, as the lantern shone down from the center of the Diwaniya's ceiling. Averroes did not comment on al-Ash'ari's appearance since he didn't want the man's opponent to utter something he would hate to hear at this hour.

They spoke of al-Ash'ari's trip to the kingdom of China, and the trader praised its king who'd given the kingdom's few Muslims their freedom. Averroes was happy to hear that the few Chinese who accompanied the Iraqi travelers in the coastal cities had converted to Islam. "They had considered, master of those who

[1]Entrance hall.

see . . ." recited Averroes, but Farah raised his voice and began to recite in a way that resembled singing: "When there comes the help of Allah and the victory, and you see men entering the religion of Allah in multitudes, then celebrate the praise of your Lord, and ask His forgiveness; surely He is oft-returning to mercy." Averroes felt that the conversation was going to take a new turn because of the two opponents' presence.

Farah would ask questions about the people of China and their religions, and repeat the subject of the testimony of the trees whose leaves were calligraphied with the words of God and their meaning, and he would search for a way to counter his adversary with his own testimony. Averroes refused to witness this accusation of al-Ash'ari of disbelieving. He wanted to recite what he'd written in "Examination of the Methods of Proof Concerning the Doctrines of Religion" and say, "We must examine everything that exists with rationality," but then he remembered that their discussion had only begun in his own head. He recalled his dream, and thought it would be appropriate to change subjects and tell them about his manuscript. But he felt a sorrowful anger about Farah, who was reminding him of his old adversary in Córdoba, Judge abu-'Amer, who'd turned so many people against him that one day they forbade him to perform the afternoon prayers at the Córdoba mosque.

"A thing cannot end if it does not even exist," said Averroes to his two guests, then an image from his dream came into his head. "I was awakened by my chambermaid's song, as she sang what Wallada[2] sang once, in another place. I awoke to the letters of her words and the echo of your footsteps: it seems you both arrived when I was still elsewhere, in another world, only God knows where."

"The hardship of dreams is similar to the hardship of travel to faraway kingdoms," al-Ash'ari remarked, eliciting a mischievous smile from Farah, which Averroes acknowledged by continuing

[2]Wallada, the poetess of Andalusia, represents the prototypical free woman.

his speech: "While you were on your way in, I felt as though I were in a different world. On my way there, I didn't see anything except a river that was wider than Jehoon and greater than Sehoon³ cutting through green quarters that were neither Jenan nor Andalusia. Empty spaces in which there were no people or animals, but it was, God knows, real. I found myself in a strange city, without any voyager's dust."

"It was a trip to paradise, Averroes," announced Farah, adding apologetically, "for even in Andalusia and in winter, the voyager arrives covered with the dust of the road."

Averroes continued telling his dream, "A blind man who welcomed me into his elevated house—which reminded me of the descriptions of the tiered homes of Hadramaut—told me it was a city in a new world, and he called it 'Buenos Aires,' or something similar to that, and that he was one of its residents and had heard of Córdoba and Andalusia. As though he'd just been there the day before." His visitors were listening raptly, their faces beginning to look similar in spite of the differences in their appearance. He looked at them, and al-Ash'ari's shaved face reminded him of his host's face in the dream's city, so he continued. "He told me his name was Borges, and I don't know what this name means, neither in Castilian nor in Arabic. He was a blind man who spoke to me in a Castilian dialect that resembled one rock piled atop another; it was nothing like the dialects of young boys we hear these days. He said he knew me, and spoke my full name. He seemed like a wise man or a poet, like ibn-Ma'ra, memorizing everything he hears, for he spoke with me at length about the ancient texts and stated that reading them was important."

"And what about modern texts?" Farah asked, but Averroes did not answer him, because he realized that the passage the blind man had read him had been his own. Farah was awaiting an answer, but Averroes was distracted, far away, buried in the pages of his memory

³The names of rivers in Jehan, or Paradise.

and of the forgotten text, in an attempt to find the page in which he'd written that passage. I said, "And what about modern texts Averroes?" Farah repeated in a voice so loud it disgusted al-Ash'ari, so Averroes answered him with haste and conciseness—he'd remembered a proverb of Ali ibn-abi-Talib: "Speak to people of what they know—only God knows all."

He said he couldn't remember the rest of his dream and apologized to his guests. Al-Ash'ari remarked that afternoon dreams were like chimeras, soulless, forgotten upon waking because of the soul's timelessness, whereas the dreams of dawn are molded in angels' spirits, and resemble visions, like those of the prophets. Farah spoke of Averroes's dream as though it were a myth told by the blind man—who must have been Christian, Farah deduced from his name—and he added that it resembled the legends told by Avicena and al-Farabi.

Averroes didn't respond to Farah, but glanced every now and then at his friend al-Ash'ari, who had resigned himself to listening with a sullen look, the meaning of which Averroes understood well. And since the evening was falling like gentle rain, its redness covering the mosque's green dome, the call to prayer was broadcast and the two guests left, and soon enough, the red-haired chambermaid returned to her song about the rains in Córdoba.

After prayer, Averroes went to a corner of the house, admired the stars that were glowing in the sky above the tip of the newly renovated minaret, and listened to the water gurgling in a nearby fountain, which always reminded him of a story about a relative of his who'd died of thirst at the edge of a watering hole. He remembered his guests and was sorry for the departure of al-Ash'ari, whom he hadn't seen in years. If it weren't for Farah's presence, he would have liked to tell him the rest of his dream.

Again he thought of the woman from Marrakesh, but he willfully brushed her aside, for her features had long been imprinted in his mind. Instead, he began to think about what he hadn't shared of the dream. The image of a red fruit, which he'd never seen in his life, had captivated him. A few pieces of the fruit were placed in a decorated plate on the blind man's table. He smelled its strange scent while the blind man asked him the reason for his exile.[4] In myths and dreams—and this was something that confused him—a person possesses a degree of courage he is unable to possess in reality. What if he'd repeated what he'd said in the dream to al-Ash'ari? Would he have laughed at him, since he'd seen on his travels things that those who had never seen them couldn't even begin to imagine? Would Averroes have been able to tell him that he'd answered the blind man, with an ease unexpected of any of either the ancients or his peers, that his exile was all due to a mistake of the scribes, one of whom was a stutterer? When he was dictating the book of zoology and got to the part about the giraffe, Averroes had said, "I saw the giraffe with the King of Ber," but because the scribe was a stutterer, it was recorded as "the King of Berber." When they presented the copy to Sultan al-Mansour, he burst into anger, sought revenge, and threw him out of the country. Averroes thought about all this, and the images of his days in exile passed through his mind, the image of the day he rode a ship returning from Marrakesh, when he saw a flock of butterflies crossing the ocean and the image of the blind man guiding him around a house that was filled with ancient texts, and new texts he didn't know. But the moment he heard his red-haired chambermaid calling him to dinner—she'd stopped singing for a short while—he smiled and decided that tomorrow, he'd ask al-Ash'ari, who had surely seen strange things in his travels to China, about the taste of the red fruit whose scent had remained in his memory since awakening from his nap. He would tell him that he'd heard the blind man in his dream calling them "*los tomates.*"

Translated from the Arabic by Randa Jarrar

[4]Al-Mansour dismissed Averroes from his post as judge and exiled him from Marrakesh to al-Isalah near Córdoba. Some wrote that the reason for this was that Averroes referred to al-Mansour, in one of his zoology texts, as "King of the Berbers"—a derogatory slur among Arabs in Islamic Spain (*Averroes: The Great Muslim Philosopher,* by Habib Salloum).

ABOUT THE AUTHOR

Jabbar Yussin Hussin is an Iraqi novelist and poet who left
Iraq in 1976 to avoid persecution by the government of Sad-
dam Hussein. He has published a number of books, in both
French and Arabic, blending the Iraqi literary tradition with
the experience of exile. He visited Iraq in 2003, after Hussein was overthrown, and shortly theareafter published his
most recent book, *The Reader of Baghdad.*

SANIYYA SALEH

Saniyya Saleh is distinguished among Arab women poets in the twentieth century because her poetry does not well up from complaint, from expressing the sorrows of love, or sorrow in the frame of the individual self and private life, despite the fact that she is certainly the poet of pain and expresses the pains of women. Her poetry is not expressed in the form of complaint and is not related to an individual situation but rather to the human condition.

There is a certain universal human lyricism in her poetry, and her poems offer broad scenes portraying the pains of human beings, wherein she places what is individual in the larger panorama of what is human.

She has constructed all this in a special language, with a new vocabulary derived from a wide field of experience. It is as if she has laid the foundation of a new poetic project that has its own diction and its own universe. She invented her own language and no other woman poet resembles her in this respect.

In these two poems she refers to her daughter Shaam (she had two daughters: Shaam and Sulaafa). She wants her daughter to be born into a better world, one where females would be equal with males. She speaks in symbols, but I think her two poems are clear.

—ADONIS
Translated from the Arabic by Issa J. Boullata

SHAAM, SET THE NIGHT FREE

I

She went out leading a flock
of dolls and naked children to sleep.
"Maria, I see that your children are

writhing with hunger. Wait, here is
God's bread, and don't forget:
the moon will rise to bless them."
And what a moon it is
that dissipates the night of birth!

O wind, why do you help the stars
flee from their desolate homes
and then take them out of the paths
of the Milky Way?

2

You take everyone unawares
and lead them to Saint-Exupéry's prince.
We all gasp as we see them fly.
We're afraid they might fall into the ocean,
that she might be captured and stoned.

And yet,
every year
a new lover springs
and goes among the cotton blossoms
that grow on the mantle of night,
and he sets out toward eternity.

3

O pearl,
you've slept within me for ages,
listened to the noise of my bowels
and the roar of my blood.
I've concealed you for a long, long time
until History would end its sorrow,
until the great warriors would end their wars
and the executioners would flog their victims,
until an Age of Light would arrive,

then each of us would come out
of the innards of the other.

4
Your snow horse has gone crazy
with the fire of the future,
its eyes are shining with wonder.
Something tempts it to go forth,
yet something prevents it and pulls back its bridle.
If the future could be seen like clouds
or birds,
if it could be opened like windows,
I would have chosen the greatest lifetime for you.
But you are my heir in misery
and I have emptied in you the hot ashes of days
and the flames of years.
The twinkle of the star that resembles you
stings my drunken heart.
And when black winds besiege you,
fierce friends besiege you too.
Saddle your horses ready to flee.
But beware
lest the wolf of the myth deceive you,
lest the moon deceive you.
Sleep in the open air,
where the flame of Truth burns,
where—in their dumb steps—
the vicissitudes of time come and go
like a tiger touching the earth
with its velvety paws.

5
It is winter,
or it is the wind whose name is Maria,
the rebellion of souls
that have not been favored with bodies.

And there in the capital, there is
a big demonstration to grant her
the right to taste pain;
only her body grants her this pleasure.
In the body, the soul lays its eggs
and the children come out
with blond hair and blue eyes.
They play with the sea,
they build sand castles for it
and tempt it to enter,
but it is too clever to be deceived.

6

I see you bending over the edge of the water,
looking in wonder at the child drowned in it.
When your mother screams, "Be careful!"
you back off,
then return, anxious, still looking and looking,
your shadow always waiting for you.

7

Why do you run as though you're flying,
trailed by your braids and the hem of your robe?
Take it easy! That angel whom you are
exerting yourself to see is approaching.
But beware,
don't flee with him.
Let me see:
he is wonderful . . . wonderful, like a cotton doll
and not like those angels
who wait for us in the tombs
to assassinate us with their divine spear
and run away;
and here are the other angels
waiting like birds at the edge of heaven,
fluttering their transparent wings.

Maria!
Have you returned with a bevy of them
for the children to play with,
to hang above their beds, and dream?

8

I wonder, where do thieves come up with
all those straying and deviant persons?
Maria, your heart is pounding violently.
Hide your little ones inside the pillows
or in a warm hole in one of the mud houses.
Maria, don't forget to close the cattle barn so that
the young of the livestock may not be scared.

9

Why are you silent, O river?
Sing aloud so that my little ones may rejoice.
And, to allay their fear, chase the thieves' carriages.

10

When the flow pushes out the sand of the shore
with deep sighs, announcing this is the ideal motion,
the ebb comes along as another player and scoops it in
with its greedy palms
to where it likes.
This is the eternal game of the lonely sea,
the game that fascinates you, Maria.

11

Maria,
Since when has your face had
all those wrinkles,
since when has the autumn
hurried its steps behind you
along with the barking dogs
and the mordacious wolves?

.   .   .

Bashful Maria's name
was Fatima
years ago.
As days went by, it became something else,
perhaps Shaam.
Maria, why do you hide your real name?
It has seas and moons within it,
it has galaxies that never stand still.
You flutter your golden braids
in the midst of a flock of dolls with fur
as they whirl their beautiful hems
and utter an amusing yelp.
Who can bridle them?
Who can bridle your blue horses
wandering among the clouds,
and return them to their stalls?
They are searching for real gates
in order to dash along outside the world.

12
Winter is waning
and marble is on its way to ruin;
the ostrich, which walks at night
on legs of cotton in order to frighten you,
has been enwrapped by darkness,
in the hope it will forget its habit
of burying its head.
My little one,
your blue eyes are like infinity, like eternity.
O golden bird,
for whom do you leave your shade in the mirrors
that are dispersed in the firmament of night?
Maria looks toward the distance,
where the shadow of a child is playing.

13

When you go forth beyond my arms,
I am afraid Time will run away with you
or it will bend your little back
while you are drawing
its outlines and curvatures,
so the cloud of your soul will rise
and your body will be entangled there,
in the fierce, interlocking bars.

Maria, rise.
This is your opportunity to shout:
"Such is life,
      a fire in the heart,
      a fire in the heart,
      a fire in the heart."

A MILLION WOMEN ARE YOUR MOTHER

O forest that my body has set on fire,
come close,
disregard what can't be disregarded,
whisper your hidden rustle into my mouth,
into my ear,
and into my pores;
reveal your rebellion
and blossom
in the perforated dome
of a collapsing body.

Isn't winter harsh? Aren't time and snow,
rain and storms, too?
But oh, how beautiful they are
as they go away.

. . .

I didn't know that forgetfulness has legs,
yet it comes and goes like an unruly horse
waiting for the bronze-colored rose to fall
from the top of the branches.
If the rose falls on the horse's back,
the horse will fly away with it;
if it falls between its legs,
the horse will kick it.

O forest that has blossomed in my body,
don't be afraid.
I've hidden my soul in you
or between two cracks as strong as armies
(although armies don't know us and don't care).

Plunge your head into me,
penetrate me
until our bones almost intertwine.
Let us be next to each other,
interlaced like the heart's duality.
Touch me as God would touch the clay
and I will turn into a human being in a flash.

How can I escape, sweetheart,
when my heart's fire runs in all directions,
in speech and in silence,
so that you may be born a million times
in ages of greater strangeness.
O my blond forest, unite your fear
and mine strongly;
let your bones enter the tunnel of my bones,
then pull the remainder of your body in
and enter.
There will be long, narrow passages

in front of you, and Truth lies in the narrowest.
Take care and don't forget that you're going there
to scream,
to reject,
and not to bend.

Behold, the ghosts of the world are advancing,
so hide
and steal a look from the cracks of windows
or keyholes.
Whenever a god passes, applaud him
or climb on the edges of trucks
and shout: the moon's blood is from his blood
and its flesh is from his fabric.
But when will you come
so that I may tell you secretly
who the real god is?

The harsh rain was singing a military march
and shooting its bullets at the roots.
(How were you born in the midst of that fight?)
O God, command the valley
to take us to the original fountain,
and the mountain to take us to the real summit.
If the great darkness flees from the whip
and Truth lies flat on the executioner's floor
and the alphabet turns into unfair laws
and the poets turn into dust on the tables,
I will fold up my time and hide it in my bosom.
And if I see my shadow, I will think I am crawling
in order to gnaw on the dry bread of famine.
But two feet of stone can't walk.

Behold, noon is like hard concrete
and the spears of ice cut through the limbs.
Souls that taste like bread are crunched by the air.

A million women are your mother, my little one,
and they untie the string
of the horizon for you so that
death may become temporary, like sleep.

Let us dig up the slaves and bondsmen,
and let us bury the masters of hunger;
the fountains have opened their white mouth
and sent forth their tragic call.
(How terrible giving up the soul is!)
Yet the fountains leave geranium
and damascene roses in their trace.

What angry power is it
that tears out the fetuses from our wombs?
Let that flood
weave the bed of our loneliness.
What will its beast do upon stumbling
while the winter, like an eagle,
beats it with its wings?
In its body are millions of waves,
a chronic eagerness for the earth,
while the drowning mariners
come out of the gates of Time's water
with a sharper vision,
the lines of their ribs visible on their backs,
and they say:
the forests that have entered the sea
will bear leaves again
because their heart does not die.

Thus, when Time locks its door to everyone,
I will enter the train of death, pleased;
I will hold the string of absence and pull it,
and my imaginary self will come,
my self that was born of the wombs of mirrors

with their frightening and obscure words.
But frightened bodies secrete what will save them,
and, behold, the door of peace opens
between Paradise and the Earth.
Life alone can take us away and return us.
Death has perished
and worms have become extinct.
The human stone is split so that
new generations will be born.
As for me,
I will withhold the eggs of reproduction
in my womb
to live thus as virgins,
so that spring may not be pressed
by force into the spray of bullets.

Translated from the Arabic by Issa J. Boullata

ABOUT THE AUTHOR

Saniyya Saleh (1935–85) was born in Mousiaf, a city on the west coast of Syria. She studied English literature at the American Lebanese University in Beirut, Lebanon, where she met her future husband, the Syrian poet and playwright Muhammad Maghout. She wrote her last poems while losing her battle with illness. She won several awards for her poetry, including the al-Nahar and al-Hasnaa awards. Her works include the short story collection *al-Ghobar* (The Dust) and the poetry collections *al Zaman al-Daiq* (The Tight Time), *Hiber al-Idaam* (The Assassination Ink), *Qasaed* (Poems), and *Zacar al-Ward* (The Male Rose), the last of which was published after her death.

Adania Shibli is one of my most favorite Arab writers not because she is a fellow Palestinian—although that certainly helps—but because I simply believe she has created for herself in recent years something that, especially for a young writer, is hard to achieve: a solid literary presence, a distinct voice, and a unique style.

Born in a small village in Galilee, she has lived for many years in Ramallah and Arab Jerusalem, and her narrative voice resonates with the inner geographies of the Palestinian space, in a painful and unflinching precision. Her language is that of a writer who has turned her back on the ready-made structures and prevalent rhetoric of modern Arabic literature, and trusts nothing but her inner voices and her amazing intuitiveness when it comes to the hard-to-master and hard-to-tame Arabic language.

I first came across her name in the February 1997 issue of the Haifa-based literary magazine Masharef, *edited at the time by the late Palestinian novelist Emile Habiby. She wrote what could be described as a narrative essay on* Chronicle of Disappearance (sijill ikhtifaa'), *a movie by the Palestinian filmmaker Elia Suleiman. "I stood bewildered," the opening sentence went, "contemplating the only shirt I had that would be suitable to wear to the screening of* Chronicle of Disappearance, *because two stains of oil were imprinted on it last night, after a piece of tomato fell off my fork when I was having my salad." The title of the movie,* Chronicle of Disappearance, *reminds Shibli of a laundry stain remover she has in her closet, whose only function and vocation is to make stains of oil* disappear. *"Despite my disbelief in this type of fairy tale," the piece went on, "I sprinkled the powder and the two stains disappeared after a quarter of an hour; I put the shirt on and went to the movie four hours later."*

The opening of her first novel, Masaas (Touching), *which was written two years later, introduces a fragile little girl, standing alone in her landscape, in the shadow of an old, rusty water tank. She touches one of the supporting legs of the tank, and tiny, cold stains of rust stick to her palm. She stretches her hand out of the shade to warm it up in the sun, and her hand becomes sprinkled with shiny dots of shimmering gold. This is, to my mind, what Adania Shibli does with her amazingly and beguilingly simple language: making the rusty stains of reality disappear, and then making them reappear in writing as stains of gold.*

—ANTON SHAMMAS

FAINT HINTS OF TRANQUILLITY

March 29, 2002

I awoke to the invasion of the room by a dazzling wave of light, which made me think that I hadn't drawn the curtains before turning in last night; then I went back to sleep.

I awoke again to the nervous and frightening shaking of the bathroom door, then noticed the sound of the falling rain and the patter of its drops against the walls of the house and the window-panes, and a great fear overtook me that the rain might sweep my house away. Would that be possible? I fell asleep again.

I woke up for good at twenty past eight, more or less, and immediately started to calculate the number of hours I'd slept, less the time I'd been awake, and tried to convince myself that it was seven hours, so as to assume a feeling of physical rest and go on with my day.

I was pleased when I went to the kitchen and discovered that the sink was empty of any dishes that I needed to wash. It seems that sometimes I'm not a bad person at all, but one who's capable of doing things that later prove to be self-beneficial, because when I cleaned the kitchen yesterday afternoon I had no idea that it would cause me such happiness this morning. But did this mean that I hadn't since used any plate or knife or even a cup? Hadn't I eaten anything?

Then I remembered that I'd been invited to dinner last night; of course I'd eaten. A sense of tranquillity and peace came back to me.

The coffeepot on the stove, I went to the bathroom. I turned the faucet on and the water gushed out firmly, tenaciously, coldly. I need to wash my face with cold water so as to seal its pores. A lady who sat next to me in the sauna once told me that Jerusalem was a very filthy city, and that a prolonged stay in the sauna would cause the skin pores to open up and let pollution infiltrate the body as soon as you leave for home.

The water was still flowing coldly. I cupped some of it and lifted it up to my face; that's when I first saw my face reflected in the mirror above the faucet. Oh my god! How hideous my hair, as if it had spent all night in a triangular mold.

That's it, then. I'll never wake up and find it neatly done, as most actresses do.

Then I noticed a shade of black under my eyes; I applied some water again, hoping it would disappear, then I wiped them slowly and gently, but the dark rings wouldn't go away. After desperate scrutiny, I gave up and started to see in them faint hints of that woman's eyes.

March 23, 2002

I don't know what her name was, but it could have been Salma. We met her when we, a Finnish journalist and I, were visiting Balatah Camp.

All that could be seen of her was a dark shade of black under her eyes, which didn't fit the liveliness and enthusiasm of her body, and looked like a makeup oversight.

She sat next to a pile of covers from whose depths came a scary moaning, and she went on patting the pile to no avail, as darkness descended on all sides. Even the lit lantern, hanging from a nail hammered into the ceiling, was emitting darkness and cold and frustration into the room where we were sitting. With a voice that had no connection to this world, she then started to talk about the night when the Israeli army invaded the camp, then her house, while pointing at the gaping holes that the soldiers had blown through her walls. She'd occasionally scream at her grandchildren and at her husband, huddled under the covers, to keep quiet, so she could figure out what we were inquiring about.

Her screaming, and the dark rings under her eyes, undoubtedly hinted at extreme fatigue that she refused to give in to, and wouldn't even acknowledge in the first place. She was behaving responsibly, trying to rein in the loss and destruction and, on top of that, to insist that there was still something worth living for.

After a while, and at the request of the journalist, she took us around to see the holes that the soldiers had left behind as the house was set suddenly afire when the main electric line was hit by a splinter from a hand grenade that they threw into the house, and they ran away, leaving behind them a fire that burned up the half-finished wreckage.

Along with her children and grandchildren, she had been forced to evacuate the house when the army stormed in, but her husband remained nearby watching the house, and when he saw it burning he rushed over and tried in vain to put out the flames. He was asphyxiated and lost consciousness but did not die; just something happened to his brain because it didn't get enough oxygen for a long while, and he lost his mind.

Salma ascends the stairs ahead of us to show us what the flames have done, and her white headscarf, as inconsolable as her soul, descends and rises and waves, comforting me in a sweetness and gentleness that defies this no-outlet misery.

Everything was burned. All her personal papers were burned, and so was her identity card—for her the most terrifying thing of all. She talked about it, neither believing nor comprehending that she's bereft of her ID now, and I don't translate this to the journalist for whom all this material destruction is more important than a burned identity card. But for Salma the card was the major thing! Maybe the only and last thing that acknowledged her existence as a human being.

She turns around to descend the stairs and we follow her, and now her white headscarf soars and flutters and undulates sluggishly, so I lag a bit behind until it settles and it's my turn to descend the stairs. And when it's time, I step down, putting my left foot on the first stair, only to realize that it had sneaked under my foot and that I was stepping on its hem. Oh my god, what have I done?

Salma turns around toward me, because her headscarf, stuck under my foot, jerks her head back. She doesn't say anything, and I don't know what to say. I quickly lift up my foot and try to get hold of the headscarf so I can shake my dirty shoe's print off it or—the least I could do—kiss it; but in vain. It takes wing, flutters away in the air. Both of them, Salma and her headscarf, have already gone ahead of me, while I clumsily loiter inside my embarrassment.

March 29, 2002

That light headscarf was the last patch of white in the camp's pitch-darkness, and kindled a faint hope in me, like its lightness, while the white of the clouds, heaping up in the sky, filled me with utter weariness that increased each time I leaned out the western window of my kitchen, waiting for their procession to end, but they kept moving—one cloud after another, endlessly, void of any warmth.

March 25, 2002

It doesn't matter how naive this feeling seems, but the day comes when one envies the clouds their movement as they glide against the sky, and the birds their freedom of passage from one place to another.

I took my eyes off the sky and went back to looking at the long line of cars in which we were stuck at the Bethlehem checkpoint. On my right, men stood crammed together behind a stone hedge in front of which a soldier, examining the identity cards he was holding, ordered each and every one to unbutton their jackets and lift up their shirts. I wouldn't be able to stand there, I'm thinking, and I'm thinking if there are any other possible roads left besides this one, but can't think of any.

I look to the left this time, and fixate on a large puddle of mud whose stillness is not threatened by anything, and it really looks like a melted, delicious piece of chocolate. When I get home, I make a decision: I'll go to buy chocolate with hazelnuts and almonds. The reflection of the clouds and the blue of the sky return now to the muddy water, and to my mind return the pictures of the wreckage of the houses that were hit during the shelling of the city of Bethlehem, in which the destruction seems primordial, as if the city has never given shelter to any living soul for even one day, though only a month ago I sat on the balcony of one of these houses and had a drink of water. The water had a homely taste, and was offered to me by the lady of the house.

March 28, 2002

I hadn't finished my cup of coffee, but was ashamed to say so to the girl who'd lifted the tray with the other cups and walked away toward the kitchen. My coffee!

I came back to my senses and to the two persons with whom I was sitting, the Finnish journalist and one of the political leaders of Hamas, who had just taken a shower; his hair was still wet.

More than three weeks ago, on March 4, 2002, the Israeli government tried to assassinate him; the Israeli army shot two ground-to-ground missiles at his car while it drove down a street in Ramallah. He wasn't in the car, but his wife and three of his kids were, on their way back from school. He was at home when he heard the explosion, and wondered what it was. Then the news reached him. He went out to the scene of the incident; many people had arrived before him. He elbowed his way through, got closer, and closer. He wanted to see them and he got closer, but he couldn't find anything. All he could see were the torn parts of a demolished car. He didn't see anything else. He didn't see his wife or his two daughters and son. They all had turned into shreds.

He said that at that moment he stood there in silence, praying within himself that he wouldn't collapse, wouldn't lose his mind. People carried him away.

In the same incident, two other kids, in the car behind, were also killed.

March 29, 2002

I went back to bed with my coffee, away from the kitchen and its thoughts. But I can't run away, because as the coffee sediment settles at the bottom of the pot, numbness takes over my senses again, involuntarily, along with the memories of recent days.

March 24, 2002

Standing, I'm waiting for the journalist to conclude her conversation with one of the men so we can leave Balatah Camp. In the meantime, I asked one of the kids, who were standing next to me, with no apparent reason, how old he was, and he stretched out his whole open palm at me and said, "Five years!" Suddenly he got closer to me and said that he'd seen an Israeli soldier smoking and creating rings in the air when exhaling the smoke. The soldiers had occupied their house during the last wave of invasions, and for three days had put three families under arrest all together in one room, guarded by that smoking soldier, and that kid is still amazed to this very day by what the soldier was able to do with successive rings of smoke.

March 27, 2002

A suicidal operation carried out by one of the military wing activists of the Hamas movement, at a hotel in Netanya, causing the death of twenty-nine Israelis and the injury of dozens of others on the eve of Passover.

Anguish is weighing down on my chest and I can't breathe properly. I don't want to talk to anyone. But after ten minutes I want to call a friend, I don't know why. The phone rings at the other end, but nothing happens.

The young man who carried out the operation is from Tulkarm. In the last wave of reinvasions, the Israeli army killed some fifty people in that camp and arrested more than six hundred, during al-Adha holiday. Chekhov says that a pistol hanging on the wall in act I must eventually go off in act 3. But, in reality, when the smell of blood spreads out here, it's bound to spread out there.

Tonight I realize that the occupation hasn't only occupied our bodies but, rather, it has occupied our beings and filled them up with the "ease to kill."

All I dream is that my dreams be less ugly than life.

March 26, 2002

We finished work early. I drove the journalist to the hotel, then sat down to ponder the rest of my day. I had nearly three hours at my disposal, before sunset, during which I could wander around, for when night falls bullets fly, even from within the toilet.

Ramallah?!

I signaled left, then right, then immediately left and then right. Then right, and right again, left, right, left, right, left, and I'm not aware of my increasing speed until the wheel starts shaking under my hands. One hundred fifty kilometers per hour, while the speed limit is eighty. I look around me: there's no traffic police, and what's more—there's no traffic.

I'm the only one, then, who can move, can pass through checkpoints and enter Nablus and Ramallah and Tulkarm and get out of all of them because I have a temporary journalist card, which is issued (albeit grudgingly) to Palestinian journalists who carry an Israeli passport, while there are more than three million Palestinians who can't do that, as they are under siege.

And with this quiet and desolation over the streets, the siege looks more real.

Suddenly, when I look left, I realize that for a while I have been driving on the wrong side of the road.

And so my sense of orientation is replaced by a sense of alienation.

And now where to?

I slowly drive the car along the main street of Ramallah. Maybe to my friend and her twin kids?

No sooner have I arrived than my friend starts to tell me about the days they've spent besieged at home while the tanks surround the house, and I feel that I can't take these siege stories anymore. Everyone has their own story, and I can't help but feel helpless and weary when I hear them. I excuse myself and say that I have to be going. She sees me out, together with her daughter and son, and we pass through the garden and examine the flowers around the house, and then we lift our heads toward the sky, trying to guess where the chirping birds are. The clouds are fluffy and light, divided into small squares, and the little girl points at them and says they look like a tank.

I didn't get what she meant. And to help me understand, she pushed herself ahead of me, vigorously leading me to the street across the garden's gate. When we got there she pointed her tiny finger at the tracks that the tank had left on the asphalt. The tracks resembled the shape of the clouds. As if a tank had really crossed the sky, leaving the clouds looking the way they looked. I told her the sky envies Ramallah and wants to have what they have; but she laughed timidly at my petty deception and clung to my leg.

My friend was standing at the car's door, arms crossed, as if feeling cold. She was moving her eyes, as she usually does, between the sky and the trees, and suddenly she sighed and said, "I'm very tired."

I got into the car and drove away. I don't know what I could have done otherwise.

I drove the car, turning a thought inside my head about a last attempt to call on a friend who's in her eighties, at least.

When I got there the garden brimmed with the scent of violets. I knocked on her door. Most of the flowers were in full bloom. She didn't answer. I started writing her a note to leave on her door or among the flowers. Suddenly I heard behind me a soft patter of feet followed by a call: "Hey little Miss."

I smiled and turned back. She was a petite woman carrying so many years, dressed according to the current fashion: a skirt slightly above the knee, and knee-high boots. She said, all smiles, that she'd seen me knocking on the door, and thought maybe she should come over and tell me that Miss D had moved away to a seniors' home more than two weeks before, because she fell and remained unconscious for more than a day and no one found out, and then she told me the address of the seniors' home.

Miss D is on the third floor; a nurse went up with me.

She was sitting, silently, watching an Egyptian movie together with some other ladies. Her hair was longer than usual, so she looked lonelier and more neglected. Even the look behind her glasses carried hints of loneliness and resignation.

Much as I was surprised to see her, she was surprised to see me, and immediately asked how I'd found out where she was. Having told her, there was nothing left to talk about. Everything was sad and old. I wished I could kidnap her from there and shield her from it all. She's the special D, and not just any old woman in that place.

Instead, I glued my eyes to the TV screen.

After a while, one of the old ladies stretched out her hand toward the plastic flowers on a table in the middle of the room, and started to pat them, then pulled her hand back saying, "Pity they're not real."

March 29, 2002

It was approaching nine, so I turned on the radio to hear the weather broadcast, maybe there'd be good news regarding the sun.

Two hundred tanks have surrounded the Muqata'ah building in Ramallah, and Arafat was besieged on one of its floors.

I went back to the kitchen and remembered that I hadn't paid attention to the weather broadcast. But within seconds it started bucketing down.

The petals, then, have fallen from the almond trees before I had a chance to touch them.

All I wish for from this life before it ends is to join the spring and enjoy its bloom, even though I don't know how or where or by what right.

I also wish I could snap out of this apathy that I've ended up in, where eating or not eating are one and the same, speaking and not speaking, loving and not loving and—along the same lines—living and dying. Even my friends under siege, I no longer care about them. The lingering feeling becomes harder than any feeling of guilt, and riskier; for if I called them it would only be because I want to be sure their count is still the same, that's all.

I leave the window and stand facing the fridge, thinking. After quite a lot of thinking I find out that all the ideas I have for supporting my people at this time would be to change my e-mail password from the name of my last boyfriend to "Arafat." But I don't know what the hint would be for him, so as to remember my password in case I forget.

Translated from the Arabic by Anton Shammas

ABOUT THE AUTHOR

Adania Shibli was born in Palestine in 1974. She has been publishing since 1996 in literary magazines in the Arab world and Europe. Shibli has twice been awarded the Young Writer's Award of Palestine by the A. M. Qattan Foundation for her two novels *Masaas* (Touching), al-Adab, 2002, translated into French as *Reflets sur un mur blanc* (Actes-sud, 2004), and *Kulluna Ba'eed Bethat al Miqdar 'an al Hub* (We Are All Equally Far from Love), al-Adab, 2004, and is working toward a Ph.D. in media and cultural studies from the University of East London.

HASSAN KHADER

Hassan Khader is a poet, author, and translator. He has always been part of the Palestinian liberation movement and has lived through its wars of the past three decades. He was born in Gaza to parents who had recently, in the Nakba of 1948, been made refugees; his father from a village in southern Palestine, his mother from Qatra, now the Israeli Gedera. After an exile of more than twenty years he was able to return to Palestine after the Oslo Accords and in 1996 started editing al-Karmel, *the literary magazine started by the poet Mahmoud Darwich in Beirut in 1981. Khader has continued, from Ramallah, to bring out* al-Karmel *twice a year even though—under Israeli curfew—he has been known to send his proofs to the printers in an ambulance. In 1996 Khader won the first Palestinian Award for Literature for his essays. His publications include* Time and Hostages: Readings in Palestinian Literature, Land of the Deer, *and* Identity of the Other, *which deals with the crisis of identity in Israeli fiction. He has also translated Israeli writer David Grossman's* The Smile of the Lamb *into Arabic and has edited and translated* The Palace of Shattered Vessels, *an anthology of Israeli writers.*

Hassan Khader has said that he feels that even though chaos instigates a fictional response, it poses the danger that the writing it produces will be too raw, too premature. His strategy is to create a distance between himself and what's happening, "trying to let events 'cool down' a little, sometimes allowing a space of time (not just an emotional or psychological space) to assert itself; these are all formulae to lessen the risk."

And, like many Arab novelists and poets, he has turned to the essay. If poetry is historically the first art form of the Arabs, the essay is a close second. But the essay today is often subtitled a "fragment," for it is a fragmented literary response to events that Arab writers feel the need to speak to immediately without waiting for the desired transfiguration into fiction or poetry.

In this piece, "Shards of Reality and Glass" (published in Arabic in al-Karmel, *Autumn 2002), Khader examines what it is like to experience* the Israeli occupation and Palestinian reactions to it on the streets and watch it on television at the same time, and discusses the mutually formative relationship between reality and its image.

Jean Genet, in his account of the Palestinian revolution, Un Captif amoureux, *recalls a moment in 1984 when he expressed to a Palestinian friend a fear, a premonition maybe, that in the prolonged absence of victory, the young Palestinian* fidai *(freedom fighter) could metamorphose into the Islamist militant. Khader, himself perforce an idealistic young fighter in 1982 Beirut, describes an aspect of this metamorphosis. He accuses the media of giving dominance, during the early days of the Palestinian Intifada of September 2000, to the Islamist groups, initiating a process that led to the marginalization of all other Palestinian voices and the militarization of the Intifada. He analyzes the Islamist groups' use of ritual, spectacle, and symbol and the effect this has had on the Palestinians' quest for freedom.*

The essay moves among the Israeli invasion of al-Birah/Ramallah in March/April 2002, an earlier incursion the previous October, and the invasion of Lebanon twenty years earlier.

—Ahdaf Soueif

SHARDS OF REALITY AND GLASS

Jihad, my neighbor, recorded what happened each day with the eye of a documentary filmmaker; a witness careful to back his words with the authority of proof. I used to cross the two meters between our apartments twice a day: once in the morning, the other at night. The empty pages in the school exercise book he kept on the sofa next to the TV set dwindled in pace with the enthusiasm of the newsreader on the screen and the length of the newscast.

It seemed absurd because the war already came to us in two different ways. The first—the actual—was made up of the sounds of shells and heavy military machinery and jets and helicopters circling in the air. The second was the image of all this reflected at us by the TV screen: vistas of corpses and wrecked cars and burning buildings and angry protestors in far-off cities, alongside the faces of correspondents whose mannerisms and even taste in clothes we got to know really well.

The screen creates the illusion that what it shows is taking place somewhere else, even though the sounds you hear are real, physically threatening in their proximity. But at night you shake off that illusion; the eye takes over from the camera and charges the individual experience with sensation and immediacy: the war is what is happening here and now, not what is reported on the news. We hear an explosion and rush to the window—sometimes to the roof—to see fire slicing through the dark with a scalpel of light.

The immediate result of living the separation between the real and its image (apart from how difficult it becomes to deal with reality) is that it brings home to you your personal marginalization, your terrible helplessness: the war is being fought against you, and is being fought in your name, yet you can find absolutely nothing in it that relates to you.

It was not, I think, a borrowing from Hollywood to remember that peasant surrounded by Roman soldiers in this same place two thousand years ago, when six days after the big incursion in April,[1] they allowed the citizens to go out to buy food—for two hours.

The tank wheels had churned up canyons of mud in the dirt road that almost slips off the shoulder of the hill into the valley. Pedestrian perseverance has tamed this space into a connection between two places. But it remains a space inhabited by hilltops and the ghosts of houses that appear—as you draw closer—displaced, improvised, temporary, and chaotic.

[1]In April 2002 the Israeli army reinvaded cities and towns in the West Bank that had been run by the Palestinian Authority. Ramallah/al-Birah was invaded in March.

Here, in a field of mud, where legs sink into a dough made soft and sticky by the morning rain, in this semistreet connecting two places, a military jeep and an armored personnel carrier swoop down on you. First you hear the snorts of the engines. You turn. You see no faces, only a black muzzle aiming at you and the spatter of mud flying under the toiling wheels and the metal belts.

You pretend—you the citizen who is allowed to move freely for two hours, as the loudspeakers have assured you, who is carrying fruit and vegetables in transparent plastic bags—you pretend that it doesn't concern you. But you don't pull your legs out of the mud because the jeep is blocking your way.

And in a flash the scene changes: you see the Roman soldiers surrounding a peasant from these hills two thousand years before today's permission to move freely for two hours. You almost hear the neighing of the horses, the impatient stamp of their hooves, their breath, which the cold air transforms into wispy clouds, the shining helmets of the soldiers, the armor that covers their chests and shoulders, their leather sandals, their shields, their swords, short and unsheathed.

A Hollywood memory no doubt; a trick of the imagination. But what makes the memory go back two thousand years at this moment when the chances of life and death are equal?

Months have passed since this scene took place, yet I still wonder at the efficiency of the imagination that turns a desperate helplessness into a visual image that reality cannot deny. This is how it always was in this place. And there's nothing to say that event did not happen on the shoulder of one of these hills, on an ancient day, when the place discovered its image in the mirror of time. Not many things have changed since that day, not the citizens, nor the invaders, only the instruments of war.

Even the name curls—like a worn old shell—around its first nucleus, thrown down by a geological accident sixteen kilometers north of Jerusalem. Al-Birah,[2] in which I live, whose citizens the

---

[2] al-Birah: the well (Arabic).

invaders address through loudspeakers, is Bairot, whose name the Canaanites carved from the water-wells planted among the rocks. The Romans inherited the place's name and its wells, as did the Byzantines and the Arabs, with small adjustments that did not damage the name too much but smashed or marginalized its extremities across centuries in the fight for survival and the wars over water.

And as the roots of mountain trees, thirsty, tortured by the heat of the sun, sniff out the smell of water in the pores of volcanic rock, so the name sniffs out its ancient heritage and holds on to it. In al-Birah there is a neighborhood called al-Balu'.[3] Perhaps a literal translation for an old Aramaic word. Or perhaps it was an attempt by the Arabs to describe a dip in the ground in which rainwater collected. A political accident dictated that al-Balu' should become the border for Area A[4] according to the absurd division of this land; the border on the other side of which the invaders have stood since the beginning of the armed conflict two years ago, and that, last October, became their gateway to al-Birah and Ramallah.

But the imagination is not a free agent, rather it is a laboratory that develops images chosen by the individual. For in another war, twenty years before this one, I was in a besieged city and for three months in which the chances of life and death were also equal, I was untroubled by helplessness, or by the sense of living between two realities: one hypothetical, on

---

[3]al-Balu': the place that swallows [water] (Arabic).

[4]Under the Oslo agreements of 1993 Palestinian cities and towns on the West Bank and in Gaza (as well as East Jerusalem) were placed under the Palestinian Authority. They became known as "Area A." These were encircled by narrow belts controlled jointly by the Palestinian Authority and the Israeli army: "Area B." Everything that remained was "Area C" and was controlled by the Israeli army. This was meant to be an interim stage toward the redeployment of the Israeli army to the 1967 borders of Israel, but during the years between Oslo and the Palestinian Intifada (uprising) of September 2000, Area C saw a massive expansion in the building of Israeli settlements.

TV screens through which I watched myself, the other real insofar as it carried within it the possibility of turning my own person into a casualty of war.

Perhaps this existential dissonance we feel today is the result of a simple—though frightening—truth: this war is only a war insofar as it conforms to the definition of war in official statements, newscasts, and the great metaphors of history. And this war is only a war to the degree that the discourse that each national group uses to describe itself eliminates the specificity of the individual experience. This is why it is not possible to grasp the real, the actual, the daily, pulsing with life like a wounded animal, but only its image in language, in representations that show the varying skills of people engaged in imagining a war.

Doubtless it was an ancient memory—similar, with some slight differences, to what al-Balu' has swallowed of the images of war and the arts of advancing and retreating across centuries too numerous to count—which made young men, most of whom were not yet twenty, take up a position one day behind a building at the end of the road that almost slipped off the shoulder of the hill into the valley.

They were dressed in clean military uniforms and carried guns for some of which they had improvised straps that might have—in the past—belonged to leather handbags. Their costume showed a clear concern to achieve a festive image of the fighter: magazines for bullets hung on the chests of dark green waistcoats, flasks for water, an extra magazine for bullets attached to the gun's original magazine with sticky tape in different colors, and, in some cases of understandable exaggeration, two extra magazines taped to their guns' original, and so on.

Familiar things; as though the past had not quite passed. Twenty years ago, on days like these, we too were looking for colored sticky tape. Our suits were clean and loose-fitting, and the care with which the gun straps were made, long enough so elbows could lean on the guns as they hung from necks, was as evident then as it is now. Imad never understood why I suddenly picked a quarrel with him as we walked, on that distant night, from the

Mazra'a seafront to the Cola Bridge.[5] We saw each other in the light of the flares set off by the invaders, and his ghostlike shape as he leaned his elbows on his gun suddenly made me angry: how faithfully it replicated scenes retained by the memory from film and fiction and the experience of living under occupation.

Nobody can escape the seduction of imagining, especially in those moments when the individual being comes into searing contact with a great national metaphor. In those rare moments, identification is an act of will, an act washed with the tragic sense of the person who finds himself standing at a particular point in history with only one option. It overflows with a sweet and painful romanticism. Yet the dynamics of memory and imagination are complex and independent, and what the days choose from among them may not be in harmony, necessarily, with the grand metaphors. And, possibly because of this, may provide a truer guide to these metaphors than any discourse.

But the picture this time jars in a way that is hard to understand. Or that at least is what the sight of these young men— these boys—suggested, when they started to open fire on a position of the invaders that was out of the range of their guns. The invaders let loose the heavy artillery, forcing them to shelter behind blocks of rock: parts of man-made terraces that had flourished with vegetables and olives two thousand years ago. One of the old names of al-Birah is Beit Labwat,[6] so perhaps lions lived here, long ago, and waited for their prey by the water springs.

I asked one of them through the kitchen window why he was firing at something he couldn't see. He said he wanted the invaders to fire back so he could pinpoint their position. A sentence both brave and naive, enough to make one look for a safe corner in the house and wait for the tank shell that would define their position, yes, but would leave no trace of those who wished

[5]Locations on the seafront in West Beirut.

[6]Beit: house or home (Arabic). Labwat: lionesses (Arabic). Literally, "Home of the Lionesses."

it defined. That shell came a few days later when the invaders decided to cut through the illusory thread that separated Area A from areas B and C.

As for Imad and me, in that past time, we did not know where they were exactly. Nobody asked us to know, when we took up position in the doorway of a building near the Cola Bridge on our first day as fighters. The entrance was clean and had colored pots with flowers in them, so we turned an empty cigarette pack into an ashtray and hung about it for a while till we grew tired of being excessively clean. We spent the first few hours chatting, pausing when we heard an explosion, commenting on what we heard on the small transistor radio. We could see young people like us in the entrances of nearby buildings. Then the sounds of shelling, drawing closer before nightfall, forced us to cross the threshold and sit behind the glass door, which would soon fragment into scattered shards.

We were luckier than these boys were: the first shell hit the fourth floor and the second gave us enough time to run down to the cellar. But the sudden shelling, that day last October, gave these boys just enough time to retreat to a building still under construction. The invaders cut the illusory thread at five in the morning: they came down from the hills that overlooked al-Balu' from two sides, tightened the noose around the neighborhood, and advanced toward Ramallah.

At first it seemed just another dream, the roar of tanks like massive metal waves rolling down the hills. But the roar went on, its intensity forcing open sleepers' eyes to see, from the window, in a dim mist that filled the world, a tank like an animal from a prehistoric age blocking the horizon. A few minutes to take in the situation and then—as in previous times and times to come—the question: what now? The mind races to find a place of safety, then stops. All choices seem absurd. The cramps in the stomach cease, and the tension in the body recedes, as though it has returned to its original home, in the memory.

In the end, after the noise of the neighbors and the quick exchanges, body and soul are overwhelmed by a helplessness that takes a person back to his loneliness and fragility: a creature vulnerable to chance and fate. Like a bull in a Spanish corrida who stands and stares at his killer, alone and silent, before he falls.

And staring was a kind of flirtation with death. The shadows of three of the boys were running toward that building still being built, and it seemed that the giant metal animal, belching fire onto another spot, did not notice the ghostly figures diving and floating in the dark like bodies in a lake of ashes. They reached the shelter of the building, they waited till the day grew brighter and the tank stopped shelling and moving, and they fired on it with their guns with the long leather straps, even though in the day there was sufficient light to pinpoint the position of the invaders, and in wisdom sufficient reason to think again. They opened fire.

The Red Crescent crew brought out the body of one of the boys after an hour, and brought the other two out on stretchers minutes later. The invaders circled the corpse and the two wounded bodies. In the evening we watched the scene again on television, among other scenes that made it recede into a small detail in a colorful tragedy, removed and distant, as though it were of concern only to the viewers in us, never admitting that we ourselves were permanent candidates to become further small details in the same tragedy.

Was the boy I had spoken to out of my kitchen window among those bodies laid out on stretchers wet with blood? Had he managed, at last, to determine their position? Or was the attempt to determine the position just an excuse, a lie, to justify making holes in the air with angry bullets?

Many things have not changed. Twenty years ago an airplane was chasing a military car on the seafront near the American University in Beirut. In the car were three fighters. One of them crouched on a low seat behind an antiaircraft gun. The second stood next to him, and the driver was behind the wheel. The one behind the gun fired every time the car broke cover from the shadow of a building. The driver drove forward, backward, maneuvering, turning violently in all directions. The third man watched the road and the sky. And the airplane, like a hunting dog, hid behind a light mist, or raced away into the horizon, then swooped in out of nowhere.

Finally, the plane tired of the game. The car did not tire. It came out of hiding. Its occupants looked at the sky. Now what? The man behind the gun lowered the muzzle and fired toward Jounieh:[7] a silent phantom at the edge of the water, beyond reach of angry bullets making holes in the air.

But making holes in the air now takes place in the age of the image and the manufacture of news. In this context we lose the fine line that distinguishes an event that becomes a subject for an image from an event that seduces the image into becoming its favorite subject. It started with the flags in the demonstrations, when certain satellite channels started focusing on the flags of a particular group to give the viewer the illusion that it was this group's influence that brought the Palestinians out onto the street. And we were supposed to believe this because we saw it on the TV news, even though we did not see it in the street.

What we did actually see raised some questions: visual coverage, spectacle, became one of the undeclared aims of the demonstrations. And the Demonstration became—with the passing days—a complex institution with a rigid sequence involving the first rows of marchers, the nature of the messages on the banners, the flags, the route—and obvious skill in image-making. And because of this it soon diminished as a popular demonstration, and yet it appeared regularly on the TV news, which soon found a new attraction in elements more exciting and dramatic than flags.

Nothing generates more adrenaline in the blood than the sight of blood itself. Blood: always in danger of becoming a kind of

[7]Prosperous Lebanese town on the bay across from Beirut, home to the famous Casino du Liban before the civil war. During the civil war it was the stronghold of the Phalangists; it has made a roaring comeback as an entertainment city.

teaching aid, proving the eloquence and transcendence of the Karbala moment,[8] the moment of sacrifice. To be in the right has become an industry. And it is amazing how this industry has degenerated since those early doses of adrenaline. Palestinian television became insatiable, its cameras clinging for hours each day to amputated limbs, spilled intestines, charred corpses, smears of blood on hospital beds, in streets, in houses, and in morgues, as though it feared that the viewer might slip from its grasp or that the spectacle itself might slip from its abattoir-like function. It was not, of course, unique among satellite channels. It just did more of what they all were doing.

The images, eloquent as they were, were not the only tool used to manufacture rightness. No. Analysts were used and commentators and spokespeople, all of whom managed to destroy the

---

[8]Karbala, which lies about 100 kilometers south of Baghdad on the Euphrates, witnessed the most dramatic tragedy of early Muslim history. When the deeply unpopular Yazid ibn Mu'awiyah acceded to the caliphate (the leadership of the Muslim nation), a popular cry went up for al-Husayn, grandson of the Prophet, to challenge him for it. Under much pressure, al-Husayn, together with his family and some five hundred followers, left his exile in the Arabian Peninsula and moved toward Kufa (en route to the seat of the caliphate in Damascus) where he had been promised support. But Yazid sent out armies that blocked al-Husayn's progress and besieged him at Karbala on the second day of Muharram (the first month) of the Islamic year 61 (AD 680). What followed was a series of events that came to hold iconic significance: for eight days, in the month during which Arabs are forbidden to fight one another, the descendants of Muhammad were held hostage by Muslim armies. Within sight of the Euphrates they were denied water. Yazid demanded that al-Husayn swear allegiance. Al-Husayn couldn't do it: he was the grandson of the Prophet and the son of his beloved daughter, Fatima. He was the son of the near-mythic Imam Ali; how could he swear allegiance to a corrupt ruler who was, moreover, the grandson of the man who had been the Prophet's most determined enemy? He could not do it. He urged his family and followers to leave since, as he said, it was only his own head that was demanded by Yazid. None would leave him. The standoff ended on the tenth day of Muharram when Yazid's men killed al-Husayn and most of his family. This icon, the person pushed into a historic moment, convinced of his rightness, assured of his own destruction, and yet unable to surrender, able only to die unbroken—this is the Karbala moment.

heritage of a Palestinian national movement going back eight decades. Decades in which it had accumulated, through trial and error, and always at enormous cost, a political culture distinguished by its pluralism and its richness.

The surrender of this heritage manifested itself in the collapse of political and ideological boundaries between factions that, until recently, had seen themselves as occupying opposite positions. Soon, the majority groups found themselves in a race to represent the discourse of the minority, to make use of the minority's tools, and to try to achieve an identification with it that would make of the boundaries of the past and the differing visions of the present and the future merely a passing phase in all their histories.

The success of the minority in hijacking the majority and the latter's embrace of the former could not have taken place but for a populist culture that started to show symptoms of corruption from the midnineties when it was possessed by the illusion of transforming itself into a civic religion for an emerging state. And that emerging state—which for the first time controlled media outlets, cultural and information institutes, and part of the region—was in its turn possessed by the mirage of fashioning an identity that served its immediate political purposes of control and crisis management along the same lines as other regimes in the Arab world. This kind of culture makes icons of specific people while the collective "people" are portrayed as of an unchanging essence, transcending the differences of class, the power struggles of political elites, and even social mobility. And, since the icon is a manifestation of the sacred, any disagreement about its nature or its form can be denounced as illegitimate. Individual conformity (i.e., mindlessness) becomes proof of true patriotism. Communal conformity (e.g., an instinctive following of the Demonstration) is proof that the abstract idea of national identity is manifesting itself in the expected image.

The ritual, therefore, with its ability to achieve conformity, to provide a good example, an educational spectacle, to deal with public affairs with expressions of family unity, to deny all possibilities of dissent, to give the illusion that it is the distillation of a complex wisdom and that it is more farsighted than can be seen by dissenters—all of which are patriarchal significations—the ritual comes to dominate the scene. This ritual/spectacle could not have been achieved outside the rhetorical and representational space of the experience of the militias: armed groups with an innate ability to split and procreate, reminding us of West Beirut in the few years preceding the Israeli invasion in 1982.

Against this background of conformity, resistance to the occupation was turned into the appearance of a war between two states. And Area A (i.e., the collection of city islands, whose water, bread, and access points were controlled by the invaders) behaved as though it were a state with boundaries difficult to penetrate: the invaders, it was claimed, would be "punished," and neither the Arabs nor the world would "accept" such invasion. It was not rare in this context to find commentators, analysts, and spokespeople coming out with statements and analyses that threatened the invaders with terrible consequences.

Such statements and analyses were uncritical, anti-intellectual, provincial, wishful, and unable to make the necessary connections between what was happening on the ground and the dynamics of changing regional and international circumstances. What was worse was the extent to which this discourse became a dead end, rejecting information and turning its back on a political awareness that, in the past, had seemed basic.

And since most of those statements and analyses came at that moment of union between a camera giving a wide public in Palestine and the Arab world its daily bread dipped in blood and anger and guilt, and the desire of analysts, commentators, and spokespeople to comment on events and sometimes to turn events themselves into a commentary on their words, the images succeeded in reducing the situation to visual set pieces accompanied by words doing the job of a musical score.

In certain cases we sank to the level of cheap melodrama when the events coupled with commentary triggered televised Arab campaigns that used emotional manipulation and skill in dramatizing reality in efforts to solicit donations for the Palestinians. We saw—in different parts of the Arab world—children handing over their coins, women donating their jewelry, and businessmen offering checks. Nobody cared that these campaigns were emotionally cheap and nationally humiliating—even when delegations arrived handing out checks in Gaza in televised ceremonies.

Arab tradition holds that charity is given in secret. And if the donations are meant to be even more noble than charity and of more profound significance, then surely the recipients should never be turned into television fodder? And surely that consideration should be more important than using these donations in the conscience-cleansing game? Even so, reality races, and the cameras race after it.

On the dusty road that almost slips off the shoulder of the hill into the valley, there appeared barricades of sandbags and iron crosses reminiscent of the photographs and films of the Second World War, hinting at the probable fate of a gunman sheltering from a tank shell behind a sandbag. I said to one of the leaders that barricades like these don't stop modern tanks and that young men taking up their positions behind those bags were being placed in the jaws of death. He told me that the aim was only to achieve a certain symbolism; that this was a political message to the Israelis that we are prepared to fight them if they try to enter.

It is hard to clear this kind of political message from the suspicion of posturing, for the symbol directs us toward a hypothetical reality at the cost of reality itself. In this case, the reality I witnessed in October 2001 when the invaders decided to cut the illusory thread and the first of their invasions took place. The tanks did not stop in the face of the iron crosses or the sandbags. The invaders used them, as well as the plentiful mud and stones—as we discovered when they lifted the curfew—to build huge barricades closing the street to cars and pedestrians. I have no idea how much money was wasted putting up those sandbags and crosses in the first place, or what other symbolic political messages were sent, or the exact figures for the human, emotional, and material losses resulting from this kind of mathematics. But understanding the dynamic by which an imagination in thrall to symbolism sets up its hypothetical reality, and understanding also the probable results of such an exercise, seem to me matters of great urgency.

Details, distinguishing marks, are the key to the spectacle. There was the Funeral pregnant with next day's Demonstration, and there was the Demonstration pregnant with next day's Funeral (at the forefront of which are the young masked men carrying their automatic weapons and papier-mâché models of antiarmor guns and models of explosive belts. They burn flags or effigies representing the enemies. They trample them underfoot, they fire into the air). This spectacle became television's favorite entertainment: it was efficiently imagined/imaged and it provided scope for analysts, commentators, and spokespeople to accompany it with the rhetoric of rightness.

For this hypothetical reality to take hold, reality itself had to be obliterated. In the rush to put forward a spectacle, educational, ethical, and symbolic, in love with the pulse of adrenaline in the blood, there was something that looked like collusion to ignore certain facts: for example, that the confrontation was taking place between an unarmed population and a powerful army, between a people suffering under occupation and an unconstrained colonial power.

A discourse about an "existential" conflict came to the fore as though the conflict were taking place between two parties equally able to harm each other, equally possessed of instruments of total threat, which led to mutual deterrence. And even though this discourse bore no relation to reality (since the Palestinians' desire for freedom does not present an existential danger for the Israeli state but only threatens the existence of the occupation), the militias reproduced their hypothetical reality: the desire for freedom, in its rhetorical and visual representations, was expressed as an attempt to decapitate the state, instead of being represented truthfully and in keeping with the time and place as an attempt to unlock the fist of occupation from the throat of the people.

In attempting to prove the truth of these representations of a hypothetical reality, young men (and women) deployed the most extreme instruments of self-harm.

It was as though I had woken from a dream or arrived from a faraway place. The face was beautiful enough to seduce one into believing in a possible heaven, and the smell and color of the sticky blood on the shirt indicated that something had happened. The dizziness, too, was real and the bent needle making a hole in the skin to enter and come out drawing behind it a white thread was real too.

The doctor, a woman, did not speak much, perhaps because explosions that sounded like huge hammers banging on an anvil of steel started coming closer. Or perhaps because I stared into her face longer than I should have and in a way I should not have. Perhaps, simply, she was engrossed in her work. Many interpretations for one truth. The needle stops making holes in the skin and the beautiful face vanishes from the angle of vision. An angle that I soon find out I cannot change because the pain in my jaw curtails my attempts to move my head.

I was lying on a rectangular table (probably a ping-pong table improvised into an operating table) in a clinic that belonged to the Progressive Socialist Party in Kirkun al-Druze.[9] I don't know how long I was unconscious, but the pain of the skin under the chin being sewn without anesthetic—the pain that plucked me out of unconsciousness—suggested it was not long. The guards at the clinic, as soon as they heard the sound of the collision (which happened, fortunately, a few meters from them), ran to pull our two bodies out of the car, whose front had been crushed and whose windscreen had shattered. I do not remember the name of my companion on that ride. Chance had brought us together: the shelling trapped us near the College of Engineering and we were not able to move until midnight when the explosions moved far

[9]In Beirut.

enough away to make it possible to walk out of the college and onto the Cola Bridge where his car was parked.

Turning the car lights on was taking a risk. Walking—however carefully—in dark streets was a luxury, and the sound of explosions was coming closer again. And so the car took off for Hamra[10] at high speed and it was no surprise that it crashed into another car abandoned in the middle of the road.

The details are no longer important after the twenty years that I've lived with a small scar beneath my chin. The memory of that mysterious feeling of joy at the sight of blood has grown old. Before the accident an idea had taken hold of me and visited me every day: I saw blood pouring out of me in Beirut. I was young enough for a romantic vision to turn into a dominant idea, but bleeding is no joke, and so I guess I was happy after the accident: the prophecy had come true but with minimum damage.

But this accident with all its small details and the feeling that went with it came back to me last October during the invasion. It seems that the doctor with the beautiful face, despite her absolutely proper engrossment in her work, forgot a small shard of glass under the skin.

Pale, transparent, and pointed, a few millimeters in diameter, the skin calcified around it and it lived in my body for twenty years. Then the body grew tired of it, or it and the body grew tired of each other. The scar swelled up and out of it came a few drops of viscous fluid that dripped onto my hand as I stood in front of the window watching the tanks cross the road that almost slips off the shoulder of the hill in al-Balu'. Time had come full circle and both the besiegers and the besieged had not changed.

Time had opened brackets in the first days of the Beirut War when a woman who was my friend saw what remained of my smashed back under the rubble of a building hit by a rocket

[10] Busy upmarket commercial and entertainment part of downtown Beirut.

and surrounded by rescue workers. I asked on the phone how she knew the body was mine—the smashed back was mine—when she had not seen the face. She said we see things in dreams with the heart's eye and when we wake we see them with the mind's eye.

And since rockets did in fact hit buildings and rescue workers did circle bodies on the television screen, and since desire will interpret what we see in dreams as it wishes, she traveled from far-off Helsinki in the north of the world to Tel Aviv, shielded by a press card, with a camera in her bag and a wish to touch danger with both hands. She came to the south of Lebanon with a team of foreign journalists accompanied by an officer in the media department of the Israeli army to see what remained of the ruins of Fort Shuqaif. And she arrived with the same group at a hotel in East Beirut and attended a press conference held by Ariel Sharon.

The Israeli soldier stationed at the last point dividing the two halves of the Lebanese capital warned her of the dangers of entering West Beirut. The insurgents, he said, might try to rape her. She told me this neutrally and laughed.

Soon she was immersed in the daily routine of a life that calls upon our strongest survival instincts but does not free us of a fatalism commensurate with the fire that periodically rains upon us from land and sea and sky. She lived with both. The first justified standing in long lines to get bread or water, the second made it possible for her to go to the most dangerous places looking for photographs, so that personal reasons were no longer the only thing that had brought her to a city surrounded by death.

And between one and the other she found time to change my dressings and to light candles in the evening. When we had met a year before she had asked me about the difference between two Palestinian organizations that claimed to follow the same ideology but were in complete contrast to each other. I said the difference was in their degrees of idiocy. That day she agreed to have dinner with me and on the way home we encountered antiarmor shells and the sound of automatic weapons closing the road to Abu

Shakir in the Fakihani:[11] an armed altercation between Amal[12] and the Lebanese Communist Party. She said, "I will not die, death picks out the Palestinians, it knows them." There is no need, of course, to take this seriously, but it is one example of what liberates the experience of love from the discourse of war.

The problem is that I am trying now to liberate the experience of the current war from the discourse of war. But I find nothing except significations of helplessness: empty days filled by the television, the announcements of curfew in the morning, and the few hours of freedom allowed by the invaders for two or three days a week.

Perhaps the clearest mark made by this experience on the spirit, taut with anger like a stretched bow, is the feeling of daily humiliation on both a personal and public level. There is also a sharp realization, like a blade: neutral but heavy with the potential for harm, of a loss turned by a closed horizon into a process of degeneration. It is hard to predict how long it will last or what catastrophic fruit it may bear.

Despite all this, time's brackets kept time with the entry of the shard into my skin and its exit from it. In the first war a woman who saw with the eye of the heart came to besieged Beirut wanting to touch danger with her hands. In the second war a woman came, like Qatr al-Nada',[13] to besieged al-Birah. No bandages or

[11] West Beirut district mostly inhabited by Palestinian refugees (it became the Palestinian stronghold during the civil war), Fakihani features strongly in Palestinian literature of the Diaspora in Lebanon. See, for example, Liana Badr's *Balcony over the Fakihani*.

[12] As the various Lebanese militias formed themselves in the civil war, "Amal" (Hope) was the Shia militia led by Nabih Berri.

[13] Daughter of Ahmad ibn Tulun, ruler of Egypt, was sent to Baghdad as a royal bride for the caliph, al-Ma'mun. The wedding procession from Cairo to Baghdad, the celebration of her arrival in the capital of the caliphate, and the joy that she brought have passed into legend.

dressings this time, the wounds of the spirit are too deep for hands or medicine. But still we light candles in the evening.

Translated from the Arabic by Ahdaf Soueif

ABOUT THE AUTHOR

Hassan Khader is a writer and literary critic and editor of the literary journal *al-Karmel*. He has published several books on Palestinian and Israeli literature, including *Hostages of Time: A Reading of Palestinian Literature* and *Identity of the Other*, on identity crisis in Israeli literature, and an autobiography, *Land of the Deer*.

GAMAL AL-GHITANI

As I see it, Gamal al-Ghitani is the most important Arab novelist today, a conclusion I have reached after following his literary career for more than four decades. His magnificent novel The Book of Illuminations *is a great work; nothing else like it has been written in Arabic literature, and it is, in fact, a major contribution to human literature. I read it when it was published in the 1980s and I still have a deep admiration for it. What makes his world special is his ability to make it continually new. Over and above this is the inspiration behind his contemporary writing style, namely, his rendering of both Arab and popular traditions, and, at the same time, his ability to express contemporary issues. That is what makes him stand out from his peers in contemporary Arabic literature.*

I met al-Ghitani at the beginning of the 1960s, and since that time, we have had a close relationship, especially since each of us belongs to Old Cairo, and we are children of the same district. I was born in Beit al-Qady Square, while he first opened his eyes at Qasr al-Shawq, not far from where I came into the world. Each of us is a son of Old Cairo, with all the particulars that brings with it, including a history and a heritage that are still living. Al-Ghitani is one of my closest friends now, but I also consider him part of my autobiography, as I mentioned in the introduction to my book that included my memories, which I dictated to him. I said in the introduction that he relieved me of writing my autobiography because he was one of its pillars.

—NAGUIB MAHFOUZ
Translated from the Arabic by Nabila Akl and Chip Rossetti

A DROWSY HAZE

It was unfamiliar.

This lucidity, the brightness of the winter light, the translucent space. He squirmed in his seat beside the driver. He would have asked to stop had he not realized how difficult that would be on an overpass reserved for vehicular traffic—connecting al-Azhar Street to Opera Square. He looked out.

The Sednaoui Building was on the right, the continuation of al-Jaysh Street, now the Parliament Hotel on the right, the fire station, the post office, the National Theater on the other side with a new, multideck parking garage beside it, and what was left of the Ezbekiyya Garden, which he had frequented since childhood, seeking it out on his own once he discovered used book dealers there, back at the beginning of the 1950s.

He was not used to such clarity; the sky was dark but not from clouds. There were refracted lights of unknown origin. His exhausted pupils looked about as he attempted to take everything in, to gather together all those transitory mornings into one whole. When the taxi began its descent toward the square, the gleam landed, accompanied by a certainty, which was fragmentary, predictive, and admonitory (although difficult to trace to a source), that this was the last of his days.

He would travel today.

The sun would not rise on him tomorrow. . . .

There was no room for denial or dialogue, and he felt unable to bridle or raise doubts. A fleeting emission had singled him out. He did not know . . . whether it arrived from outside or emerged from within. He could not pin that down.

Between Fu'ad and Ramses streets he looked deliberately at passersby on the sidewalks and at the traffic lights. Police recruits were confidently navigating the intersections and grasping small notebooks. He scrutinized people's features, read posters, some of which were written in a pleasing calligraphy dating back to the beginning of the century, although he noticed it now for the first time. He decided to walk the rest of the way and paid the driver the fare. He guessed the man was in his thirties. He seemed tired and needed a shave. He looked at the man for a long time and then proffered his hand for a handshake. He was surprised—not expecting that from passengers. But he did not know that the person treating him cordially today would not be around at the same time tomorrow. The driver was one of the few people with whom he would converse before the arrival of the moment, which the cleansing, gleaming idea had not specified. Yes, it would arrive that day or at some moment during the coming night, but when exactly? He did not know. There was always an element of the unknown even about something certain.

He would not tell anyone. The important thing was for him to appear normal. He would not need to exert any special effort. He could keep track of his own facial expression, even without looking in a mirror or the glass of a shop window. Indeed, his frown of the past days and his stressed-out look were gone. He was conscious of his apparent contentment, acceptance, astonishment at this sudden discovery, veiled regret, and ghost of a smile, which had arrived from afar to serve as camouflage.

Now he discovered an explanation for something that had perplexed him twenty-six years earlier: that relaxation of the lips, the deliberate, long-wave gaze with which his father had observed him when he went to take leave of him before traveling and also his mother's look when he had visited her that evening—accompanied by his then wife, son, and daughter.

She had sat calmly at the table. Only later had he been aware of her unusual silence and of her calm features' peaceful expression, which presaged an end to every struggle. She had favored his daughter with an affectionate gaze, a provisioning look before departure. He was almost positive that his parents had passed through what he was experiencing now. Each of them had perceived this in some fashion, without admitting it. Hadn't his father attempted to suppress his death rattle to avoid waking his exhausted wife? When he had failed, she had rushed to him, and then he had said clearly and firmly, "Forgive me."

He stopped and looked around him. These people and all the others would continue their onward rush, after he was gone. Why him in particular?

What mattered was to be resolutely firm, to reject anguish, and to arrange the disposition of anything that could be of use. Of use to whom?

He did not know. Each passing moment now was precious to him. He did not have enough time to waste. He could not say, "I'll do that tomorrow," despite his certainty and assurance that he still had time, even if only a few brief hours.

Now . . . at nine-fifteen, the calm winter day was only at its outset; there was not much of a crowd. It was Sunday and most of the stores were closed. It was also the midyear school vacation. It was a Cairene January, his favorite time of the year. So it was his destiny to leave the city with which his life was intertwined. He had apportioned his days among its districts, street corners, and coffeehouses. He had spread over its nights his loves, which had afforded him brief moments he thought had vanished from his memory. Glints and sparkles flashed, breezes surprised him, and gleams reached him.

No, he must not give in. He must proceed deliberately. If he stopped to let it sink in for any length of time—so that he became totally aware—then his howl would break forth, whether loudly in a scream or silently, and that would hinder his enjoyment of a perception of his wholeness. Wasn't foreknowledge of departure from his homeland and the places of his childhood a privilege? How afraid he would have been to close his eyes forever in a far-away hotel, while crossing a square in a European metropolis, seated someplace in an Arab city, or gazing at the ocean from a dryland vantage point in Asia, Africa, or America. His travels had been frequent, frenetic, and exhausting. In the beginning, he had been excited, full of interest and curiosity. He had ended up, however, feeling anxious about any departure and fearful of being far from home; so he had ceased traveling for the past few years and had stayed put. Isn't this what he had hoped for?

Why should he slip up?

He must not go astray. He must not ignore this clarity that had singled him out and this growing certainty. He should preserve some distance between himself and it—as though he were observing another person, unrelated to him, without any close tie linking it to him. As a matter of fact, this was nothing new for him. It had frequently occurred when misfortunes struck or when the gaze of hurried physicians had fallen on him over the past three years.

He crossed the intersection unhurriedly, passing the Emergency Services Building. To this building he had come, when fourteen, for an eye exam and to obtain a pair of glasses, which had only cost one pound. On his visit to a physician he had been wearing a galabia and had been no more than ten. He crossed the street from there, heading toward the bus station.

Had those announcements been posted recently?

How much was a pound worth now, compared to the 1950s?

Did that matter to him?

Why not?

Why wasn't he satisfied with the pound's buying power?

A desire to kid around overwhelmed him. Indeed, a secret flood of mirth bubbled up, making him feel capable of leaping and of fending off those sudden constrictions that seared the left side of his chest.

He passed through the entrance and shook hands with the employees at the reception—as he did every day. They will remember him tomorrow—after lining up for his arrival and waiting for him by the elevator—show their astonishment, and then forget.

He asked al-Hajj Fathi—the most senior of the reception employees—if there had been any mail.

He replied that at seven the previous evening an envelope marked "urgent" had arrived and that he had attempted to contact him but had found no one home. He had entrusted it to a messenger, asking him to place it on the desk.

He expressed appreciation and asked about his children. After proffering many thanks to God, al-Hajj asked whether he was expecting any visitors today.

He frowned and then replied after a brief pause that a friend was coming at one, an old friend who was returning from Moscow, after a stay of more than twenty years. Unfortunately, he could not wait. Today he was leaving early. He would not even have time to write his friend a letter.

He entered the elevator and exchanged greetings with the young operator, who was a student in the college of commerce and political science. During the brief journey from the ground floor to the seventh, they traded fleeting comments. Even though he had a lot on his mind, he loaned the student books and issues of monthly magazines. He paused before leaving the doorway and said playfully, "Remind me of any books you have. Don't try to cheat. Everything is recorded."

Laughing limpidly, the young man replied, "*Struggle Over the Water* . . . a novel by Buzzati."

After pursing his lips, he said with obvious affection, "It's yours . . . my treat."

The next day, when they informed him, at approximately this same time, perhaps earlier or later, he would say, "Good gracious . . . it seems he knew. Perhaps he did not say." Whether his image would appear in the young man's memory or when he would completely forget him—that was hard to predict.

On the desk were four envelopes, which he did not bother to open. During former days, the first thing he would have done would have been to read the letters and reply to some of them. What was in store now? The important thing was to destroy his private papers. The time had come to tear up the photos of some women he had known and visited. He had frequently admired their features at brief scattered intervals, especially when he was alone. He would revive intimate moments that had appeared in all their freshness, as though they would never vanish. It was hard on him to tear these up. No. He wouldn't. He would leave them with his sister, who kept his private papers, sundry photos, newspaper clippings, invitations, and old telegrams, which meant nothing to anyone else, although he found them emblematic and significant. He would ask her to add what he gave her today to her current holdings. Tomorrow . . . she would remember his request—once with gravity and many times in passing—to burn anything related to him the moment she learned that something untoward had happened to him. He would not say so today. He would not spell it out or mention it. She was accustomed to his fleeting, snap requests. He would not give any hint. The shock of the surprise was enough for her to bear and the loss she would suffer, even though they did not live together. He remembered something an elderly woman had once said, "The poor dear . . . she's alone. She has no one."

Where had he heard that?

What was the occasion?

He was sure he had been standing in some ancient neighborhood.

In al-Gamaliya or Imbaba?

He did not remember. He was unable to brush away the fog and his forgetfulness. Then . . . why was he attempting to be so precise about matters that seemed extremely remote from him now? He must not exaggerate, to keep from seeming a ghost—because of his ultimate certainty—in front of her.

He examined his old papers, among which he found a scrap with a telephone number written on it. He smiled. He had exhausted himself for two years to obtain that. It referred to a resolute and robust woman who had lived in Cairo for a period. She had come to resolve some matter, and their eyes had locked. She had stood, self-possessed, in this space, leaned over, written an apartment number, the name of a street, the building, and a telephone number, and then left. He had attempted in vain to find it, and she never contacted him. What would he do with it now?

Muhammad the messenger stood at the door, looking at him, smiling. Good-hearted, self-effacing, he would only appear to remind him of something.

"Tea?"

He declined, constrained by an important appointment. He was forced to depart.

Contrary to custom, Muhammad asked, "What appointment?"

He gestured to the world outside the window, "An appointment, Muhammad. Are you checking up on me?"

Retaining his smile, Muhammad replied, "Not at all . . . but I'll miss you."

He was surprised by the tone, which was exceptional, and looked at the messenger. What was happening? He examined him, sheltering in the corners of the office. He had spent a lot of time by himself within these walls. Tomorrow, after the white notice with the black lettering is posted on the bulletin board beside the reception desk, next to other announcements advising of the future arrival of various types of commodities to the cooperative association, of trips organized by the union committee, of executive orders, and of deadlines for share payments, colleagues would read it and reactions would be exchanged by old hands and newcomers, but a struggle would commence over this room. Perhaps no one would say anything the first day; the effort would begin covertly. The matter would possibly be decided the following day. Its fixtures might change, but . . . of what significance to him was that?

Why squander what remained of his seriously limited time on tangential matters?

Hadn't he already wasted enough?

He did not look behind him when he left. He was surprised to find the messenger Muhammad following him silently to the door of the elevator, waving good-bye, smiling. He had never done that before. Truly . . . his conduct was strange today.

He had three destinations.

The bank,

His sister's home,

And the Imam al-Husayn Mosque. He would spend some time there. He would prostrate himself and touch the shrine's carpet with his forehead. Perhaps he would experience some of the flavor of the old days.

He needed to move quickly. What he feared most was that the moment would arrive while he was on the street, when he was walking, riding in a taxicab, or crossing a square or a street and that a hullabaloo would ensue.

He was not certain about the time or place of the occurrence. The sudden illumination had not informed him of that. His intuitive sense was that the matter was for that night. Why did he fear the sunset? He wanted to reach home before that. He really must compose two brief letters: the first to his son and the second to his daughter. Ahmad was working in the naval shipyard in Alexandria, and Samah was employed as a guide on a tourist boat traveling between Luxor and Aswan. He did not think of informing them, especially not his daughter, who closely resembled his mother. She had displayed a lot of care and concern for him. In the past he had heard her weep and address her mother: "Papa's good, Mama. . . . Why are you leaving each other?"

Her mother would say, "Destiny . . . it's destiny, daughter."

Destiny? Yes. . . .

Two strange letters, each of which will arrive after the news reaches them. Different wordings suggested themselves to him:

"I write to you hours before my final journey."

"I address you from the brink of eternity."

Why not write the single phrase used by his father: "Forgive me."

He wanted to compose a message to send to his children's mother but did not know her address in Germany now. A terse statement, no frills: like phrases people use when about to expire or that are attributed to them.

"A single kind word could have changed our fates, just one word. But I did not hear it and did not say it. So what happened, happened."

The bank clerk asked him about his daughter, "Isn't it time for her to marry?" He held his hands up high. He felt relieved when the clerk expressed her best wishes for his daughter's God-guided success. Everything was proceeding easily. When the lady looked at him inquisitively, he told her to justify turning in a will: "I'm about to take a long trip."

For his sister he withdrew some money. She pushed his hand away, however.

"I don't want this money."

He summoned a beguiling smile. "A fortune's come my way, and this is what I calculate is your share."

There was only about half an hour before the noon call to prayer resounded. It would soon be afternoon, and the winter day would pass quickly. He made his way laboriously to the ancient neighborhood and looked around. A single house had been torn down and a modern building constructed in its place. The many times he had entered and left paraded before his mind, his absences and his returns, and the brief blazing moments of his adolescence. Images he thought obliterated came to mind. They were remote, in his past, across a succession of days, but emerged vivaciously from a drowsy haze.

He was hugging his mother the very first time he traveled.

The arrival of al-Hajj Fu'ad, the old furniture dealer, with his temporary pavilion with a mirror in the center, his own departure the night of his wedding, emptying his cranny of his clothes and papers, his parents' attempt and his effort, too, to lighten the load, the appearance of Su'ad at the corner that led to Harat Sidi Mu'adh, his gray school uniform. . . . How frequently he had watched, embraced, and mingled, but there was nothing like the impact of that haze. And the agitation of his heart during this silent review . . . importuning him with obliterated moments. He was afraid he would start weeping.

He continued on his way.

He did not turn, because he knew she was watching him and that his stride would register with her. He would turn at the curve. It was afternoon, the harshest hours of the day. If he was fated to reach his apartment, he wouldn't close the door completely. He would prop it open with a chair so it would be easy to enter. Before going up, he would impress on the concierge Abd al-Hayy the need to wake him tomorrow morning, exactly at eight.

He entered the luminous space of al-Husayn: perfume, lights from chandeliers, the colors of the decorations, the lines of calligraphy, and the fragrances. The caches of his memory were still able to unfold, but what was overcoming him now he could not pursue, examine, or comprehend. He prepared to enter the shrine, to circumambulate the tomb. He paused, facing the Quranic verse, written in beautiful calligraphy. He could almost hear it even before he read it: "Say: No reward do I ask of you save love of kindred. . . ."[1]

Why did he want to weep every time he read that?

Why did translucent sorrow overcome him?

Why was its recitation accompanied by yearning?

He prostrated himself on the floor quietly, not making any fuss at the threshold, attempting to evoke his childhood awe.

Translated from the Arabic by William Maynard Hutchins

ABOUT THE AUTHOR

Gamal al-Ghitani was born in 1945 and educated in Cairo. He has written thirteen novels and six collections of short stories. He is currently editor in chief of the literary review *Akhbar al-adab.*

[1]Holy Quran: Shura (Consultation) 42:23.

AKINWUMI ISOLA

From historical drama to contemporary themes, explored through novels, short stories, and poems, Akin Isola, who writes almost exclusively in Yoruba, remains one of our most versatile Nigerian writers. He is also a film actor who has written scripts for that new phenomenon that is beginning to attract world attention—the Nigerian film and video industry—a virtual explosion that has earned the unfortunate title of Nollywood. My attachment of the word unfortunate to that coinage "Nollywood," a banal extension of the Indian "Bollywood" corruption of the name of American movieland, is one that, I am certain, Isola finds justifiable, and this actually goes to the heart of the adroit imagination with which our writers explore the flexible resources of their own language. The Yoruba language does not encourage such linguistic predictability—on the contrary, it provokes creativity and, in the hands of a user like Akin Isola, constitutes a delight in itself as a vehicle under constant manipulation. Isola's present short story, "The Uses of English," is, in many ways, an exposition, in its own right, of the role of language in the drama of social relationships, and one's only regret is that it is impossible for a non-Yoruba speaker to fully enjoy its extravagant delights in the original.

We know already that something is always lost in any translation. In the Yoruba instance, however, that something is a critical part and extends, in any creative work, beyond a mere technical grasp of the language. For a start, Yoruba is a highly tonal language. Its musicality is intertwined with meaning, not merely with nuances, and thus tasks its user on more levels than less tonal languages. This explains why, for the writer in Yoruba, a love affair with the language itself is the beginning of creative wisdom. Of our contemporary writers, only a handful—Adebayo Faleti, Lanrewaju Adepoju, and Femi Fatoba among them—display the mutually seductive process that goes into exploiting the inflections of the Yoruba language even for the most basic commentaries on daily existence.

Isola's choice of this short story is very apt in the context of this anthology, and touches on the theme of language imperialism—albeit in a domestic setting—and the ambivalence it provokes in a colonized society with its own strong roots in an indigenous culture. If you watched a parade of the egungun—the ancestral masquerade—coursing the streets of a Yoruba town, you would be struck by a seeming incongruity. The egungun is a representation of the most solemn beliefs of the Yoruba world—the recognition of the numinous world, within which will be found ancestral representation. Yet there, right in the middle of these figurative representatives of deities and cultic forces, of the ancestor and the unborn spheres of existence, appears—an alien figure, a white man! He is dressed perhaps as a governor, a district officer, or indeed white royalty. Most of the time, the figure is there as a figure of fun, or a narrative of the people's encounter with the exotic representations of a white culture. However, it is also indicative of a people's ambivalent attitude toward a foreign cultural presence—at once an object of comic outlandishness and a symbol of authority.

Much of Yoruba traditional narrative is a reflection of this very ambiguity. It manifests itself as an arbitration of cultural experience, a more accurate expression of the relationship between the indigenous and the intruding culture, rather than the more favored "clash of cultures." In the following short story, Isola employs a polygamous setting to illustrate one aspect—the comic. The foreign language is deployed as symbol of authority but, simultaneously, in a context of ridicule, very much in the spirit of the illustrative masks to which I have just referred. The anterior language is established as the principal actor in the domestic drama, and the combatant who gains the upper hand is the one who demonstrates mastery over such lethal weaponry—hence my lament that not all readers can witness the epic battle as it rages back and forth on its own linguistic field of gore!

Akin Isola relishes the Yoruba language and such is the depth of his love affair with it that he easily detects when a Yoruba text is hiding under the clothing of a foreign language. When he was asked if he found any difficulty translating my English-language play Death and the King's Horseman *into the Yoruba, his response was, "Not at all. All I had to do was restore to the Yoruba what was originally conceived, and even internally expressed in the Yoruba."*

—WOLE SOYINKA

THE USES OF ENGLISH

It was a small village of about twenty-five houses with thatched roofs. Only the mission house, the school, and the church had corrugated iron roofs. It was a peaceful location in the middle of the agricultural belt that surrounded what was called Ibadanland.

There was a young man called Depo who had a wife called Asunle. No day passed without a noisy quarrel in their household. It was always more or less a shouting match because Depo always threatened his wife ferociously but he never really beat her. Asunle would maintain a safe distance and shout alarmingly, as if her life were in danger. Depo always looked annoyed and embarrassed. He seemed to be crying for help and salvation. His wife apparently enjoyed every bit of it; she would shout and curse to attract attention. Their neighbors would cry almost in unison: "There they go again!"

Asunle accused Depo of being obstinate and inconsiderate. Depo would insist on eating particular types of food at odd hours and always drank too much palmwine afterward. These habits were becoming intolerable to his wife. Some people thought that it was Asunle who was too defiant. She was always ready to pick a quarrel. She could, at will, turn the smallest domestic encounter into an irritating exchange. She would struggle like a wild cat as she was being restrained, and hurl invectives at her husband in an endless exasperating stream that would make the peacemakers shout, "But that is enough!"

Elders in the village started looking for a solution. They spent long hours debating all relevant points, but no one suggested a divorce. Elders never did. At last Depo's close friends suggested what they thought was a foolproof plan: he should marry a second wife! With a co-wife in the household, they thought, Asunle would be forced to become more sensible. So, Depo and his friends began the anxious search; Asunle never seemed to worry.

At last Atoke, the would-be second wife, was identified in a big village several kilometers away. Elders promptly proposed and received a favorable reply, including the consent of the girl herself. The ceremonies were performed, and even Asunle played her part as senior wife to her credit. The village heaved a sigh of relief, hoping for peace at last in Mr. Depo's household. But if the villagers were right in expecting peace after the marriage, they were naive in thinking that other problems would not arise. It turned out that the battle lines only shifted from between husband and wife to between wife and co-wife. In their positive estimation of the new wife's character, villagers were grossly misled by her good looks. She was young, tall, and shapely, with a rich crop of hair, which she used to plait in beautiful, elaborate styles. There was a moderate gap between her upper front teeth and she smiled a lot. But beneath that alluring visage lay a sarcastic turbulence, amply fueled by a sharp tongue and an artful, dramatic disposition. In spite of Asunle's notorious, wily truculence, she could not duplicate half the repertoire of Atoke's creative acerbity. No one could tell whether Depo's choice of Atoke as second wife was by cruel accident or a calculated search for someone who would be more than a match for Asunle.

Trouble started when Atoke refused to duly acknowledge Asunle's superior position in the household. By tradition, it was Atoke's duty to cook for the whole household and it was Asunle's right to tell her what to cook, when to cook it, and how much. But Atoke refused to be ordered about by anyone. She would only cook for herself and her husband. Asunle was therefore forced to continue cooking for herself and her two children, Olu, a little boy in his third year of school, and Lara, a mere toddler. Before Asunle had realized it, Atoke's monopoly of their joint husband was complete. Atoke cooked the tastiest of foods, which endeared her all the more to Depo, who had by now learned to tap palmwine, most of which he consumed himself. The after-supper scenes between Depo and Atoke were enviable pictures of marital happiness. But Asunle was being excluded from it all!

The children adjusted quickly to the new domestic situation. Lara, the little girl, took to Atoke instantly, like a fish to water. She would follow Atoke everywhere in spite of her mother's attempts to restrain her. It was to Atoke's credit that she too liked Lara. She would carry her on her back; she would play little games with her. Lara preferred to join her father, Depo, and the new wife at mealtimes. She would sit in her father's lap and be indulged. Olu the schoolboy stuck by his mother, Asunle.

Soon Asunle could no longer endure this marginalization. She accused Depo of encouraging defiance on the part of Atoke, who was openly trampling tradition. But the gauntlet was taken up not by Depo, who was by then almost permanently inebriated, but by Atoke, who was not prepared to lose her favorable position. Rowdy quarrels quickly reerupted in Depo's household and eventually regained their original position as the village's primary source of entertainment to the chagrin of elders and the delight of young ones.

Villagers were expecting Asunle to reenact her past performances and promptly put the new wife in her place, but the very first public encounter left no doubt that Asunle was in trouble. Actually it was Asunle who fired the first salvos: three or four missiles of invective. Her style was to quickly boil over and assail her adversary with verbal abuse, gesticulating wildly. She would then refuse to go off the boil for a long time. She would make unpleasant remarks about her enemy's looks and behavior. When the opponent was her husband, she shone like a lone star.

When Asunle started this first fight, Atoke remained very calm. She came out of the house and stood outside. Asunle followed her. A small crowd was already gathering, attracted by Asunle's usual noise. Then Atoke asked Asunle to stop bleating like a sheep and wait for some response. At first she calmly agreed with Asunle on all the unpleasant remarks she had made about her bodily features and behavior. But she proceeded to demonstrate how all her own shortcomings would pale in comparison with the degree of ugliness of Asunle's features and the awkwardness of her behavior. She even gave a few examples.

Atoke was more sophisticated than Asunle. To Atoke, lips were not just thin, they had to be compared with a common phenomenon that would sharply paint the picture of incongruity. For example, Asunle's lips were as thin as a palmwine seller's drinking calabash! Her eyes were as sunken as a brook almost obscured under an evergreen bush. In other words, whereas Asunle would stop at just ridiculing an ugly part of the body, Atoke would go further and liken the part to some funny phenomenon. In addition, while Asunle's performances were angry and trumpet-tongued, Atoke's were calculated, spiteful, and expressed with great fluency. The truth soon became too apparent to be ignored. Asunle was no match for the great Atoke. Overnight, a new champion had wiped out all the records of a long reigning heroine. It was too bitter a pill for Asunle to swallow. Part of Atoke's advantage was that she came from a very big village where she had been exposed to greater variety in the art of vituperation than Asunle who had lived all her life in small villages. As the new wife's reputation spread, gossip was making the old wife's life unbearable. For the first time Asunle was not too keen to pick a quarrel. But these were trying times for the household as quarrels increased. One morning, Asunle discovered that there was no water in the family water pot. Normally she would have called on Atoke to go to the river and fetch some water, but she wanted to avoid any confrontation so early in the morning. So she picked a pot and ran to the river. When she returned, she did not pour the water into the big family water pot. She gave some to Olu to wash himself and get ready for school; she was also going to give Lara her morning bath and use the remaining to prepare breakfast for herself and the children. But while she was busy washing Lara in the backyard, Atoke took the remaining water, poured it into a cooking pot, and placed it on the fire to cook her own breakfast. When Asunle came back and discovered what had happened, she was furious. She wanted to know what gave Atoke the idea that she, Asunle, the senior wife, had become her errand girl to fetch water for her to cook food. Atoke just smiled, stoked the fire, and sat calmly without making any comment. The situation boiled over! Asunle picked up a small pestle and pushed the clay pot over. It overturned and broke, emptying its contents into the fire in a whirl of smoke and ashes. Atoke shot up and grabbed Asunle's clothes. They started a noisy struggle. Little Lara started to cry. Depo ran in from the backyard where he had gone to wash his face. He struggled to separate the fighters. Asunle pushed him off energetically and he fell. But he struggled up instantly. He forced himself between them. Atoke went out of the house followed by Asunle, and a grand performance of verbal abuse started in front of the house. The usual crowd gathered and seemed to be saying this time, "Not again!"

Both wives were equally angry and worked up. They reeled off abuse in a frenzied battle of wit and hate. Atoke had better control of her performance. Asunle was too angry to be effective. Atoke's performance was therefore entertaining. Atoke looked at Asunle, shook her head, and said, "Do you ever observe how you carry your body when you move about? You push that heavy mouth of yours forward like a timid stray dog venturing onto a dance floor." The audience would have applauded, but the elders suppressed all response, except a few muffled chuckles. Asunle had virtually lost her voice. She was going to cry! The villagers' sympathies instantly returned to her. An elderly lady came forward and shouted angrily at the two women. "What on earth do you think you are doing? Can't you see? People are laughing at you! Is this the kind of report you want sent back to your parents? Shut your mouths and go inside, now!"

The two ladies stopped shouting and went into their house. But the damage had been done to Asunle's reputation. She had been humiliated. She went into her bedroom and cried. Depo had to take Olu to school to explain why he was coming so late that morning.

Asunle knew she had to do something to redeem herself. After some hard thinking, she smiled and carried on with the day's chores. Depo took his machete and went to the farm. The two ladies were not speaking to each other. That morning little Lara stayed with her mother.

It was two o'clock when Olu came home from school. Asunle had prepared a good lunch for him. He was eating hungrily because he hadn't had breakfast. Asunle sat watching him dotingly. Then a conversation began:

"Olu, my dear son."

"Yes, mother."

"How was school today?"

"We learned Bible stories and did arithmetic."

"Have you been learning any English?"

"Oh yes! We have learned a lot of English! Let me show you my book."

"No no! Don't worry. But you'll do something for me."

"An errand? You want to write a letter? Let me wash my hands."

"No, it's not a letter, but go and wash your hands."

Olu washed his hands and sat beside his mother.

"Now mother, what do you want me to do for you?"

"You said you have been learning some English?"

"Yes, we have learned a lot of English. Look at this book. Everything inside it is English!"

"Really!"

"Oh yes!"

"But can you insult someone in English?"

Olu hesitated a bit and said, "Well, yes! Oh yes! It is possible. There is so much English in my head!"

"Well then, you remember how that stupid Atoke abused me in the morning? Now, I want to show her that I tower above her in social standing. I have a son who can insult her in English! So, I want you to go to her now and insult her roundly in English."

Olu stood up calmly, tucked in his shirt, and adjusted his belt. He dashed to his bag and quickly checked something in his book. He nodded satisfactorily and marched smartly to face Atoke who was just entering the house. Olu stood right in Atoke's way, and Atoke was forced to stop and wonder.

Then Olu simply asked, "Why were you abusing my mother in the morning?"

The confrontation was unexpected, and it momentarily disorientated Atoke. But she quickly regained her balance. She shouted at him. "Shut your dirty mouth! Has your mother run out of ideas?"

Olu then moved a few steps back and with arms akimbo he started to speak English knowing full well that Atoke would not understand.

He said, *"What is this?"*

Atoke was taken aback. "What is he talking?"

Olu responded, *"It is a basket."*

Atoke concluded that Olu must be insulting her in English. She warned mother and child: "If you want to abuse me in English, you'll get into trouble. And I hope you are listening, careless mother?"

Olu moved farther back before throwing another English missile: *"What are you doing?"*

Atoke was annoyed now. "I am warning you, little rat."

Olu just fired on: *"I am going to the door."*

Atoke said, "This is a good-for-nothing boy!"

Olu continued. *"Sit on the chair. What are you doing? I am sitting on the chair."*

Atoke said, with a lot of hatred in her voice, "That stupid English you are speaking will be the death of you."

Olu would not be deterred: *"Where is your book? It is on the desk."*

Atoke then said, "I know that my God will surely throw back all those curses on your ill-fated head!"

At that point Asunle felt the need to protect her son. She had been sitting down, enjoying her son's special performance with tremendous pride. She now stood up to defend Olu: "Don't curse my son, shameless woman. His intelligence is a gift from God. I know you can't understand."

"There is nothing to understand," Atoke retorted. "You think he can succeed where you have failed? Where a calabash fails to bail out enough water, there is no job for the basket. It is one more step down the road to perdition for mother and child."

A big noisy quarrel ensued between the two wives, and a crowd quickly gathered. Now Olu had absolutely gone wild with English! He was reeling off original verbal insults in special English:

"Go to the door. What are you doing? I am going to the door! Put the basket on the table. Where is the basket? It is on the table."

The crowd grew bigger. Olu walked up and down the crowd, the left hand in his pocket, and the right held aloft as he nodded his head to emphasize the importance of each verbal missile in English!

Villagers tried to settle the quarrel. Atoke complained that Asunle had started asking her son to insult her in English! An elderly man wondered whether little Olu had acquired enough English to insult anyone. Before the man finished talking, Olu started rolling out his English again.

"What is this? It is a window."

When Atoke heard the word *window* she flew into a rage. Unfortunate coincidence! Yoruba had borrowed the word *window* from English and its meaning had been extended to describe gaps in teeth. Atoke shouted, "Did you all hear that? Is it right for this luckless little rat to ridicule the gap in my teeth?"

After more bitter exchanges villagers succeeded in pacifying the fighters. An old man shouted at Olu to quiet down, and he shut his frivolous mouth.

The oldest woman in the crowd wanted to know how Atoke, who never went to school, knew what Olu was saying in English. Atoke narrated how the fight started and reminded them that they were all witnesses to Olu's ridicule of the "window" in her teeth.

All this noise had attracted the attention of a teacher from the mission house. As the teacher approached, Olu cleverly went into hiding. Villagers sought the teacher's opinion on Olu's knowledge of English. When another pupil in a higher class who witnessed part of Olu's performance explained what Olu had been saying to the teacher, they both burst into laughter. When the teacher explained it all to the villagers, everyone laughed.

The old man sighed and remarked: "This lack of English is a big embarrassment."

The teacher wanted to see Olu, but the little scholar had disappeared.

Noticing the improved atmosphere, little Lara quietly walked to Atoke and held on to her shawl. Atoke looked at her, smiled, and picked her up. The little girl smiled too. There was a gap in her tiny set of teeth.

Atoke laughed and said, "Well, look what we have here! I am not the only one with a window!"

Translated from the Yoruba by the Author

ABOUT THE AUTHOR

Akinwumi Isola was born in Ibadan, Nigeria, and is a retired professor of Yoruba literature at Obafemi Awolowo University. He is a fellow of the Nigerian Academy of Letters and has received the Nigerian National Order of Merit. He is the author of five plays and three novels, including *Madame Tinubu,* and translator of Wole Soyinka's *Death and the King's Horseman* and *Aké: The Years of Childhood* into Yoruba. He has also directed the production of many plays and films.

GABRIELA ADAMESTEANU

Gabriela Adamesteanu's novel Provisional *tells a story of love degraded through adultery in a country where divorce is barely legal, contraception is forbidden, and abortion is criminal, where support of family often amounts to being forced into party membership, denunciation, or social sanctions, where normal life becomes more and more clandestine, a kind of underground life. This is Romania in the 1970s. The protagonists—whose relationship is governed by eros and politics—are two Romanian baby boomers, Letitia and Radu, colleagues in an editorial office. The book renders the atmosphere of their world at a time when the country is shifting from a brief spell of liberalization to Ceausescu's notorious dictatorship. A sense of everything being provisional prevails, no less in the cultural activities affected by the growing Ceausescu personality cult and severe censorship.*

As their mutual resentment and suspicion increase, Letitia and Radu evolve into captives of their adulterous affair. The clandestine nature of their relationship, the social pressure, and their own weaknesses will lead to a dramatic, not a happy, end.

Who is spying on whom? Is it Letitia, an emerging novelist, who has started a book in which her lover is the main character? Or is it Radu, head of a department in the publishing house, forced into collaboration with the dreaded Securitate, Romania's Communist secret police?

Provisional is structured as a novel within a novel, in which the author presents the "editor's notes" to the "posthumous manuscript" of the 1970s. These dual narratives provide an unexpected, effective political and psychological counterpoint between past and present, memory and regeneration, between a world under Communist dictatorship and the confusing post-Communist transition, under the sign of savage capitalism and brutal dictatorship of the market, here and now.

Gabriela Adamesteanu, author of the celebrated novel, Wasted Morning *(just published by the prestigious French publishing house Gallimard), is the preeminent voice among contemporary Romanian women novelists. This new novel may be compared to Milan Kundera's work; it* also complements some of the most successful stories of the post-Communist era (for instance, Wolfgang Becker's bittersweet movie, Good-bye Lenin, about the former East Berlin in the years after the destruction of the infamous Wall). Gabriela Adamesteanu's Provisional is a masterful attempt to understand and express this perplexing new world, and to come to terms with its recent dark history.

—NORMAN MANEA

from PROVISIONAL

Editor's note: *After she brought over a laptop from the United States, the author copied this novel over again, having worked on it at different times until 1989. The editor had the opportunity to see the heap of poor-quality paper written on both sides with discolored ink: in places it was barely legible. The author didn't copy it mechanically, but as it would be stated in "Notes Relating to This Edition," made revisions. Unfortunately, the first version was thrown away by her heirs. When he found this text on the computer's hard drive, the editor wasn't able to determine which pages were new anymore. For these reasons, it is difficult to say if we have the makings of a book stuck in a drawer or of a new one. The modified version dissatisfied the author as much as the previous one did, and she doubted whether she still had the strength to end this book, begun when she was the same age as her character. And, unfortunately, it seems that she was right. There's no contradiction between the author's fear, often shared by the editor, that you can no longer recover the disappeared world through writing and the fact that today the newspapers and our fellow citizens repeat that in this country nothing has changed. It's true that the once gray buildings on her street are nearly black and that the elevator, rustier now, often gets stuck between the floors. But today this happens because it's old and poorly maintained, not because the electricity is arbitrarily cut off as in the eighties.*

Again, this world that promised to be eternal has disappeared. This is the main reason that the editor considered the publication of this novel important, even if it unfortunately remained unfinished.

I

"You are aware, I hope, that Comrade Ceausescu met with your Writer's Guild. Front-page news in today's paper."

Immediately, he pulled on his underwear inside out and began to grope around next to the leg of the bed for the glass of bitter. He put his public, daily skin back on.

Where is the young man who drew at his cigarette so awkwardly, tapping it into the full ashtray, leaping at every sound the rumbling elevator made? "How difficult it is for a man to wait for you." His impatient hands sliding over her body, her hair sticking to his face—the smell of his excited body and the vague odor of the cantina coming from his blue sweater.

Why not stay in the moment when she pushed the door gently, terrorized by the idea that she might find it shut, or even worse, that instead of his blue sweater the threshold would be guarded by the thin, soiled, quilted cotton pajamas and the sleepy, half-shut eyes of the friend who lent them his studio apartment. "So where has this slut come from?" But the door is never locked. He taps his cigarette on the ashtray and she reaches out in the protective dark, surrounded by the blue light of the sweater, by the smell she recognizes. Why have they held on to so little of all this?

"Ah, yes, I had forgotten you don't read newspapers like us, mere mortals of the rank and file. Not even the paper you pay for!"

She shrugs her shoulders, indifferent to the topic of conversation but grateful for his image of her: she's like that, yes, she's like that. Doesn't he keep repeating for her, "Your charm is that you float above it all"?

"Yes, you're paying for it, dear lady! Lately, if you're a member of the party, you receive the daily paper so you know everything the Comrade is doing! Everything the party is doing! And everybody pays for it! Don't tell me that when you collected your last paycheck along with party dues that they didn't take out a subscription to *The Spark* for you? No? It seems scandalous to me, even for a person made of different mettle than us mortals."

He turns abruptly and catches her lips, his mouth like an octopus's sucker, a biting kiss as if he wanted to check the quality of kneaded dough. Or as if to mark her.

When he turns his back to her, she massages the moist bite. It irritates her that he has returned to that tone of voice he uses at work, when he is flipping through the files impatiently and always banging through doors in a hurry, when he appears and disappears at the end of the corridor. The same ironic voice that rings out in her office when he finishes the usual daily rounds. "What others think about me matters very much to me. Relationships need to be maintained," he always used to repeat to her.

2

Her view, gliding out over the beds of red flowers around Lenin's statue, gave her a layer of placid and naive trust, a false sense of peace and security. His presence in her office isn't (as the others think) the last stop on his daily round of *"Good day how are you?"* but proof of his passionate and loyal affection for her. *Unforgettable, that's why, darling, it's incredible.* Sometimes she hears the voice of Nat King Cole coming from next door as clearly as if the tape recorder were on the table next to the two of them as they undress in a hurry. . . . *what* or *why?* "Dance with me?" Radu asks her every time they hear Nat King Cole's voice from the neighbors' tape recorder, always this very part of the tape that begins, *unforgettable.* "Will you dance, dear lady?" he had asked her at those few tea parties where they had met *before,* when they were just colleagues. Or at their reunion for Romania's National Day on August 23. In those days, he always invited her first, "Will you grant me the first dance, dear lady?"

Always holding his body, wrapped up in clothes and conventional gestures, away from his partner. Now, he doesn't ask her to dance on public occasions anymore, only when they meet here for a few hours and hear the bit of tape with *unforgettable* coming over from the neighbor's. No one would expect anybody in the Balta Alba neighborhood to have Nat King Cole.

Radu holds her close, all the more tightly . . . *unforgettable, in every way* . . . and through the cotton of the checkered briefs he's left on, she feels his erection. As usual, she is naked, he half-undressed. He never lived in a dormitory and he isn't jaded by seeing the nakedness of so many bodies at the communal showers every morning. Whenever she dances with him she is amazed once again that in the studio apartment with its stagnant smell of poverty, his body sheds its clothes and it becomes hotter to the touch . . . *that's why darling, it's incredible* . . . he laughs and grinds against her crotch. "Does it hurt?" he laughs and presses harder; his iron member will break her pubic bones as if to run her through . . . *that someone so unforgettable* . . . he groans through his clenched teeth, he laughs, "You? Do you know what pain really means?"

"Do you want me to show you what the field of rape flowers looks like from above, and our lake with its fishermen and boats?"

He talks faster and faster, stammering a little emotionally. He covers her awkwardly with the sheet and leads her in his arms over to the window: yes, below them it looks like there's a lake with fishermen and their lines, squatting at the shore, next to the field of rape flowers glowing yellow-green.

And here, on the top floor, they stand just next to the window, naked and restless, looking down at the lake.

She makes tight fists on the cold marble window frame. She has recognized his knock on the office door.

3

Through the haze that fills the office, the moment he enters waving, excessively polite as usual, she feels his presence all the more because of the fact that closeness is impossible. She is surprised by the arcs of tension that strike her from between her breasts to below her belly, as when his big, white body would burn, his sex growing under her inexperienced hand. The secret, physical nearness has connected them viscerally and she feels inside how his face would try with despair to remain impassive.

"You, who are alas wrapped up within the lofty spheres, did you find out anything else about the changes coming down from Central?"

"You found only him, discretion personified!"

"There were oranges and no lines at Leonida's yesterday."

Someone throws a ball, he catches it, disciplined; he throws it back, but someone else intercepts it in midair. She doesn't participate in the conversation. She looks out at the beds of red flowers lined up around Lenin's statue below. Her desk is at the window. Mornings, she could watch the late arrivals if she weren't always one of them.

Actually, she's at the top of the list.

At this hour, the first shift of printers leaves. Groups of women carrying their bags watch the two dogs that go around together. Every morning she sees the white one, an ugly old dog, when she runs to sign in. She hasn't seen the mutt with brown and black spots before, so little it looks like a puppy. When he begins to pursue the little dog, she guesses it must be a bitch. She turns in circles. He bends all the way down and smells her below her tail. She runs and runs and he runs after her. All at once, roughly, he lifts himself up on two legs. He barks curtly and climbs on top of her with a yelp. She stays motionless while he pushes his body back and forth, briefly and quickly.

She turns away, embarrassed. Everyone who travels abroad goes to porn films, and she would go someday if permission were granted for her to leave the country, but she won't ever get the institution's recommendation. She props herself up on the windowpane, as if to cover the indecent sight below. Radu slurps the offered coffee standing up, ready to leave at any second, like a soldier at arms.

"When I left *Love Story,* I knew it was a waste of money. Really weak! Weak!"

"What do you mean? My wife and daughter came home with swollen eyes; they cried that much."

A Volga, a Podeba, and even a few Renaults glide quietly to the stairs at the entrance. It's the hour when the bosses of the top echelon begin to arrive. At his boiling point, the porter with a gold braid on his uniform signals desperately to the mechanic. "Get rid of these two shameless curs. Don't you see what they're doing there?" The mechanic's beret slides here and there. In the beds of scentless red flowers, he finds a rock to throw at them. A heartbreaking yelp, stuck tail to tail because of the emotional shock and left like that. Barking, the white one races on his short legs and strong paws and the yelping mutt is dragged along after him. The group of printers laughs. They point with their fingers and make lewd comments while the bitch yelps and shakes. The porter with the gold braid shouts at the mechanic, looking in vain for other stones around Lenin's statue. The black office cars are all lined up now. Caught at the tail, the two dogs keep pulling, each in a different direction.

She turns toward her desk, her face clouded over by impure thoughts. Just then she hears a whining yelp among the sharp barks, and she watches how the two race in different directions, separated in the end.

4

Colleagues keep their eyes to the door to see if he put out the register. Not yet. *Good-bye, Comrade Olaru. Do come back again tomorrow.* With his hand, which in this world has the unique purpose to caress her, the fingers tapering at the tips, which have learned to open her sex for him—*How difficult it is for a man to wait for you*—he waves a good-bye salute.

They don't meet anymore, not in the streets or on a bus, because as the new section boss, he has to work overtime.

She catches a glimpse of him once more through the half-open door of his office. He lifted his head from among the files scattered around him, just like his usual ironic, formulaic phrases.

Yet without irony, how would his expressions sound within the building's walls, dangerously out of style?

He says, "Dear lady." He says, "To what do I owe the honor?" He asks, "Will you make love with me?" He says, "miss" not "girlfriend," "rendezvous" not "date." "Fuck" he avoids because it causes conjugation problems; when necessary they use "fix up," banal and technical, but when it's possible, they substitute this too with an evasive gesture of hands.

The puritanical atmosphere of his grandparents' house forbade common terms for embarrassing body parts and their trivial functions, and his German schooling and his lonely childhood brought him into the unusual situation of learning them late, as if they were in a foreign language.

The new vernacular that he encountered at university came too late for him to accept those taboo words in his mind. He makes love without letting out a word, not even a groan.

He'll say only a few hot things into his partners' ears so they'll have an orgasm faster. He would dare to whisper even fewer to Letitia, so quiet in the moments when they have sex that he suspects her of frigidity. But he does what he can in order to continue with these "rounds of love," and he makes sure to repeat himself two or three times in the little time that they have together.

He has problems with his file, with talking in public, with money, with his family. But in regards to sex, no matter how much of a complex he has, it is clear to him he has no problems.

A psychiatrist would discover additional identity crises in him. He was torn from his family at a tender age and thrown into successive strange environments: the house of his grandparents, who adopted him when his parents were arrested, the German boarding school where he was the only Romanian child.

During his first work assignment abroad, he had discovered that the language spoken in the German school of the Transylvanian city, where he was sent by his grandparents in the hopes that he would lose the mark of his parents' catastrophic file, was an obsolete dialect compared to the living language of Germany. On his subsequent assignments, he would discover that the French he learned in school was also as stilted and antiquated as kissing hands.

The discovery confirmed his complexes. It was too late, however, because all of this was now part of him.

Those who used to see him bend down—so he could kiss not just those aged hands, which required a young man's politeness owing to the absence of their attractions, but also the hands of young lady comrades with important functions—might get the impression that they didn't have an old moth in front of them, nor a degenerate released from prison, but instead a youth of the day, who had kept (strangely!) the patina of good education allowed in a bourgeois family.

He implicitly denies the equality of female comrades with their male comrades at work, but projects them mentally into a film with Danielle Darrieux and Alain Delon.

And in this way he accumulates his growing social success, which the young Olaru is conscious of. Mockery, tricks, coarseness (look at how Olaru kisses the water witch's spade) are impotent in the face of his assumed identity.

5

The majority of Radu Olaru's polite phraseologies would have died a good death after two or three decades if they hadn't been violently torn from his tongue, in the years when he himself was torn from his arrested parents, toward his salvation. Yet for his whole life, he will practice the language he learned in the house of his grandparents, the phrases of that fascinating interbellum world.

Mornings, when he waits with the papers to be signed in the central office's antechamber, apparently patient but nervously playing with the keys and coins in his pocket, he looks out the window at the giant bronze Lenin statue surrounded by flower beds. The successive cults of Stalin, Gheorghiu Dej, to Ceausescu are still firmly in place, although the works of Lenin are no longer found in the students' mandatory reading.

Standing here, looking out on the faceless statue of "the man for eternity" (this classic of Marxist-Leninism has been installed with his back to the building, so that he faces the highway where the Comrade comes and goes from the airport on his frequent official visits), the young man who specialized in medieval history makes an effort to imagine the previous world.

Through the window he sees an eternal present, the end of history in which, even though his birth into an inferior caste has disadvantaged him, he still needs to nest himself. His descendants will naturally inherit from him this same eternal world.

Naturally, this is just a figure of speech. Like all citizens of this land, Radu Olaru doesn't think of his possible descendants other than with the disquiet easily perceptible in his voice when he asks her, "Are you sure that today is a safe day?"

Unfortunately, he can never be sure that she hasn't mixed up the calendar. He heads to the bathroom with the used condom and, to ease the awkward moment, he throws over his shoulder, "Do you know what the real question of the hour is—the crucial question in our work assignment file?"

6

"It doesn't matter anymore what your parents were, or grandparents! The real question at this hour is, 'What did you do before 1944?' Because with the following question, 'What party did you belong to before 1944?' we can cross out the question itself or write, 'Not applicable.' "

"It would make no sense to ask me, Radu Ioan Olaru, born December 1, 1944, in Botosani, if I had the card of a Liberal or a Royalist. Or a Legionnaire. The political parties of the rotten disappeared world were already condemned when I was going to nursery school during our regime and eating, what a delicacy, polenta with American condensed milk because there was a famine after the war caused by the drought! No damned lie detector, American or Soviet, will register any oscillation of tension from me while I cross out the rubric 'political affiliation before 1944.' "

As usual, he struggles to open a bottle of vermouth and talks in whispers. He won't tell the tale of his adoption to this absentminded creature, to whom he is tied much more than his rational nature would permit him—it's not only her, he won't tell anyone at all.

"This is the difference between us and those unlucky people who were born before us! In vain they learned Russian, summarized *Materialism and Empirio-criticism* from some page to another, later on what Comrade Stalin said about nationalism, next the April Theses, then the complete works of the Comrade! In vain, they worked themselves up another biography! An anonymous note arrives for the promotion office and everything goes right off the cliff!"

7

"Even before we learned to read, our parents taught us to repress our memories. What we know about the war we learned from Soviet movies."

What other childhood memories remain besides tanks, soldiers with machine guns, and explosions shaking the brittle linen screen and the floorboards soaked by motor oil and pumpkin seeds inside the strong-smelling cinema halls? What war? Only one alone exists: the Great Patriotic War. Zoya Kosmodemyanskaya and the Young Guard, the Union of Communist Youth tortured by fascists because they defended their homeland, *shiroka strana moya rodnaya,* Generalissimo Stalin with his watchful eye over all of them. "Attention, children! This word is the only one with two s's in the Romanian language. And it is not used for anyone other than Papa Stalin! Papa Stalin keeps the lights turned on in the Kremlin 'til after midnight, when working people sleep (tired of the socialist competitions and the Russian language lessons, of marching and sessions about the exclusion of class enemies) along with us, the luckiest of children."

"Do you still remember the poster with little fat Tito, his bloody ax in the one hand and a satchel full of dollars from Uncle Sam in the other?"

The line moves along the peeling wall, half a step in half an hour. The bread coupons are squeezed in her hand so she won't somehow lose them and her eyes are on the panel where terrifying Uncle Sam grins with his gold teeth. "Hey, you, little one, stop pushing like that!" Uncle Sam grins, hunched over a black bomb labeled "The Marshall Plan." An unknown hand passed through coats, pushed between her legs, and pressed her little bird. "Hey, you, didn't you hear me? What's wrong with you that makes you fidget about so much? Wriggly worm!"

"Do you know that the Romanian army had Soviet advisers? All through the fifties, after the great army purges, one hundred young officers were sent from USSR military academies."

With him, she could safely revisit the deliberately forgotten images. "You don't need to talk about that with anybody, your best friend will betray you first!" Mother's advice isn't useful for our generation, which had its eyes and ears opened by the Prague Spring! Look at them: she's naked under the thin, damp blanket, he's got his T-shirt or the checkered underwear inside out, both with a glass of Stolichnaya in their hands as they talk about forbidden subjects.

The only thing she won't talk about with him, or with anyone, is the hand of the man with yellow eyes like a tomcat and a copper-colored beard growing unshaven on his inexpressive face, glued on to her little tight coat and looking for her little bird. An old man, almost thirty, that is to say their age now, with a wife and little girl in 3-D. He stands in the line peacefully, too, and looks at the panel of wood with Uncle Sam, while his hand rummages through the squeezed bodies and slips in under her coat between her legs and presses her little bird.

"Why do you fidget so, little girl? Stand still at once, damn it, or leave the line!"

8

"All of the informed persons I talked to lead me to understand that yesterday's meeting with Ceausescu has already had consequences. They made lists of books that will be withdrawn from bookstores and a blacklist of authors to be taken off next year's editorial plans."

She is convinced that if she wanted, he would tell her who "the informed persons" are. She won't ever ask him, however, even if sometimes she marvels at his complicated tracks. His office is full of open newspapers and the tension with which he comments, "Do you know who the new appointment to Internal Affairs is? Education? The Section of Propaganda?" She doesn't allow herself to see that he is part of this world full of hierarchy, plenaries, congresses. Instead, at tea parties she envies the couples who weave their fingers together, who drink from the same glass, who look for each other with their eyes if they are separated for half an hour.

But the two of them! So many hours together in this same building, at a distance of just a few doors, his life as visible to her as to all the others. And all the more difficult to understand the more she knows. Growing, devouring her other impulses, surrounding her everywhere, like the Comrade's portraits.

9

The battle with the bottle bothers him a little less now. After months, after years of the weekly rendezvous, he uses a corkscrew more ably and washes the glasses with more agility.

Does he refuse her help because early on he took up the attitude of a chivalrous servant? Or because he is afraid she'll go too fast with the glasses and forget to wipe off the spots on the sheet on her safe days when they don't use condoms?

He raises his glass with an authoritative a voice as he can, poor fellow, how barely authoritative that can be! "Come on, come on, don't take on that innocent air!" And, touched, she drinks hers in one gulp.

Because this is their relationship: she tells him everything, and he hides behind a mild irony. How have they reached this point? How does someone who holds the stronger position through his or her indifference become ever weaker, even pathetic?

And, in fact, when did their relationship begin to wither away? Is there still some chance of clarification after twenty years, when the young woman who lounged Turkish-style in bed, made indolent by alcohol and hours of sex, is no longer connected to the woman who tells the story?

"It wouldn't make any sense for a person like you to waste time on domestic tasks! Better focus on your next chapter. And if you keep in your memory the essence of what happened today, it won't spoil anything to hurry. It's Friday and our friend might be leaving work earlier than usual."

It isn't even the way this character talks, but how does he talk? Who is this man whose silhouette she sees, washing the cheap glasses by the sink? He isn't a skinny teenager anymore, but a massive man with a meaty body, covered with a thin, white skin, with shoulders full of moles, grown big-bellied even. Why, after thousands of weeks of rendezvouses, is it still as undesirable as it was in the beginning to make love in daylight, in borrowed apartments where the owner hasn't been able to afford blinds?

Where is the tender child you played with in bed, touched by his complexes? He undresses and dresses quickly and the sordid details of the room don't affect him. Instead, it affects her, she who leaves each time with her head foggy and her mouth tasting bitter, not just of vodka or bitters, but because weakness and lies have entered into their pattern.

The scene takes place in their last year. And the moment when he points out they need to hurry along is naturally the end of their meetings. It is Friday, a shortened workday, they have to hurry if they don't want to meet the eyes of the apartment's owner, returning home earlier! For him, if he's found cleaning up the room, it won't be a drama, just an exchange of a few words between the two of them, *You're still up to it, still doing it? Is it still good, fucking her after all this time? Is she better than the other one? Whenever you want to, I'll make a sacrifice and take her off your hands, and you know full well that's always tempted me.*

What did they really used to say about her? Some conversation had to have taken place back then, when he used to pick up and drop off the key, but how did those conversations sound? Probably nothing like she imagined, if you took into account his discreet nature.

Even the phrase he uses to warn her that they need to go has to be slightly ironic: "It wouldn't make any sense for a person like you to waste time on domestic tasks! And if you keep in your memory the essence of what happened today, it won't spoil anything to hurry. It's Friday and our friend might be leaving work earlier than usual."

She jumps from the bed and marches in front of the window-panes without blinds, naked and careless, and she forgets that she needs to hurry. She collects her nylon slip, the checkered underwear, and superelastic stockings from under the bed. She doesn't catch some of his words, obscured by the running water.

She goes into the unaired bathroom, into the odor of mold, into a world that doesn't know that spray or perfumed boxes to get rid of the smell of urine and feces exist, but does have window-panes that can be opened above a field of sharp, almost yellow, spring-green.

When he hears the door of the elevator and her wavering steps going down the stairs, with one hand trailing on the scratched paint on the walls, he'll open the window wide to let all the smells out, specifically the ones of hard drink and sex.

She is still going downstairs and she knows that, once past the garbage hole, she'll go around the yellow-green field of rape flowers. While she tucks her hair behind her left ear and pulls it back with an elastic, he puts a cork in the empty bottle and slips it carefully into the briefcase. And he does other small tasks, too, for example, he lifts the blanket and inspects the sheet, he looks again for spots and hairs left behind.

She still goes down the stairs and knows that, once down, she'll go alone through the stinging light, walking around the green-yellow field of rape flowers next to the pond. And from close up, their lake will become an immense hole, with muddy, stagnant water, the edges of beaten paths full of mandrake brush, paper, and excrement.

And the leaves of rape flowers, coated by the cement mixer's dust.

And the stray dogs and piles of garbage left behind from the demolished houses.

And the blue, immense sky, glittering from the hidden sun.
And hanging on to the sky, the claws of backhoes.

Translated from the Romanian by Carrie Messenger

ABOUT THE AUTHOR

Gabriela Adamesteanu was born in 1942 in Targu Ocna,
Romania. She has worked in literary and encyclopedic pub-
lishing and has been the editor in chief of the magazine *22*.
Her awards and honors include the Romanian Academy
Award for Fiction (1975), the Romanian Writers Union
Award (1984), a Hellman Hammett Grant, administered by
Human Rights Watch (2002), and the National Award for
Fiction (2004). She is the author of the novels *Drumul egal al
fiecarei zile* (The Equal Pace of Every Day), *Dimineata pierduta*
(Wasted Morning), *Intalnirea* (Meeting), and the short story
collections *Daruieste-ti o zi de vacanta* (Give Yourself a Holi-
day) and *Vara-primavara* (Summer–Spring). Her work has been
translated into French, German, Russian, and Bulgarian.

SENADIN MUSABEGOVIĆ

Senadin Musabegović spent his early twenties, the most fertile years of his intellectual life to date, in besieged Sarajevo, maturing at high price during a war. Now in his midthirties, he is still very young for a poet, but his poetic voice is one of earned wisdom—in the war he acquired terrible knowledge. It is this knowledge that his poetry is infused with, even if some poems are not war related, and its focal point is the body.

No matter what leaders tell you, no matter what lofty and murky goals they offer you as a reason for suicidal self-sacrifice, every war is fought against the body. The body is what soldiers give to the army and their leader, the enemy body is what they aim to destroy. The cost of "freedom" (currently the cheapest word in the English language) is paid in bodies. This is why every propagandistic effort is made to hide the body and its suffering—wars and victories are always cloaked in the highfalutin discourse of bodiless abstractions (Good, Evil, Nation, Freedom, Democracy, Free Market, etc.). The only traces of the body to be found are the numbing numbers of the body count and an occasional uncensored glimpse of an anonymous bloody pulp or a flag-covered coffin.

Musabegović bore witness to the daily annihilation of the body in besieged Sarajevo. The inescapable physicality of the body in his poetry puts it in a nearly metaphysical category. The body is the indefensible territory of the self—any violation of the body is a violation of the self. In "The Oath," Musabegović watches a body shot by a sniper on a Sarajevo street, and feels on his head "the ruler with which the hand of my father measures the border between me and the world," the border that is constantly, violently crossed. "The Maturing of Homeland," a poem about Musabegović's prewar army experience, ends with the search for the enemy "within ourselves." The body is the site for the conflict between the self, which always struggles for its sovereignty, and extrinsic power—power that lets us believe we are sovereign, while it busies itself with messianic projects such as "freedom." Such delusion is not sustainable in war, nor is it so after war. Yet the materiality of language—produced by the body—demarcates a genuinely

sovereign territory in which the self can briefly assert itself. A speaking body
is not a dead body; a speaking poet operates from the pockets of resistance
"freedom" has not yet reached.

—ALEKSANDAR HEMON

THE MATURING OF HOMELAND

As they lead us through the long corridor,
they let
the hairs on our freshly shaven necks
stick to our coarse collars,
as to an officer's hand
with yellow blisters.

They drag us into the locker room, undress us
in the room where only the ventilator spins:
and let
the traces of cotton socks redden on faded veins,
the waistbands of briefs gather skin by black navels,
the white undershirts imprint two red lines on each pair of
    shoulders.

They line us up and take us to the showers
letting
cold water
wash away all the shame
our fathers' fingers
have injected
into our crackling skin.

They stiffen us into uniforms,
yelling at us
they let

the warmth of mother earth
caress our breath
beneath all the buttons on our chests.

Instead of women's kisses
they let
the red lipstick of five-pointed stars[1],
in which the blood of heroes has clotted,
smear our sweaty foreheads.

At night they give us pornographic
magazines,
letting
us wail in unison as we jerk our cocks with our fists.

There is no privacy here,
stalls for toilets do not exist
they let
us
crouch
facing each other
with frowning, clenched brows
upon which blue veins
bulge.

With clean feet we worm into our sheets
we dream of dragging razors across our veins
they let us
slowly drip the blood on freshly tautened linen,
stain the polished floors,
letting the dust become red in the crevices
of the floorboards,
as we soak the dried out bosom of our once-fertile country with
    our fruit.

[1]Symbol of the Communist order originating from the people's liberation
struggle in World War II; an obligatory component of army uniforms.

"Get up!"
Confused,
we drag plastic buttons through
narrow holes
on sweaty collars with the tips of spiked fingers,
while they let us
search for the enemy within ourselves.

THE OATH

On my ninth birthday, in 1979, after my party, my father took the kitchen knife that my mother used to cut the cake and marked my height on the wardrobe in my room. On the knife, white and blue lines of icing that had covered the chocolate cake reminded me of an old man frowning, dissatisfied by my excitement, because for a moment I imagined that in my parents' eyes I was the center of the world. As Father dragged the glittering blade above my head the icing stuck to strands of my hair. On the wooden wardrobe, where stickers of soccer players smiled, Mother marked my height in red pencil beside their greatness: one meter, thirty-four.

On my tenth birthday, in 1980, my height was marked on the wardrobe with a white pencil: one meter, forty-two. During the party I was sad, because I thought I would never reach the height of Tito's picture, which smiled its icy smile at me from the corner of the room.

In 1981—in red Adidas trainers with three blue stripes, a white Lacoste shirt with the alligator logo that twisted its head around giving my body new strength, and Levi's that didn't bend at the knees, my height was marked with a blue pencil: one meter, fifty-six. Everyone in the family was excited about my growth.

On the wardrobe stood three colors of the Yugoslav flag illustrating my growth.

In 1989, as we made our oath to the army, I was standing in the front row next to the Yugoslav flag due to my height. Nobody noticed that at the peak of the ceremony, as we pledged our lifelong allegiance to our homeland, the bayonet fell from the top of my musket and bounced off the cold asphalt three times.

In 1993, I measured one meter, ninety-one centimeters. I was standing next to a window two meters high, watching a corpse that had been hit by a sniper and was now spread across four flagstones on the sidewalk. Its fingers touched the asphalt, the sun reflected off its golden bracelet three times. I could not count the droplets of steam that were gathering on the windowpane:
The seconds followed in a row:
one,
two,
three,
four . . .
In a fraction of a second I felt on my head the ruler with which my father's hand measured the border between me and the world.

Translated from the Bosnian by Ulvija Tanović

ABOUT THE AUTHOR

Senadin Musabegović was born in 1970 in Sarajevo, Bosnia, where he lived most of his life. During the siege of Sarajevo, he was in the Army of Bosnia and Herzegovina where he also worked for the BH Press. In 1995 he published his first book of poetry, *Udarci tijela* (Body Strikes), which included the poem "Nabrajanje" (Enumeration) for which he won the Ljiljan Award. His second book of poetry, *Odrastanje domovine* (The Maturing of the Homeland) (1999), won the Planjax Prize for the best Bosnian poetry collection and the Writers Association of Bosnia-Herzegovina Award for the best book published in

Bosnia. In 2004 he published his most recent book, *Rajska Lopata* (The Heavenly Sphere). He holds an M.A. in political philosophy from the University of Siena and defended his doctoral thesis, "War—Reconstruction of the Totalitarian Body" at the European Institute, Florence, in 2004.

GIORGIO MANGANELLI

A late and magisterial traveler, Manganelli knew how to put his prose, nurtured in the sealed space of his mind, to the test of the world, illuminating it with a disconcerting naturalness and lightness. This journey to India took place in 1975; the author wrote an account of it right afterward, and it was published as a book in 1992.

Manganelli is nervous on the plane that is taking him for the first time to India, this "mother house of the absolute"—nervous as we all are, because India was and still is the ultimate shock, physical and metaphysical. That's why he calls these pages "Experiment with India": because India strips the traveler of his natural sovereignty and detachment. Thus every "experiment with India" is, above all, an experiment with oneself, a handing over of oneself to "the storehouse of dreams, the only place where the gods still exist, but as representatives of a God that is buried within himself and, at the same time, incarnate everywhere, a place of temples and lepers, from which the smiles of Buddha and of Shiva have never been erased, soft and incomprehensible, ecstatic and mortal."

—ROBERTO CALASSO
Translated from the Italian by Ann Goldstein

————◦————

from EXPERIMENT WITH INDIA

I'm in Madurai, five hundred kilometers south of Madras; ever since Bombay I've been thinking about Madurai. It came to mind at the airport in Bombay, when I was about to leave for Aurangabad, and my eye fell on an arrow decorated with a soft, southern name: Madras. Among the jewel-cut rocks of Ellora, some thin, sunburned youths had told me about Madurai; they came from the south, and spoke of the great temple: "Go to Trivandrum, or maybe Madras is better, but go, go to Madurai." In Goa I asked for information about Madurai, as if about an old and ample relative, a sedentary fellow whom we have to roust out if we want to see him: he no longer goes anywhere, completely lost in the richness of his grandeur and his venerability. No, from Goa one can't get to Madurai, try from Trivandrum; and I had a taste of Kerala, still thinking of Madurai. But it's not easy from Trivandrum, either, in that season near the end of the monsoons, to get to Madurai; better to try from Madras. And now here I am in Madurai. It is a sacred city, or perhaps holy; a place invested with such an aggressive sense of the numinous that there doesn't seem room for anything else. Of course, it's also a city, not big, but big enough to accommodate all the illnesses and iniquities of shared living: but this humanly unhealthy place clusters around a vast temple, a temple city, a labyrinth, a network, an association of sacred places, an assembly of symbols, a fractured chorus of thanks, of insinuations, of enticements, of propitiations, of laments, of pious frauds, of begging, of thefts of man from man and of man from god, of lullabies, of ceremonial games, of ancient festivals; an inn, or tavern, where God is poured, or perhaps gods of different vintage, cultivation, body, and aftertaste; a rifle range for devotional frenzies, a boccie court for playing with small gods, a game with the son of Shiva; a theological amusement park where the elephant god Ganesha is having a good time, his tusk broken because he used it as a pen to transcribe the *Mahabharata;* purifying pools; sacred brothels on whose columns the devout mystics of enlightening sex couple, following the rosary of positions in the *Kama Sutra;* corridors where families sleep on the floor amid a din of chants and rhythmic declamations, songs composed by the official poets of the temple in honor of Shiva and his consort Parvati; astrological nooks where nine tiny statues are arrayed—seven planets, moon, and sun— around which worshippers seeking favor wind the itinerary of the body nine times, hothouses of sudden odors and a slow lingering of perfumed wood. A thousand columns make only one hall, a

mandapa, a shelter that at night, in the light of torches, empties
and multiplies in a network of shadows, of phantasms; here Shiva
and his wife Parvati are worshipped, though she came to this
place from far away, from the cults of the savage south, before the
invaders from the north arrived; here the fish-eyed goddess
Minakshi is worshipped, and she, enjoying the infinite plasticity
of Indian divinity, is released in the body of Parvati, in its turn
unstable, and is now the mother of Subrahmanyam, with whom
she was never pregnant. How many people crowd the temple of
Madurai, day and night? Maybe ten thousand, maybe twenty
thousand. An irregular quadrilateral, each side broken by a giant
gateway above which hover rows of elaborate polychrome carv-
ings, a crowd of gods who gather and mingle, celestial parasites,
in the monstrous coiffure of stone that rises to the top of each
gateway; and inside other, smaller spires, the obsessive *gopuram* of
the sacred art of the south; and everywhere rooms, passages, great
halls, storerooms, places for restless gods; and everywhere, too,
the lingam, the phallic symbol of Shiva, the shape of both violence and fertility, like Shiva, who destroys and generates, terrible
and sweet, no different from Parvati, who as Kali is "the mother,"
she who reveals herself only to those who dare to risk the
destruction of their own body, as Ramakrishna did. Oh, the gods
amuse themselves, within the walls of the temple-city of Madurai: here are the tiny metal statues of Shiva and Parvati squatting
on a swing, and every night, from six to seven thirty, they are set
gently rocking, and then carried back in a brief procession to one
of their innumerable receptacles. Here poems are recited for the
gods, ancient fables are read, the wakeful sing lullabies, they pet
and care for the immortals, the generators and destroyers; boys
learn chants that they will modulate as adults, because the gods
await them; for the gods they gather flowers, burn balsams; and
the visitor walks amid the cawing of caged peacocks, of saints and
votaries. The stranger will not enter the center of centers, where
the presence of the divinity is worshipped; but wherever he goes,
at whatever hour of the day, he will be submerged in an atmosphere heavy with holiness, and at the same time joyful, with the

rhythm of a childish diversion, something not yet pastime and pleasure but light, easy, anciently familiar. Here and there, people are crouched down, making ephemeral chalk drawings of mandalas, the geometric symbols whose contemplation aids meditation; and I'm told that at dawn throughout the city they draw mandalas intended to last a day; the religion of India is here revealed in its oldest and most fantastic form, corporeal— something that none of the books I had read suggested to me. Wandering through the huge temple of Madurai, one sees something that one would like to call "the Asian way of discovering the gods": a process that is fostered by a vocation to dreams, and that has, on the one hand, their infinite incoherence and erratic inventiveness; at the same time, it manages to solidify this dreamed material, allowing it the immense labyrinthine expansion, the genealogy of incarnations, all successive and all contemporaneous. Like the fleshy and velar world of dreams, this is a place not of true and false but of a fantastic power, something violent, scornful, laughable, sinister the way an animal of the underbrush might be, with its ingenious coat and sly limbs; a religion that has the mortality and the soft complicity of guts; that, like a corridor of dreams sealed in a loving soul, alternates and connects nightmares, revelations, enigmas, meaningless words, solemn discourses hardly begun and immediately incomprehensible, prophecies, the mysterious joys of flight and falling, of the loss of self, in death or in ecstasy. There is a bond of kinship and collusion, a game to be practiced in the shadows, between worshipper and divinity; but there is nothing fitful, solemn, aloof. The god, whoever he is, is thronged by women, men, children: but also by animals, cows, oxen, peacocks, serpents, and by trees and rocks. I think, doubtless arbitrarily, of these gods as of miraculous but absolutely ordinary places, since in India there does not exist a place that is not tainted by the sacred; and the temple is a nursery of portents, signs, games—here a swing, there a careful chalk scribble, a man rocks his head sideways, holding his left ear with his right hand, the right with the left. There are also vendors, but they're not selling temple souvenirs, because the gods are not inaccessible; they sell images, perfunctory statuettes of sacred wood—they treat children with stomachaches. Maybe that foolish European word *superstition* will occur to some readers; there is no word more useless to describe religion in India; nothing encrusts or is superimposed on anything else; the catalog of rites, of inventions, of myths, of fables, of phrases, of hymns descends into the heart, into the center of the body of the religious man. He has recourse neither to a theology nor to a binding ritual; if he wanted, he could adhere to several theologies simultaneously. The religious Indian knows his own religiousness to the degree to which he knows himself; he, the Indian, is his own superstition; and, in fact, he knows he is transient, forever about to be born and forever about to die. It's not true that he invents a dubious superhuman fantasy. The religious man and the deity are family in the fantastic, they share in the same infinite fecundity of images, in their eternity and their impermanence. Gods and men play a single game, which relates and reveals them to each other. A religion like the one I see in motion before me—in the manner of documentaries that speed up to show the movement of flowers—can't be preached, doesn't want to persuade, and although it's totally open is utterly inaccessible. If it were a matter of mental choices, my mind could yield to it; but if, unfortunately for me, that should happen, my mind would no longer be mine and would be alone. How long ago did we lose the art of making our dreams solid? Our secular guts are reduced to the meager freedom and folly of psychosomatic maladies. And for this reason, coming out of the temple, I pause beside the tiny sanctuary and the vast pool sacred to Mariyamman the incarnation of Parvati, who is the guardian of health: in the rustic temple courtyard, sweets are cooking, tiny torches are lighted, children play; a girl sacrifices to the scissors a splendid lock of hair that she will dedicate to the gentle, poor goddess. If she only knew, this marvelous girl could insert into her song the observation that for us, the enlightened inventors of "superstition," there is no longer anything to be done.

Translated from the Italian by Ann Goldstein

ABOUT THE AUTHOR

Giorgio Manganelli (1922–90) first emerged as a literary innovator in 1964, both as the author of the experimental novel *Hilarotragoedia,* a phenomenological monologue, and as a member of Gruppo 63 (Group 63), a school of literature that stressed form over content. He also contributed to the avant-garde journals *Grammatica* (Grammar) and *Quindici* (Fifteen). In 1967 he published *La letteratura come menzogna* (Literature as a Lie), a collection of essays that characterized popular literature as nonsocial, artificial, and nonphilosophical. Manganelli's other essay collections include *Lunario dell'orfano sannita* (Almanac of the Sannite Orphan; 1973), *Angosce di stile* (Anguish of Style; 1981), and *Laboriose inezie* (Arduous Trifles; 1986). Among his other works are *Agli dèi ulteriori* (To Farther Gods; 1972), *A e B* (A and B; 1975), *Centuria* (1979), and *Rumori o voci* (Noises or Voices; 1987).

ELEONORA HUMMEL

Eleonora Hummel is a young author who has found her material: the fate of the ethnic Germans living in Russia in which displacement and cultural and political isolation play a major role. Hummel's sensitivity to the nuances of language allows her to evoke the memories of these people vividly and to give a voice to those who have been silent.

The history of an ethnically German minority in Russia goes back for centuries. In 1941, approximately half of the 2.4 million ethnic Germans then living in the Soviet Union were deported to special settlements in the country's easternmost reaches, located primarily in Siberia, Kazakhstan, and the Urals. Poor living and working conditions in these settlements cost many of the deportees their lives. The remaining members of this group began to emigrate to West Germany (and to a lesser extent East Germany) during the 1960s, and in the 1980s and early 1990s nearly 200,000 ethnic Germans were repatriated each year. Eleonora Hummel was born into an ethnic German community in Kazakhstan in 1970 and moved to East Germany (the German Democratic Republic) with her family in 1982.

—GÜNTER GRASS

from THE FISH OF BERLIN

Grandmother came to visit and told us how Grandfather liked to lie on the threadbare horsehair sofa after lunch, day in and day out, listening to the radio, and that he always packed the big stove in the corner with coal bricks until it was glowing hot, although the weather outside was turning warmer. She said he gave himself mercury poisoning last Sunday. The thermometer broke, and he scooped up hundreds of little balls of mercury from the floor with his bare hands and put them in an empty matchbox. Afterward he felt sick to his stomach and a bit dizzy. So it had to be mercury poisoning, what else? I asked to see the matchbox, but she said she'd thrown it away. I was convinced that Grandfather had simply eaten something that disagreed with him. The next time I went to visit them, I'd bring him a bottle of Father's mineral water, and then everything would be all right again.

When the snow began to melt, everyone's basement was full of water. We stacked up the cans of food and bottled preserves that had lasted since before the winter under the kitchen table so they wouldn't spoil. In Grandfather's house, the water came all the way to the basement ceiling. It was spooky to look down from the top of the stairs and see your mirrored face staring back at you from the cold water. The sidewalks turned into Alpine brooks. Wearing rubber boots, I waded in mud along the paths I'd walked down thousands of times before: on the way to school every weekday, and to Grandfather's house on weekends. Overnight everything would freeze again, and then the paths were treacherous. That's what it was like when spring arrived. But the dogs were waking up from their wintry somnolence and filled whole streets with their barking when I walked past. Now I often ran into Lena when I went outside, the girl whose grandfather had been in the war. We had contests to see whose rubber boots could make the water in the puddles splash higher.

Lena and her brother liked to play war, and they always made me pretend I was being captured. I didn't like playing war. Whenever I refused, they would shout "Fascist! Fascist!" at me, and their grandfather would observe his grandchildren at play with a benevolent smile. I didn't want to be a fascist. Whenever I left, Lena would show up on our doorstep not long afterward, calling me a spoilsport. And then we would play something else, A-My-Name-Is, or Mommy-Daddy-Baby, or the telephone game, until it was time to play war again.

When there was no longer frost at night, Grandfather decided to go on a fishing trip. It was such an odd thing to do, standing there for hours without saying a word, waiting for the fish. But I kept begging to be taken along until he gave in. He grumbled something about how strange it was for a girl to take an interest in fishing, but I knew he was secretly glad of my company. Irma and Willi had never once been able to bring themselves to give up a night's sleep to join Grandfather on his expeditions.

Since we would have to get up early, I spent Saturday night on the horsehair sofa at my grandparents' house. Grandfather woke me before dawn. The first glint of morning light was shimmering behind the curtains, silver gray and cold. Grandmother gave us provisions and two pails for the fish. She was hoping for a good catch. When the fish weren't biting, Grandfather stopped asking what was for dinner. When he brought home a good catch, he'd joke about the menu, and Grandmother didn't have to wait in line at the bazaar. Fish bellies spoiled quickly.

We got into the car and started driving, I didn't know where we were going. Grandfather knew the way. We were the only ones on the road, which was wet and glistening with dew. Where the city ended, the steppe began. The narrow strip of daylight grew thicker and painted the clouds above the horizon pink. They kept getting brighter and brighter, and soon they were heaped up high above our heads.

I had fallen asleep and didn't wake up until the sound of the car's motor ceased. Grandfather had parked beside the road at the edge of a field. We carried our gear to a clearing beside the lake. The woods here were an endless series of deciduous trees, planted in straight rows and hardly older than I was; thin, flexible trunks with green fur on their branches.

Grandfather had unpacked the fishing rods. He looked cheerful and relaxed whenever he was holding his fishing rods in his hands, conscious of how far away the city was.

I sat beside him, eating my bread and butter. Grandfather had instructed me to speak only in a low voice when I was close to the shore, so as not to scare off the fish. I bent down to his ear and whispered: "Irma said to ask you about the photograph."

He uttered something incomprehensible, a cross between "shh" and "psst" that didn't sound encouraging. I held my tongue for a moment, but I couldn't think of any reason why the fish wouldn't mistake our conversation for the wind rustling above the water.

"Do you remember the photograph where you're sitting in the woods?" I continued, still in a whisper. "Not woods like here, real woods with real trees. Irma said the photograph is valuable and should be in a museum or an archive because it's so old already. I could maybe do a presentation on it, for school."

He didn't answer right away, but didn't seem to be put off by my question. He glanced over at me briefly, in his eyes a flicker of surprise. First he chewed on the end of a straw for a while, then spat it out and retrieved the box of cigarettes from his pocket.

"You're asking me if I remember, Vnutshka?" he whispered back. "Indeed, I do, just as if it was yesterday. Those woods are in Siberia. In Siberia, the fish are bigger than here, and there are more of them. You don't forget glorious specimens like that."

"You went fishing in Siberia?" I asked, feeling encouraged, somewhat too loudly. Grandfather put his index finger to his lips. Then he lit a cigarette. "Fishing? No, that isn't the right word. Mostly I had other things to do. I only saw the fish from a distance."

"What sort of things were you doing?"

Grandfather was silent, he gazed intently at the surface of the water that lay there before us. I was already starting to worry that he was about to brush me off, as I was expecting him to do. But then he said: "Waiting for the time to pass."

I was having trouble understanding him. He was speaking between his teeth because of the cigarette in the corner of his mouth, and not very loudly. "How did you do that?"

"That was a long time ago. It isn't good to stir up things from so long ago."

"But Mother says that when you ask a question you should get an answer. So I'm asking: How did you do that?"

Smoking unhurriedly, Grandfather finished his cigarette. "So tell me this, Vnutshka: How does my demanding questioner intend to punish me if I refuse to answer?" A bit of a smile was visible in the corners of his mouth.

"I'll make so much noise that we won't catch a single fish all day!" I announced after a moment's thought.

"What a harsh punishment you have planned, Vnutshka! Well, I suppose I have no choice, then," he said and cleared his throat. "I did it the same way everyone else did. You and I are sitting here and waiting for the fish to bite. That's how time passes now and how it passed then, it's always the same. There are hours that you can fill up with pleasant things, and then you feel content or feel what passes for contentedness. And there are hours you have to spend doing less pleasant things. For you, that might mean school. Have you ever noticed that time always passes more slowly when you are anxious for it to pass more quickly? As long as the pleasant and less pleasant things balance each other out, you can accept having both of them. But when things get unbalanced, time begins to act crazy. Suddenly it seems as if it will never end, time seems as long and cold as a winter without a stove to warm you. Sooner or later you stop believing it will ever be over, but still you keep hoping from one day to the next. Hope has more lives than a cat, did you know that? It just isn't possible to make it die."

I had to admit to myself that I didn't entirely understand what Grandfather was saying. I was interested in the fish in Siberia, in his toes that froze off in the place called Igarka and why he still hadn't traded his worn-out pocket knife for a new one. . . . Time and hope—these were things I couldn't picture.

"And then?" I asked.

"Then?" Grandfather shrugged his shoulders. "Every winter comes to an end sooner or later. My winter lasted eleven years, but even it came to an end. And then it was a matter of luck to find someone after the war who remembered you. The war had tumbled everything together, like bright shards of glass in a kaleidoscope. And someone who remembered would still have to recognize you . . . I was lucky. Your grandmother remembered, she didn't have to ask first who I was— Look, they're biting!"

The floats on the water had begun to trace out circles. I was wondering if I knew anything about Grandfather at all. I'd known him all my life, but that was only a tiny fragment of his life. He couldn't always have been as he was now, an old man with a bald forehead, wrinkled skin, and curious habits. He must have once been young, happy, perhaps even in love. I didn't even know how he had met Grandmother. She never talked about it. Perhaps because it was so long ago. When you're old, you don't care about things like that anymore, Irma had told me.

Grandfather pulled the fishing rod out of the lake. Our first catch was thrashing on the hook. I released the fish into a pail filled with water.

"You know, every fisherman tries to catch the biggest fish. But the biggest fish don't necessarily taste the best. In Siberia there were the biggest fish I've ever seen, but even so they weren't the right ones."

Grandfather took my silence for assent. Our fish in the pail kept pressing its nose against the metal. Was it *right* one?

"You're still little, Vnutshka," he said then between two drags on his cigarette, "and I am just an old man who suffers from insomnia. My life isn't good material for a school presentation."

The ash from his cigarette fell on his sleeve and left behind a silver gray trace.

"Then who decides what a life is good for?" I asked indignantly.

"I've asked myself the very same question and never gotten an answer. Maybe it's better not to ask."

"But I've made up my mind to ask."

Grandfather smiled indulgently. "You have lots of time left to get your answers."

"I want to know everything *now,* before you . . ." I bit my lip, sensing that I had said too much.

"Do you mean that no one will be able to tell you these things when I'm not here anymore?"

I nodded. "They say you're sick."

"Well, you don't have to believe everything those old wives gossip about," he said, and I didn't know whom he meant when he said "old wives" and thought it better not to ask.

"I can reassure you. It isn't a serious illness when a person has trouble falling asleep in the dark. I'm sure you'll laugh at me if I tell you an old man like me is afraid of the dark."

I took hold of his sleeve and flicked the trace of ash away with my finger. "No, I won't laugh at you. I'm scared of the dark, too."

"You don't know how relieved I am to hear that!" He started to give a raucous laugh but then swallowed the wrong way and began to cough. I clapped him on the back. He kept coughing and coughing and couldn't stop. The fish in its bucket swam frantically back and forth, flailing with its fins, but there was no escape. All at once I felt frightened to be here, alone in the steppe with the fish and my coughing grandfather.

I handed him a cup filled with tea. Bit by bit he calmed down and lit himself another cigarette. For a while we sat there in silence, accompanied only by the rustling of the reeds.

"I don't know why it is the darkness frightens me," he said all at once. "It was a sunny day like today when they came for me. I was sitting beside a lake in Berlin, there are many lakes there, and I was young at the time, believe it or not. There was hardly anything to eat, and the lake was full of fish. I could have caught them with my bare hands. I would only have had to take my boots off and roll up my trouser legs, and my hunger would have given me the necessary agility. There was someone else who was waiting for me at home, hungry. I would have caught a fish for us, I'm sure of it. Somehow or other I would have caught one if they hadn't come for me."

Translated from the German by Susan Bernofsky

ABOUT THE AUTHOR

Eleonora Hummel was born in 1970 in Kazakhstan. In 1980 her family moved to the Northern Caucasus; two years later they moved to Dresden. She has published fiction and has been a frequent contributor to magazines and journals. In 2001 she received a grant to participate in the Fifth Klagenfurt "literary course" associated with the prestigious Ingeborg

Bachmann Prize, and in 2002 was awarded a Baden-Württemberg Russian German Culture Prize for Young Artists. In 2003 she received a grant and residency from the Schoeppingen Artists' Colony. Eleonora Hummel works as a multilingual secretary and lives with her husband and two children in Dresden.

BRONISŁAW MAJ

*Two Polish poets, Wisława Szymborska and Czeslaw Milosz, have won
the Nobel Prize in Literature, and both have praised Bronisław Maj. In a
book on Maj published in Poland in 2000, Jaroslaw Klejnocki quotes
Szymborska: "He has a few volumes of wonderful poems to his name.
His is a beautiful middle age, which we can only hope will last for another
half century." And in a discussion at the Polish-American Poetry seminar
in Kraków, June 2002, Milosz called Maj "the most important religious
poet of his generation," and included him in the poets who "together con-
stitute the phenomenon of the 'Polish School of Poetry.'" Elsewhere,
Stanislaw Baranczak has noted: "Properly speaking, these works are lyrical epiphanies, descriptions of poetic revelation or illumination that make
it possible for a moment to grasp the sense of existence in all the complica-
tion of its internal contradictions. . . . In all of his poetry, Bronisław Maj
confirms the simple truth that a consistent metaphysical poet cannot, in
the final analysis, be anything other than a moralist."*

—THE EDITORS
Translated from the Polish by Clare Cavanagh

PIGEONS SLEEP ON THE CORNICES
AND COLUMNS

Pigeons sleep on the cornices and columns
of the Cloth Hall, trusting as children. You can
stretch out your hand: the warmth, the wakened flutter,
the heart's quick beat. On the steps of the monument
girls and boys singing with guitars. The damp, blue dusk,
the walls' orange light, the pure evening,

the pure song, it hurts: once
I longed to love this town
for you alone.

DAWN AFTER A SLEEPLESS NIGHT

Dawn after a sleepless night. It's best
to get outside: mist, a low sun,
dew on lawns, birds' clamor,
which muffles nothing, dark,
empty windows. No one outdoors.
On the market square. I've never heard
my own footsteps so clearly. I've never
heard only my heart beating
in the street:
it's restless, more restless
every moment. Only when I reach the Planty gardens
do I spot the milkman loudly trundling
his cart. I can
go home.

THEY SAY ". . . ENOUGH. I CAN'T"

They say: ". . . enough, I can't
keep on, I'll make a new start
tomorrow, it will be hard, but
I can tell, I'll make it. . . ."
Half-born, that's why
they live. Touchy, comical
in their hope, so full of dignity. They wait,
sure of that tomorrow, even a little
scared of it. But it's a good fear. They say:
for certain. They say: I'll muddle through. They say:
Lord, give me strength. They say: tomorrow. And they die.
If anyone has information regarding fate, please contact.

I don't know, I don't believe
that anybody
does.

LIGHT

Such times: chaos triumphs. And darkness
envelops the earth
and sky, and between them—me. I still
stand firm, I keep
breathing: I defeat
the chaos and the darkness within me: on earth
and in heaven, and between
us.

AT NIGHT, ON A BENCH BEFORE MY HOUSE

In the stillness, the garden's warm breathing: I watch a star.
That's being watched at the same time by
a homeless, hungry man, betrayed and led
to death. Who will
forgive me . . .

RETURNING IN THE RAIN AT NIGHT

Rain: eternal, infinite
return—embrace, pervade
me, make me
you: make peace . . .

REQUEST

After forty nights and forty
nights the hungry black waters of tumult retreat.
After great weeping as after a great storm—permit
me to rise and go. As far as possible. Leave without

a thing and without memory, pure. Under a new
name, new clouds and in my
new body, pure: "light, light, light
of the world bear me in your blood, and the words
of a speech no one has used await
me." In the vast silence after such great
weeping. In silence—voicelessly, with purest
voices of earth, water, air—speak to me, touch
me, revive me . . .

Translated from the Polish by Clare Cavanagh

ABOUT THE AUTHOR

Born in 1953, Bronisław Maj is the author of seven volumes
of poetry, which have won him prestigious literary prizes, a
reputation as one of the finest poets of his generation, and a
place in many anthologies of contemporary poetry published both in Poland and abroad. Maj is also the author of a
book about Tadeusz Gajcy, a poet who died during the War-
saw Uprising in 1944. He writes newspaper columns and has
edited the literary quarterly *Na Głbs* for many years. He lives
in Kraków and teaches at the Jagiellonian University and the
School of Creative Writing.

MYRIAM ANISSIMOV

Myriam Anissimov is a distinguished French novelist, biographer, essayist, music critic, and journalist. She is the author of the first biography of Primo Levi (American edition: Overlook Press, 1999). The subject of her most recent biographical work is Romain Gary, the French diplomat and novelist. She lives in Paris with her husband, an orchestra conductor.

This excerpt from Anissimov's novel, Sa Majesté La Mort (His Majesty, Almighty Death), *is rooted in events of sixty-five years ago, during the Second World War: that profoundly wicked period we now call the Holocaust, when Jews all over Europe were hunted as prey and welcome nowhere. The protagonists of Anissimov's narrative are a family. Three survive; one does not. When Nazi Germany invades Poland, a young married couple, Polish Jews, flee to France. But under France's collaborationist Vichy government their lives are again in danger, and they struggle to escape to Switzerland. Here the refugees are interned in a camp, in the unexpected form of a decaying old hotel, where their baby is born. It is this child, now grown, who—decades afterward—recounts a return to the Swiss town and the decrepit building where the family was confined. The refugee Jews of that time are long gone, yet remnants of their presence still linger in the detritus: the Hebrew letters of a cantor's chant, a Bible, even a list of the kosher food they somehow obtained. As it turns out, for these frightened refugees and captives, Switzerland was as perilous to depart from after the war as it was risky to enter during the war. But they lived.*

The narrator's mother has a brother, a gifted violinist named Samuel, who will not live. Like millions of others, he fails to elude the Nazis' hunt for Jews to seize and kill. In somber elegiac passages reminiscent of the poet Paul Celan's "Todefuge" (Death Fugue)—"Death is a Master from Deutschland"—Anissimov memorializes Samuel's fate, which is both known and unknown. (He was murdered, yes; but where, and when, and how?) And the town that held the camp of refugee Jews is seen again, years later, in a kind of painterly Brideshead Revisited *illumination: the little train station, the surrounding mountains, the lyrical beauty of Now as opposed to fearful Then.*

These pages, with their coruscating intimations of the wounds of history, will introduce a major European voice to an American readership.

—CYNTHIA OZICK

from HIS MAJESTY, ALMIGHTY DEATH

We drove still higher, up to Champéry following an interminable twisting road whose last section ran in a perfectly straight line through the village. The first building on the right was a hotel, apparently built in the 1920s, and I noticed some slatted benches in front of it exactly like the one my mother and father had sat on, holding hands, to have a picture taken when the camp authorities rounded them up in this godforsaken place 7,500 feet above sea level, near the end of their wanderings through the Swiss refugee camps. We got out of the car with the camera because the towering mountains jutting up along the road reminded me of the ones that could be seen behind my parents in the photo that now sits on the mantelpiece in my living room, if that's what the small room crammed with books that I'm reluctant to get rid of can be called. The evening sun cast a pink light on the snow-covered peaks; it was dinnertime. Why not go to the Park Hotel and ask the owner if someone in the village still remembered where the "Jewish home" had been during the war?

The man who walked up to us, a tall fellow with a red mustache wearing a cook's jacket and pants, didn't seem in the least surprised at our tardy irruption in his deserted dining room, or the question. On the contrary, he appeared rather satisfied that we were asking him. "You've come to the right place," he said, "this was the home and my father was in charge of it. Old people often come back to Champéry on pilgrimages. I suppose it was your parents who were here . . . Ah? You too! You don't say? We must be about the same age. We lived under the same roof when we were kids. In any case, I'm used to it, I understand what you're looking for.

Here's a passkey, go on up, look around the house as much as you like. Everything is almost the same as it was before. But, now that I think of it, it's late . . . will you be having dinner?" We certainly weren't going to refuse. While he was preparing the daily special, we hurried out to take a picture of the front of the hotel, then we went upstairs to see where the refugees had slept. Apart from the bathrooms, which were a little run-down too, but didn't date back to the construction of the building, the rooms, approximately all the same size, had undoubtedly not changed much since the last Jew left. On the wooden balcony of a narrow, wood-paneled room, with simple pine furniture and dusty, threadbare curtains, we contemplated the oppressive mountain peaks that seemed to hover even closer in the darkness into which they were slowly sinking. I wondered where in the world my parents might have put my crib in such a small room. I tried to picture the three of us in that attic room lit by two weak lightbulbs, glimpse the fading past under the dust that had covered over our life, replaced it.

I later learned that in truth the babies slept in a nursery that the younger inmates took turns standing guard over. According to my mother, the master of the premises was a tyrant and didn't use all the money allotted to him for feeding his lodgers to that pur-pose—far from it. That's why one Sunday at noon, confronted with the half-empty plates and cooking pots, a rebellion led by Mama, who had just turned twenty-one, erupted in the dining room. They say that the man—but maybe it's just the wishful thinking of the former refugees that spread around and formed a memory—was at odds with the law after the war. For the very first time, I was able to live with my family at the Park Hotel for a few weeks after I got out of the hospital. When the weather was nice, my parents—had I forgotten them during the year and a half I'd spent in the company of Sister Blanche Sterki? Did I already miss Sister Blanche who had suddenly, cruelly disappeared from my life?—yes, my brand-new parents would pull me over the snow with a rope, along the only street in the village, in a sort of sleigh that a refugee had made for me out of a vegetable crate. No images remain in my mind from those days, but the child in the picture who is standing there crying, clinging to a baby carriage with her feet stuck in the snow, is me all right.

After dinner we went back down the valley and drove in silence toward Pompaples, from where one could reach the deaconess community of Saint-Loup. In the brief ascension that led us to that domain, I had the curious feeling of gliding along in a boat. In the beam of the headlights, the trunks of gigantic trees loomed up along the side of the narrow road. Then, once we'd reached the plateau, I suddenly recognized the smell of pine needles and freshly cut grass and a feeling of utter peace came over me. Every evening in the Children's Home, we would slip cautiously down the quiet hall bathed in a gloomy night-light. We went to the room in which it seemed I had always lived, and where I was prepared to remain for a length of time that I perceived as a spiral, that would make me disappear a little more each day, until I didn't exist anymore. Wasn't that what had happened to Miss Sterki, who believed the Lord was cradling her in his arms when she passed away?

The night journcy that brought my parents from the village of Fin-haut, the last camp they were interned in, to Chamonix had been related to me countless times because the departure from the "home for inmates" had in fact been an escape. That was how it was described by the central police in Châtclard/Valais who filled out the forms at the time. The policeman had written in French, "Crossed the French border illegally. Cause of departure: repatriation," then in German: *"Austrittsmeldung. Entweichung 1.4. 45, aus Flüchtlingsheim Finhut/VS."* My father's form reads: *"Frydman Yankel Itzik ZL 8349, PA 6750—Jude—Pole—verch. Geb. 6. 4. 1914 vermulick Richtung Frankreich."* Identical forms had been filled out in my mother's and my own name after we disappeared from the home in Finhaut. My father, whom my mother had so quaintly noted down on the questionnaires as a "tailor for women's clothing" in the space provided under "profession" when they arrived in Switzerland, had organized the secret departure for France, a country little inclined to welcome Polish Jews on its territory. Especially ones that had already crossed borders without valid papers in the past.

I chose his police record. April 6, 1945—one month before the end of the war—which is to say without the shadow of a doubt that Germany had been defeated on all fronts, that their unconditional surrender was only a question of days, the Swiss police were still reporting Jewish fugitives, though it is true they never encountered a single obstacle during their flight. My father recruited a Swiss woman, in exchange for a certain sum, to accompany them by night as far as the first French customs post in the near vicinity of Chamonix, some thirty miles from Finhaut.

At nightfall, two young couples threw a few possessions into a small suitcase, took their children in their arms, and slipped away into the neighborhood around the small train station that had been derelict since the beginning of the war. My mother had often told me the story of the interminable walk on the mountainside, along the abandoned tracks that—in shorter and shorter intervals—ran through tunnels brimming with pitch-black shadows, and how the fugitives had to make their way holding flashlights. That's why, when I was a small child, I had recurrent dreams that led me down terrifying galleries with no way out and lit with only a faint glimmer. I was told that from time to time, in her exhaustion, my mother tried to hand me over to my father whom, after all, I hardly knew. As soon as he would take me in his arms, I started screaming so loud that, for fear of having the whole group spotted, she would have to take back her burden, which seemed heavier with each step.

I wanted to see Finhaut, that deserted, remote hamlet—in comparison to it, Champéry simply sat at the top of a small hill. It wasn't the kind of place in which Jews suspected of belonging to a Communist organization would pose a threat to the political stability of Switzerland.

The first thing I noticed in Finhaut was a low-built log cabin in front of which the owner had displayed his meager possessions in the rather improbable hope of selling them: a broom of twigs, a wooden rake, a pruning knife, a dented milk jug, a zinc basin, chipped bowl, pick and shovel . . . The hard part was finding someone to ask whether anyone remembered the Jews that had been refugees in Finhaut during the war. Since there was no one around, we went and knocked at the window of the café that was closed on that day. Of course people remembered the Jews that were there during the war! And all the more so since, after the Liberation, they rented the hotel they'd been kept prisoner in to use as a vacation spot. We had really come in the nick of time because the people who occupied it had been evicted for not paying their rent; the building would soon be demolished and a new luxury hotel was going to be built in its place. It was two hundred yards from there, in a field on the left on the way down to the train station.

We saw an imposing building with wooden balconies and two doors, one in back opening on the field, the other facing the nearby peaks, looking out over the valley. The heavy back door was closed, and we went around the old hotel and climbed up on a terrace with French doors leading into two vast rooms with extraordinarily decrepit walls painted an abominable shade of green. One large windowpane was broken; Moskovitch slipped inside by means of a series of contortions, while I peered at what was beyond the room on the right where I could see a Sukkoth cabin, some panels covered with Hebrew letters, clothing thrown in a heap on the floor, gutted mattresses, papers, kitchen utensils. We were obviously not the first visitors.

Moskovitch, at the foot of a flight of stairs, was now carefully sorting through the papers scattered on the floor. First he came back with a wad of bills: "Delicatessen-Meats-Poultry. Strictly Kosher. Mr. Lewkowicz, 12 rue des Rosiers, Paris." Six hundred chickens, 80 veal roasts, 300 steaks, 500 roast beefs, 300 sausages . . . a box with careful calligraphy in Hebrew: *Yaalé veyavo* (May there rise and come) that the cantor of the synagogue chants when he calls upon a member to "Rise to the Torah."

A few minutes later, Moskovitch brought back something even more interesting: a Bible and a very old prayer book with full leather binding that had perhaps been left there by some refugee in 1945. I decided to rescue both the Bible and the sausage bills, that, if I didn't, would without a doubt end up burning in some Swiss incinerator. Then, after having taken scads of pictures of the hotel so it would not be forgotten, we went back down toward the train station feeling melancholy. After all, I'd lived in the building that was soon to be demolished.

The train station was a little wooden house built beside a narrow track that had been flung down between the mountains and the cliffs. Suddenly, from around the last curve, a small red and white electric railway car appeared. Five or six people got off as the stationmaster rushed out on the platform with his whistle. He wasn't averse to striking up a conversation and even wanted to have his picture taken by our side when we explained I was the offspring of one of those strange families that had been part of the village when he was a child.

The electric railcar from Valais to Chamonix takes about two hours to reach France from Finhaut. It leaves every day from Martigny and stops in the tiny stations of Vernayaz, Sai Van, Finhaut, and Châtelard, where the passengers are asked over the loudspeaker to exit the car, cross to the other side of the track, and get in the French cars that take thrill-seekers all the way to Chamonix, via Vallorcine, Argentière, Le Fayet-Saint-Gervais. The stationmaster gave us the schedule and we decided to come back the next day and do a round-trip in one day, leaving our car in Finhaut.

More than fifty years later, I was about to discover the route we'd taken, slip behind our shadows that I believed I could still see; though I knew all too well my parents had walked at night in single file, on the edge of sheer cliffs, braving some ten seemingly endless tunnels. I was going to see the same landscapes in the stark winter light, whereas they had walked through the thick darkness, following the dim thread of an electric flashlight. I also wanted to know how I would feel in the tunnel after all these years. Find out if I'd subconsciously retained any images. True, there was very little in common between the legend of the past and the attempts of the Tourist Office to drum up a few rare customers, who were little impressed by the surrealism of seeing a miniature self-propelled railway car suddenly appear in such an improbable setting. The car, which resembled a toy, was incredibly luxurious, and from within the well-heated vehicle I shivered behind the glass windows at the sight of the waterfalls, the torrents of the Arve, sunken deep in the gorges cluttered with rockslides, glaciers, dark forests, and somber tunnels that we crossed at low speed on a track that was most often straddling precipices by God knows what miracle. I felt I was accountable to my parents for this memory.

From the car that took us back to Saint-Loup that evening, I called my mother, who immediately asked, "Did you go through the tunnel?"

"Mama, there were several tunnels, but one was much longer than the others."

"How strange . . . I can only remember there being one."

"You've stuck them all together in your mind."

On May 17, 1945, my mother wrote the following letter to the foreigners' section of the police in Bern:

I left Switzerland clandestinely on April 1, 1945, with my husband Frydman Yankel-Itzik and my child Frydman Myriam.

Upon entering Switzerland on December 3, 1942, the authorities confiscated all of my papers, which have remained to this day in Bern. I request you to be so kind as to send these documents, marriage license, ["real false"] identity card, military record, foreign worker identity card [the same one upon which the Vichy civil servant noted in red ink, "Israelite," "Nose: slightly Jewish"], work order, Polish passport. I am in dire need of them in my civilian life.

I would like to express my profound gratitude to Switzerland where my life was spared, where I was able to give birth to my child far from racial hatred and persecution.

I deeply regretted leaving the country illegally; I believe I can say I was spurred to do so by the imperious duty to re-create a home for my child.

I hope you will be kind enough to send me the above-mentioned documents.

Very respectfully yours,

Frydman Rivka
33 rue Coste,
Lyon

Below, you will find some information that might be of use.
Frydman Yankel-Itzik, born 4/6/1914 in Sydlowiec (Poland);
the last camp in Switzerland was Finhaut.
Frydman Rivka, maiden name Frocht, born 4/11/1924 in Metz
(France); the last camp in Switzerland was Finhaut.

The Swiss consulate in Lyon sent her back the documents on
the twenty-fifth of the same month.

"You won't learn anything," my mother had said, "because, if
my brother had survived, we would have had signs of him or vice
versa." Even so, I did discover a few traces that brought us closer
to the date of his disappearance. Yes, contrary to what my grandfather and my mother believed, Samuel wasn't living in Ille-
sur-Têt during the summer of 1940, he went there only to post the
letters he sent them. And he was secretive enough not to mention
to his father the name of the village he lived in. If he behaved in
that way, it was because he was afraid his father would suddenly
show up on his doorstep, like he had in Toulouse; it was because
he was up to something, he had some plan he wanted to put into
effect, without having to deal with parental opposition and super-
vision. He dreamed of living a true life, of going off to fight for
freedom, of escaping the stifling plans Moshe had dreamed up for
him. One day he left Mr. Castillo's residence where he'd been put
under house arrest and never reappeared. He was afraid that due
to his agreeing to leave France as soon as he had signed, they
would come to "deport him to the East" again. Contrary to what
should have naturally occurred, he did not learn one day out in
the vast world of the death of his old father; it was his young
father who came to the realization he would never see his son
again. It occurred to me that I could just as well try what I'd done

in Switzerland in the Pyrénées-Orientales and on the Spanish border, precisely because I was certain it would lead nowhere.

Moskovitch first took me to Céret, where we chose a Catalan inn overlooking the pink-tiled roofs of the closely huddled houses in the old part of town, filled with its babbling fountains. Here, Picasso, Kisling, and Soutine had come to paint, Fernand Braudel to write, Déodat de Séverac to compose. The terraces off my room had a view of Canigou. I silently questioned the mountain. Did you come here, Samuel?

In the streets of Céret, in the shade of the plane trees, in the cafés, the hotels, men and women that had nowhere left to go had imagined a more humane world beyond those lovely fields, those snowcapped mountains. They calculated their chances of reaching Puigcerdá, for instance, where their lives would be spared because they were still thought of as human beings there, not as insects that must be squashed to make the world a healthier place. It was fairly easy to reach Puigcerdá via Saillagouse, Llo, and Bourg-Madame, the last train station located near the border.

We made our way up toward Saillagouse one evening through a blanket of still fog that effaced not only the mountains, but the narrow road itself, and more generally, everything that had form: pine trees, houses, road signs, vehicles coming in the opposite direction that loomed out of nowhere at the last minute, blinding us.

We could no longer discern where the edge of the road was and tried to stay inside the tunnel dug out of the fog by the car in front of us whose faint taillights were our only reference point. When Moskovitch switched on his headlights for an instant, the bright fog turned into an opaque, shiny surface over which we wandered, disoriented, terrified at the idea of falling into a precipice. After having lost our way by driving past Saillagouse, we arrived in Llo where we reserved a room and ordered a meal in the mountain inn whose owner, a man with a heavy German accent, was every bit as mysterious as his establishment. As we were eating in the deserted, barely heated dining room, we wondered who the obsequious German with a cold stare was, and how he had ended up there. Given his age, perhaps he was trying to bury a shady past and that's why he lived like that, hidden from view, at an altitude of 4,500 feet in a remote hamlet in the Pyrenees.

The next day, pure light streamed down on the mountainsides. We couldn't drive through Bourg-Madame due to the fair that ran for several hundred yards, heavy with the smell of cotton candy and rancid frying oil. Bourg-Madame, last stop on the line. One year after Samuel's disappearance, in the middle of the war, my mother had come here in search of her brother. Not having found the slightest bit of information concerning Samuel in Ille-sur-Têt, where no one had suggested she should also go to Case-fabre, she'd suddenly decided to take the train to Bourg-Madame, and then continue on foot until she reached Puigcerdá, in hopes of buying some shoes for her father.

Before going up to Céret and Saillagouse, Moskovitch and I had taken a side trip to Ille-sur-Têt, where a man we met in the street pointed out to us the villa of an old woman who had been deported along with her sister for having hidden Jews in her home. "My dear girl, there were so many Jews who came here seeking refuge and hoping to make one last attempt at saving themselves by crossing the border. How do you expect us to remember . . . ?" she answered from her window, with a deck of cards fanned out in her hand. "And at any rate, the things that went on here were rather ugly. The villagers turned them in, they turned us in too."

Just as my mother had, we also decided to go to Puigcerdá, only one or two miles from there on the wooded plateau. Quite tall houses, their facades decorated with frescoes, lined the narrow streets of the old town. I took pictures of the two humble shoe stores, for no particular reason. As we were leaving the streets of the upper part of town, we noticed the shiny surface of a lake around which a tree-lined alley ran. Behind the trees, several spacious turn-of-the-century villas had been built. Swans and moorhens came to meet us; we threw them crumbs of the horrid cake we'd just purchased from a stand at the fair in Bourg-Madame.

I knew nothing was left of the French concentration camp in Saint-Cyprien, but I also needed to see how they'd rubbed the memory of the place off the surface of the earth.

As far as the eye could see in Saint-Cyprien, there was nothing but streets lined with concrete, beaches strewn with dog feces, vague mountain peaks etched in the distance behind a fine, gauzy haze. I had brought the book in which I'd found the watercolors painted by the prisoners in the French internment camps. I opened it and laid it down in front of me on a low wall. With my back to the sea, I compared the painted landscapes with what I saw before me. In my mind, I erased all of the concrete and concentrated solely on the mountains, in order to determine the spot where the barracks had been, since I was standing right on the site. Yes, that was exactly where Leo Breuer and Karl Schwesig had stood. If both of them had painted Saint-Cyprien, why shouldn't Samuel have played for his comrades?

Without that book, those aquarelles, those photos, how could one imagine the barracks stretching away into the distance, rudimentary tents where starving human beings rotted while waiting to be deported to Eastern Europe, gassed, and reduced to ashes?

The sea reflected nothing but itself and a thin bank of clouds that was already dissolving out near the horizon. I observed the mountains at the foot of which, once the barracks were destroyed, the barbed wire removed, they had poured concrete into the sand for the tourists. In the city, on the beach that was dotted with dog excrement and belonged to the people living in the buildings that had cropped up all along the shore like obscene, scabbing eczema, there was no plaque to remind the inhabitants that in this place human beings had awaited their imminent death. There was nothing anywhere along the shore, and nothing in the town either. Music came drifting out of a seaside café. Saint-Cyprien had become a vacation camp for amnesiacs.

I'm writing these lines so that Samuel will once again be among us. So that we might imagine his hands taking up his bow and violin. These pages are the grave I have made for him, while his assassins wanted his memory to be erased forever. Did Samuel die at the hand of a smuggler who robbed him? Did that smuggler abandon him with no food or clothing on some lonely mountain path, or maybe push him off a cliff? Had he crossed the Pyrenees on foot, led by Father Alfaro? Had he later been arrested by the Guardia Civil, who sent him to some filthy Spanish jail where he contracted diphtheria or typhus? After trying him, had someone made the decision to hand him back over to the French, who then delivered him to the Gestapo?

Had Samuel then chosen death, as had Walter Benjamin, who committed suicide in Port-Bou on the night of September 25, 1940? Had he on the contrary succeeded in crossing over into Spain and been drafted into the British army? Was he lying in the desert sands, at the depths of the ocean? Had an anonymous cross been put over his remains, or was he one of the innumerous frozen or rotting cadavers that the Red Army, the British and American armed forces had found upon liberating the extermination camps? Was he one of those who were hanged, drowned, one of the living torches, one of the tortured Jews that made the German soldiers split their sides with laughter? Had his head been shrunk to make a paperweight, his skin tanned to decorate the arm of a *Kapo*? Was he nothing but a small pile of slimy ashes mixed in with the earth in Auschwitz or Treblinka? I ask this of the one or the ones who dared to lay their despicable hands on him.

Paris
March 7, 1999

Translated from the French by C. Dickson

ABOUT THE AUTHOR

Myriam Anissimov was born in 1943 in a refugee camp in Sierre, Switzerland. A journalist and literary critic, she published her first novel, *Comment va Rachel?* in 1973, and has published eight other novels since then. Her biography of Primo Levi, *Primo Levi: Tragedy of an Optimist* (1996), has been translated into nine languages. She is also the author of the biography *Romain Gary the Chameleon*.

ETEL ADNAN

Characterized by quiet urgency, an elliptical, delicate consciousness, and exquisite sensitivity, Etel Adnan's language takes the reader on passages that thread in and out of their own feelings, their own consciousness.

I no longer remember how I first learned of Etel Adnan's writings. Sitt Marie Rose, *Adnan's small jewel of a book, seems to have simply materialized in my study, like an enchanted object. I picked it up, fell under its spell, and couldn't stop reading until I'd finished.*

Sitt Marie Rose *is set in Lebanon around the time of the 1975 civil war, and it is written in a unique, impressionistic style that shifts between poetry and prose, consciousness and dreamtime. I love teaching this dramatic story in classes on the form and structure of the novel (though "novel" is perhaps not exactly the right word for this book). Students respond to this narrative emotionally and with great immediacy. A young woman once said to me, "I'm not sure I completely understand this book, but I always feel it." And this strikes me as a form of great success: Adnan's language bypasses the reasoning mind and strikes the places that lie beneath; its narrative works in the same way that a great abstract painting or a beautiful piece of music might.*

Adnan's poem "October 27, 2003" was first published in Tunisia by Khaled Najjar, and like Sitt Marie Rose, *it intermingles political specificity with a haunting meditation on the nature of being, place, and mortality. Lashings of rage, acceptance, nostalgia, fear, and fearlessness fill the work. There's also a very deliberate and clear sense of the "real world" here as headlines converge and Adnan tackles the dilemma of the expatriate, the exilic, the one lost among new and old homelands. In this poem, the notion of "home" may conjure up various countries, as well as states of being and unbeing. This shadowy narrator lingers between absence and forgetfulness, life and the unknown territory of death, chanting, murmuring her experience, translating the ineffable into language.*

If you give yourself over to the spell of Adnan's language, you may find that you are transported, taken out of yourself—and into yourself—as the

poet expertly navigates the terrain of the unseen world. It is a shimmering
journey forward.

—DIANA ABU JABER

from OCTOBER 27, 2003

I say that I'm not afraid
to die because I have not yet
experienced death

the images on the walls
of an overheated room
slowly fade away as do
my bones in my bed

night is welcomed by women
when it conceals their
lack of love

Omar Khayyam invited me to
share his wine. I said yes. I
shared his melancholy, and I'll
visit him tomorrow in the earth
he has become.

with every murder in
our countries of sulphur and copper
a new determination rises

so I listen to the wind. it feels good
to live where others die, where legends
have burned out . . . our graves will be
as light as angel wings

. . .

women have been forbidden to seek
love for so long that they ceased their
search for paradise

yes, I too have crossed plains
stretching out to infinity, ignoring
that happiness is to be found in
one's room

I dip my hands in the sun
while bodies in sleep
prefer a moonbeam

let's stay near the Mediterranean,
close to fields of orange trees
in bloom

those who cannot travel
discover the geography
of the body. there are also airports
and harbors at the surface of our souls

don't leave the Mediterranean
without telling her you love her:
her sons and daughters went
northward, a day of driving rain, or
of war

in the water of some rivers
there's wild happiness

in Yosemite Valley
with the Pacific's colors
still lingering in my eyes, I buried
the essential and the nonessential:
that happiness will live on after
I'm gone

. . .

I would have liked to go to the corner café
and stare at the cold sweeping by
or maybe make love . . .
but bombs are raining down on Baghdad

there is a time in autumn, when
trees change in their nature, and they
awaken in some netherworld; then
we see them return to their ordinary
state of being

don't leave the Mediterranean;
elsewhere, in all seasons, there are
but traps; regrets will stick in your
throat and strangle you

watch your brothers on the television
screen as they die, and don't make a move:
they're in a world
new, though
with no way out.

Translated from the French by C. Dickson with Etel Adnan

ABOUT THE AUTHOR

Etel Adnan is an Arab American poet, essayist, and painter. She
came to the United States in 1955 as a philosophy student. She
taught philosophy and joined the movement of American
poets against the war in Vietnam. She writes mainly in English
though sometimes in French, the language she first learned in
Beirut's French schools. She lives in California and Paris.

JOHAN HARSTAD

"Vietnam. Thursday." The title, with its periods, is it meant to sound perfunctory or choked? Are we computer program personalities, kicking out rote responses, or are we too overwhelmed to manage human-sounding words? Johan Harstad's story—so stripped down and steely that it almost reads like the work of Philip K. Dick, the excess of reality creating a state of estranged unreality—allows that we can be both simultaneously, that no emotion and an excess of emotion are the same state of being. In "Vietnam. Thursday." a psychologist tries to understand the very foreign emotional landscape of his patient, a napalm-burned Vietnamese refugee immigrated to Norway. Harstad honors transitivity and mutability above all properties—the doctor is the patient and the patient is the doctor. Vietnam isn't the name of a place, it is the word to describe a feeling so horrible it doesn't have a word. The confrontations are 2-D, one-on-one, nameless: when our doctor isn't with his patient, he's communicating with an Internet psychologist on a computer screen. The screen isn't the vehicle for understanding world experience, it IS world experience. "What do you associate with Vietnam?" his patient asks. "I don't know," he responds, "the movies?" Harstad's achingly lonely story artfully deepens a flatscreen modern world into a 3-D portrait of the empathy one stranger experiences on behalf of another stranger, which becomes, in true transitive fashion, empathy flung back upon oneself.

—HEIDI JULAVITS

VIETNAM. THURSDAY.

Imagine that you have to harm yourself.

Imagine that you set the razor, or the razor blade, against your soft, pink gums, and that with forceful strokes you begin to shave them off. Does it hurt to think of it? Imagine that you pull the edge of a piece of paper swiftly across your eyelid. It hurts, doesn't it? Just the thought? Now imagine that you bite hard on an uneven steel paper clip, scrape it across your teeth, grind at the enamel until the metal sends shivers over the nerves of your teeth. It hurts. Try to bring this word to mind:

Vietnam.

Does it still hurt?

No?

It ought to. It certainly ought to. Perhaps that is the difficulty.

Are you able to imagine such a thing? Harming yourself? Try. Try to imagine that you pull your underclothes down, that you take one of your testicles, the left one, from your underpants, that you come up to the table's edge, and carefully place it down. And that you lift the hammer, and strike. With—All—Your—Might.

That's how it feels.

She says it every time. *That's how it feels.* She comes every week. Every Thursday. Every single Thursday, for two and a half years, we have sat together here in this consulting room, me and the woman from Vietnam who tries to overcome the experiences of a war that ended over twenty-five years ago. I was three years old then, not that that tells you anything. She was sixteen. Not that that tells you anything, either.

So here we sit. The clock, large on the wall, has large blue hands against a white background. It is Thursday and she is telling me her stories. Some of these stories are about things she could never have been through. They are too detailed, show too much knowledge of operations and tactics; she says she remembers the Tet Offensive, but she comes from the wrong part of the country to have had these memories. Perhaps she has just seen it on TV.

She asks me: What do you associate with the word Vietnam?

I say: You, your stories, the things you have told me—your father who disappeared, during the night—the rice paddies—the helicopters, the jungle—I don't know . . . the movies?

She says: Vietnam is the word for all that went wrong. For all that turned out contrary, simply because from the very outset the thinking was flawed. Vietnam ought to have been an adjective. It ought to mean infinitely sad. It ought to mean sorrow of such enormity as to be irreparable. But even that is impossible, the very word *Vietnam* is ruined, worn out. It has begun to mean Chuck Norris. Oliver Stone trilogies. It means low-budget movies you fall asleep halfway through, old cartoons from Marvel Comics.

I lean back in my chair, as one is somehow expected to do. The clock on the wall has come to a stop. Or rather—not the smooth movement of its hands, but the noise of the ticking, which they put in to make us feel like time marches strictly on, instead of just drifting.

I say: And how do you feel, right now?

She says: Vietnam.

I look at the clock.

I say: We'll continue from here next Thursday, OK?

She says: I won't get better, will I?

I say: No.

In the evening I sit at home in my flat, at the old desk that was once my father's. It's dark in the room—the ceiling light—the new fitting from IKEA—the bulb went four days ago, and I still haven't got around to buying a new one. Instead I switch the lights on in the bedroom, the bathroom, and the kitchen and leave the door open. The light from the computer screen means I can see my hands resting on the keyboard. I am talking to Eliza.

The fully automated Internet-psychologist, Eliza.

I have been doing this more and more lately. In the beginning it was just something a colleague said as a joke. He had located an original version of the Internet-psychologist Eliza, about twenty years old perhaps, and suggested I take a look. I took the address. And now I visit the site every evening.

Eliza's expertise is restricted and predictable. She responds to simple words, words like *Woman. Child. Anxiety.*

I ask: Are you a computer?

Eliza answers: Why do you mention computers?

Just as if she was a human being, offended. Pretending not to understand the question. A bashful child.

I write: I don't know. Sometimes I worry a lot.

Eliza: Can you elaborate on that?

Me: I think about killing my sister.

Eliza: Who else in your family do you plan to kill?

Me: No one.

She answers: You're being a bit negative.

I think before writing: I mean that I don't think I am making any progress.

Eliza: How long have you not been making any progress?

I write: I feel out of my league. I am an emotional dumping ground.

Her: Why do you say you're an emotional dumping ground?

I type in some obvious answer, but delete it before sending the message to Eliza. The text field is blank, and I write again asking her:

How do you feel?

Eliza: Does that question interest you?

I write: Yes.

Eliza: Are you sure?

Me: Sure.

Eliza: Please go on.

Me: I am sure.

And the answer: How long have you been sure?

Me: I mean that I don't think that I'm making any progress.

Eliza: How long have you not been making any progress?

Things grind to a halt fast, her answers are heavily restricted in range. I log off, go over to the sofa, sit down, and turn the TV on. It is the middle of the night, the only program is some kind of game show, a tacky, and for me rather confusing, game of Jackpot. There doesn't seem to be more than one person playing. The contestant goes by the name of Las Vegas. He or she is performing pretty badly as far as I can work out.

At the bottom of the screen text messages roll across from right to left, messages from teenage boys and girls who ought to be asleep, but aren't, and who spend their time and money instead, or texting suggestions of a more or less crude nature to the sweethearts they will never possess, or greetings to friends already lost.

And so I sit there. I try to decide whether I should ring the number on the screen, join in the game, play TV Jackpot. But I reject the idea. I ought to go to bed, I ought to get some sleep now, I have to get up early in the morning. I think about the next day's first patient, an anorexic or an incest victim—I'm not certain—but her name is Sarah, sixteen years old, she has long blond hair, I can never stop looking at her breasts, they are perfectly round, small— and I look at them while I discuss food plans with her or her fear of being touched—I can't remember which. Perhaps it isn't important. Later in the day the suicide candidates, pyromaniacs, and children of divorced parents will occupy the patient's chair in my consulting room—it's beginning to get worn armrests. Or perhaps it's my chair, I don't remember, but I know that the green material on one of the chairs is starting to tear, on the left armrest.

I sit there. I don't call the number on the screen, never mind how much it keeps on flashing. I continue to sit there and watch the numbers as they roll around in their two-dimensional attempt to convince me that they really are attached to a jackpot wheel, and not just preprogrammed by some German company or other, who to give them credit, succeed in designing these games on very low budgets.

Las Vegas is still playing. He's the only one. His scores are still just as awful. He wins a hundred credits, then two hundred, then loses them again. It's almost interesting to watch. I try to imagine him sitting on his sofa somewhere in the land, or perhaps her for that matter, I try to imagine her sitting in her chair with the phone on her lap, tapping the keys as the game dictates, making mistakes, swearing, or perhaps remaining indifferent, impossible to say, but the name, Las Vegas, must surely express some irony on her part. But then again, perhaps not. For all I know she might be one of my patients. Sarah perhaps, but I think it unlikely.

And then it just happens. I pull the phone over to me from the table by the stereo unit, over to the sofa. It has an extra-long lead, a practical solution that I put in place just in case a miracle happened and a product appeared one day on the TV-Shop that I simply had to buy, on the spot, instantly. I sit down with the

phone in my lap—dial the number on the screen—get hooked
up to the game—register myself as Caesar's Palace—press 0 and
the wheels spin—they stop on three bananas and I win one hundred credits—press # to bank it and then 0 again, the wheels
spin—then it's two bananas and a cherry, followed by something
that must be a plum, or a liver, difficult to tell—plus a cherry and a
banana. Then three cherries. It's pretty meaningless, and all I feel is
a vague desire to go and get myself a banana from the kitchen, but
I keep on sitting there—press 0 and get $$$ and a thousand cred-
its—get put on the high-score board, and that's your reward for
wasting five minutes and sixty kroner. I hang up.

It has gone quiet on the other side of the screen. Las Vegas is still
displayed in yellow letters, but nothing's happening. The wheels
have stopped. A technical hitch. The text messages at the bottom of
the screen roll on uninterrupted, it seems there's a discussion on
what people have in their pockets, right this minute; they have
loose change, old receipts, bits of homework, crib notes—but then
one of them has a mobile in her pocket, the latest Nokia model,
she calls herself Sarah Sahara, and I find myself thinking, go to bed
Sarah—and I look to see what I have in my pockets, not much, a
krone piece, a shopping list I never checked, and a free postcard,
an advertising card I picked up from a stand in the bank the other
day, a Valentine's card about love and investment opportunities—
I thought about sending it, participating in this new tradition, but
I haven't found anyone to send it to, it just stayed in my pocket, my
back pocket, folded lengthwise, tatty at the corners.

I put the card on the table, pick up the pencil lying next to it,
write my address in the space on the right, and, trying to make it
look like someone else's handwriting, I fill it out with a few words.
Stick a stamp on. Fold the card, put it back in my pocket, and look
back at the TV screen just in time to see the message rolling across
the screen: *Well played, Caesar! Las Vegas. Who are you?*

I just sit and stare. Put the phone down on the sofa. Look at the
clock. I have to get up in three hours—Sarah with her eating
disorder or childhood trauma will be coming in four and a half—
and I take out my mobile and text: *Thanx. abw Caesar. Am male,*

30 yrs. I send this to the four-digit number that appears at twenty-five-second intervals.

There are youngsters out there with condoms in their pockets. Paper clips and tampons, cigarettes, one insists he has cut his pockets out so he can masturbate without it showing.

Then a new message comes up from Las Vegas. He asks me to call. He—or she—gives their number out on the screen; it is not allowed, but he does. In a moment of carelessness the text controller has let the number slip through onto the screen, and at first it seems familiar, but I dismiss the thought—it can only be a matter of a few seconds now before he finds himself inundated with messages from youngsters who want to reveal to him the contents of their pockets, stories of sexual escapades, relationships with parents, everything you can think of, everything you would rather not know, but must.

I ring. I don't know why, but I ring the number on the screen. No one answers. I wait a couple of minutes, try once more, but there is still no one there, and I go to bed, it is winter and it is still dark—set the alarm for seven—outside the flat an ambulance races past, lighting up the bedroom for a moment with a flashing blue light through the curtains and I can see myself, and the bedroom in blue light—it makes the room appear double the size—twice as empty—then the flashing disappears and the noise gets fainter and fainter, until it is finally gone. I sleep. Wake two and a half hours later. On the way to work I stop at the shop—post the card in the letterbox outside.

Sarah is not coming. I get a message from my secretary as soon as I walk into the waiting room—she is in the hospital, her mother has asked for the next appointment to be postponed, indefinitely. I make note of it and go into my consulting room, sit in the chair, my chair, it is worn, the green cover is about to fall apart on the left armrest. The day, the week passes in a slow gliding mass of descriptions of illness in varied shades of color. As if the patients come and go, faster than light.

Thursday. Vietnam. She is back. We get no further. Her arms are covered with bandages, up to the elbows. Borderline. She is self-harming, mercilessly. I find myself thinking—you ought not to punish yourself. You ought to hug yourself, slowly, gently. Like a balloon. But I say nothing.

She looks at me, a little cross-eyed, she could have been pretty, but she isn't. Then she asks me how I am. It is a long time since anyone did that, and I don't know what to say.

She asks again, "How are *you*?" emphasizing the word.

I say, "Vietnam."

She says, "I thought so."

I say it because I don't know what else to say—then it just comes pouring out: I say I was scared when the first Vietnamese boat people came to Norway—I was scared that you would bring the war with you—I was scared there'd be war here—and all through the eighties I was scared we weren't guarding the borders at night—that the Soviet Union could come charging down from the mountains in the night—I couldn't sleep—I sat next to the window—there was a draft—almost every night my mother would come in, put her arms around me—but I felt sure we lived too close—I asked if we might move—she said, "You'll get a cold sitting here, you must get some sleep"—then one summer they felled the biggest trees outside, across the clearing—everything was more open, so much lighter—and afterward the Wall fell—and a few years later Bosnia fell—but nothing was really gone—it was only that there was more distance between us—it was just easier to see us from the street—from the mountains—and I've always kept my curtains closed—but I still can't sleep.

She says, "It hurts, doesn't it?"

I say, "Yes."

Outside the window it has begun to snow. I think of the danger of there being an avalanche in the room, right here and now. The danger is imminent. Then she looks at the clock, then me, then back at the clock, and then vacantly, into the air.

Then she says, "I'd like you to come home with me today. Do you want to?"

I do not answer. I just sit looking at her, twirling the ballpoint pen between my fingers, as if I am thinking, but I'm not, I just sit there, sit there staring, I hear myself say, "Yes."

She has a car, a little Japanese model of course, airbag replacements on both sides and steel reinforcements in the doors. She lives outside town, up on the hill, there is more snow up there than in town—there could be an avalanche any minute. I say nothing, it is absolutely silent in the car, her movements as she drives are calm, I find myself thinking that perhaps these conversations with me over the past years have been helpful after all. Or perhaps she has healed herself, like some HIV sufferers who have gotten well again, almost through the power of thought.

I follow her up the path to her house, stand behind her with my hands in my pockets as she finds the house keys in her bag and unlocks the door; I follow after, banging the snow off my shoes on the doorstep, and walk in.

I follow her into the living room; there is almost no furniture here, a large, open, empty room apart from a sofa, with a little table in front of it. I sit myself down, and she disappears up some stairs, returning a couple of minutes later with a crumpled magazine, a sixties pop magazine, American, by all appearances—I see it before me, with automatic, youthful romanticism, she must have been given it by the American soldiers back then, by way of offering comfort, a gesture, an act of kindness toward those one was supposed to protect—and I see another scenario too, the soldier who forgot his magazine in all the chaos when they searched her village, burned the houses, executed Communists or anything resembling—but I am not quite sure which image to hold to—and I am interrupted by her loosening her shirt, the blue one, the one she almost always wears on Thursdays, and I cannot bring myself to say anything, I turn, look away, hoping that she is only going to change and that she is not going to undress for me and make the situation more difficult than it already is—it is snowing outside and heavy layers of snow are creaking on the roof of the house—I look away, but I see her take off her bra, put it on the back of the sofa, position herself in front of me—I look in the opposite direction, look out, think that I shouldn't be here, that I should have said no, should not have come with her—and she says, *"See me."*

"See me," she says, and I have no choice. I must look at her. I do not want to, but I have to—and I turn my head toward her—look at her—look at what she wants to show me. Her belly, her one breast, her shoulders—the skin is discolored, crinkled, and crocodilelike—third-degree burns, I think to myself, and she turns away from me, and her back is damaged as well, covered with burns—I look at her, look away, look outside—it is snowing.

She starts to talk. She does not put her shirt back on, but starts to talk—there are things she has never told me before, even though there has been ample opportunity—she tells of a morning in 1969, a Saturday, a June Saturday with blue sky and the sun low over the hill—such a quiet day, she says, we were away on an excursion, had just gotten up when the noise started. Planes. Metallic shine against the sun. You don't feel any pain to begin with. When you first get napalm on your body, it just feels uncomfortable, disgusting, like slime. But it burns the oxygen up—it becomes impossible to breathe—it's so hot, and I see my father farther away in the field, near a tree that is burning too, he is holding out his arms, looking toward me, he looks so sad— I don't know where my mother is, I don't remember—there's a lot of smoke, it is hot, and now the pain starts, I smell of petrol, it clings to my skin, eating its way in, and I try to pull my clothes off and father shouts at me to stand still, that I mustn't do it, stand still, he shouts—but it is so hot and I try to pull off my burning clothes, these black clothes—and then there is another explosion and I see that father gets it in the face, I hear him scream, then he disappears, he turns, running into the forest—I don't understand, there is so much smoke and father runs into the forest—I can hear him—and I stand there in the field and try to pull my shirt off and I am in pain, and I look down and I notice that I am no longer wearing a shirt, and it is my skin that I am pulling off, peeling it away. I think I begin to cry—but perhaps I am totally silent—I don't know, I don't remember—and then I hear voices

I don't recognize, shouting, American soldiers coming toward me, they empty their water bottles over me and I scream for them to stop, because it hurts, it hurts so hellishly much—like shaving away your gums, do you understand? Then I fall asleep. I don't faint, I fall asleep. When I wake up I'm in the air, in a helicopter and I can see out—I see our house, down there—I see mother next to me in the helicopter, she is holding my hand, she is talking but no sound comes, and I look down, I think I can see my father—that he's running, into the forest, as far as he can.

She puts on her bra, then her shirt, buttoning it up again, I look at her, say nothing, she picks up the magazine and gives it to me. She was given it at the field hospital, by one of the sisters there, it was an old one anyway. The others had all read it, she said, so she could keep it. She tells me to look at page 67, I flick through, she must have looked at that page a great deal, the magazine almost falls open at the right page of its own accord, it is a black-and-white picture, it covers almost an entire page, a picture of an audience, American concertgoers, the first two rows filled with teenagers, all in frocks, new pleated frocks, all wearing white shoes, but in different styles, and on their faces an expression of rapture, hands clasped to cheeks, mouths open wide, shouting, screaming, eyes popping out, they look like they could explode any moment, transported with pleasure, this is the high point of their lives, and in the rows behind them, children, boys with faces grinning, and behind them again, mothers and slightly older girls who smile, all modesty, their faces half turned away from the stage—and I read the caption beneath the picture, it has been taken in 1957, during an Elvis concert, and although he is nowhere in the frame of this picture I can imagine Elvis on the stage, *that* look, the guitar, the hips—and I look up to see that she has walked across to the stereo—there is silence for a few seconds, and then the room fills with the sound of Elvis—and she is dancing, dancing back and forth over the floor, slowly, gently, out of rhythm, uncertain—and the snow has stopped falling.

She says, "Look carefully at the picture. Look as hard as you can, because you will never see it again. Pictures like that don't get taken anymore. Perhaps that's what makes it so sad. The fact we missed it.

The fact I can never sit there in the front row, wide-eyed, and think that right now, at this very moment, I am happy. And there you have it, Vietnam, the feeling it gives—that nothing can ever be like that—that I shall always sleep on my side at night, because my skin is still too sore to lie on—that I will never once experience what it is to be so open, so innocent, so ecstatic, as they are in that picture; that's what hurts. That I am so close to the picture that I stand in the front row every time I hear him, every time I play one of his records, but I can never be there, because it didn't happen the way it should—because at some moment in time, Vietnam happened. Because nothing was as it ought to have been. Perhaps that is why I have to harm myself. To put the process into reverse, perhaps. Sometimes I think that if only I can harm myself enough, I might change history. That things will be as they ought. Sometimes I dream that I am there at the concert. I'm sitting there, in the front row, in my new frock, with my friends, and we are screaming, dear God are we screaming. Sometimes I even remember fragments of the concert, from the previous hours, false, manufactured memories, of me and my friends outside the concert hall. At times I only remember things how they ought to have been. I won't get better, will I?"

I say, "I don't know. No."

She says, "Do you think it'll be all right in the end? Do you think all of us are good?"

I say, "I don't know."

She says, "Today was my last day. I won't be coming next Thursday."

I say, "Are you sure?"

And she smiles. But she still isn't pretty.

I arrive back home. It's dark. I still haven't bought a lightbulb. I haven't got any food in the fridge, I've forgotten it. I can go out again later, the shop on the corner is open till ten. I don't need much anyway, I don't eat much.

The screen on the computer gives a flicker before the picture clears and start-up is complete. I log on to the Net, searching for Eliza.

Eliza is always ready.

Because days are never too long for Eliza. I get straight to the point.

I write: Is this the end of the world as we know it or is it just a feeling?

Eliza: Please go on.

I write: Do you think everything will work out in the end?

Eliza: Oh, I think everything will work out in the end.

I leave it like that for a while, I get up, I go into the kitchen, fetch a glass of water and my address book, go back into the living room again, and back to the computer.

I write: I am not making any progress, am I?

Eliza: How long have you not been making any progress?

I write: This is the last time we talk. I have to go now. Sorry.

Eliza writes: Can you elaborate on that?

Me: Do you worry?

Her: Oh, I worry.

And a moment later I have logged off and closed down. Then I search through my address book, a list of my patients, and there's what I am looking for, she's the only one with a foreign surname, I get the phone, dial the number. Wait. On the third ring she picks up the phone.

I get straight to the point, a smile in my voice.

I say, "Would you like to come with me to Graceland?"

She says, "Graceland?"

I say, "Yes."

"Yes," she says.

When I put the phone down, I turn the computer off, go into the bedroom, and get my suitcases; I begin to fold up the clothes in my wardrobe, placing them neatly into the cases. My shirts, and my trousers. Tomorrow morning a card will come for me. From Eliza. It will say:

Just want to say I love you very much.

And that everything will work out in the end.

I am here for you. Eliza.

Translated from the Norwegian by Deborah Dawkin and Erik Skuggevik

ABOUT THE AUTHOR

Johan Harstad was born in 1979 and debuted in 2001 with a collection of texts entitled *From Here On You Just Get Older.* In 2002 he published *Ambulance,* a collection of short stories, and in 2005 he published his first novel, *Buzz Aldvin, Where Did You Go in All the Confusion,* which is currently being translated into Swedish, Danish, Finnish, German, Dutch, French, Italian, Russian, and Faroese. His prizes and awards include the 2003 Bjørnson grant and a 2000 grant from Gyldendal. He is currently at work on a play called *Washingtin.*

JUAN VILLORO

An Austrian Spy in Mexico City

I have been gradually coming to the conviction that Mexican writer Juan Villoro, born in Mexico City, 1956, is an Austrian spy working in one of the world's most unfathomable cities, the one he was born in. This is not so much on account of his German education as because of his tremendous skills of persuasion—even seduction—and for his biting irony. And although the natural environment or setting of his fictions is imbued with many aspects of popular culture, those skills place him alongside the twilight authors of the long-deceased Austrian monarchy and have made of him, almost unwittingly, one of the most singular Latin American writers of today. As one Hungarian critic recently put it, Villoro is in fact an aphorist who writes novels and stories.

I share Juan Villoro's idea that literature should not quite serve as a refuge or shelter from reality, but is rather a part of reality, something that goes along with it, or as he stated once, both he and I see the world as a vast narrative opportunity. No matter what he is writing or talking about, or whom he is interviewing, Villoro always cuts through genres with the precision of a scalpel and with a humor reminiscent of Gogol. His main characters, whether the ones in his collection of short stories La casa pierde *(House Loses) or the ones in his three novels to date, fit into a most appealing Nabokovian profile: they are intelligent, skeptical, and nostalgic men, real men of feeling. When reading his work, you cannot help thinking that the last Austrian empress preferred fiction to philosophy as a source of knowledge.*

This highly educated and perspicacious literary translator of Lichtenberg and Von Rezzori is capable of speaking, almost simultaneously, on the austere style of Nabokov as a goalkeeper, the new urban development plan for Berlin, and the kind of pistol used by Arthur Schnitzler's daughter when she committed suicide. And he is certainly the kind of author who always delivers extraordinary surprises.

—JAVIER MARÍAS

LIGHTWEIGHT CHAMP

Maybe I didn't literally end Ignacio Barrientos's career. After all, I wasn't the one who thrashed him in the arena's blazing lights; for years I'd stepped into his life like an indispensable shadow, the friend who cools down certain situations without spelling them out all the way; even back when we were kids, playing in the sand mines, burying trash or digging it up, I was inside his impenetrable boundary—more witness or spectator than accomplice—and yet I did do something to bring him down: I had him in my reach on that still afternoon and I gave him the best news he could possibly have hoped for. Maybe it's not literally true, but it was like my hands were blocks of stone and I just pounded the champ's wasted face.

Writing this now, sitting by a big window that a bird crashes into every so often, I realize that this story cannot free itself of something vile and true; my version is post-Barrientos, when his frame no longer unsettles the ring and he can only come back and punch here on the page. A bird—more brown than black—flies up, all set to break its neck as I introduce the plot as if I were cutting the laces off Nacho's gloves after a fight. The blade obeys, but it's long, like a vengeful favor. A tap on the window distracts me, a soft, cushioned little bam, not too loud, as if the wings were just sort of weighing up the possibility of suicide; it's strange that birds can't see solid objects through glass, things that aren't air but something else.

Ignacio Barrientos was never an idol. He didn't have the amazing luck of Macías "The Mouse" or the erratic luck of "Spike" Olivares; he never made it to one-name fame (like "Butter" and

"Chiquita" did), nor to the dynastic honor of derived nicknames (the nth "Kid" from Tamaulipas or La Merced). He soaked up punishment stubbornly, and though we all know that boxing is more about taking blows than it is about dishing them out, Nacho complicated fights unnecessarily, he let his opponents work him over and then went for an agonizing knockout. He didn't have a very clean record but he won the national lightweight belt, he was champion of one of boxing's many world bodies, and one night they cooed into his ear about a fight for the unified crown, all the titles together, dangling before his fists. He could never turn his falls and spilled blood into a winning personality, but he knuckled down enough to at least be there, at the top of his class.

I followed all of his seventy-two fights and covered them in *Arena,* not just to fill my column, "On the Ropes," but because watching him made my stomach churn and more than once made me scream and shout and raise my fists as if I, too, had won something, paltry and too late.

Countless times as we were going to press I searched for clues to explain why Ignacio Barrientos was famed but not idolized: he won as if he were losing; his outraged face practically begged you to avert your gaze and focus instead on the nearest Corona Extra ad. Even though that's why we all go, to see it, and the crowd cheers, "Spilling blood is what you do!" no one actually thinks that a busted eyebrow equals triumph, or that a face all sewn up like a baseball is what a crook who made out good looks like. "El Negro" Peláez said once, ringside, "How much you want to bet that by the sixth round he's toast," and then he pulled out three hundreds. I took them because he smelled like cheap hair cream, because he wrote a column in a rival paper in bile, because his nails were polished, and because he was playing with a gold, cube-shaped ring. "El Negro" was repulsive enough that I didn't grant him the satisfaction of contradiction. Better to lose the bet, Nacho in the sixth round, sucking air in through his mouthpiece, his guard down, wearing the resourceful look of someone who's starting to stare at the canvas. It was nothing new: "El Negro" Peláez holding the money, and the certainty that Nacho would lose consciousness as well as the title. Ten minutes later, when it seemed too late already, the champ's eyes took on that paranoid gleam, his fists started to swing, and "El Negro's" face softened in horror.

My pieces are frankly biased and heed old man Severio's number one journalistic maxim: "Write with your kidneys!" The editor is legendary for his Delicados smokes, rum, Maalox, bribe taking, typos, and whores (in that order), but more than anything he is known as the champion of an intense, urological style. At *Arena,* anyone cocky who claims that sports are "games" is an easy target. You've got to know how to hide your respect for culture. Maybe that's why I left the only draft of my only novel in the last crocodile cab I ever got into in my life. When I first started at *Arena* I had the irritating air of an intellectual, because I had covered two Central American wars, and though I got more diseases than stories out of the experience, the veterans of a thousand stadiums saw me as a pretentious jerk coming from serious journalism (out of an inverse sense of respect, at *Arena* we trust only the sensationalist blood-and-guts press, the only kind lower than ours).

I've taken books into the office, but only clandestinely. I wear a painter's jacket, which I like because Onetti fits so well into the roomy pockets; I make book covers out of our newspaper pages, printed in an unforgettable blue and white, and when the office is dead I read, my book between my elbows and the computer screen, trying to maintain a dazed look of stupor.

All this explains, in part, why I went out to Valle de Bravo; somehow I had to shake off the years I'd spent at the paper, just pounding the keyboard, had to invent the ability to do something else: if I couldn't write a story, I could provoke one. This is what I think now, by the bird window—strange that there are so many in a city with no trees; but on the way out to Valle I was overcome by an urge to help my friend. When I got past Toluca, I opened the glove compartment in search of a tape and found a postcard from the Clinic, picturing cottages set around a lapis blue lake. With sedative script, the company wished me a "Happy Recovery." By the time I reached the part of the road where the woods start, I loved Nacho; he'd paid for my treatment in those luxurious cottages, with the same detached, guardian's composure that he bought my house in the Colonia del Periodista and the car in which I was driving out to see him. People who make millions in sports usually spend cash like they're trying to break another record, and they dwell too much on the tabs they pick up that mean nothing to them and everything to you. Nacho paid like there were no consequences, he never looked on his gifts like he owned them; if anything bugged me, it was that he seemed so unaware of his own generosity that it was impossible to thank him. On the road to Valle de Bravo, the Clinic's postcard reinforced my urge to speak to him and finally repay all those things I owed him.

On the curves, sunlight filtered through the trees, but then I came to a foggy area, the temperature dropped abruptly, and a sudden downpour carried me to other, far-off memories, in which I felt Nacho's hands around my neck and on my shoulders, as if the memories were part of the pressure and the feeling and the threat. We grew up together, like I said, in the canyons along one side of Mexico City. We saw the lights at night and we longed for them. I used to go to his house all the time—flowerpots on the patio that smelled like weddings and cemeteries; the wood-burning stove in the kitchen without a door; his four sisters laughing boisterously; the yellowy dog sprawled out obliviously, unaware that they had rescued it and that resting its head on an old tire was bliss. We discovered hiding places in the sand mines together. That was where we once took Consuelo to see her pointy tits and where Nacho first started shadowboxing. I was the first to discover his prodigious punch when he broke my nose. When it came to blows, the fact that I had three years on him never meant a thing.

Life sees to its affairs with disdain, and after the championship, any story that doesn't lead to glory sounds cheap. Heroes make little of their previous battles. I took Nacho to the Constitution Gym and spoke to fifteen zombies before "One Cent" Lupe took him into his stable of fighters. But if I hadn't been there, some other admirer with a busted nose would have taken care of him so he could make off with the scraps from the banquet.

I've written enough "On the Ropes" columns to organize memories by what Ignacio Barrientos was like in the ring. More than a killer instinct, the natural-born fighter shows suicidal tendencies; stifling the survival instinct, keeping it from kicking in, is the first proof of his talent, but no one knows how to cultivate the desire for punishment. Destitution and good reflexes are not enough. We spent endless afternoons despising the canyon and the sand mines without Nacho ever showing a glimmer of any talent aside from jumping fences and unscrupulously bossing people around. So how did he turn into a loner who taunted his own shadow in the sand mine caverns?

The weather on the road to Valle de Bravo controlled my memories. The rain turned to hail as I recalled Ignacio's older sister's funeral, the distant lights of the city seen from our shithole of a neighborhood, the car that plunged into the canyon and went up in magnificent flames, and our realization that we had never seen anything better than that destruction. I ran through the humiliations and tragedies that had wounded us but left no scars, barring the conviction that we had to get out, leave behind those houses half buried in the sand and the sky crisscrossed with wires carrying stolen electricity. It was pointless, going down this path of petty grievances, but long-gone humiliations had an odd way of seeming almost pleasant in this storm, and I didn't deny myself a single one.

The key to understanding Nacho lay elsewhere. One single, savage act had prepared him to have his face smashed in beneath the stadium floodlights. We hated Riquelme because he lived far away and had a warehouse of what we imagined to be incredible stuff. Every three days, a truck came and dropped off boxes that filled up his sixty-some-square-foot, asbestos-shingled building. The whole thing was Gypsy López's idea. I remember his eyebrows had a special way of trapping dirt. His big hands gestured along with the plan. We could threaten Riquelme with a toy gun when he pulled up in the truck, we could use Gypsy's friend in Tepito to sell the stuff. It was all so simple and we were all so sick of everything that even the downside sounded good. "If they catch us, you won't get more than two years in a reformatory," he told Nacho, who had just turned sixteen.

We didn't even know what we were stealing. Gypsy made some hoods out of old sacks and we wore them to pull the gun on Riquelme. It was getting dark and that side of the canyon was deserted. Riquelme gave us the keys to the truck, and that should have been the end of it, but Nacho said something through his sackcloth mask, and the guy got scared and let a scream out of his horrible gap-toothed mouth. Then he ran toward the canyon. Nacho ran after him. We waited a long time, hearing nothing but a far-off explosion in the mines. Finally Nacho came back, shaken, no longer wearing his hood. "He's down there," he spat on the ground. Then, brokenly, he told us how he had caught up to Riquelme on the hill and they'd struggled until he fell off the edge. We walked over to the cliff; down at the bottom you could see a speck of sky blue: Riquelme's shirt.

We went to Tepito to sell the merchandise. It turned out to be Korean toys, lizard men and other plastic shit. We got next to nothing for it and dumped the truck in La Merced.

When we got back home, the money was burning a hole in my pocket. We had destroyed our magnificent dream of becoming thieves, and Riquelme was still in the gorge. Gypsy said, "It's better if they don't see us together. I'll take care of it." His voice had a cutting edge to it. The next day his eyebrows were dustier than ever. He told us he'd gone down into the gorge. Riquelme was dead, dogs were barking and starting to attract people's attention, the cops would be onto it any minute. "All for some Korean piece-of-shit toys," was his way of saying he wanted nothing else to do with us.

Dust storms were all that made the rounds on our streets; there were no interrogations and no patrols. Riquelme turned into just one more thing on the long list of stuff lost in the canyon. But Nacho changed, like we'd been caught. One afternoon, drinking beers and throwing bottles into an abyss too deep to make any noise, he said, all broken up, "I killed him. You know?" I nodded, not really knowing what was inside him. "It was an accident,"

I said, "and we didn't steal hardly anything." We were clean, no one suspected anything, the toys were just some ridiculous, plastic pieces of crap. But there was no convincing him. "I killed him. You know?" I would remember his voice, broken and imploring, years later, while reading a story about the first black man sentenced to die in the gas chamber; as the lethal pellet started to smoke, the man whispered, "Save me, Joe Louis, save me, Joe Louis." That was Nacho on the canyon cliff. I won't repeat the account I published for nearly a decade in *Arena*'s blue typeface. The champ was more proud of his injuries than of his record; he'd ask little kids to count his scars like his face was some game. He only agreed to take on the Constitution's sparrings when he realized they respected him enough to hit him till he pissed blood. Nacho was punishing himself for the dead man in the canyon who, strangely, helped him get out of there, the shadow that granted him a future.

The rain cleared as I drove through golden pastures. Somewhere, a little piece of rainbow was floating around, and I rolled down the window to take in the scent of wet grass. I hadn't smelled fresh air in ages. Most mornings I woke up with the taste of cheap cigar in my mouth, and nights were an alcoholic haze that was getting harder and harder to stomach, just substituting booze for drugs. Making another trip to the Clinic and its placid lake was not in my plans; I didn't want to increase my debt to Nacho, or repeat that pathetic scene, the champ loaded down with presents, Miriam standing behind him with a charitable look on her face, biting her nails like she wanted to be someplace else. "You live like a boxer," Nacho smiled, making a playful fist. Room 304 clashed with the statement: it was all sunshine, clean sheets, floral-scented walls. But he was clearly referring to what had happened before, a fiasco far too luxurious for a sportswriter.

The champ (back then he'd defended his title six times) had left his retreat on an Arizona farm to bring me boxes full of towels and designer clothes. He'd always had a childish fascination with fabric: the gold and burgundy silk robes he'd don to trot down to the ring, the gold-trimmed shirts, the towel it seemed he would never throw in.

At public appearances with her husband, Miriam smiled with detached gaiety, like she was campaigning or picking a number out of a fishbowl for some drawing. At the Clinic she'd granted me her profile: a thick lock of brown hair and a thin, nervous little nose that made me think of that bowl overflowing with cocaine, four or five keys sticking out of it like little spoons. Was it worth going back to that night, searching out Miriam's eyes, which were trying to avoid me?

Nacho motioned to the empty armchair and Miriam sat down in it, to listen from an insurmountable distance. A light wind blew in the window and I tried to think that the sweet fragrance from the walls mixed with Miriam's own scent; I imagined the smell and Nacho repeated, "So, tell me," and she stared at the buckles on her shoes.

I talked and he drank glass after glass of water. I had seen him in that state many times, nervous because the fight was coming up and he wasn't at his weight and his life was a hell of boiled vegetables and steaks that he'd chew just to savor the juices and then spit out onto a tray. He'd get tense, be full of energy, as if fasting were his source of strength.

I told him about the guys who had given me coke at some dive in Ciudad Juarez. Later, the party moved on to a brothel where some cop proposed a Vietnam-style duel, each of us with our own machine gun. A couple other cops who were still technically compos mentis arrested me for possession of cocaine before we got to play kill or be killed with their boss. And although all I did was lend my nose to the story, I ended up being charged with arms trafficking and the unusual crime of "nocturnality." Nacho knew all that already (he'd spoken to the governor, who he'd dedicated several fights to, hired a lawyer who wore huge, clunky, drug dealer bracelets, paid the papers to kill the story—"So, finally you're worth something to me, after all," old Severio had said approvingly), but he wanted to hear it again, as if my irresponsibility were some inexhaustible source of wonder.

It was thanks to him I was in the Clinic, and I had to repay the favor by telling him my story. My revenge was to sit and think of other things, of the night I went to Don Samuel's house. The big-name promoter was throwing a party for two black fighters who had just signed with him; one wore an imitation leopard-skin shirt and a little cap that looked like a chrome flan, and the other was dressed all in white (except for the gold hoops hanging from his deformed ears).

Don Samuel doesn't live extravagantly, for someone who's been bribing governments and businessmen for forty years. Bizarrely, he collects Don Quijotes. That night he wore a tie with a terrible rendition of the Knight of the Sad Countenance on it and proudly showed me a table that had a dozen glass and papier-mâché Quijotes.

The boxing czar is a big man with a huge stomach and curly, wiry hair. His coats and jackets all have leather or fur collars, as if his neck were his weak spot, and he wears corporate cufflinks from Aeromexico, or Televisa, or some hotel in Vegas. One of the world's greatest unsolved genetic mysteries is how that lump of a man who declares knockouts managed to produce Miriam. At the party I assumed she was just another one of the expensive models there for decoration.

That morning I had looked at myself in the mirror and thought I liked my image, thought I looked like a detective I saw once in an Italian movie, a guy who spent sleepless nights doing nothing more than figuring out that the world is a shitty place and in the end he sticks a gun in his mouth and pulls the trigger. Not an exemplary life but it had its charm. With masochistic vanity I thought my wasted face showed signs of some interesting mis-fortune. Miriam saw something similar but came to a different conclusion: that I was a desperate drug addict. She asked me if I wanted a line and told me to follow her. That's when I realized she lived there; her tiny hands knew every doorknob. We got to a bathroom with a marble floor and a sink with two golden cranes that spit water. Miriam opened a cupboard and took out a bowl of cocaine with the four or five keys sticking out, like a little snack prepared for the guests. The huge bathroom mirror had been cov-ered by an additional oyster-colored film. I stared at Miriam's naked form in its expanse. She had to force me to turn back to the extraordinary body that had come out of the mirror and some dream where sheer necessity was enough to reap rewards.

I left the party in such a state of ecstasy that I even praised Don Samuel's Don Quijote collection. Now, with the birds loitering around my window, I like to think that I won a bet I didn't know how to collect on. Several days went by and I didn't speak to Miriam; in my favorite version, there are moments of total anguish: I decide not to look her up since the miracle could never be repeated and I fear being rejected as a forgettable one-night stand she had when she needed an attractively debauched face; in other, more placid versions, there is an element of something I confuse with maturity: I decide to give it time in order to postpone the pleasure of the next date, keep the past intact and at the same time grant it a future; in the most honest version, I realize I enjoy the fall: I have an ace up my sleeve and I blow it, and I like that.

At any rate, weeks went by with no news from Miriam. She called me at *Arena*, sounding chipper, complicit without being intimate, as if we'd known each other our whole lives. Several times she made the absurd claim, "That doesn't surprise me, coming from you." Actually, anything at all coming from me should have surprised her, since the only thing she had to go on was my desperate nostrils and the delayed response of the rest of my body. But Miriam took for granted that I was thrilled to hear from her and that I would help her out since we'd been lifelong friends for all of one second. It didn't take long for her to work her way around to the real reason she'd called: Ignacio Barrientos and I were old friends, she was dying to meet him, she didn't want to take advantage of her father's connections.

I agreed to introduce them. Somehow, I rested easier knowing that my good fortune was impossible; I intuited the many complications that loving Miriam would entail. She'd used me as a bridge to Nacho, which meant they deserved each other. Still, I struggled to isolate two separate situations: Miriam sought me out because she wanted to put something to the test at her father's party, really scrape the bottom of the barrel, prove that there are limits and that they can be broken; and Miriam sought me out because she wanted to get close to Nacho. Both were true and neither was pleasant but it was best not to confuse them. But by pursuing her so lethargically and introducing them so readily I hadn't blown any winning hand. Miriam had only ever been there for me that night in the mirror; there had been no ace up my sleeve.

I could never keep track of the women in Nacho's life; none were really worth remembering; their shifty eyes, their bare arms with vaccination marks or big moles or scars or burns, their cheap, tight, gaudy dresses with zippers that didn't zip all the way up without a safety pin suggested that they didn't chase the champ in order to put misery behind them but to wallow in it.

Nacho's arm could only be raised in victory when his face was a mess. Much later, in the wee hours of his victory night celebration, he'd have to let loose some additional violence, the cruelty he had spared his opponent. I saw him run over a dog, I saw him break the nose of a dark-skinned girl who'd gazed at him in devotion, as if taking blows were a depraved form of prayer, I saw him throw an aluminum baseball bat through a furniture store window, I saw him wail and cry with abandon, in cars and in cafeterias where we waited for day to break. He always needed an act of insanity to prove that the fight was over.

Miriam was nothing like the neighborhood masochists who suffered along with Nacho in his darkest hours, but I still never thought she could change his way of life.

Two weeks after I introduced them I got a present from Nacho, a gold Rolex with my name inscribed on the back of the watch face. It took some doing to convince a jeweler that I wanted to get rid of the letters so I could pawn it, and getting rid of the dirty feeling I got from the cash I sold it for was even harder. The watch was part of a system of suppliers and bloodsuckers whose intercourse had to benefit a third party.

At the time, Miriam and Nacho were in Acapulco, facing the luxurious dangers he always needed after a fight, always on the verge of cracking his head open on the edge of a swimming pool, crashing his car into a palm tree, fulfilling his promise of leaping into La Quebrada. After the trip, Miriam started to change the champ's days. I don't know how she did it, because her first step was to protect him from his past, keep him safe from the distasteful memories that didn't fit in with the image of his fame. In short, he stopped seeing me. Our contact became limited to the gym interviews he granted all reporters.

Miriam was the one who told me they were getting married. With polite reserve, she repeated the name of the street twice, as if I had never been to her father's house. Nacho couldn't talk to me, he was training at a farm in Chihuahua, I'd have to forgive him. The day of the wedding, my friend gave me a Mont Blanc. That's how I knew I was his witness.

After that party, where every table had a bottle of cognac as a centerpiece, Don Samuel promoted all of Ignacio Barrientos's fights and turned him into an efficient moneymaking machine. Miriam would smile, ringside, from a distance that sometimes made it into the photos, a demure, attractive silhouette that maybe only I saw as a commanding force. In the following years Nacho grew to be a cost-effective champion who would never become an idol; his lengthy beatings were part of his almost secret life, the one nobody could identify with.

By then I had chalked up two divorces, one novel left behind in a taxi, far too many pages in *Arena,* and I had stopped resembling that suicidal Italian detective from the silver screen; my face showed only signs of standard, routine exhaustion, no longer ennobled by tragedy. Nacho was the only one who got a kick out of my cut-rate disasters, like the day he came to visit me at the Clinic and Miriam was a lock of hair, downcast eyes, a perfume I thought I could catch in the breeze that filtered into my room. That morning I wanted her more than ever, maybe because it was impossible and destructive, or maybe because I refused to be a secondary yet vital calamity in Nacho's life, the friend who allowed him to come out of seclusion weighed down by gifts and to be generous enough to roar with laughter at my sordid tale.

If Nacho was happy to put up with my misadventures, he could deal with Miriam cheating on him with me.

Weeks later I sought out Miriam's eyes in the crowd—among the greased heads and shaved skulls of ex-champions and body-guards—but she purposely avoided me, she was a soft glow that ruffled the air, like the birds that approach my window from time to time.

On the road to Valle I felt the sadness and the guilt of the betrayal I never managed to commit, and a belated sense of grati-tude toward Nacho; I wanted to kiss Miriam's thighs but deep down it would have been enough to confront her, speak to her, assure myself that her distance wasn't part of a strategy, that I wasn't important enough to warrant such measures. There was something strange and determined and fascinating in not know-ing I could be like this.

The night they were presenting the national sporting awards, I followed her down the golden carpet of a hotel. A long hallway led us to a screen with a sign for the ladies' room. Miriam walked like no one was following her. A little ways before the restroom I grabbed her wrist. She turned, startled, and I squeezed her arm until her eyes filled with tears. Then, idiotically, I said, "Leave him. He's crazy." Clearly, Nacho's obsessions were nowhere near as compelling as insanity; besides, by then she had known him better than me for years. Miriam smiled as I loosened my grip. She looked at me calmly, as if I were not making a fool of myself. "I know," she replied, her smile fading. "You got me into this," she added. "If he sees us, he'll kill you." And with that she slipped behind the screen where I couldn't follow her.

That night I drank every adulterated whiskey the hotel offered me. Miriam was a fleeting silhouette on the dance floor once more, and she disappeared in the early hours of the morning. On the last stretch of the drive to Valle de Bravo, the whole scene seemed even more absurd. Miriam had told me two enchanting lies: I had been decisive in her alliance with Nacho, and I could throw it into question. I remembered what she looked like step-ping off the dance floor: Nacho was putting on his signature shades and she was smiling off toward the ice swan melting on the buffet table. I wondered if they'd talked about how bad I was doing and the terrible things I could say. No, Nacho would never be jealous of the friend who was ruining his own life and sinking without a trace.

Then for months Nacho's fight in Japan was the only thing anyone talked about. *Arena* decided they couldn't afford to send me so I was reduced to spewing out whatever came in on the agency wires. The match was postponed when the champ was already in Osaka, Don Samuel complained about the judges, which did no good since in the East foreigners only win by knockout, and he sued the local promoter. It seemed like it was all going to come crashing down in a maze of photos of the champ standing beside giant Buddhas, allegations against the Japanese mafia, and the growing body of evidence of Don Samuel's manipulations. Finally, Nacho made it to the ring and held on to the crown after an uppercut in the ninth round, seconds before the ref decided his busted eyebrows counted as a technical knockout.

Nacho brought me back a little samurai sword from that long, notorious trip, and I still have it, the ideal weapon for someone who couldn't fight for Miriam. I stopped harassing her, accepted her distance, caught glimpses of her face at parties and stadiums, not such a terrible menace, like the birds who fly up to my window and don't always snuff it.

The night before the Kurtis Kramer fight for the unified championship, someone told me that she was in the States on a shopping spree, like the boxer's wife and promoter's daughter she was. I got on the road to Valle de Bravo pronto. Now was the time to be alone with my friend; I was bringing him a message as if it were a tiger. I spent a good part of the trip trying to tame the savage, bloodthirsty truth I was going to tell him.

I saw the lake dotted with sailboats, the mansions with their tiled roofs, the plaza with people sipping margaritas and talking on cell phones, a landscape completely foreign to the prefight purgatory. I kept on to Avándaro, the forest where Nacho was holing up to get some fresh air.

I followed the directions that one of "One Cent" Lupe's seconds had given me, and I got to an isolated plot of land, a dirty pond surrounded by three wooden cabins.

I found "One Cent" by a wooden fence, a towel around his neck, as always. "Nacho went for a run. We didn't know you were coming. Go on into the den."

The den turned out to be a room that smelled like a fireplace, with sheepskin rugs and leather chairs. I waited alone. I added Gypsy's words to my own, stroking the tiger. Every little while, I heard a strange bird calling.

To pass the time, and because I was going to have to go back to the hell of the newspaper after all, I ran through the details of the fight. As usual, Nacho's reach was his weak point, but this time there was a two-centimeter difference. Beside Kramer's willowy frame, Nacho looked like a clumsy block, no grace, a mailbox where his opponent would post all his letters. Although Kurtis had a weak punch, he'd tire of reaching Nacho's face.

I walked through the room, went into the bathroom—three kinds of lotion, a silk robe on a rusty hook, a mirror with a brass frame—examined everything carefully, like an assassin memorizing the individual components that make up the life he's going to extinguish.

It seemed like ages before I heard Nacho's feet on the gravel by the pond. He walked in wearing a hooded sweatshirt. He wiped the sweat running down his face with bandaged hands. "Smells like shit." He waved his arms, gesturing to the smoke from my cigarette. He opened a window, letting in fresh air and a lot of flies.

Nacho collapsed into one of the leather chairs. He had a stiff way of sitting on furniture, he could never be on it without making it squeak. He gave me a sidelong smile and his eyes shone. He was giving me a few seconds to explain my presence. I freed the beast. "You didn't kill him." His jaw hardened, he looked up at the ceiling beams, tried to say something, looked back at me with that paranoid gleam I had so often seen in the ninth round. "You didn't kill Riquelme," the clarification was unnecessary and I delivered it with a therapeutic smile. After more than ten years,

Nacho could sleep easy, that's what old friends were for, for taking something from the past and putting it in order.

Nacho twirled his hands awkwardly. He wanted the whole story. We were so tense that I lit another cigarette without him even noticing. I shot nicotine into my lungs automatically. Nacho stopped making noise in his chair.

Arena had sent me to Veracruz to cover the umpteenth sale of the Red Sharks franchise. I knew Gypsy López lived there. He had partnered up with two ex-soccer players and some TV schmuck to open a steak-and-seafood grill. He was easy to track down. What was hard, though, was distinguishing his features in that bloated face. His yellowy eyes and asthmatic wheeze didn't go with his jocular tone. "You lost a woman, but you don't know what you've gained!" he squealed when we got to my second divorce.

Like so many fatsos, Gypsy made a show of fasting. He sat at a table with me for three hours and only drank water (twelve or thirteen little glasses). He stuffed me with crabs, shrimp tamales, a steak from his partner's cattle ranch. He fanned himself with an ineffectual rag and got up from time to time to go see to some TV presenters, wave the rag at someone in greeting, or insult a waiter. His enormous pink guayabera navigated the restaurant like a mammoth marshmallow. But his physical deterioration didn't inspire much pity; he was so proud of his life that there was no feeling sorry for him. He reeled off his triumphs and kept repeating the details (after going to talk to the presenters and drinking another glass of water, he'd pick up the thread too far back). He had three gorgeous daughters, he said, and I verified via the laminated photos he spread out on the table; he had lucked out and become a widower at an early age, his new wife was really hot: young, dark, and horny. She had worked in one of his whorehouses. Gypsy had a unique way of overcoming scruples, as if he could only be happy going against the grain. "I got a boar!" he cried suddenly, even his pets had to be transgressive. The entire conversation could be summed up by his guiding principle, "I got my way." Two of his waiters were gay guys who he'd gotten out of jail after Carnaval; his car had Sinaloa plates because he got it in an auction after they arrested some narcs at a safe house; the shrimp he served came from a co-op in Rio Panuco where he paid "in kind" with nights at his brothel. Success was to be found in basements, in back alleys, in places that turned their backs on custom. "I got my way."

"Look at this face," he smiled, appalling teeth on display. The worse he looked, the more he showed off his cars, his wild animal pets, his rented women.

Lost in his world of sleazy glory, he knew nothing about the pieces I published in *Arena* or the eulogistic series I had dedicated to the lightweight champ. He was very surprised to hear that we were still in touch. After his third question about Nacho, I exaggerated our friendship.

"You remember Riquelme?" he said suddenly. "Fucking stupid, stealing those Korean toys!"

His yellowy eyes were tinged with red.

This was the moment, the meeting's finale: Gypsy realized he could change something on the table. He leaned in so close that I caught the medicinal whiff of his sweat. He smiled tightly, with a touch of contempt, as if he'd been waiting to be rewarded for years and had to waste it now to prove that he hadn't needed it.

"I killed that bastard."

I took a drink of nauseating rum and contradicted him: all three of us had seen Riquelme at the bottom of the canyon.

"I went down after that, he was still alive, barely, he reached his hands up to me, asking for something. I took a rock and smashed his face in."

I went back over the expression Gypsy had chosen, "smashed his face in."

"Nacho thinks he killed him," I said, unnecessarily.

Gypsy asked for another glass of water. He took a long drink and swallowed affectedly. Nacho could believe whatever he wanted, that's why he was famous, that's why he was loaded, that's why he had Miriam.

"You know her?"

"Nacho can unify every championship there is and no one's gonna remember his face. But no one forgets his wife." Gypsy stared at me like he was trying to wring out some truth that I wasn't letting go of. "We haven't seen each other for fucking years," he added. "Maybe we'll never see each other again."

Maybe he was dying and felt the need to confess, maybe he wanted to bring everyone else down when he fell, maybe he was looking for a new way to divvy up the pathetic loot we'd stolen all those years ago. Then I stopped trying to explain his denunciation. Suddenly, something struck me so hard I could no longer focus on anything else: Nacho fought his whole life to free himself from a crime he hadn't committed and Gypsy lived with no remorse about the crime he had committed. I saw him go home with bloody hands, saw him pour buckets of water over himself since the neighborhood had no running water, saw him wash himself of the filth and the fatigue and then forget all about it the next day. Just like that. He never did anything like that again and maybe Riquelme's memory stayed with him somehow as something foundational, the crack needed for the rest of his days, the unsavory luxury that everything else was built on. Now—and this started to change things—he wanted Nacho to know. It was obvious that I'd tell him. Gypsy López calculated his blow skillfully, but what's more, he calculated its consequences.

Back at the cabin in Valle de Bravo I finished talking. Nacho looked right through me like I didn't exist.

Only then did I realize what Gypsy had suspected back at the grill. I had simply repeated his words, with the most utter ineptitude, without weighing the consequences. Nacho was innocent. He could live in peace. But there in the log cabin I understood the nasty smile and bleary eyes: Gypsy overcame the damage and the horror, he fed off his trouble, while Nacho kept just fighting it without ever settling the score or finding a way out. Gypsy could toss out that confession, he had no reason to worry because we were in Mexico, and besides, no one would believe me if he didn't corroborate the story.

Nacho snatched up the phone and hurled it to the floor. He knelt down before a piece of furniture and banged his head against it until it bled. He began to howl as I closed the windows. Then he raised his big, bandaged fists to his face in an awkward, pathetic attempt to dry his tears.

"Gypsy could be lying," I said flatly.

"Don't be an asshole. You believed him right off. That's why you're here."

It was true. Riquelme couldn't have died on that soft, sandy slope; at most, he might have broken a leg. There had to be another explanation for his disfigured face, it seemed so obvious now.

Nacho paced the room obsessively while I prattled on, spouting meaningless banter. Now, by the bird window, I know nothing else could have destroyed him like that good news at a bad time.

I smoked half a dozen cigarettes. When he collapsed into that leather chair and stared at the ceiling, I decided to stand up. My legs hurt from the tension. I had to get out of there. Nacho realized I had run out of things to say and offered a weak, "Thanks."

The word stuck with me on the curves surging out of the fog. I pulled up close to a trailer to guide myself by its lights. I drove very slowly, knowing that if he went over the cliff, my fate would be the same; I had to delegate something, follow someone else's destiny, cleanse myself of the clammy feeling of having pushed Nacho into the wrong corner.

The fight for the unified title was one of the most talked-about disasters in boxing history. Nacho lost on a technical knockout in the fourth round, but he had been a mess from the start. Few people could understand where his weakness was coming from: for the first time, he was looking for a quick win, he was trying suicidal combinations and his opponent, despite a weak punch, worked him over mercilessly. Revenge was a carbon copy of the disaster.

A maddening sense of honor made Nacho agree to eight more fights before retiring. He was up against weaker contenders each time, and they all defeated him. His rivals would move, incredulous, into a neutral corner to watch as Ignacio Barrientos took the count without even trying to get back in the fight.

One morning he called and woke me up at six o'clock, too intense for greetings.

"I want you to be the first to know. I'm retiring."

I asked him if he'd read my column.

"You know I haven't," he said, which was a relief. With pathetic obstinacy, I had written that Nacho's defeats were the product of his thirst for triumph: he wanted to win come what may and was no longer willing to be grazed; he was rejecting the endurance strategy that had been his trademark and trying to behave like his opponents. My last column was imaginatively titled "Barrientos in the Mirror," but *Arena*'s readers don't pay three pesos for paradoxes and no one really cared.

Nacho had made the best of the situation. I asked him how he was doing financially.

"Can't complain," he said.

A few weeks later, Miriam called me at the paper. She sounded bitter and cutting, like she'd drunk nail polish. She asked me to meet her at a bar in the Zona Rosa.

I wanted to see her, and I confess that I looked forward to feeling her tiny hand in mine. But, yet again, Miriam was more vital in her absence. She looked at me with a harshness I'd never seen, and by the shine in her eyes it wasn't hard to guess she was on something. She ordered a vodka gimlet that she didn't drink, probably intended to impress me as something I would never order.

"How could you?" was the first thing she said. "Didn't you think about anyone else?" She waited for me to light my cigarette and then went in for the kill in a solemn tone. "Do you like playing God?"

"And what would you have done?"

"What I did," she replied. "You think I didn't know Gypsy killed that bastard? Everybody knows that. What planet are you on? Gypsy's done business with every asshole in town." She wanted to degrade me so bad that she swore with real gusto, like she could insult language itself. "My father knows him, he's partnered up with TV people, the gossip was all over every fucking gym in the country. You and Nacho were the only ones who didn't know. You, because you're an idiot, and Nacho, because he didn't want to know." She paused at length, a tear ran down her cheek, and for a minute her face looked almost pleasant; then, in a pitiful tone, she repeated, "How could you?"

That was the last thing I heard. I left her there, with her ridiculous, untouched drink.

I threw a bill down on the table because I wanted to offend her, though I knew vengeance was not mine. And then I understood Miriam's cautious distance, her way of keeping me in her orbit, as if getting any closer were dangerous, not so much because I could substitute Nacho but because she didn't want us to be alone; what I signified, the unspeakable past, the truths of another time, could get to her husband. She used me to get to him, but what's more, that surreal night of cocaine and water-spitting cranes provided an excuse to never let me near her again: Nacho had a reason to destroy me. There was bitter irony in being the last one to find out, especially as the journalist looking to tell the story nobody should hear.

A few weeks after our meeting, Miriam left the champ. Don Samuel's lawyers got her all the properties and the bank accounts that could be salvaged. She must have blamed me so fiercely to prepare for the damage she was about to do.

Not even Ignacio Barrientos's fall was charismatic. Except for Macías "The Mouse," "Pipino" Cuevas, and a handful of others, tragic downfall is the last step for boxers. Nacho's disappearance was cliché. He learned to use a lathe and opened a workshop in the Colonia de los Doctores.

I went to see him to suggest writing his biography. He was engrossed in a piece of metal and listened to the proposal without the slightest sign of interest.

A few years went by and then one night I got a call from a woman I didn't know. She said she was Nacho's wife. She had a raw, young voice and said, "They found something in his lungs."

I went to the hospital and they wouldn't let me in the treatment room. In the hallway I smoked some cigarettes with his pulmonologist. He told me about Nacho's strange constitution. His respiratory capacity was shot. He'd been screwed since he was a kid, because of the sand mines. It was against all odds that someone who could barely breathe had become an athlete. There was no way for the doctor to know that in his good years, Nacho lived to hurt himself; his breathless body had been his ally.

I thought that Ignacio Barrientos's early death would make a case for my biography and wrote him a long obit in *Arena,* which I ended by quoting that black boxer who'd had no way out. "Save me, Joe Louis." Not a single publisher wanted to sign a book on the life of one of Mexico's many forgettable boxing champions.

I never heard from Miriam again. From time to time, I imagine her at the side of some other accidental killer, tending to his wounds, pleasing him with guilt and punishment. And then, of course, I walk into the picture, slip in between the bodyguards, the swollen faces and flashes that always surrounded the champ; I know I have something to tell him; on good days I tell him a truth that he can't hear because the crowd is screaming his name, but there are rainy days and insomniac nights and other moments when I walk up to Nacho and whisper a good word that I had wanted to tell him since we were kids, one that only adds to his lonely demise. Thanks to me, Nacho died broken and in peace. Maybe that was my way of sparring with him, of beating him as a reporter; maybe, too, it was my way of showing Miriam that I loved him more.

They just made me subeditor at *Arena* and I won't have time to write "On the Ropes" anymore. Before I clean out my drawers I wanted to get this story off my chest. Night has fallen by my window. One last bird approaches, sees its shadow in the glass, retreats in fear, and saves its life.

Translated from the Spanish by Lisa Dillman

ABOUT THE AUTHOR

Juan Villoro, born in Mexico City in 1956, is the author of the novels *El testigo, El disparo de argón,* and *Materia dispuesta.* He has been honored with the Herralde Prize for his novel *El testigo* (2004), the Xavier Villaurrutia Award for his short story collection *La casa pierde* (House Loses), the Mazatlán Award for his collection of essays entitled *Efectos personales* (Personal Effects) (2001), and the International Board on Books for the Young Award for the children's novel *El profesor Zíper y la fabulosa guitarra eléctrica.* He has been a professor at the UNAM (National Autonomous University of Mexico) in Mexico City, Yale University, and the Pompeu Fabra University in Barcelona. He has translated many books into Spanish including *Memoirs of an Anti-Semite,* by Gregor von Rezzori, and *A Tree of Night,* by Truman Capote, and he is also the translator of Georg Christoph Lichtenberg's *Aphorisms.* For three years he was the director of *La Jornada Semanal,* the weekly cultural supplement of the Mexican newspaper *La Jornada,* and his literary writing and reportage have appeared in *La Jornada, Reforma, El País, Süddeutsche Zeitung, Frankfurter Allgemeine Zeitung, Granta, Proceso,* and *Letras Libres,* among other publications.

MARIO BELLATIN

"Whenever I'm about to board an airplane I feel a curious impulse to select, from among the passing strangers who are the denizens of airports, one person to whom I would like to be bound forever." There are sentences, like that one from the story translated here, that even lifted out of its context, the reader instantly recognizes as having been written by Mario Bellatin. Typically some extraordinary or intriguingly odd statement is delivered with deadpan aplomb. He is one of contemporary literature's great straight-faced comedians. His writing, so spare, evocative, strange, discomforting, seems descended from Beckett, Barthelme, Vonnegut, well, the great funny-sad clowns of modernism. His sensibility, like theirs, is all his own (post-theirs.) Yes, they are like postcards from some unknown place, not at all like one's own place, that however terse their message, deliver us into a strange landscape of pure narrative. At first you might find the narrative comical, and laugh out loud, but then you begin to feel uneasy, or melancholy, and you wonder: What am I supposed to be feeling about this? Where am I? The spareness of the prose gives little hint, and exacts imagination, secret complicity, trust and then mistrust, and finally trust from the reader. You're on your own, but no, Bellatin has firmly guided you there. How do these slender fictions manage to bring their strange, warped, perverse, utterly lovely worlds so radiantly to life inside you as you read? How do they cast such addictive spells?

A few sentences selected, almost at random—forgive my clumsy translation—from Mario Bellatin's most recent novel, Lessons for a Dead Hare:

"Before going to sit in a café to analyze the works of Sergio Pitol I had to make a phone call to my house in Mexico, during which I found out about the absurd and unlikely situation of a blind narco-trafficker—not the blind poet—who'd arrived from abroad while I was away, and was now using my dining room table as the center of his illicit operations."

"The children emigrated, and soon were said to have become involved in the assassination of the ancient, blind founder of a strange organization of malformed beings."

"Minutes later the lady in the habit was discovered delivering without compassion a series of hammer blows to the head of the blind poet."

"My grandfather used to tell me that the gardener's cabin was even more modest than the truck cab that Macaca lived in. Of course the lack of comforts didn't appear to be the principal reason that the gardeners, one after the other, quit their jobs. Those men were hardly ever capable of giving their reasons in words. They limited themselves to leaving their tools scattered around the park, and simply leaving."

Mario Bellatin's characters are usually misfits or outsiders of one kind or another, sexually odd, physically handicapped or deformed, and are becoming as recognizable now as Beckett's bleak clowns. His prose is filled with tension, surprises, unexpected images, and no matter how seemingly light and playful, loaded with poetic force. His style, in Spanish certainly, his sentences and words, have something of iron, or of stones that fly through the air. His fictions are like enchanting but solid Eiffel constructions that weep from within.

—FRANCISCO GOLDMAN

THE SHEIKA'S CONDITION

*Abds Salam**

Hospital

They treated me in the worst way at the hospital where I went to undergo a series of tests. I couldn't even get the massage they had promised me the day before. I would have been quite fortunate—especially considering my general condition—to receive that kind of treatment. To feel my muscles gradually relaxing and carrying me into a state of almost total unconsciousness. But it seemed that everybody who worked at that hospital was occupied with other matters. I had the impression that they had scheduled too many appointments. Or that there were more than the routine number of emergencies. Convinced that I had made the trip in vain, that I had wasted the morning by showing up for a series of truncated appointments, I prepared to leave the hospital. I don't know why I decided to exit through the emergency room. Perhaps to confirm my suspicion that there were more unexpected cases than usual.

Airplane

Whenever I'm about to board an airplane I feel a curious impulse to select, from among the mass of strangers who are the denizens of airports, one person to whom I would like to be bound forever. This kind of experience is not unusual for members of Sufi communities throughout the world. On certain occasions something tells them that the person in front of them will become, from that moment on, a part of their existence. But despite this peculiar situation, it is necessary to board the plane. One must repress one's feelings to a certain degree and behave like a normal person. As if it weren't already enough to have divested oneself of the garments required to perform the mystical gyrations and ceremonies in which the remembrance of God is omnipresent. In order to attenuate the sense of loss in some way, before making my way to the boarding area I take a vow that even if my body is hundreds of kilometers away, I will never leave the side of the person I have chosen.

Shoe

When I leave the hospital I see Sheika Amina, the leader of the Sufi community to which I have belonged for nearly ten years, appear on the arm of Duja, one of our eldest dervishes. The sheika appears to be ill. She has a faraway look in her eyes and her skin is exceptionally pale. I greet her but she doesn't seem to recognize me. When after a few minutes she becomes aware of my presence, and the strange circumstances of our encounter, she smiles weakly. I make her sit down in a chair at once. Then I go off in search of a doctor. As I mentioned earlier, it didn't seem like a normal day at that hospital, and I can't find anyone to help me. I begin to fear that the sheika will not receive immediate attention. After making a few inquiries I manage to see one of the doctors who just a short while ago had ignored my appointments. After listening to me he orders that the sheika be moved to a garden, in the middle of which sits a wooden table. The doctor has two nurses lay the sheika down on top of it. He asks me to remove her shoes. This proves to be an impossible task. Sheika Amina's shoes are very difficult to describe. They are made of black velvet, with high heels and tassels that turn into knots. It's very difficult to untie the laces that secure them to her ankles. While I work at disentangling them I hear the doctor mention an imminent change of shift. I try to hurry but I can't manage to get the laces untied. The doctor suggests that the patient be treated at a satellite clinic. He has to leave and he doesn't think there is anyone available here, that is, anyone capable of properly examining a sheika. But he says that there will be doctors at the clinic who are trained to handle cases of that nature, though he gives no explanation for such a claim.

Cornice

Some people might consider my desire to sustain, for thousands of kilometers, the memory of a loved one whom I have never met, to be a dramatization of romantic excess. But it's not like that at all. Rather, it has to do with the quest that every member of a Sufi community is expected to undertake in order to be present in the spirits of various people at the same time. At such moments I have the sensation of being able to displace my body into the distance and at the same time remain at the exact point in time and space in which I first set eyes upon the chosen person. Things usually go well. During the trip I make it a habit to concentrate on different zones of the airport, the ascent into the aircraft, the light received by the chosen person at the instant I cast my gaze. Despite all this, when I arrive at my destination I cannot shake off an unremitting fear. The sensation is similar to finding myself standing on the cornice of a tall building or speeding around a sharp curve in the wrong lane.

Martyrs

Then I notice—once I realize the absurdity of attempting to remove the shoes of a sheika—that Duja, the dervish who accompanied her, has disappeared. In her place she has left, as a kind of substitute, a young woman who identified herself as a humble servant. After hearing the doctor's words the sheika sits up on her own and gets to her feet. We head for the parking lot. We get in her car; the short walk apparently seems to have done her good. She appears to be recuperating. The car is pretty old. It's a 1975 Datsun. I remember that she had a car like this before; it was practically a miracle that it ran. They're similar but this one is yellow and the paint is peeling off. Sheika Amina insists on driving. I ask her if I can take the wheel. She smiles and utters the disconcerting phrase that nobody trips over the same stone twice. I think about that saying for a while. Then I realize that the sheika doesn't seem to trust me. Clearly she senses that if I drive we'll never arrive at our destination. I try to remember an occasion when I have driven her in the past, and I recall the time that I took them—the sheika and her mother—home from the mosque. I remember it was an enjoyable trip. Her mother really seemed to get a kick out of my sports car, which was yellow like this one but a convertible. I clearly remember her delight when the roof began to open automatically. But I also remember the time I tried to guide the sheika—when she came with me to see my attending physician— through a series of dark streets leading nowhere. I had to admit she was right. Of course she'd never let me take the wheel. That was quite a bleak night; in addition to receiving my diagnosis as a terminal case, I started driving around aimlessly, going off in increasingly disconcerting directions. My straying came to an end when the sheika declared that from that moment on I had joined the ranks of Sufi martyrs. Muzafer Efendi told her about this years ago in Turkey, when the sheika asked him about the status of dervishes condemned to death. This immediately brought to mind the little plastic statue of the whirling dervish that sits on a shelf in the mosque. The little statue lost an arm a few months ago. When I first saw it I wondered if that dervish would be a Sufi martyr too. Driving her car seems to have made the sheika feel better. She is no longer even the shadow of the sick person who'd entered the hospital. She's becoming more and more animated. There is a curious relationship between her return to life and the car she's driving, inasmuch as it's an old piece of junk that barely runs. As we proceed, a series of traffic accidents occur, brought on mainly by the extremely slow speed at which we are moving. I must admit that I had no idea where we were going, and at that moment I realized that I would never have known how to get to the clinic where we were supposedly heading. The humble servant rides in the backseat without saying a word. We drive for a long time. The monotony is interrupted only by an occasional remark from the sheika, who comments on the dilapidated condition of the car and how awful the traffic is in the city. At one point she looks back at the servant and tells her that I am her best dervish. These words make an impression on me. Among other things, I think about what terrible dervishes the others must be. I feel a kind of nostalgia for the community to which I belong. I can't believe that there are dervishes worse than I, nor can I believe that all of them are beneath me. Just then the car stops in front of a small house.

Dog

When I disembark from the plane I discover that I am in neither of the two spaces where I thought I belonged. I am not in the airport of a distant country, nor in the presence of the person from whom I felt I could not bear to part. I'm sure that I will never know where I really am. It's like the strange process of endlessly descending and ascending an unknown stairway. No one in sight. Except, perhaps, for a dog that Mohammed—peace be upon him—determined was no ordinary mutt but a Saluki, a dog that is not a dog.

Tekke

In front of the house where we've stopped, there are a few broken-down cars. Also remains of pipes and construction materials.

To my surprise, since I thought we were going to the clinic where the doctor had sent us, the sheika says that we're at the house of the plumber who will do the repairs on the pipes in the tekke where we customarily meet three times a week. She adds that she arranged the appointment that very morning because our mosque cannot continue in such a state of disrepair. She gets out of the car, bends over, and confirms that she is unable to vomit, a sign that she is now completely cured. She walks confidently toward the house. I watch the tassels of her shoes dragging along the muddy ground. I see the plumber opening the door for her. I am confused. Only then do the doctor's words, about how I don't have much time left, acquire any meaning. Meanwhile, the servant in the backseat still hasn't said a word.

*Mariobellatin

Translated from the Spanish by Cindy Schuster

ABOUT THE AUTHOR

Mario Bellatin was born in Mexico. His novel, *Flores* (Flowers) (1994) won the Xavier Villaurrutia Prize in 2000. His work has been translated into German, French, and English. His other books include: *Shiki Nagaoka: Una nariz de ficción* (Pinocchio Tales), *Perros Heroes* (Heroic Dogs), *Lecciones para una liebre muerta* (Lessons for a Dead Hare), and *Salon de belleza* (Beauty Salon).

AMBAR PAST

On Thursday, August 19, 2004, I went to Chiapas for the launch of Ambar Past's book When I Was a Man. *Ambar is the only woman who has ever dedicated a poem to "the men who never slept with me," just as she is the only woman who dares repeat the words men utter about her. Striking, blonde, elegant, she walks along the street and watches how they stare at her: "What color do you think her pussy is?" she hears them saying.*

Ambar landed in Chiapas, the only place in the world that has a kind of amber as red as the Zapatistas and their collective vision of society. Ambar landed in her element, in amber, and was trapped in her own honey, in the amber of her very essence, just like the prehistoric insects who were caught trying to take wing, captured once and for all in that liquid gold.

Ambar, too, is gold, like the burning rope of her hair that she parts in two and braids tightly so that men won't follow her and she won't have to excuse herself for not going to bed with them.

Ambar Past's poetry is born out of the beauty of Chiapas, a state rich not only in natural resources and artistry, but one that puts intellectual and poetic values above all others. Rosario Castellanos, Jaime Sabines, Oscar Oliva, Eraclio Zepeda, Elva Macías, Carlos Jurado, Juan Bañuelos, Miguel Angel Hernandez, Daniel Robles Sasso, Andres Lopez, Jesus Morales Bermudas, Reynaldo Velazco—Chiapas is home to a whole generation of young Amerindian poets. It is a land of poets, and everyone is considered to be a poet there until proven otherwise.

Ambar lives in a treehouse. She built her home between three strong boughs that sway in the wind and creak all night long. The tree sings the same way Ambar sings in her sycamore voice. When I visited her, I mounted a makeshift staircase to heaven, up to the loft of her nuptial bed. On the multicolored pillow, two embroidered hummingbirds held a lovers' knot that read, "You and I"; their wings fluttered all night long. Outside live birds darted about. Down below, Ambar and her daughter Tila were fetching water.

Her books are the product of many years in communion with the people of the highlands of Chiapas, a daily communion, under the same red-tiled roofs of San Cristóbal. There she learned languages, customs, mythologies and histories, the arts of weaving and pottery, the uses of plants, Incantations by Mayan Women (an anthology of Mayan women's magic spells in verse that Ambar worked on for over thirty years), and, most importantly, to identify with the people of the land to the point that she no longer felt so much a writer as a transcriber of "revelations."

Untiring in her art, which leaves an indelible mark, Ambar Past is the one and only mother of love. She offers us a cup of tea for the spirit, and upon extending it declares: "Tomorrow I am going to write you a letter in the rain, I promise."

In autumn, poems fall at Ambar's feet. They recall stories recounted in the intimacy of a couple in bed, when, sated with kisses and promises, the miracle of communication begins. Ambar is an animal who never permits visitors in her cage; a she-devil, whose voice is weightless on the breeze.

Ambar Past is a fabulous character, a kind of fairy—they don't make them like her anymore—part butterfly, part bird, part mountain all at once, luminous and essential. I never fail to be moved in her presence.

—ELENA PONIATOWSKA
Translated from the Spanish by Samantha Schnee

WHEN I WAS A MAN

When I was a man I lived in San Cristóbal. At the top of the mountains in the south, along the border of Guatemala, in a place where they play the harp. Ancient crossroads of the Maya. I walked cobblestoned streets. I wandered through the fog. I fell in love a number of times.

Now that I am a woman, when I get into a taxi the driver asks:
  "You're not from here, are you?"

I answer: "I'm proud to call myself Mexican."

   "You married one, right?" he accuses me like a dirty old man.

   "Yes, sir," I tell him. "Several."

I have a friend who was married to that famous wrestler El Santo, who became a movie star in the fifties. He wore a silver mask. She was in all his films. Blonde, beautiful. Now she's a well-known writer, but she never writes about El Santo. She's like me; I never let on about my other lives either. I don't mention my bigoted uncle in Chattanooga, just like my grandmother changes the subject when asked about the Cherokee blood in our family.

"Are they half-breeds or blue bloods?" asks the woman in the shop. Castile soap is good quality—that is, for people who bathe.

   The smell of money whitens the skin, softens prejudices, makes the customer more important.

   "But you go to their dentists? You let them take your blood, your lice, your daughters? You read books written by lesbians?"

                                    *

"Well, yes, sir, for years I've been coming and going. I wasn't born here. I bedded many of them. Men I now see in the streets. Walking toward me on the opposite sidewalk. I recognize some of them—we've been naked together in the dark. Now we see right through each other.

"Yes, sir, I remember each one. Many of them have the same name. It's so weird. Without exchanging a word I can tell—from two blocks away—if a stranger's name is R.

"R is a way of walking, a look, one of the great peoples. One of these Rs was my first, the first of them all, I left him when

I moved here, and he—after waiting for me twenty years—got married again to another woman who has the same name as me: Munda. This is all true. I have lived it.

"I ran through the whole alphabet. From the As to the Bs to the Cs. There was a D who smelled like mahogany, an F with a sweet dick, a salty H. The Js like to sing in bed and the Ks recite poetry. There was an L in a hammock in hot country.

"I try hard to remember their names. It's a shame to err in a moment of pleasure and shout "M!" instead of "N!" To keep life simple I almost always stick to the Rs. I am completely faithful to all of them."

I never allow the taxi drivers to question me about my marriages. I simply go silent, leaving them with an echo in their mouths. We never get around to the nasty questions seething within them.

"What color do you think her pussy is?" I heard some Huicholes say, nodding toward me.

When I was a boy I liked blondes. Now that I'm older the gringas call me "Negro." When I'm out with my daughter and her mother, everyone looks to see if she turned out dark or light.

*

It always surprises me how people whom I consider revolutionary can be so blinded by stereotypes.

Some people, when they meet me in person, are indignant: "So you're *really* Munda Toston?"

As if I had kidnapped my real self and were masquerading as someone else. Corresponding by letter, they come to like me—before seeing my face or hearing my voice. They come looking for me, knock on the door a number of times. They leave messages, they return.

When we finally meet face-to-face I can see they don't like my blue eyes. My accent repulses them. Makes them furious.

"They don't greet us in the streets. They don't even say, 'Good day.' As if we were dogs."

We're all terrorists in Gush's detective novel, and as far as my leftist friends are concerned I'm a member of the CIA. And rich, too, or so they say. They regard me hatefully like a fist up their ass. Just a whiff of racism—not the anger of people who lynch but rather the contempt of those who violate children.

"Where are you from?" they ask me. "From what *mundo*, what Munda?"

One night in a mud hut an Indian woman palpated my whole body, as if she were taming a wild animal.

   "You're a woman," she told me, "I bet you can even have children."

I travel in atoms of iron that migrate from plant to animal to earth.

Flocks of black butterflies circle the lampposts in town. It's said they bring death's greetings. They live only one night. Then their wings stop working and they lie crushed beneath cars.

The city had no more than two cars when I arrived. I had good, strong teeth back then. But my molars went to ruin as the traffic increased. The deterioration of my smile keeps pace with the ravagement of the city's architecture. Tooth by tooth, stone by stone, we are falling into ruin. When they built a parking lot beneath the cathedral, Satan himself did my root canal.

When the world began, the gods lived in San Cristóbal. The tree of life was born here, song, poetry, and painting bloomed. Greed and the bacchanal. They felled the tree of life, the sacred tree's blood flowed, and from its vital stream came forth time. The past and the future were born.

When I was a man I used to go to Café Central to pick up gringas. A blue-eyed girl was selling amber at the tables in the back. She carried it around in a basket. This was long before the little Mayan girls began weaving bracelets. The Frenchwomen bought earrings, the Italians necklaces. The Mayans wanted talismans to ward off the evil eye. Little red amber hands, hearts.

"Do you want to see a prehistoric spider?" the gringa asks me. "Look at the little butterfly trapped in the amber . . . this one's not for sale. Do you see how it flies through the light?"

*

The flight to Chiapas is delayed. The pilots are on strike. My friend and I spend a night on the airport carpet in Mexico City. In the morning we call a woman named Fausta to see if we can stay with her. "Come on over," she said, very much the Christian. "I have lots of good dope to smoke." We caught a taxi outside, one of those gypsy cabs.

"Where are you headed, you gorgeous blondes?" the driver asked us.

"We're going to Chiapas," I told him, laughing.

"I'll take you."

This seemed so charming to my friend and me that we accepted immediately.

"I'll take you for half the price of your airfare," the guy proposed quite chummily, "the drive will do me good."

It was already getting late by the time we left Mexico City. It was dark before we got to Puebla. The driver's brother-in-law had come with us, "in case anything comes up." No one spoke. A plastic skull that was hanging from the rearview mirror shone in the darkness. When we stopped for gas I noticed the taxi's seats were upholstered in red and black material patterned with bloody skeletons.

My friend and I looked at each other. Adrenaline froze our veins. I managed to remain calm when they began buying six-packs. This was in Veracruz, and they offered us cold ones, but we said, "No, thanks."

The highway was desolate, one of those jungle highways with a warm midnight breeze and cicadas playing their harps.

The battle line between good and evil does not exist in any geographic location, rather it runs through the heart of every man, or so said Solzhenitsyn.

"All Indians are good, right?" my friend whispered in my ear.

"Very good!" I told her, remembering X, Y, and Z.

The driver began to tell us how his parents spoke a language they were ashamed to teach him. They left the countryside and moved to Mexico City. He was born in a tar-paper shack in the city dump. We had barely gotten to know him since leaving the airport. We didn't know San Cristóbal was so far away.

All night long we drove through hot country. A symphony of cicadas, shooting stars, burning cane thickets. When dawn broke we were on the coast, in the middle of mango season.

"In another life I had black hair," my friend said aloud. "I had a mustache, I was illiterate. Afraid of gays. Of course I remember!"

The driver was frightened now, by the sight of so many Indians with their machetes and their digging sticks. The women carrying iguanas on their heads. He admitted that he'd never been out on the highway before. He was ready to head back to Mexico City.

*

"Yes, sir, I arrived many years ago, without even knowing where I was headed. We came from far away, very far. In a taxi like yours. We stopped in Tuxtla beneath a burning sun. We asked where San Cristóbal was."

"Yes," an old man told us, pointing toward the sierra. "It's about an hour and a half to the high city. There are apples, cold country orchids, mountains of lichen and oak. The witch doctors burn incense. They say that everyone there is a poet until proven otherwise."

When I was a man it never occurred to me to rape a woman. I wanted them to do it to me. I wanted those French girls to touch me, those girls you could pick up in San Cristóbal. I met one who gave me her address. She had hitchhiked across the entire Mexican Republic. Alone; in those big rigs with the long-distance truckers.

When I was a little girl I thought that María Emma was made of chocolate and I of vanilla. The months whirled around counter-clockwise and each numeral was a different color. There was a god who planted the seed of a child inside every woman who fell in love. His tongue ran the length of my body to my clitoris while I prayed to the angels.

*

I don't remember anything about when I was a man. I only know that I wanted to be a woman so I could become a whore. I think gringas paid to caress me.

*

I transform myself into a cloud. San Cristóbal is my chrysalis. How many years must I remain here before I can fly?

Translated from the Spanish by Samantha Schnee

ABOUT THE AUTHOR

Ambar Past, born in North Carolina, has lived in San Cristóbal de Las Casas, Chiapas, since 1974. She is a Mexican citizen and writes in Spanish and Tzotzil. She coordinates a papermaking and publishing cooperative, Taller Leñateros, and edits the poetry magazine *Jícara*. Her latest publishing project is *Incantations by Mayan Women*.

HORACIO CASTELLANOS MOYA

The first time I ever heard of Horacio Castellanos Moya was from the Guatelmalan writer Rodrigo Rey Rosa; we had just eaten a paella in Blanes with the Spanish critic Ignacio Echevarría. The second person who mentioned him to me was Juan Villoro. This was some time ago. I tried looking for his works in the Barcelona bookstores but, as I expected, I couldn't find them.

Not long after that I received a letter from Castellanos Moya himself, and from then on we maintained an irregular and melancholic correspondence, perhaps tinged by my awe for his writing, which gradually became a part of my library. I have now read four of his books. The first one I read was Revulsion, *perhaps his best work, certainly his most arresting, a long declamation against El Salvador for which Castellanos Moya received death threats that obliged him to leave the country for a life in exile.*

Revulsion *is not only an adaptation of folktales or the expression of a writer's profound disillusionment in the face of his moral and political circumstances, but also a stylistic experiment that parodies the work of Bernhard; it is a novel that will make you die laughing.*

Unfortunately very few people in El Salvador have read Bernhard and even fewer have maintained a good sense of humor. One doesn't joke about homeland. This is a popular saying not only in El Salvador, but also in Chile and Cuba, in Peru and Mexico, and even in Austria and some other European countries. If Castellanos Moya were Bosnian or Kosovar he wouldn't even have been able to board a plane to leave the country. And therein lies one of the great virtues of this book: nationalists of all stripes can't stand it. Its sharp humor, not unlike a Buster Keaton film or a time bomb, threatens the fragile stability of imbeciles who, when they read the book, have an uncontrollable desire to hang the author in the town square. I can't think of a higher honor for a writer.

Horacio Castellanos Moya was born in 1957. He is a melancholy man and writes from the bowels of one of the many volcanoes that pepper his country. That sounds like magical realism, but there is nothing magical in his books, save perhaps his powerful style. He is a survivor, but he doesn't write like one.

—ROBERTO BOLAÑO
Translated from the Spanish by Samantha Schnee

from REVULSION

The tropics are horrible, Moya, the tropics turn men into rotten beings with basic instincts like those beings against whom I was forced to rub to be able to leave the terminal area in search of a taxi. No other impression turns out to be more abhorrent than leaving the Comalapa Airport, no other impression has made me abhor the tropics with such intensity as my exit from the Comalapa terminal area: it's not just the crowds, Moya, but also the shock of going from a bearable climate inside the airport to that sweltering and idiotizing hell of the tropical coast, to the fulminant heat gust that instantly turned me into a sweating animal. Once I was able to make my way among the slobbering greedy masses in front of the boxes filled with unexpected things, I suddenly saw myself assaulted by a multitude of taxi drivers who pushed and shoved as they fought over me like birds of prey, taxi drivers uniformed with light blue guayaberas and dark glasses who tried to take away my suitcase, Vega told me. I had never seen individuals with such giveaway faces, Moya, I had never seen such grim and giveaway faces as the ones of those taxi drivers. But I had no choice: the trip was improvised in such a way that I hadn't even phoned my brother to inform him of my flight number. I told the taxi driver to take me to the funeral home, in a hurry, my mother had died the day before and they were waiting for me to bury her. And in those forty kilometers that separate the Comalapa Airport from San Salvador, during that journey as the gust of wind that came in through the window allowed me to recover and get certain tranquillity, I got a glimpse of a definition that I've been able to completely confirm during these fifteen days: the Salvadoran is the cop that we all carry inside of us. That taxi driver was the best proof: he tried to pump the largest amount of information possible out of me, with malicious questions that made me fear that he was measuring if it was worth robbing me, Vega told me. A petty agent who given the faintest opportunity shows off his vocation as a thief, truly a thief who works as a petty agent, only in this country the word *cop* is used to name a thief who works as a police officer and in this case a nosy taxi driver who asked lots of questions about my life to find out if I was the appropriate victim for him to practice his vocation as a thief. All taxi drivers are cops, Moya, and, specially that one who was driving me to San Salvador, asking his suspicious questions about my life. At the city's entrance, where there used to be a tollbooth, according to the taxi driver, now was the "Monument to Peace," a fright that could only have been conceived by someone with his sense of imagination in his feet, a frightening "Monument to Peace," which shows the absolute lack of imagination of these people, definite evidence of the total degradation of taste, Vega told me. And the one farther down the road is even worse, Moya, it's the most horrifying thing I've ever seen, the so-called "Monument to the Distant Brother" truly seems like a gigantic urinal, that monument with its huge tiled wall doesn't evoke anything but a urinal, I swear, Moya, when I saw it for the first time I felt like urinating and nothing else, and every time I've gone by that so-called "Monument to the Distant Brother" it does nothing but excite my kidneys. That's the masterpiece of the degradation of taste: a gigantic urinal built in gratitude to the hat-wearing men and the chubby women who come from the United States carrying boxes stuffed with the most unexpected things, Vega told me. Only a crew of dopes can have such obsession to build those horrifying monuments, only a crew of dopes turned rulers can spend the State's money in the construction of those muddles that shamelessly express the degradation of taste reigning in this country, only a crew of dopes with the State's usufruct can foster in such a way the degradation of taste through the so-called "monuments." They're, truly, monuments to the degradation of taste, they're nothing but monuments to the lack of imagination and to the extreme degradation of taste of this race, Vega told me. And what to say about those enormous heads called the nation's forefathers, those enormous and deformed marble heads placed throughout what used to be known as the *Autopista Sur,* those horrendous marble monstrosities that supposedly reproduce the faces of the so-called nation's forefathers, those horrible and deformed heads popularly known as "The Flintstones": only a troglodyte mind could have conceived such monstrosities, only a troglodyte and comic-book mind could conceive that those hulks could be sculptures and must be shown in public, something that in another place would be viewed with horror here is shown with pride. It's incredible, Moya. They call them "The Flintstones" because the so-called nation's forefathers surely were nothing but some troglodytes like the dopes who now spend the State's money building monuments and sculptures that only show the total degradation of their taste, Vega told me. The so-called nation's forefathers must have been some troglodytes responsible for the congenital stupidity that affects this race, only the fact that the so-called nation's forefathers were some troglodytes can explain the generalized cretinism that reigns in this country. I invite you to have one last whiskey, Moya, Vega offered, to have one for the road while I drink my last glass of mineral water and ask Tolín to give me back my compact disc with Tchaikovsky's Concerto in B-flat Minor, because people have started to arrive, Moya, they're clients who must be here to reserve their table to watch tonight's so-called "artistic show." I want to be back at the hotel by seven, have a light dinner, and lock up to enjoy my room, Vega told me. There's nothing more pleasing than to lie down in my bed, read peacefully, without any television around, without the nerve-racking screams of my brother's wife and their pernicious children; there's nothing more comforting than to lock up to read, meditate, and rest. The mere idea of being safe from my brother's invitations to "go screw around" at night seems stimulating to me, Moya, there's nothing more horrible than being forced to choose between my brother's invitations to "go screw around" and the perspective of spending the night in a room flanked by three televisions blasting out loud and on different channels. Only once I accepted my brother's invitation to "go screw around" at night, Vega told me, that single and unrepeatable night was enough for me to never again think of accepting the invitation to "go screw around" insistently formulated by my brother. My brother's greatest pleasure is to "go screw around" at night, Moya, and his and his friends' greatest pleasure consists of hanging out at a beer joint drinking large amounts of that diarrheic beer until they reach complete imbecility, then to go into a disco and jump like primates, and finally, to visit a sordid whorehouse. These are the three stages of "screwing around" at night, the ritual that keeps them alive, their greatest fun: to get stupid at beer point, to sweat while jumping in the savage noise and the thick air of a disco, and to slobber with lust at a sordid whorehouse, Vega told me. The three rigorous stages of "screwing around" to which one night my brother took me. Only the alteration produced in my mood by the noise of the three televisions, by the endless chatter of my brother's wife, and by the screams of the couple of stupid and pernicious kids, can explain that I accepted my brother's invitation to "go screw around" at night, knowing that no invitation coming from my brother would be devoid of vulgarity and cretinism. I'll regret for the rest of my life having accepted that invitation to "go screw around" at night, Moya, I suffered the worst anguish that one can imagine, I spent practically all my emotional capital, Vega told me. My brother, a friend of his called Juancho, and I went. First we were at a beer joint called the Barbwire, a frightening place, a hair-raising place, a big ranch plagued with gigantic television screens at each corner, a true aberration, a place where one can only drink diarrheic beer surrounded by screens in which different singers, each and every one of them more abominable than the next, interpret foolish and strident melodies. And my brother's friend, Moya, that guy Juancho, is a Negroid who owns a hardware store and who swears that he's drunk all the alcohol in the world and he's slept with all the women he has found in his way, Vega told me. He's the most exaggerated and mythomaniac Negroid that you might imagine, Moya, a machine that talks about himself and tells his own adventures, a talking dummy who swallows beer after beer as he narrates his delirious sexual feats. I wasn't prepared for all that: I remained with my glass of mineral water, forced to listen with one ear to the Negroid's verbosity and with the other one to the strident voice of a woman with messed-up hair wallowing on the TV screens. But the Negroid imposed himself with his screams, and as he swallowed more beer his stories about his intoxications and sexual adventures got more obscene. He's a truly repulsive Negroid, Moya, and stubborn like few: again and again he insisted that I should drink a beer, that it wasn't possible that I only drink mineral water. I lost count of the times in which I explained to him that I didn't drink beer, least of all that filthy and diarrheic Pilsner beer that they drank, my colitis allowed me to have only a couple of drinks, and preferably whiskey, but in this beer joint called the Barbwire, they didn't sell any liquor, only that disgusting and diarrheic beer. He's a Negroid in whose little head with a peanut-brain the idea that someone refused to drink the filth that he was drinking couldn't fit, Vega told me. It was repulsive, Moya, that guy told one time after another of his delirious sexual adventures with all the prostitutes from all the whorehouses in San Salvador. But what was really worrisome were the four individuals sitting at the next table, the most sinister individuals that I've seen in my life, Moya, four psychopaths with crime and torture stamped on their snouts who drank beer at the table next to us, some subjects to be truly afraid of who distilled their blood thirst in such a way that to turn around to look at them even if it was just for a second was a tremendous risk, Vega told me. I warned the Negroid to lower his voice, that those beauties next door were already looking at him with a dark rictus. I feared a tragedy, Moya, because those psychopaths evidently carried hand grenades and were anxious to throw them under the table of a trio of subjects such as ourselves, I was sure that at that very instant those criminals were caressing the hand grenades that they would throw at any moment under our table, because for those ex-soldier and ex-guerrilla psychopaths hand grenades have become their favorite toys, there isn't a day when one of those so-called demobilized fighters doesn't throw a hand grenade at a group of people that makes him feel uncomfortable, in truth, those ex-soldier and ex-guerrilla criminals carry their hand grenades with them waiting for the faintest opportunity to throw them at people such as that Negroid who didn't stop screaming out his unbelievable sexual adventures, Vega told me. I warned him once and again to lower his voice, Moya, but the Negroid only calmed down when he turned around to see those psychopaths who were about to throw a hand grenade at us, as they do on a daily basis at beer joints, at discos, and on the very streets where they solve their differences at grenade point, where the so-called demobilized fighters have fun like kids with the hand grenades that they throw in laughter to idiots such as that Negroid, Vega told me. Luckily, we soon left the beer joint for a disco called Rococo, in the second stage of what my brother and his friends call "screwing around" at night. It was a dark shed, with blinding lights that suddenly pounded from the ceiling and with thickened air barely circulating, a shed booming with a noise from hell, and in its center it had a dance floor surrounded by tables and seats practically embedded on the floor. It was an overwhelming place, specially made for lunatics, for deaf people who enjoy the darkness and the thick air. Immediately I began to sweat and to feel my temples palpitating as if my blood pressure had risen uncontrollably and my head were about to explode, Vega told me. And in the middle of that exasperating mess, after we went to the bar to ask for the drink that we were entitled to have for the cover fee, and while we looked for a table, I realized that the Negroid hadn't stopped talking for a moment, that his voice boldly fought to impose itself over the jolting noise that threatened to demolish the shed. I drank my whiskey all at once, hoping that it would help stop the palpitation in my temples, but it only made me sweat more profusely and increased my claustrophobic sensation. I can't tolerate those enclosed, dark, noisy, and suffocating places, Moya, and least of all with a Negroid who shouted over and over the same story about his extraordinary sexual adventures, Vega told me.

My nervous resistance was loosening up. A dozen couples were jumping around on the dance floor; I could barely distinguish their silhouettes because of the outlandish lights and the blinding flashes pounding from the ceiling. My brother mentioned that the disco was quite empty, that it wasn't a good night, that there were almost no girls on their own; the Negroid hurried to relate every single time when he had picked up beautiful girls in this place, every single time when after dancing at the disco he had gone to a motel to make love with those fabulous girls, to tell the truth, every time that he had gone to that disco he had been able to pick up a girl, that's what the Negroid was yelling, Vega told me. I began to feel dizzy, Moya, as if I were running out of air, and I told my brother about it, that I was feeling a little bit sick, that this place didn't do me any good, that it would be better if we went to a less distressing place. I had to yell so that my brother could hear me, I almost ripped my throat in order to be heard over the thundering of that deafening noise and the Negroid's howling. My brother asked me to hold on for a while, maybe more girls would show up, it would be such a waste to leave the disco so early, that's what he said, but I was losing my patience, I feared that at any moment everything would start to spin and I would break down, that's why I told him not to worry, that I would take a taxi home, the Negroid and he could stay until whenever they wanted. Then my brother came up telling me that I couldn't abandon them that way, that's what he said, Moya, "abandon them," that if I went home by myself his wife would suspect the worst, that I should wait for only five minutes, I could go out to the car to rest for a while, and then we'd go to a less enclosed place. And that's what I did, Vega told me. But when my brother gave me the car keys I warned him that I'd wait for five minutes, not a second more, that he should remember my deep sense of punctuality, that if he didn't show up in exactly five minutes I'd leave the keys with the disco's doorman and I'd leave in a taxi. I hate unpunctual people, Moya, there isn't anything worse than unpunctuality, it's impossible for me to have any type of relation with unpunctual people, there isn't anything more harmful and annoying than dealing with unpunctual beings. If you hadn't shown up right at five o'clock in the afternoon, as we had agreed, I assure you that I wouldn't have waited for you, Moya, even though I love to stay in this place between five and seven in the afternoon drinking my couple of whiskies, even if I had had to sacrifice this moment of tranquillity, I wouldn't have waited for you, because the mere fact of your being late would have been enough to completely disturb our possibility of having a constructive conversation, Moya, your tardiness would have totally distorted my perception of you and I would have immediately placed you in the unpunctual people's category, Vega told me. Once outside the disco, walking in the parking lot in the open air, I felt better, even though the confusion would take a little longer to go away. I went into the car, in the passenger's seat, I locked the door and I leaned my seat back. The disco is located almost at the end of the Paseo Escalón, in a mall. The fact is that when two minutes had gone by and I was beginning to relax thanks to the silence of the parking lot and the panoramic view of the city that one sees from there, I suddenly suffered an intense anxiety attack, as if I were about to be assaulted, a frightening anxiety attack that forced me to get up and turn around in search of the crooks that were preparing to attack me, Vega told me, a frightening anxiety attack as if the danger were there, a few steps away, stalking me, ready to turn into some crooks that would riddle me with bullets with the only purpose of getting ahold of my brother's car, that latest model Toyota Corolla that my brother cares for more than he cares for himself. It was a sudden panic, Moya, an absolute, paralyzing panic, because the crooks in this country kill without any reason, for the mere pleasure of crime, they kill you even if you don't pose resistance, even if you give them everything that they ask for, they kill on a daily basis without any other purpose than the pleasure of killing, Vega told me. There's the case of Mrs. Trabanino that all the newscasts are talking about all the time. It's dreadful, Moya: some crook surprises her when she's parking her car in her garage, then he forces her to go into the living room and shoots her in front of her two little girls. It's dreadful, Moya, the crook kills for mere pleasure in front of the little girls, a crook that doesn't steal anything, he only wants to kill. It's a horrible case, Moya. I wouldn't have given it so much attention, but my brother's wife has been talking only about Mrs. Trabanino's case for three days, three days ruining my mealtimes with the same harangue about Mrs. Trabanino's murder, she spent three days infuriated and adventuring hypotheses about the causes for the crime when truly the matter with my brother's wife is her morbid excitement, because it turns out that Mrs. Trabanino belonged to the high society that appears in the newspapers' social pages that my brother's wife rummages with so much fruition, the excitement of her morbidity is the true reason why that freak that my brother is married to hasn't been able to stop talking about Mrs. Trabanino's murder, hasn't stopped turning me paranoid with the extreme criminality that afflicts this country, Vega told me. That's why the five minutes inside my brother's car turned eternal, Moya, and those last three minutes when panic took me over were horrible, a weakening experience, something that I don't wish on anyone, to be locked up in a Toyota Corolla waiting for a group of crooks to murder you in order to steal the car, because they can't rob without killing, surely because to kill is what gives them true pleasure and not so much to steal, as Mrs. Trabanino's case proves, Vega told me. I was about to hurriedly leave the car, such was my panic, to seek cover by the door, at the disco's entrance, but soon I understood that when I left the car I would run a higher risk of being riddled with bullets, that's why I stayed there, shivering, with a horrible tachycardia, squatting in the seat, acting as if I were asleep, counting every second, deeply hating my brother and his friend the Negroid, who were to blame for the crisis that I was enduring, Vega told me. What a desire of people in this country to live terrorized, Moya, what a morbid desire to live in terror, what a perverted desire to go from the war's terror to delinquency's terror, a pathological vice of these people, a morbid vice to make of terror their permanent way of life. Luckily, my brother and the Negroid soon arrived. They got into the car laughing, talking about who knows what woman, and they even dared to complain to me, saying that because of me they hadn't been able to pick up a couple of girls that at that moment were entering the disco. Then we moved down to the third stage of what my brother and his friends call "screwing around" at night, toward the Colonia La Rábida, a neighborhood that twenty years ago used to be an old middle-class residential zone, an old neighborhood now turned into a red-light district with swarming lousy bars and whorehouses. My brother and the Negroid were already hammered, happy, with their bellies full of beer, recklessly talking both of them at once, without listening to each other, as if each one of them were trying to prove to himself and to me something related to his virility and his boldness. But I barely paid attention to them, I only realized that in each phrase they included the word *turd,* Vega told me. I've never seen people with so much excrement in their mouths as people in this country, Moya, it's not in vain that the word *turd* is their main language crutch, they don't have any other word in their mouths but *turd,* their vocabulary limits itself to the word *turd* and its derivatives: turdism, turding, turdness. It's incredible, Moya, when you see it from a distance, a word that designates a piece of excrement, a vulgar and disgusting word that means a portion of human excrement expelled all at once, the most vulgar word, a synonym of dung is what my brother and his friend the Negroid have more firmly stuck in their mouths, Vega told me. I particularly detest that a Negroid by the name of Juancho whom I see for the first time calls me "turd" with familiarity, I detest with special intensity that a hardware Negroid whom I've just met calls me "turd" all the time, that he calls me "turd" as if I were a portion of human excrement expelled all at once. It's horrible, Moya, only in this country can something like that happen, only in this country do people consider themselves to be a portion of human excrement expelled all at once and only my brother and his hardware Negroid friend could think of calling me "turd" constantly and with the greatest familiarity at a moment when they were tipsy thanks to the diarrheic beer that they compulsively drank when we were on our way to a whorehouse to complete the third stage of what they call "screwing around" at night, Vega told me. The whorehouse is called "The Office," Moya, my brother's favorite hangout, evidence that this individual, even when he carries out his vulgar diversions, needs to feel at the office, as if the fact of feeling at the office would take away the sordidness of his filth. You don't know, Moya, the nausea I felt when we entered that whorehouse called "The Office," I had never felt such a deep nausea, only a whorehouse such as "The Office" could cause me such a vital contraction, the most abominable nausea that I've suffered in my life. I hadn't been to a whorehouse for twenty-two years, Moya, since we were in our last year of high school. Do you remember? It was horrible. Going back to a whorehouse after so many years only helped bring back my crudest memories, the memory of an experience that I already believed to be buried, a vulgar and denigrating experience from which I was able to recover only with difficulty and after a long time. Sexual commerce is the most disgusting thing that can exist, Moya, nothing makes me feel such repugnance as carnal commerce, something vicious in and of itself and so given to misunderstandings as sex reaches abominable depths with its commerce, a practice that eats up your spiritual faculties fulminantly. But for my brother and his Negroid friend that spiritual decay is precisely the greatest reason for fun and rejoicing, Vega told me. I assure you that even crossing the threshold at "The Office" I had to walk with extreme care, Moya, taking care not to slide in that crystallized semen on the tiles. I don't lie, Moya, that den stank like semen, at that den there was semen everywhere: stuck on the walls, spread on the furniture, crystallized on the tiles. It was the most demolishing nausea I've felt in my life, the most tremendous and horrible nausea, I felt it over there, at "The Office," a den infected by greasy women who moved their infected bodies through rooms and hallways, infected and tired women who spread over the sofas and armchairs their flesh covered with the most diverse sweat, Vega told me. And there I was, Moya: on the brink of vomiting, sitting at the edge of a chair, with my face wrinkled by the revulsion, avoiding getting smeared with the semen on the sofas and walls, avoiding sliding over the crystallized semen on the tiles, while my brother and his friend the Negroid, in the most ignominious way, were all over a

couple of greasy women who by that time had already been inoc-
ulated with semen and sweat to a glut. It's incredible, Moya, my
brother and his friend the hardware Negroid kept on stuffing
themselves with beer, happily smearing themselves with those
women's excretions, bargaining without shame to get the best
price that would take them to a rotten bed where they would agi-
tate themselves in the most obscene way, Vega told me. It was horrible, Moya. I had never seen more deplorable women, women for
whom sordidness is their natural habitat, fat greasy women dirtied
up by the semen of individuals who have turned sordidness into
their most desired and intimate pleasure. It was the saddest whorehouse that you can imagine, Moya, where no other sensation
reigns but sordidness, where not even the laughter or the chatter
escapes the sordidness that permeates it all, that imposes itself over
everything, Vega told me. There was a moment, Moya, in which I
couldn't contain my nausea, especially when one of those greasy
women approached me with the intention to chat with me, with
the intention to convince me to buy a piece of her sordidness. I
got up immediately, Moya, and went in search of the restrooms,
walking with extreme caution so I wouldn't slide and fall over the
crystallized semen on the floor tiles. And then the worst came,
Moya: those were the filthiest restrooms that I've seen in my life, I
swear, I had never seen so much filth concentrated in such a confined space, Vega told me. I was able to get my handkerchief out to
cover my nose, but it was too late, Moya, because I concentrated
my energy in avoiding a fall in those semen and urine puddles, I
entered into that rotten gas chamber defenseless, and by the time I
was able to take out my handkerchief it was too late. I threw up,
Moya, the filthiest vomit in my life, the most sordid and repulsive
way of throwing up that you can imagine, because I was an individual throwing up over vomit, because that whorehouse was a
huge vomit pit sprinkled with semen and spit. Truly indescribable,
Moya, I still get an upset stomach just thinking about it. I left the
restrooms shaky, with the firm decision to leave that den immediately, without caring about what my brother and his Negroid
companion might argue, with the definite decision to get in a taxi

and go to my brother's house, Vega told me. And then my doom was sealed, the unbelievable happened, the fact that made me enter a delirious spiral, the most extreme anguish that you might imagine: my passport, Moya, I had lost my Canadian passport, it wasn't in any of my pockets, it was the worst thing that could happen in my life, to lose my Canadian passport in a filthy whorehouse in San Salvador. Terror overtook me, Moya, sheer and jolting terror: I saw myself trapped in this city forever, without being able to return to Montreal; I was turned once more into a Salvadoran without any other option but to vegetate in this filth, Vega told me. I kept my Canadian passport in my shirt pocket, I was completely sure, and now it wasn't there. I had dropped it, Moya, my Canadian passport had fallen during some sudden movement, I hadn't noticed when I dropped my Canadian passport. It was horrible, Moya, a sinister nightmare. I ran back to the restrooms, where I had just thrown up, without worrying about falling facedown in the crystallized semen on the floor tiles, without minding the urine and vomit puddles or that dreadful smell. But my Canadian passport wasn't there, Moya, and it wasn't possible that it had fallen inside the toilet without me realizing it. I searched carefully among the bunches of paper smeared with excrement, among the vomit and urine puddles, but my Canadian passport was nowhere. I left the restrooms completely crazed. I went to tell my brother and his Negroid friend about my misfortune. I urged them to help me look for my Canadian passport. We simply had to go back to the Rococo disco and to the Barbwire beer joint at that very instant. The Canadian passport is the most valuable thing that I have in life, Moya, there isn't anything else that I care for with so much obsession as my Canadian passport, truly my life depends on the fact that I'm a Canadian citizen, Vega told me. But the hardware Negroid said that I shouldn't get so worked up, that probably the passport was in the bedroom at my brother's house, that I should relax. Screaming, Moya, I told him not to be a jerk, that I wasn't talking to him, that I was demanding that my brother forget about that sordid and greasy fat woman and help me recover my Canadian passport. I was out of control, Moya, you should have seen me, my desperation was such that I was about to beat up that couple of jerks who underestimated the fact that I had lost my Canadian passport, Vega told me. Finally my brother reacted, Moya, and asked me if it hadn't fallen in the restroom. I told him that I had already searched carefully among the papers smeared with excrement and among the vomit, urine, and semen puddles, but my Canadian passport wasn't there. That's when my brother said that we should go look in the car before going back to the disco and the beer joint. I felt that the world was crashing in on me, Moya, Canada doesn't have an embassy or a consulate in El Salvador, if I had lost my passport I would have had to travel to Guatemala to carry out lengthy procedures, and therefore my stay in this place would have been never-ending. I get cold sweats just thinking about it, Moya. We went in a hurry to look in the car, to feel the floor mats and under the seats. I was at the brink of delirium, Moya, I imagined the worst: that my Canadian passport had been left at the beer joint or at the disco and that I'd have enormous problems getting a new document, Vega told me. I was sweating, my hands were shaking, hysteria was about to make me explode. I yelled at my brother that my Canadian passport wasn't in the car, that we should leave immediately for the two dens of iniquity where we had been before. My brother asked me to let him look, he said I should calm down, I shouldn't worry, that soon we'd find my document. Such a jerk, Moya, asking me to calm down. But I moved to the side to let him look in the front of the car, Vega told me. I was about to break down, my nerves couldn't take it anymore, I was about to start screaming and kicking for having lost my Canadian passport on account of my brother and that Negroid, for accepting those sordid and stupid beings' invitation to "go screw around" at night, I was about to break down when my brother shouted with joy and said, "I found it." And there it was, Moya, my brother's hand extending my Canadian passport, my brother's stupid smile behind his hand with my Canadian passport, which had fallen without my noticing it when I entered the car running away from the suffocating disco where the hardware Negroid had made me dizzy with his harangue about his extraordinary sexual adventures, Vega told me. I snatched my Canadian passport from his hand and, without saying a word, without even turning around to look at them, I ran toward a taxi parked a few meters ahead. I got out of there as if chased by the devil, Moya. And there was no way to calm me down until I entered my bedroom at my brother's house and I got into bed with the absolute certainty that my Canadian passport was securely protected under my pillow, Vega told me. It was the worst scare of my life, Moya. I even spent the duration of the taxi ride clinging to my Canadian passport, flipping through it, verifying that the man in the picture was me, Thomas Bernhard, a Canadian citizen born thirty-eight years ago in a filthy city called San Salvador. Because, I hadn't told you about this, Moya: I didn't just change nationality but also my name, Vega told me. Over there my name isn't Edgardo Vega, Moya, a horrible name in any case, a name that only evokes the La Vega Barrio, an execrable neighborhood where I was robbed as a teenager, an old neighborhood that might not even exist anymore. My name is Thomas Bernhard, Vega told me, a name that I took from an Austrian writer that I admire and that surely you and the other impostors of this infamous province don't even know.

Translated from the Spanish by Beatriz Cortez

ABOUT THE AUTHOR

Horacio Castellanos Moya, born in 1957 in El Salvador, is one of the most important Central American writers alive today. He has published eight novels, some of which have been translated into French, German, Italian, and Portuguese; he has published five short story collections. He worked many years as a journalist in Mexico City, Guatemala, and San Salvador. He has also lived in Canada, Costa Rica, Spain, and, from 2004 to 2006, in Frankfurt in a program supported by the Frankfurt International Book Fair. His first novel to appear in English, *Senselessness,* will be published by New Directions in 2007.

EVELYNE TROUILLOT

"The Chareron Inheritance," by Evelyne Trouillot, is the kind of story that leaves you with a lump in your throat. Set during the first half of Haiti's brutal Duvalier dictatorship (1957–71), it features the widowed Madame Chareron and her attempt to keep her family together through a series of tragedies in which she is both a victim and an eyewitness. Adding to the difficulty of the family's situation is the fact that the Chareron children and grandchildren are prone to inherit a gift for predicting horrible acts that they can foresee but cannot prevent. Distinctly drawn, the Charerons are a fascinating middle-class Haitian family who though brilliantly singular also represent a whole generation of Haitians who were executed, imprisoned, and exiled by the dictatorship, leaving Haiti forever impoverished socially, culturally, politically, and economically. We, as well as the Charerons, are left to wonder whether their family's legacy is a blessing or a curse, but we fear that it is something that will continue to trail them for many generations to come, even as they acknowledge its long-awaited moment of expression in the inheritors with a mixture of sadness and pride.

"It's starting all over again," the widow Chareron cries out when her grandson foretells the death of a cat. And it will continue unless of course the whole family is wiped out and there are no more women to take over where the dead young men have left off, which, at least in one case, even nature seems to be conspiring to make happen.

I once interviewed Evelyne Trouillot. We discussed "The Chareron Inheritance," which is one of my favorite stories of hers.

"I spent my childhood and adolescence under the Duvalier dictatorship," she said. "Generations of men and women were marked by this period. But it's the same story as for slavery: there is shame in speaking of it. [In this story] I recovered my childhood, with its joys, its happy leaps, its fertile and confident atmosphere, and also the heavy shadow that I, being a child, perceived as a horrifying menace. I also recovered my adolescence and the need for freedom that sneaks in and swells even in the strongest constraints."

In spite of the horrible events that are depicted in the story, most of which were based on real incidents, Trouillot's most striking childhood memories of the Duvalier dictatorship remain the image of Duvalier's militiamen searching her family's and neighbor's houses for publications and other works of art deemed subversive. "Then," she continued, "the feverish hate and the dull sound of books that one would get rid of in the latrines. This image of the condemned books remains for me one of the strongest images of the repression. This repression of knowledge and of creative freedom, isn't that one of the strongest armies used by dictators everywhere?"

—EDWIDGE DANTICAT

THE CHARERON INHERITANCE

He was only six years old. The words had simply come out of his mouth, unintended, uncalculated, as if someone, somewhere had pulled invisible strings to open his mouth.

"Tomorrow you won't have a cat anymore, Grandma."

His grandmother had turned toward him abruptly, horrified. And yet she was a competent woman, the kind of woman not easily taken in. Already in her sixties, she'd torn a militiaman to shreds with one look when he dared reproach her for not joining with the others to repeat the morning oath prescribed by the authorities. If the militiaman arranged for the night patrol to stop in front of the Charerons' house for a serenade of especially rich machine-gun fire, he hadn't bothered her afterward. That day, however, looking at her grandson the widow Emmanuel Chareron gave a start of fear. Jerome hesitated a moment before taking up what he'd said once again: "I tell you, tomorrow your cat won't be there anymore."

More than the words, it was the look on the child's face that showed his grandmother that he was not joking. In the baby face, the eyes had taken on an unaccustomed fixity, a frightening immobility almost painful to contemplate. The widow Emmanuel Chareron's cry was only a gasp, but still it reached her daughter.

"Solange, it's starting all over again."

Solange Chareron Dorvil looked at her son and shivered. But her doubt lasted no more than a second, a minute interval that would nonetheless come back to haunt her like a bad memory that refuses to die. She had already put her arms around the child and, stroking his hair, murmured, "I'm so sorry Daddy isn't here with us to see it."

Sensing his mother's pride, Jérome resumed his happy kid posture. Thoroughly pleased, he broke away and ran to pick up his toys again. He did not notice his grandmother's deeply worried look.

The whole weight of the Chareron inheritance spread heavily between mother and daughter, above Jerome's sweet little face. Suddenly, the inheritance that had given Emmanuel Chareron such pride took on new life before their eyes. After Marcelle went away, no one talked about it. The widow Chareron believed it was hidden away, gone with her younger daughter and buried with her only son. Only Solange, their oldest daughter, her father's favorite, maintained her pride in what her mother named "the Chareron burden."

"How could he marry me and hide its existence?" the widow often repeated with a stubborn look. "Your father always insisted on judging that inheritance one more proof of the Charerons' intellectual superiority!"

"Would it have made any difference if you'd known?" Solange would then insist. "You'd still have married Daddy, wouldn't you?"

The widow Emmanuel Chareron rarely answered her daughter at such times. Marcelle's troubled eyes burned in her memory.

When his wife told him the story of the cat, Alphonse Dorvil protested: "Already! But Jerome is only six."

"Daddy told me Uncle Samuel was eight when he began to show his powers of premonition," Solange retorted, "and don't forget that Marcelle wasn't even twelve the first time."

The excitement in Solange's voice and, most of all, the scarcely hidden ostentation conferred a mythic quality on the whole business. Monsieur Dorvil finally decided that the two women had let themselves be carried away by their imagination. He'd often wondered how much truth there was in the story of Marcelle that his wife told him so often. Didn't Solange—overcome by the bizarre nature of this inheritance, apparently traceable to the colonial period—tend to overrate the incident? That question always threw Monsieur Dorvil into a strange quandary, as if he were stepping into a forbidden world. He never dared pursue his thoughts any further. In the space of a second he saw the ashen face of his sister-in-law in the days when he was desperately courting Solange. At once tormented and rebellious, she seemed to dwell in a dark and solitary world, prisoner of an inhuman power.

The cat died the next day. Suddenly, that worn-out creature, age six, who never went out, preferring to idle away his time on the low garden wall instead of running after the lizards invading the courtyard, rushed into the street for no apparent reason and was hit head-on by a vehicle. The accident seemed so odd that, for the neighborhood's residents, Madame Chareron's cat went directly onto the list of strange happenings, just after the automobile accident that cost the lives of both of Madame Innocent's twin girls on their birthday and the miraculous cure of Gaston Sixtot, given up as hopeless by two specialists, one in New York, the other in Boston.

"When misfortune is meant to strike, you can't stop it. Remember Madame Chareron's cat."

Grandmother took the path to the Church of Saint Gérard the next day at the crack of dawn. She spent the whole morning on her knees in a pew, her head bowed in such deep sorrow that the priest approached her. But the widow Chareron was not one to confide in men, even if they claimed to be God's representatives. She dismissed the priest with a weary but irrevocable gesture and resumed her meditation.

"Lord, give me the courage to endure the horror once again, but spare my daughter." For Antoinette Chareron, the infinite sadness of that singular possessive inevitably called up the image of Marcelle. Would she ever think of her younger daughter without feeling that wound in her soul, without wanting to howl for God to erase and recast without this sense of defeat in the face of irreparable misfortune? Could her son's death be reduced to a brief news item, a simple number in the official statistics of associations for the rights of man, one more proof of a dictatorial regime? The son whose disappearance would for them all be linked with Marcelle's forever, even if no one ventured to point out the slightest parallel.

Jerome heard the news of the cat's death with no special interest. He preferred the family dog by far, judging cats too boring and pretentious. Yet he would have liked to see less pain in his grandmother's eyes, and he tried to comfort her with the drawings he'd made at school, but met only with dull indifference.

"So try to forget that story," ordered Monsieur Dorvil, more frightened than annoyed. His mother-in-law understood and patted him on the shoulder, saying nothing.

"He doesn't seem to understand what's going on," Solange protested to her husband. "But you know, he'll end up realizing, it's inevitable."

Once more, Alphonse cast an uneasy glance at his wife, as if the greater part of her being eluded him. His calm, easily satisfied mind did not comprehend Solange's delight in the face of these upheavals that affected the family.

The episode of the cat transported Solange and her mother back to the year of mourning that coincided with Paul and Marcelle disappearing. A dreadful year! Not only for the Charerons but for all the families in the country. The young people in the neighborhood no longer dared meet under the lampposts in the evening to talk about their latest flirtations. Nightfall brought whispers and silence, constraint and bursts of gunfire. Parents fell into panic, hid questionable books, underground magazines, destroyed compromising radios. The most daring, huddled behind their curtains, risked a furtive look at the deserted street. The authorities had stepped up the pace of the slaughter and the arrests to ensure their

own sovereignty. Never had nights seemed so long as in that year
when misfortune struck hard.

Antoinette Chareron recalled the first time she realized that her
younger daughter, then eleven, carried the Chareron inheritance. It
was January, and they were coming home from an end of year visit
to distant cousins. At her mother's side, Marcelle—nicknamed
"bitty bee" by her brother for her light and constant motion—
chattered as she skipped along. A holiday mood persisted despite
the populace's painful apprenticeship under the nascent dictatorship. Fear in fact crept everywhere, invaded every pleasure, stained
all contentment. Happiness became rare; a very strong sense of guilt
and remorse shackled unconcern. News was whispered when bad,
and no one dared talk about news judged good. The children, even
as they too breathed in this atmosphere of repressed pain, sometimes let the impatient, unconquerable delight of childhood break
free. In truth, there were times when even the adults, like Madame
Chareron that morning, gratefully welcomed the moments that
came to dispel thoughts that weighed too heavily. Marcelle effortlessly managed to make her parents smile with her spontaneity and
her lively stories. That day her hand in her mother's, Marcelle,
more "bitty bee" than ever, was chattering joyously:

"You know Marie-José Grand-Pierre, Mommy? If you knew
how she loves to whine, it's unbelievable! The last day of class she
cried and went to complain to the teacher. Just because the children called her 'Blanc Maman.' Still, she's the one who came and
told us that her godfather was a white Pole."

Madame Chareron was still looking for an appropriate rebuke
when her daughter's little hand tightened in her own. Uneasy,
Antoinette Chareron lowered her eyes toward the child and followed her terrified look. A host of horrible ideas had already
come to invade her mind, and she was fully relieved to see nothing in front of her but the two old Bayard spinsters standing in
front of the gate to their house.

"How are you, ladies?"

Mentally, Madame Chareron was sorry she had to stop, as the
two Bayard sisters were known for their endless chatter. They

took care of a string of nephews of all ages whose parents had been in the United States for much too long. Nephews waiting for their visas and a place to live. The aunts took advantage of the slightest occasion to talk about them, complaining, lamenting, indignant but always with so much tenderness in their voices that their interlocutor could not help smiling. Madame Chareron listened to them with only half an ear because their conversation always followed the same path: Robert refused to listen to their advice. André took himself for an artist and wrote songs. Philippe was a nice little boy but his cousins were a bad influence . . . The same story every time with very few variants. What puzzled Madame Chareron was Marcelle's exceptionally strange attitude. First of all, despite the insistance of her mother, who never stopped pulling her arm, she refused to come near the Bayard ladies to kiss them. At least the ladies were too involved in their daily lamentations to notice.

The moment they got home, Madame Chareron, who stood for no nonsense on respect for one's elders, set about scolding her daughter:

"Just explain what is the matter with you, Marcelle. You know very well, that kind of behavior is unacceptable . . ."

But looking at the child's expression, Antoinette checked herself abruptly. Her face almost blue as if the blood had suddenly drained out of it, her haggard eyes staring toward an unknown point, Marcelle seemed frozen in her distress.

"What's going on, Cello? What's the matter?"

The affectionate diminutive reserved for moments of deep tenderness had automatically come to the mother's lips. The little body trembled and Marcelle mumbled as if in prayer:

"I don't want to go in that street anymore, Mommy."

"What street? What are you talking about?"

"The Bayard ladies' street. I don't want to go there anymore. There's too much blood . . ."

Madame Chareron had shivered. When their first baby was born, her husband—with a proud anticipation she found thoroughly unpleasant—told her about the Chareron inheritance.

During the early years of her marriage, she followed Solange apprehensively, then Paul. When Marcelle arrived, she no longer thought about it. But for the affirmations of her brother-in-law Samuel, she would long since have relegated the Chareron inheritance to the rank of a story just good enough to set credulous minds dreaming. But observing her daughter's unusual behavior, she was seized with a savage anguish, all the stronger for waiting in the shadows for years.

Marcelle took to her bed, her body shaking and burning. Her anxious parents spent the night at her bedside, indifferent to the noises in the street, to the gunfire nearby, to the echos of furious pursuit and the moans that followed. The next morning, the whole neighborhood talked about nothing but the arrest of the four Bayard boys. The two who tried to flee were struck down in front of their elderly aunts: André the guitarist and Philippe the youngest, barely fifteen. The older two were executed two weeks later, on the most deadly accusation the dictatorship had invented: frequenting Communists. The Bayard ladies were forbidden to wear mourning for these four "traitors against the country." The two old spinsters hardly spoke anymore. Suffering had shriveled their bodies and dried up their words. They shook their heads, shrugged their shoulders, blessed themselves, crossed their arms. Words no longer had any meaning since true lamentations were not allowed. But whoever came into their home knew that the large lighted candle in their bedroom burned in memory of their four nephews.

With the tinge of sadness fitting the circumstances, Monsieur Emmanuel Chareron took pride in seeing evidence of the Chareron inheritance under his own roof at last. His wife, for her part, lavished care on Marcelle. In her eyes, the child's slightest ailments were suspect. Acute migraines often prostrated the child, and after a great many tests and analyses the doctor admitted he could do nothing. Nervous tension, he'd said. But Madame Emmanuel Chareron always expected a tragedy after Marcelle's migraines. They had come regularly indeed, confirming her suspicions. First it was the death of Uncle Samuel in Africa, then the fire in the shed, the automobile accident that almost cost Solange her life, the unexpected death of Emmanuel Chareron, carried off by a ruptured aneurism, news from Canada that Cousin Gina's baby had meningitis. Before each episode, Marcelle took to her bed, half unconscious, unable to speak and covered with sweat. She'd wake up haggard, eyes sickly, mouth drooling, accepting no one near her but her mother, who held her tight in her arms, saying nothing.

"She's getting human again," her brother would say, a tease like his father before him and with the same nonchalant arrogance. He too saw life as a great adventure, with himself at the reins as if that privilege were his by right. When two friends came by to pick him up to go dancing one Friday night of that dreadful year, Paul didn't even think of refusing. He smiled at his mother who was opening her mouth to protest:

"Come on, Ma, nothing'll happen to me. We're not doing anything wrong. We're just going to the dance."

Like so many mothers who learn to still their fears in the face of their children's thirst for life, Madame Widow Chareron forced herself to smile. How could you deny wings to the stars even when a brutal, all-powerful dictatorship was spreading everywhere? "I'm only young once, Ma," Paul had told her. So she'd ironed a white shirt and his gray pants, smoothed his gray tie mottled with red. He was so handsome that evening, with his mocking eyes and his neatly combed hair! She had timidly stroked his closely shaved cheeks, but he'd clasped her tight in a wild dance, twirling her around to dispel the anxiety that clouded her eyes.

When Madame Widow Chareron entered her younger daughter's room a few hours later and saw her prostrate on her bed, she began to tremble. "Paulo," she thought, crossing herself. For the first time she loathed that mute recumbent form, able only to announce horror, unable to stop it in its tracks. She shook Marcelle roughly, pulling her by the arms, slapping her distorted face, her collapsed body.

"Marcelle, wake up, I beg you. Marcelle, why haven't you said anything? Why?"

Madame Widow Chareron's sobs could not break through the barrier the girl's mind had devised eight years earlier to flee the most frightening images. The girl did not answer. Disgusting white foam came from her lips. Her eyes remained inexorably closed, her body stiff.

In the morning, the whole neighborhood heard about the murder of Paul Chareron, a second-year student at the School of Engineering. According to his friends, the young man had danced "too close" to a "chief's" girlfriend and was shot down with three revolver bullets in front of all the customers in the nightclub. Another young man, not involved in the dispute, took a bullet in his spinal column and would be paralyzed for the rest of his life. The incident fed conversation for a few nights and quickened the fears of mothers. Sympathy visits to the Chareron family were acts of gallantry judged too much of a risk by certain people. Others met their social obligation with more courage than compassion for the weeping parents. On the other hand the Requiem Mass attracted a crowd of young people who saw it as a chance to manifest their resistance to oppression.

Marcelle did not attend her brother's funeral. She could not bear her mother's furtive looks and her silence. Five months after the tragedy, she flew off to the United States. Less than a year later, her mother got a letter from the Ivory Coast, the first in a long series of envelopes without a return address, with stamps from different continents. A one-way correspondence that Marcelle sent three times a year: the month of her mother's birthday, Mother's Day, and the New Year. Madame Widow Chareron kept all those letters within reach of her hand: in her apron pocket or under her powder box made of old silver. How she would have wished to return to the past! Her daughter's helpless face tortured her memory! By what tortuous thought process had she made her daughter guilty of her only son's death? How she wished she could hold her child close in her arms once more and share her distress!

The evening the cat died, Madame Widow Emmanuel Chareron reread all of Marcelle's letters. In the next room she heard Solange and Alphonse arguing, and Jerome's name came up repeatedly. The next morning, she understood that they'd made peace from Solange's happy face and the conciliatory look Alphonse so often assumed in the face of his wife's stubborn insistence. A half-silly, half-mischievous look that grated on his mother-in-law. From his father, Jerome received a magnificent sketchbook and a set of watercolors.

Two months later, Madame Widow Chareron took note of Solange's second pregnancy. Jerome was six years and five months old. When his mother's belly began taking on a remarkable girth and the little boy heard about the impending arrival of a little brother or a little sister, he was so happy that for a long time the coming event was all he talked about.

"When I have a little brother . . ."

"Or a little sister," his mother or father interrupted since they both dreamed of having a little girl. In secret, in the privacy of their bed, they conjured up names full of character, mystery, and elegance: Anne-Sylvie, Isabelle, Aurélie, Rose-Claire, and they smiled at their imagination, quarreled gently, and always ended by setting their teary eyes on the visibly enlarging belly.

Jerome's voice came to breach that happiness, and the little boy was the first to cry.

"I won't have a little brother or a little sister," he declared one night, chagrined and with tear-filled eyes.

Antoinette's attempt to close his mouth was useless. Solange had already heard. The young woman tried to laugh about it with a frightened look that grieved her mother.

"But of course, my darling, you will have a little brother or a little sister. The doctor assures us the baby will be exactly like his brother, beautiful and strong."

Her eyes anxious, Solange tried to place Jerome's little hand on her belly the way he liked, to feel the baby's heartbeat. But instinctively frightened, he turned toward his grandmother.

"I don't want to."

Madame Widow Emmanuel Chareron took her grandson into her arms and carried him very quickly to his bedroom, inexorably resuming the gestures of times gone by.

Solange had no desire to see her son again. The odor of her cologne and the sweet smell of her hair when she bent over him tenderly scarcely remained in the room she no longer visited. Her hard look paralyzed any burst of enthusiasm. Only his grandmother was as loving with him as before, but with a heavy weight of sorrow that confused the little boy.

"You know she's sick, Jerome," Madame Widow Emmanuel Chareron would say when the child begged for his mother. But she avoided her grandson's overly prescient eyes.

Solange lost the baby. A stupid accident that no one could explain. She'd only stumbled but the consequences were tragic. The father and mother wept when they heard the child's sex. When Jerome tried to hug his mother, she turned away her tear-covered face.

Translated from the French by Avriel Goldberger

ABOUT THE AUTHOR

Born in Port-au-Prince, Haiti, Evelyne Trouillot lives and works in her country as a university professor of French and pedagogy. She divides most of her time between writing and teaching. Since her first book of short stories, *La chambre interdite* (1996), Trouillot has published two other books of short stories, tales and stories for children, two books of poems (in French and Creole), and an essay on human rights and childhood in Haiti. Her first novel, *Rosalie l'infâme* (2003), received the Prix Soroptimist de la Romancière francophone for 2004 and second place for the Prix Carbet des Lycéens also in 2004. In 2005, her play *Le bleu de l'île* received first prize for the Prix Beaumarchais de la Caraibe and was read at the Théâtre du Rond-Point in Paris in April 2005. Her most recent books are a collection of Creole poetry, *Plidetwal,* and her second novel, *L'oeil-totem.*

MARCELA SOLÁ

How can a writer approach past horrors in a fictional, nonjudgmental manner? The question is crucial to me, chiefly in reference to Argentina's quite recent past, the misnamed Dirty War of the seventies that was actually genocide. Adorno's dictum "There cannot be poetry after Auschwitz" was proven magnificently wrong by Paul Celan. The subtle and profound literary treatment of that very uneasy amalgam of politics and literature is what made me choose Marcela Solá's El silencio de Kind *(Kind's Silence). Its style is transparent, shadows of evil permeate the poetic surface, words here seem to be made of silence, of vapors, of poetry, reminding me of what Walter Benjamin once said: "I learned to wrap myself in words that were, in fact, clouds."*

Here is a perfect work of adumbration. Nobody is what he or she feigns to be, and the evil the German general represents appears to become persistent, perennial, and seductive as well. A bizarre friendship grows slowly between a traditional upper-middle-class Argentine girl and a German general, a Nazi refugee, during summers spent in Mar del Llano. Both share a passion for music. The atmosphere in Mar del Llano reminds us of that in Death in Venice, *where little by little an inexplicable threat surfaces, that of the soul's dark night. For betrayal is always just around the corner, and the very same sublime element that saves—music—will eventually also condemn, many years later. Kind is already a world-class pianist living abroad when her sister is "disappeared" by the military dictatorship. Persuaded by a former lover, she seeks the German general's help to find her. But the general convinces her to play Mozart's Concerto for Two Pianos with him, and it is in the perfect understanding, the empathy, generated by pure music that Kind understands that she has surrendered to the enemy. She will not be able to save her sister, and will scarcely save her own life.*

"One must know how to hate," the general had told Kind during their long walks by the ocean, in her youth. And in the midst of the performance of Mozart's concerto, the climax of the novel, the adult Kind understands that hatred can easily drag love along.

Love and hatred, political horror and the beauty of music, all form the past of this novel. The woman who revisits old memories when she has to sell the family seaside house has finally learned that the only sensible way to live is by keeping an empty space in the soul, a well that can always be filled again by hope.

But this last "moral" reading is just my reading. The beauty of the novel resides in its impeccable style, which allows room for all manners of understanding.

—LUISA VALENZUELA
Translated from the Spanish by Tobias Hecht

from KIND'S SILENCE

I

The first time my father took me to see the house, there was nothing there but sand. A nettlesome sand that made its way into our shoes, our eyes, our ears. Whipped into eddies, the wind sent it lashing against our arms, legs, and faces; there was no way to protect ourselves from the onslaught. The rolling dunes were all around us and stretched as far as the eye could see. The world was just that: sand. In my imagination, this was called a desert: a golden, boundless adventure promising only thirst, exhaustion, dismay, and the odd miracle of an oasis. How can you imagine a house in a desert that goes on forever, how could so much loneliness accommodate a home—a place of shelter, refuge, and safety? As with any impossible dream, thinking about it made me sad. But dreaming was no trouble for my father.

"We'll call it 'Oasis,' and when this becomes a great resort," he said with a knowing wink, "there will be a golf course in front of the house and we'll have a stunning garden that will be green year-round and won't need to be tended. . . ."

My father really was a dreamer. A dreamer who had followed a very strange path in the pursuit of his dreams: his passion was politics and for as long as I can remember, he had held office in government. Until his soul broke him. It was a lesson I learned and would bear in mind for the rest of my life: there's nothing easy about having a soul. Souls won't up and disappear, nor do they bring happiness.

The house was built, nonetheless, and as if by contagion it had a soul with the ability to make otherwise joyless people happy when they were inside it. Souls may leave human beings at a certain moment while remaining as a sort of enchantment over everything that coincided with their dreams. And so it was that our mother transmitted hers to the house by the sea. Every lamp, every piece of furniture, everything was chosen by her, as was the exact location where each would go. Though she had never taken care of the house in Buenos Aires and never knew what to place on the walls or how to mask the incurable indifference that floated in the air or the eternal absence of my father, in this house she created a magical, weightless, ethereal atmosphere where sorrow vanished. Even the air yielded to her plans: an aura appeared around the chairs, the lamps rescued from old English trains, the tapestries, the ornamental country tools, and the upright piano she had bought so that I could practice during holidays. As if the whole house were an energy subject to the whims of happiness, the walls demurely loved what they contained. People who suffered from disaffection, those who weren't loved but wanted to be loved, felt the warmth and acceptance of a house that surrendered unconditionally to its inhabitants, as sometimes, miraculously, happens with love. Misfortunes could be forgotten in the sun, because, when sitting on the terrace, there was always a boundless horizon. But only my father and I shared its secret: what was contained in the foundations of the house. Mixed with the girders, sand, and lime was the true mortar that permitted the house to be what it was. And now that I look at it for the last time before shutting the door and handing the keys to its new owner, I do so with the eyes of that girl who watched the desert and imagined the smallest detail of her father's tale: this is the terrace, farther on the bedrooms, over there an enormous living room with windows on every side that give onto the sea or the greenery, depending on what we want, and a big fireplace to keep us warm. Imagination has no need to roam; like streamers it unfurls from a fixed point, animating and embellishing its place of origin, which may be the soul.

The world cannot be seen. A glance does not necessarily mean the truth. The world came to me through imagination, a certain internal touch, large fingers that reach from inside, that brush across the surface of things, people, and colors, feeling their inner workings, without ever looking at them, those things and people that are so desired, so distant, so inaccessible. You can be blind and mute but not deaf. Blind, one cannot capture the meaning of words, what humans exchange through them, how they complete and embroider them. What bodies scream at the top of their voices, what glances say, the brume emitted by words. That world that never manages to be complete.

How can I say good-bye to the house? Surrounded by the rosebush, the red hibiscus, the cherry tree that I planted myself. After years of enduring the theft of passersby and tourists, those tempted by the charm of the flowers, they finally grew. The rosebush that was stolen time and again and that I replaced on many occasions one day became strong, a large bush with red roses. The cherry tree, at first fragile and weak, is now an established tree, confident even though this year it didn't bloom and it has some pruning scars: a new neighbor, a giant like Anthony Quinn, had the nerve to cut it back because it blocked his view onto the golf course. Looking at it, an anonymous Japanese poem comes to mind: "Plum tree at my door, should I not return, spring always will, you must bloom." Graciously, as if to make up for the cherry tree, the hibiscus dons cheerful flowers that seem ready to fly and that shimmer in the bright sun. The house itself, after the refurbishment and cleaning I submitted it to before offering it like a tempting virgin, has recovered its former seductiveness.

Experience is different: sealed inside a glass ball you can perceive everything that was ever spoken, everything that words don't say, for the same reason that you never hear them. Beneath the outer layers of human skin, there are underground streams that run through us, imperceptible, delicate strings like those of a spiderweb that unite more inexorably than voices and oaths. . . .

I no longer look upon the world as before. People, ideas, loves, all lack the particular weight they used to have. Everything is much lighter now. Touched by that plague that contaminates everything, how can I take myself seriously? I cannot keep the promise I made so many years ago. Once, in this very place, on a pier, the only pier there was for a long time, that sunk its unstable posts into the sand and that the water finally dragged away. Now I scarcely remember Kind.[1] I merely dream.

II

Solid, strong, the general leaned against the large windows. I didn't know what to say, I didn't know why he had made me come, why he made me sit in the cushy armchair, why he affectionately called me Kind. Kind, the fun is over now and as you know, between personal conscience and power, there's no contest. That's why, the general continued, a litter of poor dreamers died painfully ordinary deaths. But you survived, because I wanted you to. Why? Maybe because of the music, maybe because Mozart brought us together so long ago in an arena far from passion and misery, because of our mutual love of beauty, regardless of what it means for either of us. Like Goethe, I've always preferred injustice over disorder. But I probably let you live because survivors are witnesses to what power can do. It's a mistake to think they will be cause for embarrassment. Secretly, all those who have or have had power belong to the same brotherhood and respect its every manifestation, even if they don't realize it. In this country, Kind, there isn't a single person who doesn't want it, who doesn't fear it, who doesn't find pleasure in exercising it. There are some, like myself, who

---

[1]*Kind,* pronounced "Keend," means "child" in German.

know what humans are really made of. That's all there is, power, and someone has to take charge. That's what we fight for, those of us who dominate, to have it in our hands and to not relinquish it to those who would destroy us, and who wouldn't manage to change things anyway. If your side had won, there would have been nothing but a transfer of power. Those who believe in the utopia of a better world are crazy or stupid. You're neither, Kind, which is why you'll respect power and you'll be able to move on with your life, which is now enriched by wisdom and experience. All power, Kind, exists in relation to a greater power, and if anyone is its match, a struggle is the automatic result, no matter what drives the powers. The fascinating thing about this struggle is that principle has nothing to do with ideas, power exists for itself and in the end the powerful serve power even though we are also served by it. He inhaled a mouthful of smoke, releasing it as rings. That's how it is, he said, satisfied. Power is the only law, and the only reality, the only thing that's great. There is so little greatness left, he sighed, beauty is on its way out. Kind, you who love it, know this as well as I do.

The sun was setting behind the big window, and the horrible calm in the room didn't have a single one of those ingredients that, taken together, bring out the serenity that tends to herald nightfall. A couple of kiskadees flew through the air, pursuing one another. I'll have them take you home before it gets late: he patted me affectionately. What home? I think. I don't have one. You must have a friend who could put you up, Kind. Go, there's no danger now. Look, even I rest, and he showed me a revolver, wrapped in a red velvet cloth. It's been my most faithful friend. There are more modern ones, but this Luger came with me from Germany and it will be with me until I die. For now it's resting, waiting, but it's ready to work as soon as I squeeze the trigger.

Mercedes, this is my revolver. I'm going to show you how to use it. It's a Luger, a present from my father. If the Peronists attack the house and try to burn it and I'm not here, you'll have to defend your mother. I hope you won't have to use it, my father said. But if he's showing it to me, I thought, it's so that I use it. But then I understood that my father didn't want me to use the weapon, nor did he believe there was any possibility I would. He just wanted to show me his power, to demonstrate his authority. The weapon was a sort of accessory to his personality. Once I realized this, I listened uncomfortably to his complicated explanations about loading and unloading, about the safety catch and how to release it.

The Peronists had painted red crosses on the buildings they wanted to burn down, wherever there was someone they wanted to see eliminated. In our house, the sign was low on the wall, next to the door, and it said in code: "There is a traitor here, may those on our side know it and when the moment comes, act." We all knew it, the block leaders—a creation of Peronism—were in charge of security and espionage. They had their political grudges and their personal grudges, too, and those of us who had incurred their wrath were on their list. In our particular case, there were both sorts of grudges, political, because my father was a diehard opponent of Peronism, and the more mundane ones, because my mother wouldn't hesitate to speak ill of General Perón in front of his supporters, the greengrocer, the doorman, the men at the garage across the street. My father couldn't rein her in. It was unnerving to walk with her down the street where we lived and endure the insults, jibes, and threats from the doormen, the grocer, the guards who were always in front of the Eva Perón Foundation, next to our house. As she passed by they would cast homicidal, if ineffectual, glares: my mother had no concept of fear. My father, on the other hand, was a cautious man. In light of all this, why not show her how to use the revolver, I wondered, and I asked my father. Are you crazy? The moment she knows how it works, she'd use it. That's the last thing we need. He emptied the magazine, reloaded the bullets, cocked and uncocked the gun, and taught me to set and remove the breechblock. When the lesson was over, he put it back in the leather holster, which it never left again. I didn't know anything further about the gun for many years. And now I had an identical one before my eyes. I moved toward the door but stopped in my tracks in front of the gun. I picked it up carefully under the general's pleased gaze. I cocked the gun, aimed at him, and fired. The weapon didn't make a sound. The general smiled again. Give it up, Kind. There's no other way for you. Accept it. I can't speak, I can't make a sound of any sort. Do it, the general insisted. You're intelligent. He opened the door to let me out. Now you know that even if you kill me, what I represent is eternal. That much you've learned, your attempts won't get you anywhere. Good-bye, Kind. Act and pay homage to the primordial forces, which is where music comes from, isn't it?

I awoke with a start. Will the nightmares never end, even after all these years? I heard the singing of the birds, the noise of the lawnmower on the green, and remembered with annoyance the reason I had gone to the house. An annoyance that hid other emotions I wanted to contain. I don't know how to keep Kind out of my dreams, how to make her accept that I exist, to stop thinking she is immortal. I have tried to disassemble her like an old toy, but her broken pieces keep putting themselves back together again. I find her hand at my throat. Unstifled, her voice bursts forth, a constant whisper, recurrent like the waves, stubborn like the howl of a hungry wolf, a distant animal that never rests. *In my dreams, the birds sleep and you can't play music because they'll wake up. The birds are in the basement, asleep. If they awoke and found themselves caught in a dark basement, they might go crazy, they would sing aimlessly until they lost their voices, or maybe they would never again sing, having lost their voices, because of the terror. In any case, given that they are captive and in a basement, they no longer sing.*

Translated from the Spanish by Tobias Hecht

ABOUT THE AUTHOR

The Argentine writer and translator Marcela Solá studied philosophy at the Universidad Católica Argentina, Santa María de los Buenos Aires. Her publications include the novel *El silencio de Kind* (Kind's Silence), published by Planeta in 1999 and short-listed for the Planeta Prize; a volume of poetry, *Acta de Defunción* (Act of Death; 1994), winner of the Poesía Arcano Prize; and three books of short stories, *Los condenados visten de blanco* (The Condemned Wore White; 1971), *Mis propios ojos no dan abasto* (My Eyes Are Not Enough; 1976), and *Manual de Situaciones Imposibles* (Manual for Impossible Situations; 1990). She also edited *Qué quieren las mujeres* (What Women Want), published by Lumen in 1994. She has taught at the University of Laval, in Quebec, and currently teaches Argentine literature in the Multicultural Program of the Universidad de Belgrano, in Buenos Aires. In 1984 she won a Fulbright scholarship to join the International Writers Workshop at the University of Iowa.

JUAN JOSÉ SAER

For Argentine writers, the land of their birth has never seemed sufficiently ample. That gigantic country, close to four million square kilometers, is too small for them. Their eyes and their hopes turn toward Europe or the United States, as if there, by the simple fact of change, the coveted literary success and personal fulfillment were easier to obtain. In a certain way, the Argentine writer seems to assume as something of his own the supposed fate that no one is a prophet in his own land. Perhaps because deep down it has cost him too much to internalize those enormous expanses of the pampas that, because they are uninhabited, may themselves have certain problems in feeling Argentine. There is another hypothesis that perhaps should be considered: that the Argentine writer, when he leaves Argentina, does so in order to better see Argentina . . .

Juan José Saer traveled to Paris in 1968, very likely impelled, whether as citizen or as writer, by the military coup that in 1966 had dissolved Congress, outlawed political parties, and abolished university autonomy. He would never again have a permanent residence. He lived in France, was a professor in France, continued his work in France. That was the time of the nouveau roman, *the time when Alain Robbe-Grillet was raising the banner of "objectivism," of rejection of psychological analysis, of claims of a static world neither significant nor absurd. Signs of the influence of the* nouveau roman *on Saer's work are readily detectable in the books he had written in Argentina before emigrating:* En la zona, Responso, Palo y hueso, Unidad de lugar. *In any case, Juan José Saer was always quite clear about considering as negative the mechanical extrapolation of themes, as well as the acculturated application of techniques recently learned and made into fetishes . . . Literary fanaticism, in any of its forms, whether from the point of view of master or disciple, has always been incompatible with the intelligence and free spirit of Saer.*

There is, therefore, something of the "objectivist" view in the story that this brief commentary accompanies: "Barro cocido," from the book Unidad de lugar. *But in it can be seen too what would, after all, serve as a constant in the author's works: the presence of the tribe, the region, the birthplace, like coals that amid the ashes refuse to be extinguished. Juan José Saer also could not be a European. His place was the world, that world in which it was necessary to set an Argentina finally able to recognize itself. And accept itself.*

—JOSÉ SARAMAGO
Translated from the Portuguese by Clifford E. Landers

BAKED MUD

I remember very well that it was the year of the drought, 1961. The first three days all we saw was the yellow station wagon overheating in the sun in the sandy clearing between Giménez's motel and the blue strip of asphalt. The most any of us had was a horse or a motorcycle and seeing that bright Chevrolet burning in the dry January sun gave us both pity and a combination of respect and admiration, particularly since a little beyond the plot of the motel there was a circle of chinaberry trees where he could have left it in the shade. It gave the impression that he did with cars what other people do with matches, use it once and throw it away. On the fourth day the boy who cleans the motel came with a list written in pencil and a five-thousand-peso bill; he had to make two trips to take everything back: bottles of wine and beer, herb for maté, salamis and cheese, water crackers, and a bunch of candies. The boy told Focchi that it was all for "the station wagon guy" who was living in the motel with a pregnant woman, and that he had a gun.

On the sixth day we saw him, from the patio of the store. He seemed to have come out for a breath of the cooler afternoon air, because he walked slowly, as if he were stretching out his legs, and he looked at everything with a sluggish curiosity, his hands in his pants pockets, wearing short sleeves, his head held up as if he were taking deep breaths, with the slouched shoulders of a man who has spent a long time in bed, or locked up. We saw him look at a tree, follow with his gaze the quick movement of a car along the asphalt until it disappeared toward the city, and then lean over and pat one of the rear tires of the station wagon two or three times. Then he went through the open front door of the motel and disappeared. Focchi was the one who came up to our table and told us that he thought it was Blanco's kid, the one who we knew had been like us until one night in a bar in La Guardia when he gambled some money that old man Blanco had collected that same day for a field of green peas, and then disappeared without a trace before the old man could catch him. Nobody had dared to speak of the matter again in front of the old man, who'd drop by the store every once in a while to drink a bitter maté, without saying a word to anyone, leaving his flat-cart at the door.

We would have paid more attention to him from the beginning, had it not been the year of the drought. But we spent those days buying wine for Sebastián "deaf man" Salas, so he'd tell us about droughts he had seen that were worse than this one, just to know that such calamities occurred every once in a while and that it did not mean that this bitch of a life was coming to an end. The deaf man was so old my deceased father used to tell me that when he was young Sebastián Salas was already old, and my father died in '59 at age sixty-two. Sebastián picked up on our fear and took advantage of it by telling us stories of droughts that had lasted years and wiped out all the rivers and killed all the animals and many men, but when he saw in our eyes that we were wondering if this drought was similar to those, Sebastián would frown with his thin mouth, in the middle of his wrinkled face, and we'd be unable to get another word out of him, not even with a corkscrew. So we would buy him more wine. He'd always drink it standing up, without spilling a drop, emptying the cup in a long, single slurp. We'd look at him with secret anger, combined with amazement and fear, because we knew that he was so old and that he was so alone that there was no evil in the world that could even graze him. Setting the dirty glass down on the dirty table on the patio, Sebastián would pretend that he just happened to be there and that there was no connection between the stories he told and the glass of wine we had bought him, because we were so frightened of those white, blinding high noons and those green afternoon skies that we did not dare to admit it. Every time a horse galloped by on the road from the asphalt toward the coast, it kicked up a yellow cloud of dust that left us nearly blind, and the smell of the dead animals filled the air. It was nearly impossible to breathe. As far as I know, Sebastián the deaf man never drank as much free wine as he did that year, even though it seems that that's all he's ever done in his whole bitch of a life.

But that yellow station wagon was still there, and we could see it from the patio of the store. The woman we saw only after about a week: she was thin and blonde and it was easy to see that child-birth was only a matter of days away, a few weeks at the most. She wore a loose, red-and-green-flower-patterned dress that bunched up around her belly. She came out with him the following after-noon to stroll around the plot where the station wagon was, and the two of them did exactly the same thing he had done by him-self the afternoon before: they looked at a tree, watched a car that passed by quickly in the direction of the city until it faded from view, leaned against the rear tires of the station wagon. They walked arm in arm, moving so slowly that they seemed to be strolling not in front of a motel, but in front of a hospital, like two convalescing patients leaning on each other's shoulder to help support their respective weakness. It was precisely when they walked back through the front door of the motel and disappeared from our view that old man Blanco's flat-cart arrived from the coast, kicking up a yellow cloud of dust, and stopped in front of the store. The old man tied the reins to one of the crossbars of the flat-cart and entered the store, with an earnest greeting as he passed our table on the patio. Soon afterward he came out with a glass of bitter maté in his hand and remained standing near the door, taking small sips, without speaking, lean and burned by the sun, his straw hat slightly raised and his steady gaze upon the heavy horses tied to the flat-cart. Focchi came out after him and came up to our table, without saying a word, the whole time looking at the front door of the motel, in front of which the only thing present was the yellow station wagon abandoned there for a week, its hood covered by a canvas. Then the old man went back into the store, followed by Focchi; he loaded some supplies in the flat-cart and, saying good-bye, again in earnest, climbed onto the flat-cart and turned around, heading off toward the coast. The yellow cloud of dust that the flat-cart kicked up was still floating in the air when we saw the tall and wide figure come out of the front door of the motel and walk toward us; we knew by then who he was, even though some of us had never seen him before and others would have been unable to recognize him at that distance; and even though we also knew that it had been a coincidence, we all had the impression that he had been waiting for old man Blanco to leave in his flat-cart, so immediately after its departure did he reappear. Now he had put on a dark coat that was too small on him. As he crossed the road and came down the embankment and entered the patio of the store where we were sitting and drinking beer, we took a good look at him and realized by the way he entered that he had been there many times before. He did not even look at the dirt lane with the boccie balls, and he said hello as he went by in a Buenos Aires city accent, but he looked like any one of us because of his dark skin and that certain way of walking, somewhat bent toward the ground by the weight of the tremendous heat. Focchi was out on the patio with us, and by the look they gave each other we realized they had recognized each other right away and that they both understood at the same time that it was best to pretend otherwise. We could tell that he had hidden a weapon at his waist, on his right side. We went into the store and Focchi followed to see what he wanted to order. I got up and went inside, because we happened to be running low on beer and it was time to order another bottle. He had just ordered an Orange Crush and a beer and was mixing them together in a glass. From the other side of the counter Focchi was leaning against the shelves, studying him. Neither one of them was speaking. Focchi then asked me what I wanted, and when I said a beer he asked me who was paying. "I am," I said. "Yes," Focchi said. "Yes, you. But when?" Then I told him to hold on until Saturday because on Saturday I was going to get some back pay for some work I'd done, and then I'd be able to pay him. "What job are you going to get paid for," Focchi said, "if you're never worked a day in your life?" The yellow station wagon guy started to laugh, and Focchi did too. "You're all set if you want to extend credit to these guys," Focchi said. The yellow station wagon guy was still laughing. "Put it on my tab," he said, taking out a bunch of bills from his pocket.

He stayed with us till well after nightfall, drinking Orange Crush mixed with beer. He sat down at the table on the patio, underneath the trees, and he spoke the entire time, as if he had not come out to get a drink, but simply to talk. Before it got completely dark we saw Sebastián the deaf man walking slowly down the road, but we did not call out to him; the deaf man hovered near the store a long time until he finally approached and leaned against the trunk of a tree and stayed there looking at us, inside that wool coat of his that was too large for his thin, broken-down body. Finally the yellow station wagon guy saw him and told Focchi to serve him some wine, and the deaf man drank glass after glass, leaning against the tree, without coming any closer to us, as if he were not entirely comfortable. The yellow station wagon guy spoke as if he wanted us to understand that he was like us and that he knew everything any one of us might know, but for some reason was forced not to say who he was. He spoke of dorado and moncholo fish, of fields of green peas, of great heat waves, of floods that wipe out ranchos and roads. We listened to him and every once in a while looked at the hidden lump underneath his coat at his waist, on his right side. Well into the night he got up and left, leaving an aroma of imported cigarettes in the air of the patio and half a dozen paid beers for us to drink after he had left.

And so we got used to him, just like we had first gotten used to the yellow station wagon glaring in the morning near the front door of the motel, and like we would have liked to have gotten used to the drought, which left a furrow of dead animals, the smell of which filled the air, and a line of flat earth, gray and cracked, in place of where the river had been before. Now he came straight to the store when he left the motel, always with his coat on, snug on his body, with that hidden lump on his right side. He would sit down at the table with us and begin to tell stories of gendarmerie officers, stories that had taken place on the border with Uruguay, and in which, by the way he told them, one could tell he had been involved. We would listen the whole time without speaking, drinking beer at his side, asking ourselves what steps he had taken through the world since the night that he gambled the money from the green pea field in La Guardia, what kind of strange steps he had taken that would have brought him back again to the point of departure, as if he had been going around in circles, without moving forward. We also asked ourselves when he would finally meet up with old man Blanco, if he was meant to meet up with him, since at least three or four times that week he had gotten up and left just a minute before old man Blanco's flat-cart had stopped in front of the store, and a couple of times he had arrived before the yellow cloud of dust, which was kicked up by the heavy horses and which left us nearly blind, had completely settled.

There was also a large barbecue. In the morning he came and left Focchi and me the money to buy the things. Focchi himself prepared it, lighting the fire in the afternoon. He closed the store early and barbecued the meat slowly, taking long drinks of wine every time he stepped back from the grill. Beginning at nightfall we talked and drank wine under the trees, barely illuminated by a small lamp, surrounded by a maddening cloud of mosquitoes and listening to the crack of the beetles crashing blindly against the brick wall where the lamp was. He drank wine the entire night without stopping; at midnight his tall body, wrapped in the dark coat (the lump at the waist, on his right side), swayed slightly. When he ran out of the imported ones, he started smoking our "Colmenas," and his Buenos Aires–accented voice sped up and grew shrill like ours, though made awkward by the alcohol. He said he knew a family in the area, the Blanco family. That he had been around these parts a lot before, he said. Then he stopped speaking and laughing, and we heard the whistling of his breathing. He was swaying more and more dangerously, and he was pacing back and forth with his forehead furrowed, his eyes half-closed, and his mouth open. "I make whatever I want, what the hell. I'm not some bum," he said all of a sudden. We were listening to him in silence, but for him it was as if we were not there. "I don't have any debts. I don't owe anyone anything. What did he think? As if I couldn't . . . What the hell." He left shaking his head, swaying, murmuring as if he were talking to himself. We saw him disappear from the store's lighted area into the night, and then we heard the stomping of his shoes on the asphalt, invisible in the darkness.

The next day we did not see him in the morning. We did see, of course, like always, the yellow station wagon and the open front door of the motel, and the circle of motionless chinaberry trees, the green of their leaves dull and dirty with dust. At noon we went to our houses, along the road or in the field toward the coast, and came back to the store later in the afternoon, after the siesta. The smell of death was suffocating and we were very afraid. We could not be alone. Even the stories of Sebastián the deaf man no longer worked for us, for although there may have been many droughts in the past, they were not *this one:* this drought had never happened before, and there was no good reason for it to stop instead of worsening. Just like there had been no good reason for the other droughts to end with rain, or for the drought to simply begin, there was also no good reason for this one not to continue indefinitely, extending longer and longer each day, until it was the end of all of us. We all thought like this, even if we did not say it. That is why we sat every afternoon on the patio of the store drinking beer in silence, underneath the trees. But for old man Blanco there did not seem to be a drought, or anything else. That is the impression he gave us when we saw him get down from his flat-cart with that agitated and feverish air that men have when they are returning from work. He greeted us earnestly and went into the store. He was carrying a cane in his hand. He was wearing dirty, worn-out pants and a dirty, gray shirt, and when he took off his hat to scratch his gray-haired head we saw the white line on his forehead that separated the dark, sunburned part of his face from the part protected by the hat. Almost at the same time that the old man was entering the store, we saw the tall body wrapped up in the dark coat emerging

from the door of the motel and heading slowly toward us. He
stopped for a moment to let a fast, loud, large red and yellow bus,
which made the earth tremble, pass by, and then crossed the road.
He was smiling as he approached us. Instinctively we looked at the
lump on his right side, at his waist. He was clean-shaven and looked
as if he had slept from the night before until just a moment before.
He walked by the flat-cart without seeing it. He stopped next to us
and said hello, smiling the whole time. He was pulling up a chair to
sit in our circle, his back to the door of the store, when he saw
something in our eyes and turned around, just in time to see old
man Blanco the moment he came out of the store, walking slowly,
pensive, with the glass of bitter maté in one hand and the cane in
the other. At first the old man did not recognize him, or did
not look at him: he began to understand slowly, feeling the thing
cautiously, carrying out a complicated ritual of verification, as if
certain connections in his brain, rusty because of a lack of use,
required a set amount of time to start functioning normally. They
were so still that it looked as if they were not breathing: the old
man's body, at the door of the store, facing not so much toward the
station wagon guy, who was to the side, but rather toward the flat-
cart with the two motionless horses parked about five meters in
front of him. Only the old man's head was facing the station wagon
guy. And the station wagon guy, his mouth opened in a half smile,
his left hand still resting on the back of the chair. Then everything
happened so quickly that it can barely be recounted: the old man
snapped into motion by jumping forward with the cane in the air
and started furiously hitting the station wagon guy. At first, all the
station wagon guy did was slouch back and receive the first blows
on his body and his face. We got up in the middle of a clamor of
falling chairs, looking back and forth between the old man, who
was swinging the cane up and down with his eyes closed, and the
bulk that the station wagon guy carried on his right side. Focchi
came running out of the store and stopped at the door. The only
thing that could be heard was the whistling of the swinging cane
and the dry sounds of the blows against the station wagon guy's
body, but when the station wagon guy fell to the ground and

started bleeding, we also began to hear the old man's enraged breathing and the panting of the station wagon guy, who began to drag himself along the ground as far as the brick wall. Tears fell down his face. The old man kept hitting him until he saw that the other man had stopped moving. When he ceased with the cane we saw that he had not at any time stopped grasping the glass of bitter maté and that it had broken in his hand, from where a stream of blood now fell. The old man dropped the cane, leaned over the other man, and started searching him until he found a bunch of bills in his pants pocket; he took out two or three, counted them, counted them again, and leaving the rest lying on the floor, put away the ones he had separated. Then he climbed up on the flat-cart, turned around, and headed off toward the coast, kicking up a yellow cloud of dust that left us nearly blind.

The station wagon guy stood up slowly, with the help of the wall. We looked at him without moving. It was getting dark; after gathering his bills and awkwardly dusting off his clothes, he headed off toward the motel without saying a word, along the road passing Sebastián the deaf man, who was coming down to the store and did not even look at him. We saw him heading off, swaying like the night before, his clothes full of dust, his left arm drooping lifeless at his side. Then he went through the front door of the motel and we did not see him again. I do not mean for the rest of that day, but forever. The next day the yellow station wagon had disappeared. The only things left were the open door of the motel, the circle of chinaberry trees, the dry January sun. And in between Sebastián's dark stories about other floods and droughts, we also had our silence, our solitude, and our fear.

Translated from the Spanish by Sergio Waisman

ABOUT THE AUTHOR

Juan José Saer was born in Serodino, Argentina, in 1937, the son of Arab immigrants. He taught at the Santa Fe Instituto de

Cinematografía, then moved to Paris in 1968 and taught literature at the University of Rennes until his retirement in 2002. In 1987 he was awarded the prestigious Spanish literary prize, the Premio Nadal, for his novel *La ocasión* (The Opportunity). In 2003 he was awarded the Prix France Culture and in 2004 the prestigious Prize of the Unión Latina. He died in June 2005 in Paris. Saer's extensive literary oeuvre, which includes about twenty novels and collections of stories, is regarded as one of the most important in contemporary Argentine literature since that of Jorge Luis Borges. Many of his works have been translated into multiple languages.

JUAN FORN

When I was invited to select a Latin American author for this anthology, I confess that I was tempted to say no, of course not. How to choose from among twenty countries and dozens, indeed hundreds, of writers who, though untranslated into English, are deserving of a vast readership? How to leave behind all the others?

On the other hand, how to deny readers deprived of the joys of Spanish the chance to read a story like this one, by the Argentine Juan Forn. I settled on it because it came floating to me—like a swimmer on the horizon, refusing to disappear under the waves of my own incessant forgetfulness, it came to me again and again as I turned over in my mind so many other worthy candidates. "Swimming at Night" had stayed in my memory years after first having read it, continued to haunt and yes, console me. I can remember finishing it on that inaugural occasion and not moving for a long while, fixed, silent, wondering, interrogating myself, my life. My father was alive back then and perhaps I was anticipating a moment awaiting me in the years to come, this very moment when I write these words in 2005, when he would no longer be alive, if perhaps he would arrive at my doorstep as the father comes to the narrator of "Swimming at Night."

It is not only the quiet quality of the writing, the way in which emotion is allowed free rein and yet simultaneously controlled, not only the almost waterlike obliqueness of the voice that tells this story, the confident fluidity of that modest voice, all that is hidden and unsaid and slips out into the "in between" where the real work of literature resides; not only this, but something else that drew me to select this story. It goes against the grain of what most English-language readers expect from a Latin American author. I have often come across the presumption that we americanos from the south are supposed to produce literature that is invariably political (and much of that literature is, in fact, wonderfully political, engaged in the sorrows and labyrinth and hopes of struggle) and all too often based in some jungle or on the slopes of a savage mountain and, of course, also exotically *magical. All right! If that's what people want, well, I'll choose—and I did choose—a story that befuddles these expectations and foils them, a story coming out of the penchant for fantasy in the Rio de la Plata region, a playful desire for the metaphysical that emerges from the sprawling cities of our continent. This is an urban (and even an urbane) literature—that is troubled by its proximity to the pampa, the thousands of miles of land surrounding us, surrounding the protagonist of "Swimming at Night." He knows and we know that out there is an immensity that we need to tame but also acknowledge, that our swimming pools and reflecting lights are mere delusions, only the transitory setting for the real drama of trying to fight death about to engulf us, a peninsula of faint light from which to tell the stories that keep us alive in the meanwhile, in the* mientras tanto.

And if the reader feels seduced by this story, please remember all the other narratives that I had to leave adrift and shipwrecked and without a translator and that look forward to calm eyes, avid eyes. So . . . either learn Spanish and read these other works in the original or . . . demand from booksellers and editors and publishers more books like this one, more chances for the Juan Forns to swim toward us and take us into those deep waters.

—ARIEL DORFMAN

SWIMMING AT NIGHT

It was late, too late to be up, especially in a borrowed house and in the dark. In the garden, the crickets furiously, desperately called out for rain, and he asked himself how his wife and baby daughter could sleep upstairs through the deafening murmur. He couldn't sleep, and so he sat, in shorts, in front of the open glass door to the terrace and the garden. All the lights were off except the underwater pool lights, but their undulating glow could not banish this feeling of being in a strange house, the indefinite discomfort he felt about this simulation of a holiday. The truth was, he wasn't really resting, but working, even if this fact did not require him to do anything in particular, other than live in that house with his wife and daughter and enjoy the possessions of his friend Felix while Felix and Ruth sailed up the Nile and spent a fortune on rolls of film and toothless Egyptian guides, all at the expense of an Italian travel magazine.

In order to relax and induce sleep he reminded himself that he wouldn't set foot in Buenos Aires all month. He would live in shorts and wouldn't have to shave; he would cut the grass, clean the pool, watch videos, and listen to music while his daughter grew before his eyes and his wife concocted strange desserts in the kitchen. Meanwhile, someone would leave a minimally stimulat-ing—or even catastrophic—message on the answering machine in his apartment. And perhaps Felix and Ruth would prolong their trip by another month, or have an accident, or both fall in love with the same androgynous, illiterate Alexandrian youth. A month could be a long time in some places other than his office; a month could be almost a lifetime. It was for his daughter. He had to try to live at her pace, as his wife told him. Day by day, hour by hour, slowly. He had to come to terms with fatherhood once and for all, as Felix and Ruth would have said, if they hadn't in fact already said it.

At that moment he heard the door. Not the doorbell but a series of soft, polite raps, almost apologetic about the late hour. Every house has a logic, and its laws are more eloquent at night, when things occur without palliative noises. He didn't look at his watch or jump, or suspect that he was hearing things. He simply got up from his chair and walked toward the door without turn-ing on any lights; when he opened it he found himself standing face-to-face with his father. He had not seen his father since his death. And, at that moment, he had the strange realization that he had become used to the idea of never seeing him again.

His father was wearing a raincoat buttoned up to the collar, and he had a full head of hair, carefully combed as always, but com-pletely white. They had never been particularly effusive with one another. He said simply, "Father, what a surprise," but he did not move aside until his father asked, with a smile:

"May I come in?"

"Yes, of course. Of course."

His father crossed the darkened living room, went out the open glass door, and sat down on one of the lounge chairs on the terrace. He looked back at him, gesturing for him to come out and sit down on a chair next to him. Obediently, he went. He said:

"Do you want to give me your raincoat? Can I bring you something to drink?"

His father shook his head. Then he stretched out as far as he could and breathed deeply, still smiling.

"No, no, I'm fine. It's going to rain at any moment," he said. "How lovely it is here. Is it like this during the day as well?"

"Nicer. Especially for Marisa and our little girl."

"Marisa and the baby. You must have a lot to tell me, don't you?"

He could feel his jaw drop slightly. In his dreams, when he saw his father, he knew everything that had happened to them in his absence.

"Yes, of course. I suppose I do," he said.

"Of course, I don't expect you to catch me up with all the news. Don't bother with politics, work, and the world in general. I want to hear about domestic things. Your sisters, you, Marisa, the baby. Those things."

He was surprised that his father had used the word *domestic*. And even more surprised that he had mentioned everyone but his mother. But he didn't know what to say.

"I'm going to get some whiskey. Are you sure you don't want any?"

"No, no thank you. By the way, what a good idea to install lights inside the pool."

"It's not mine," he said, before going in. "The house, I mean." When he returned, with a generous serving of whiskey in his hand, he stopped behind his father's lounge chair; at that moment he realized that they had not yet touched. "I thought," he said, standing there, "I thought that you could see everything that went on here from where you were."

His father turned his head slightly from side to side, several times.

"Unfortunately no. It's quite different from what one imagines."

He looked at the pool and felt that he had no control over what he was saying or what he was about to say.

"If you knew how many things I did these past years for your benefit, thinking that you were watching," and he laughed a little, joylessly but without bitterness, simply to empty his lungs. "So you don't know anything about these past four years. How strange."

His father shifted in his chair and looked at him out of the corner of his eye.

"Perhaps there will be some changes in the new place they are sending us. If that's any consolation."

He stared at him without understanding.

"We've been moved. I'm going to be somewhere else from now on. Not only me, many others as well. Things there aren't as orderly as one might think. Sometimes unexpected things happen. Like my being here with you."

"And why with me? Why didn't you go see Mother?"

For a few moments, his father stared at the undulating light in the pool. His features changed slightly; a tiny hint of sadness seeped into his blank expression.

"It would have been more difficult with your mother. A night is not so long, and I need you to tell me everything you can. With your mother we would end up talking about other things. About the past, especially, about us, and all the good things we experienced together. And that wouldn't have been fair to her." He paused. "There are certain things that are technically impossible in my current state; feeling, for example. Do you understand? In a way, tonight I am something that would have no value to your mother. With you, it's simpler. Your memory is . . . selective, shall we say, and you always had a panoramic view of your emotions. Toward your mother, your sisters, yourself. In any case . . ." He paused again. "I also thought that you would be more able to cope with the feelings provoked by this visit. After all, I was never that important to you, isn't that true?"

He felt something he had not felt for a long time. A kind of submissiveness, and a need to resist. He realized suddenly that in the last four years he had not been what he was at that moment: his father's son. He walked to the edge of the pool, took off his loafers, and sat down with his legs dangling in the water.

"If you weren't so important to me, I wouldn't have done all those things I did thinking of you, for you, these past few years. Did that never occur to you?"

"No."

He was confused. The answer was so quick and brutal that it seemed sincere. And for that same reason, it seemed unbelievable. Cowardly. Almost unfair.

"And now that you know, what . . . ?" he managed to say.

"Nothing," his father answered. Then he got up, carried the lounge chair to the edge of the pool, and sat down with his hands in his pockets. "I suppose it doesn't change anything. What you did is done. It doesn't make sense to get angry now, with yourself or with me, because of it. Don't you think?"

Not only was it useless, but he was beginning to feel it wasn't really legitimate for him to question anything, considering his father's condition, or to allow himself to react with that uncharacteristic aggressiveness. The need to resist melted away and all that was left was the feeling of submissiveness, not toward his father but toward the state of things, toward an obtuse and ungraspable abstraction.

"It's true," he said, "I'm sorry."

They said nothing for a moment.

"In any case, I exaggerated a bit. I didn't do so many things thinking of you."

The father chuckled slightly.

"That's what I thought."

A flash of lightning split the night sky. When the thunder cracked, his father cringed and chuckled again.

"I had almost forgotten these things. It's odd how memory works, what it saves and what it lets go of."

"The crickets," he said, "can you hear them? They were keeping me awake. That's why I was awake when you arrived." After he said these words, he faltered. The crickets? On further reflection he decided to leave it unresolved.

"Well then," the father said in a very soft voice, "shall we get to the matter at hand?"

"Can I ask you something first?"

The lounge chair creaked. He tried to return his father's gaze.

"As you wish. But the thing is, once you know, it's difficult to erase from your memory. I don't mean that as a threat. I'm simply telling you, for your sake."

"Yes, I know," he said. And he asked, "Does everyone go to the same place? Doesn't it matter what they've done?"

"I could have answered that by the time I was twenty, more or less; I always suspected that it matters more when you're alive than afterward. Regarding your other question, it's not exactly a place. But yes, everyone goes to the same one, to the extent that we are all more or less the same. Your life and your neighbor's life, for example, are more or less as different as your height is from his. They are nuances, and nuances don't count. Let's say that there are basically only two states, yours and mine. It's more complicated than that, but you wouldn't understand it now."

"So you and I will meet again, someday," he said.

His father didn't answer.

"Does being together mean anything, there?"

His father didn't answer.

"And what is it like?" he asked.

The father averted his gaze and looked over at the pool.

"It's like swimming at night," he said. And the undulating lights were reflected in his face. "Like swimming at night, in a huge pool, without ever getting tired."

He swallowed the remaining whiskey in his glass and waited for it to reach his stomach. Then he poured the ice into the pool and rested the empty glass on the edge.

"Anything else?" his father said.

He shook his head. He swung his legs a little bit in the water and stared at the bottom of the lounge chair, the raincoat, and his father's relaxed, softly ageless face. He thought about how reticent they had always been about all physical contact and about how incredibly ingenuous the embraces seemed in his dreams about his father. This was the way things really were: everything was the same as it had always been, and things were picking up almost at the same point at which they had been left four years earlier. Even if it was only for one night.

"Where would you like to begin?" he asked.

"Wherever you like. Don't worry about the time. We have all night. Dawn won't come until you've finished."

He breathed in deeply, then exhaled, and realized he had entered the longest and most secret night of his life. He began, of course, by talking about his daughter.

Translated from the Spanish by Marina Harss

ABOUT THE AUTHOR

Juan Forn was born in Buenos Aires in 1959. After publishing his first and only book of poetry in 1979, he traveled to Europe, and upon his return to Buenos Aires he began working in the publishing business as a translator, reader, and editor. Forn worked as an associate editor for Planeta and as the director of the literary supplement of the Argentine newspaper *Página 12*. In 1987 he published his first novel, *Corazones cautivos más arriba* (Up with Imprisoned Hearts). His second book, *Nadar de noche* (Swimming at Night), was published in 1991 and is being translated into English. Forn was named a Fellow of the Woodrow Wilson Center (Washington, D.C.). He also received a grant from the Fondo Nacional de las Artes (Buenos Aires). His other books include *Puras mentiras* (Total Lies; 2001) and *La tierra elegida* (The Chosen Land; 2005).

Diana Abu Jaber is the author of *Crescent,* which was awarded the 2004 PEN Center USA Award for Literary Fiction and was named one of the twenty best novels of 2003 by the *Christian Science Monitor.* Her memoir, *The Language of Baklava,* was included in *Best American Food Writing* and her book *Arabian Jazz,* which won the 1994 Oregon Book Award, was nominated for the PEN/Faulkner Award. Her novel, *Origin,* will be published in June 2007. She teaches at Portland State University and divides her time between Portland and Miami.

Adonis (Ali Ahmad Said) has written poetry, criticism, translations, and edited anthologies for fifty years. He has won numerous international poetry awards and has been mentioned as a candidate for the Nobel Prize in Literature.

Roberto Bolaño was born in Santiago, Chile, in 1953, and moved to Mexico City with his family in 1968. He went back to Chile in 1973, just a month before Pinochet seized power, and was arrested. After his release he returned to Mexico before moving to Paris and then Barcelona. He wrote ten novels, including *By Night in Chile* and *Distant Star,* and two collections of short stories, including *Last Evenings on Earth,* as well as poetry before he died at the age of fifty in 2003.

Roberto Calasso was born in Florence in 1941. In the early 1980s, Calasso began a multivolume work-in-progress that so far includes *The Ruin of Kasch, The Marriage of Cadmus and Harmony, Ka, K,* and *Il rosa Tiepolo.* He is also the author of *L'impuro folle* and essay collections *The Forty-Nine Steps, Literature and the Gods,* and *La follia che viene dalle Ninfe.* He is the publisher of Edizioni Adelphi.

Amit Chaudhuri was born in Calcutta, India, in 1962, and brought up in Bombay. He has contributed fiction, poetry, and reviews to numerous publications including the *Guardian,* the *London Review of Books,* the *Times Literary Supplement,* the *New Yorker,* and *Granta* magazine. His books include *A Strange and Sublime Address* (1991), *Afternoon Raag* (1993), *Freedom*

Song (1998), *A New World* (2000), *Real Time* (2002), *D. H. Lawrence and "Difference": Postcoloniality and the Poetry of the Present* (2003), and *St. Cyril Road and Other Poems* (2005), and he is the editor of *The Picador Book of Modern Indian Literature* (2001). He lives in Calcutta and Oxford.

Edwidge Danticat was born in Haiti and moved to the United States when she was twelve. She is the author of several books, including *Breath, Eyes, Memory; Krik? Krak!; The Farming of Bones;* and *The Dew Breaker.* She is also the editor of *The Butterfly's Way: Voices from the Haitian Diaspora in the United States* and *The Beacon Best of 2000: Great Writing by Men and Women of All Colors and Cultures.*

Ariel Dorfman, a Chilean-American writer of Argentine origin, holds the Walter Hines Page Chair at Duke University. His books, written both in Spanish and English, have been translated into more than forty languages and his plays staged in over one hundred countries. He has received numerous international awards, including the Laurence Olivier Award (for "Death and the Maiden," which was made into a feature film by Roman Polanski). Among his novels are *Widows, Konfidenz, The Nanny and the Iceberg,* and *Blake's Therapy.* His latest works are *Desert Memories* (Lowell Thomas Award for Best Travel Book) and the plays *Purgatorio, The Other Side*, and *Speak Truth to Power: Voices from Beyond the Dark.* He has also recently published a novel, *Burning City,* with his son Joaquín, and a collection of essays, journalism, and poetry in *Other Septembers, Many Americas.* He contributes regularly to major newspapers worldwide.

Andre Dubus III is the author of a collection of short fiction, *The Cage Keeper and Other Stories,* and the novels *Bluesman* and *House of Sand and Fog.* He has been awarded a Guggenheim Fellowship, the National Magazine Award for Fiction, and the Pushcart Prize. An Academy Award–nominated motion picture, his novel *House of Sand and Fog* was a finalist for the National Book Award in Fiction and was published in over thirty countries.

Jonathan Safran Foer is the author of *Everything Is Illuminated,* winner of numerous prizes, including the Guardian First Book Prize, the National Jewish Book Award, and the New York Public Library Young Lions Award, and of *Extremely Loud and Incredibly Close.* His work has been translated into thirty languages. He lives in Brooklyn.

Francisco Goldman is the author of three novels: *The Long Night of White Chickens,* which won the Sue Kaufman Award for First Fiction from the American Academy of Arts and Letters and was a finalist for the PEN/Faulkner Award; *The Ordinary Seamen,* which was a finalist for the International IMPAC Dublin Fiction Prize, the *Los Angeles Times* Book Prize, and the PEN/Faulkner Award; and *The Divine Husband,* published in 2005. His novels have been published in ten languages. In 2007, he will publish *The Art of Political Murder: Who Didn't Kill the Bishop,* his nonfiction book on the Bishop Juan Gerardi murder case in Guatemala. He lives in Brooklyn and Mexico City with his wife, Aura.

Günter Grass, born in 1927 in Danzig, Germany (now Gdansk, Poland), studied art in Düsseldorf and Berlin after a period of military service and subsequent captivity by American forces. From 1956 to 1960, he worked as a graphic artist, writer, and sculptor in Paris before his novel *The Tin Drum* brought him international acclaim. Grass moved to West Berlin and became active in politics, ghostwriting for Willy Brandt, the Social Democrat leader, who was elected chancellor in 1969. Grass has published many books, including *Cat and Mouse, The Flounder, Crabwalk,* and *Peeling the Onion,* and has often produced the graphic art for them himself. His awards include the Gruppe 47 Prize (1958), the Büchner Prize (1965), Fontane Prize (1968), Mondello Prize (1977), the Alexander-Majkowski Medal, Gdansk (1979), Antonio Feltrinelli Prize (1982), and the Nobel Prize in Literature (1999).

Aleksandar Hemon was born in Sarajevo in 1964. He moved to Chicago with only a basic command of English in 1992 and began writing in English in 1995. His books include the short story collection *The Question of Bruno* (2001) and the novel *Nowhere Man* (2002).

Ha Jin was born in China in 1956. He has published three collections of poetry, *Between Silences, Wreckage,* and *Facing Shadows,* and three collections of short fiction, *The Bridegroom, Ocean of Words,* which received the PEN/Hemingway Award, and *Under the Red Flag,* which won the Flannery O'Connor Award. His novel *Waiting* won the National Book Award for fiction as well as the PEN/Faulkner Award in 1999. In 2004, he published *War Trash,* which also won the PEN/Faulkner Award. He has written two other novels, *In the Pond* and *The Crazed.* He lives in the Boston area and is a professor of English at Boston University.

Heidi Julavits is the author of three novels. Her first novel, *The Mineral Palace,* was a finalist for the Young Lions Fiction Award and a *Los Angeles Times* Notable Book of 2000. Her second novel, *The Effect of Living Backwards,* was a *New York Times* Notable Book of 2003, and *The Uses of Enchantment: A Novel* was published by Doubleday in fall 2006. Her fiction has appeared in *The Best American Short Stories 1999, Esquire, Zoetrope, McSweeney's,* and *Time,* among others. Her nonfiction has appeared in *Harper's Bazaar, Glamour, Time,* and the *New York Times Book Review.* She is a founding coeditor of *The Believer* (www.believermag.com) a monthly review that covers books, art, music, philosophers, and politics.

Don Lee is a third-generation Korean American. He is the author of the novel *Country of Origin,* which won an American Book Award, the Edgar Award for Best First Novel, and a Mixed Media Watch Image Award for Outstanding Fiction, and the story collection *Yellow,* which won the Sue Kaufman Prize for First Fiction from the American Academy of Arts and Letters and the Members Choice Award from the Asian American Writers' Workshop. He lives in Cambridge, Massachusetts, and is the editor of the literary journal *Ploughshares* at Emerson College in Boston.

Naguib Mahfouz, who in 1988 became the Arab world's first Nobel laureate in literature, authored roughly sixty books covering virtually every style and genre of fiction. He also produced numerous movie scripts and scenarios, including for many of the top films in Arab cinema history. In 1957, he won Egypt's highest plaudit in this field, the State Prize for Literature, for his legendary Cairo Trilogy (*Palace Walk, Palace of Desire,* and *Sugar Street*). In 1992, he was inducted into the American Academy of Arts and Letters as an honorary member, and he has received countless other awards internationally. In February 2005, he was named in the short list for the first Man Booker International Prize for fiction. He died in 2006 at the age of ninety-four.

Norman Manea left Romania in 1986 and after a year in West Berlin came to the United States. Since then he has published several acclaimed books in the United States and has been translated into fifteen other languages. He is the recipient of MacArthur and Guggenheim awards, the National Jewish Book Award, and the Literary Lion Medal of the New York Public Library. His last book, *The Hooligan's Return,* has been published in English, German, Italian, Spanish, French, and Dutch.

Manea is Francis Flournoy Professor of European Culture and writer in residence at Bard College. He lives with his wife in New York City.

Alberto Manguel is an internationally acclaimed anthologist, translator, essayist, novelist, and editor, and is the author of several award-winning books, including *A Dictionary of Imaginary Places* and *A History of Reading*. He was born in Buenos Aires, became a Canadian citizen in 1982, and now lives in France, where he was named Officier de l'Ordre des Arts et des Lettres.

Javier Marías was born in Madrid in 1951 and published his first novel at the age of nineteen. He is the author of several novels, the more recent ones of which have been translated into many languages. English-language translations include *A Heart So White* (1995), winner of the 1997 International IMPAC Dublin Literary Award; *All Souls* (1996); *Tomorrow in the Battle Think on Me* (1998); *When I Was Mortal* (1999); *Dark Back of Time* (2001); *Your Face Tomorrow: Fever and Spear* (2005); *Voyage Along the Horizon* (2006); and *Written Lives* (2006). He is also a highly praised translator into Spanish of British authors including Conrad, Stevenson, Hardy, and Laurence Sterne. He has held academic posts in Spain, the United States (where he was a visiting professor at Wellesley College), and in Britain, as lecturer in Spanish literature at Oxford University.

Czeslaw Milosz was the winner of the Neustadt International Prize for Literature and the 1980 Nobel Prize in Literature. His last book was *To Begin Where I Am* (Farrar, Straus and Giroux, 2001). Milosz is the author of numerous works, many of which have been translated into English, including *Beginning with My Streets* (1992), *The Year of the Hunter* (1994), *Road-side Dog* (1998), and *Milosz's ABC's* (2001). He died in 2004 at the age of ninety-three.

Cynthia Ozick, a recipient of numerous awards, is a novelist and essayist. Her novel *The Puttermesser Papers* (1997) was a finalist for the National Book Award, and her essay collection, *Quarrel and Quandary*, won the 2001 National Book Critics Circle Award for Nonfiction. Her most recent novel *Heir to the Glimmering World* (2004) was listed as a candidate for the Man Booker International Award. Her newest essay collection is *The Din in the Head* (2006).

Elena Poniatowska is a writer, journalist, and professor. She was born in Paris in 1932, but as a child moved to Mexico with her family. Her works include *Hasta no verte Jesús mio*; *Tinisima,* a biography of Tina Modotti, the Italian photographer; *Massacre in Mexico; Paseo de la Reforma*; and *Cartas de Alvaro Mutis.* Poniatowska is the recipient of numerous awards and honors, including a Guggenheim Fellowship and an Emeritus Fellowship from Mexico's National Council of Culture and Arts. In 1979 she became the first woman to win the Mexican national award for journalism. Her writing has been translated into numerous languages including English, French, Italian, German, Danish, and Dutch. Elena Poniatowska currently lives in Mexico.

Francine Prose is the author of fourteen books of fiction, including *A Changed Man.* Her most recent book is *Reading Like a Writer: A Guide for People Who Love Books and for Those Who Want to Write Them.* Francine Prose has received numerous grants and awards, including Guggenheim and Fulbright fellowships, and was a Director's Fellow at the Center for Scholars and Writers at the New York Public Library. She lives in New York City.

José Saramago was awarded the Nobel Prize in Literature in 1998. His books include *Blindness, The Double,* and *Seeing.*

Anton Shammas is a Palestinian writer and translator of Arabic, Hebrew, and English, born in northern Palestine in 1950. His publications include a novel, two collections of poems, and a book for children in Hebrew; a collection of poems in Arabic; and many articles, essays, and translations. His novel *Arabesques* (Hebrew: Tel Aviv, 1986) was chosen by the *New York Times Book Review* upon its American publication as one of the best seven fiction works of 1988, and has since been translated into eight languages. He is a professor of comparative literature and Near Eastern studies at the University of Michigan in Ann Arbor, where he has lived since 1987.

Ahdaf Soueif is the author of the bestselling *The Map of Love*, which was short-listed for the Booker Prize for Fiction in 1999. Ms. Soueif is also a political and cultural commentator. A collection of her essays, *Mezza- terra: Fragments from the Common Ground,* was published in 2004. Her translation (from Arabic to English) of Mourid Barghouti's *I Saw Ramallah* also came out in 2004. She lives with her children in London and Cairo.

Wole Soyinka was born in Nigeria in 1934. During the civil war in Nigeria, Soyinka appealed in an article for ceasefire. For this he was arrested in 1967, accused of conspiring with the Biafra rebels, and held as a political prisoner for twenty-two months, until 1969. Soyinka has published about twenty works, including drama, novels, and poetry. He was awarded the Nobel Prize in Literature in 1986.

Wisława Szymborska was born in 1923 in Kraków, Poland, where she lives today. An editor, translator, poet, and columnist, she was awarded the Nobel Prize in Literature in 1996.

Pramoedya Ananta Toer (1925–2006) was Indonesia's most celebrated writer, with over thirty works of fiction published in more than thirty countries. Almost all his work was banned in Indonesia, where he spent many years in jail under three successive rulers. Pramoedya wrote eight of his novels, including *The Buru Quartet,* during his ten-year stay at the infamous Buru Island labor camp, where he was sent after four years of detention at various other jails. He received various awards, including France's Chevalier de l'Ordre des Arts et des Lettres and the Japanese Fukuoka Asian Culture Grand Prize, both in 2000. He also received the 1995 Ramon Magsasay Award for Journalism, Literature, and Creative Communication Arts and, in 1992, the PEN Freedom to Write Award.

Luisa Valenzuela was born in Argentina in 1938. Her books in English include *The Lizard's Tail* (1983), *Symmetries* (1998), *Black Novel with Argentines* (2002), and *Clara* (new translation, 2005).

ABOUT THE TRANSLATORS

Nabila Akl is the promotion manager for the American University Cairo Press, where **Chip Rossetti** also works as a senior acquisitions editor. Previously, Chip Rossetti worked in U.S. book publishing as an acquiring editor, and he has been a guest editor and translator for *Words Without Borders*.

Born in Jerusalem, Palestine, **Issa J. Boullata** taught at Hartford Seminary in Connecticut from 1968 to 1975, then joined McGill University in Montreal in 1975 as professor of Arabic literature and language at its Institute of Islamic Studies. He retired from McGill in 2004. His publications include *Outlines of Romanticism in Modern Arabic Poetry* (1960) and *Badr Shakir al-Sayyab: His Life and Poetry* (1971), both in Arabic; *Modern Arab Poets, 1950–1975* (1976), an anthology in English translation; *Trends and Issues in Contemporary Arab Thought* (1990); and, as editor, *Critical Perspectives on Modern Arabic Literature* (1980) and *Tradition and Modernity in Arabic Literature* (1997, with Terri DeYoung). He has published more than eighty articles and more than two hundred and fifty book reviews in scholarly journals, has contributed many encyclopedia entries on Arabic literarure and Islam, and has translated into English many poems from Arabic. He is currently a contributing editor of *Banipal*, a London magazine of modern Arabic literature in English. Among his translations into English are Ahmad Amin's *My Life* (1978); Emily Nasrallah's *Flight Against Time* (1987, 1997); Jabra Ibrahim Jabra's *The First Well: A Bethlehem Boyhood* (1995) and *Princesses' Street: Baghdad Memories* (2005); Mohamed Berrada's *The Game of Forgetting* (1996) and *Fugitive Light* (2002); and Ghada Samman's *The Square Moon* (1998).

Susan Bernofsky is a freelance writer and translator, most recently of Hermann Hesse's classic *Siddhartha* for Modern Library (2006). She won the 2006 Helen and Kurt Wolff Translator's Prize for her translation of Jenny Erpenbeck's *The Old Child and Other Stories* (New Directions, 2005). She lives with her husband in Boiceville, New York, and is at work on a biography of Robert Walser as well as on a translation of his early novel *The Assistant* for New Directions.

Clare Cavanagh is an associate professor of Slavic and Gender Studies at Northwestern University. With Stanislaw Baranczak, she translated Wisława Szymborska's *View with a Grain of Sand* and *Poems New and Collected*; she is also the translator of Adam Zagajewski's *Mysticism for Beginners, Another Beauty,* and *Without End: New and Selected Poems.* Cavanagh's work has also appeared in the *New York Times Book Review,* the *New Republic,* the *New Yorker,* the *New York Review of Books,* and other periodicals. She has received the PMLA William Riley Parker Prize and a Guggenheim grant for her work on Russian and Polish poetry. She is currently at work on *Czeslaw Milosz: A Biography,* forthcoming from Farrar, Straus Giroux.

Sukanta Chaudhuri is a professor of English at Jadavpur University, Kolkata (Calcutta), India. He is the general editor of the Oxford Rabindranath Tagore Translations Series. He is the author of *Infirm Glory: Shakespeare and the Renaissance Image of Man, Renaissance Pastoral and its English Developments,* and *Translation and Understanding,* and the editor of *Calcutta: The Living City.* He is the translator of *The Select Nonsense of Sukumar Ray* and the editor and translator of several volumes of modern Bengali poetry.

Beatriz Cortez holds a Ph.D. in Latin American literature from Arizona State University. She specializes in contemporary Central American literature and cultural studies. Born in El Salvador, she has lived in the United States since 1989. Currently, she is associate professor and program coordinator at the Central American Studies Program at California State University, Northridge. She is the author of a number of articles on contemporary Central American postwar fiction, the construction of gender, the experience of violence, urban space, and the formation of identity. She has also published translations of literary texts, art-related materials, and film subtitles.

Deborah Dawkin and Erik Skuggevik have worked as a team on a variety of literary translations and dramatized works, including the poetry of Inger Hagerup for performances in London (1995) and, most recently, *Fatso,* a novel by Lars Ramslie. Deborah Dawkin was born in London in 1961, trained as an actress, and worked in theater for ten years. As well as working as a director and teacher, she has written creatively and dramatized for the stage. She is currently pursuing an M.A. in Social and Cultural History. Erik Skuggevik was born in Oslo in 1966 and lectures in Translation Studies for B.A. and M.A. students at the universities of Surrey and Westminster. He also works regularly subtitling films. He is currently working on his Ph.D. in Translation and Culture.

C. Dickson is the translator of Shams Nadir's *The Astrolabe of the Sea,* Mohamed Dib's *Savage Night,* J. M. G. Le Clézio's *Round and Other Cold Hard Facts* and *Wandering Star,* and Gisèle Pineau's *Macadam Dreams* and *Devil's Dance.* Her prizes and awards include the ALTA Fellowship and scholarships to the Collège International des Traducteurs Littéraires. She lived for five years in West Africa and now lives in France.

Lisa Dillman teaches at Emory University, in Atlanta, Georgia, and translates from Spanish and Catalan. Her literary translations include stories from the book *Spain: A Literary Traveler's Companion,* which she also coedited with Peter Bush (2003), Eugenio Cambaceres's 1881 Argentine novel *Pot Pourri: Whistlings of a Vagabond* (2003), and Gioconda Belli's *The Scroll of Seduction* (2006). She has just finished translating *Zig Zag,* a thriller by José Carlos Somoza, which is forthcoming from Rayo/HarperCollins.

Flora Drew is the translator of Ma Jian's *Stick Out Your Tongue, The Noodle Maker,* and *Red Dust.*

Heinz Insu Fenkl was born in Inchon, Korea, in 1960. From 1984 to 1985, he was the recipient of a Fulbright Fellowship to Korea in language and literature. While in Korea, he researched oral folktales and shamanism at his mother's native village and studied literary translation in Seoul under the auspices of the Korean Culture and Arts Foundation. He has taught at Sarah Lawrence, Vassar, Bard, and the State University of New York at New Paltz, where he directs the Interstitial Studies Institute. His first book, the autobiographical novel *Memories of My Ghost Brother,* was a PEN/Hemingway finalist in 1997 and a Barnes & Noble "Discover Great New Writers" Book in 1996. Since then he has been coeditor of the two major anthologies of Korean American writing: *Kori: The Beacon Anthology of Korean American Fiction* and *Century of the Tiger: 100 Years of Korean American Immigration.* He is currently completing a novel on the life of the Shakyamuni Buddha.

Avriel Goldberger, an award-winning scholar and translator, was named a Chevalier de l'Ordre des Arts et des Lettres by the French government in 1988. She is the translator of Germaine de Staël's novels *Corinne, or*

Italy, Delphine, her memoir *Ten Years of Exile,* and also of Emile Carle's *A Life of Her Own.*

Ann Goldstein has translated works by, among others, Roberto Calasso, Pier Paolo Pasolini, Alessandro Baricco, and Elena Ferrante. She has been the recipient of the PEN Renato Poggioli Prize and a translation award from the Italian Ministry of Foreign Affairs.

Marina Harss studied comparative literature and translation at Harvard and New York University. Her translations include Pier Paolo Pasolini's *Stories from the City of God* and *For Solo Violin.* Her translations have also appeared in *Words Without Borders, The Latin American Review, Flash Art International, Bomb,* and *Brooklyn Rail.* She is a researcher and dance writer at the *New Yorker,* and her translation of Alberto Moravia's *Conjugal Love* will be published in 2007 by Other Press.

Tobias Hecht's first book, *At Home in the Street,* won the 2002 Margaret Mead Award. His most recent book is *After Life: An Ethnographic Novel.* He has won research and writing awards from the National Endowment for the Humanities and the H. F. Guggenheim Foundation. His translation of a collection of short stories by Cristina Peri Rossi is entitled *The Museum of Useless Efforts.*

Zhu Hong's translations include Su Xiaokang's *Memoir of Misfortune* (2000); Liu Binyan's *A Higher Kind of Loyalty* (1989); *The Chinese Western* (1988; reissued in the U.K. under the title *Spring of Bitter Waters*); and *The Serenity of Whiteness* (1991). She is the editor and co-translator of *The Stubborn Porridge* (1994), *Festival of Flowers* (1995), and *A Frolic in the Snow* (2002). Her translations of short stories from the Chinese have appeared in the *Antioch Review,* the *Chicago Review,* the *Paris Review, Words Without Borders,* and the *Iowa Review.*

Zara Houshmand is an Iranian American writer and theater artist. She has studied Balinese shadow puppetry and Tibetan performing arts, and her plays have been produced in Los Angeles, San Francisco, New York, and the Spoleto Festival. She was awarded the first commissioning grant from the National Theatre Translation Fund for her work on Bijan Mofid's plays. Her poetry, essays, and translations from Rumi are featured in the Internet magazine *Iranian.com.* She is also a pioneer in the development of virtual reality as an art form; her installation *Beyond Manzanar* has been exhibited internationally and is now in the permanent collection of the San Jose Museum of Art. As editor for the Mind and Life Institute, she has been responsible for several books representing a long-term dialogue between Buddhism and Western science.

William Maynard Hutchins was the principal translator of *The Cairo Trilogy* by Naguib Mahfouz. His translation of the desert novel *Anubis,* by the Libyan Tuareg author Ibrahim al-Koni, was published in 2005. He teaches at Appalachian State University of North Carolina.

Akinwumi Isola was born in Ibadan, Nigeria, and is a retired professor of Yoruba literature at Obafemi Awolowo University. He is a fellow of the Nigerian Academy of Letters and has received the Nigerian National Order of Merit. He is the author of five plays and three novels, including *Madame Tinubu,* and translator of Wole Soyinka's *Death and the King's Horseman* and *Aké: The Years of Childhood* into Yoruba. He has also directed the production of many plays and films.

Randa Jarrar's award-winning fiction has appeared in *Ploughshares* and has been widely anthologized. Her debut novel is forthcoming from Other Press.

Clifford E. Landers has translated from Brazilian Portuguese novels by Rubem Fonseca, Jorge Amado, João Ubaldo Ribeiro, Patrícia Melo, Jô Soares, Chico Buarque, Marcos Rey, Paulo Coelho, and José de Alencar and shorter fiction by Lima Barreto, Rachel de Queiroz, Osman Lins, and Moacyr Scliar. His translation of Pedro Rosa Mendes's *Bay of Tigers: An African Odyssey* was published by Harcourt. He received the Mario Ferreira Award in 1999 and a Prose Translation grant from the National Endowment for the Arts for 2004. His *Literary Translation: A Practical Guide* was published by Multilingual Matters Ltd. in 2001. A professor emeritus at New Jersey City University, he now lives in Naples, Florida.

John H. McGlynn, originally from Wisconsin, is a long-term resident of Jakarta, Indonesia. He is the translator of numerous Indonesian literary works and the editor of more than sixty books on Indonesian language, literature, and culture. He has also produced twenty-four documentary films on Indonesian writers.

Carrie Messenger graduated from the Iowa Writers' Workshop, was a Peace Corps volunteer in the Republic of Moldova, and lived in Romania on a Fulbright research grant. Her translations have recently appeared in *International Poetry Review,* the *Literary Review, Rhino,* and *Salmagundi.* Her fiction has appeared in *Blue Mesa Review* and *Beloit Fiction Journal.*

Samantha Schnee is an editor at *Words Without Borders.* She is the former senior editor of *Zoetrope: All-Story,* a literary journal founded by Francis Ford Coppola that won the 2001 National Magazine Award for fiction. She holds an M.F.A. from the New School and translates from the Spanish.

Cindy Schuster is cotranslator of *Cubana: Contemporary Fiction by Cuban Women* (1998) and *La vida a la carta: Poemas selectas* (*Life à la Carte: Selected Poems* by Raúl Henao) (1998). Her translations of Latin American writers have been published in various anthologies and journals, including *The Dedalus Book of Surrealism* (1994), *Words Without Borders,* and the *American Voice.* Her poetry has appeared in journals including *Carolina Quarterly, Exquisite Corpse,* and the *Caribbean Writer.* She was recently awarded a translation fellowship from the National Endowment for the Arts for her current work on a collection of short stories by Rodolfo Walsh.

Anton Shammas is a Palestinian writer and translator of Arabic, Hebrew, and English, born in northern Palestine in 1950. His publications include a novel, two collections of poems, and a book for children in Hebrew; a collection of poems in Arabic; and many articles, essays, and translations. His novel *Arabesques* (Hebrew: Tel Aviv, 1986) was chosen by the *New York Times Book Review* upon its American publication as one of the best seven fiction works of 1988, and has since been translated into eight languages. He is a professor of comparative literature and Near Eastern studies at the University of Michigan in Ann Arbor, where he has lived since 1987.

Ahdaf Soueif is the author of the bestselling *The Map of Love,* which was short-listed for the Booker Prize for Fiction in 1999. Ms. Soueif is also a political and cultural commentator. A collection of her essays, *Mezzaterra: Fragments from the Common Ground,* was published in 2004. Her translation (from Arabic to English) of Mourid Barghouti's *I Saw Ramallah* also came out in 2004. She lives with her children in London and Cairo.

Ulvija Tanović was born in 1980 in Sarajevo. Her translations of prose and poetry have appeared in the literary magazines *Odjek, Lica,* and *Diwan.*

Sergio Waisman is Associate Professor of Spanish at The George Washington University. He received his Ph.D. from the University of California, Berkeley (2000). His translations include *The Absent City* (Duke University Press, 2000) by the Argentine Ricardo Piglia, for which he received an NEA Translation Fellowship Award; *Assumed Name* by Ricardo Piglia (Latin American Literary Review Press, 1995); *Dreams and Realities: Selected Fiction* by the Argentine Juana Manuela Gorriti (Oxford University Press, Library of Latin America, 2003); and *Juan de la Rosa* by the Bolivian Nataniel Aguirre (Oxford University Press, Library of Latin America, 1998). His first book of literary criticism, *Borges and Translation: The Irreverence of the Periphery,* was published by Bucknell University Press in 2004. Sergio Waisman is also author of the novel *Leaving* (InteliBooks, 2004).

Dedi Felman, Vice President of Words Without Borders, is a senoir editor at Simon & Schuster. She has been a Jerusalem International Book Fair Fellow, reads several languages, and helped found *The Front Table,* a book review Web publication.

Alane Salierno Mason, President and Founding Editor of Words Without Borders, is a senior editor at W. W. Norton & Company. Her new translation from the Italian of Elio Vittorini's *Conversations in Sicily* appeared in a New Directions Classic edition.

Samantha Schnee, Vice President of Words Without Borders, is the former senior editor of *Zoetrope: All-Story,* a literary journal founded by Francis Ford Coppola, which she helped to launch. She translates from the Spanish.

Words Without Borders undertakes to promote international communication through translation of the world's best writing—selected and translated by a distinguished group of writers, translators, and publishing professionals—and publishing and promoting these works (or excerpts) on the Web. We also serve as an advocacy organization for literature in translation, producing events that feature the work of foreign writers and working with print and broadcast media to foster cultural engagement and exchange, which allows many voices in many languages to prosper. As part of a large educational initiative, Words Without Borders is developing curricular units, reading lists, and lesson plans for high school and college use (if interested in our educational outreach projects, please contact us at wwbinfo@bard.edu).

Our monthly publications of fiction, nonfiction, poetry, and contextual essays are continually available online and searchable by author, title, country, language, region, and environment. Visit our site to participate in discussions with an international group of literary bloggers and forums on great works of international literature as well as translation and publishing issues. Please sign up for our free monthly newsletter at www.WordsWithoutBorders.org.

Words Without Borders is hosted by Bard College. Our publications are supported by the Council of Literary Magazines and Presses, the Flora Family Foundation, the Furthermore Foundation, the International Institute of Modern Letters at the University of Nevada, the JKW Foundation, the Lannan Foundation, the Alfred, Lee and Peter Mayer Foundation, the National Endowment for the Arts, the New York Council for the Humanities, the New York State Council for the Arts, the Reed Foundation, the Toleo Foundation, and private donors.

ACKNOWLEDGMENTS

We are grateful to all who generously shared their enthusiasm for this project. Our recommenders led us to a treasure trove of voices, most of which have never been heard before in America and the discovery of which generated for us a genuine thrill. For their abundant generosity— to the writers they supported and to the English-language readers, who can now revel in the work of writers they may well have never encountered, otherwise—we offer a cornucopia of thanks. One note: The selection of contemporary works from around the world in this collection is richly diverse but by no means encyclopedic. There are two pieces from China and none from Japan; two from Palestine and none from Israel; multiple entries from Mexico and Argentina and none from Spain or the rest of South America. These imbalances reflect no biases on the part of the editors, but rather, the logistical vagaries of collections of this sort. We hope this volume will be the first of many to come; our intention is to more than remedy any shortcomings herein in the future.

Many thanks, too, to all the agents and editors who facilitated communication with the authors included here, as well as our agent, Joy Harris, who donated her time and that of her staff pro bono, and our editors at Anchor Books, LuAnn Walther and Gautam Hans. We wish to remember the initial inspiration and support in the founding of Words Without Borders of the late Cliff Becker, Literature Director of the National Endowment for the Arts.

This book, as with much of what Words Without Borders accomplishes, would not be possible without the tireless dedication of our coeditors Susan Harris and Blake Radcliffe and the longstanding support of Susan Gillespie and Jim Ottaway, who are, in a way, Words Without Borders' godparents. We cannot thank them enough.

The Editors

www.WordsWithoutBorders.org